Dr THOMAS McCOOG, S.J. Archivist of the
British Province, completed his doctoral
studies on the foundation of the English
Province of the Society of Jesus at the
University of Warwick in 1984. He now
spends some months every year at the Jesuit
Historical Institute, Rome, editing
documents for volumes of *Monumenta
Angliae*. He is the author of *The Society of
Jesus in Ireland, Scotland, and England,
1541-1588: 'Our Way of Proceeding?'*

D1067994

THE RECKONED EXPENSE

*EDMUND CAMPION AND
THE EARLY ENGLISH JESUITS*

THE RECKONED EXPENSE

EDMUND CAMPION AND THE EARLY ENGLISH JESUITS

Essays in celebration of the first centenary of Campion Hall, Oxford (1896–1996)

Edited by
THOMAS M. McCOOG, S.J.

THE BOYDELL PRESS

First published 1996
The Boydell Press, Woodbridge

ISBN 0 85115 590 1

The Boydell Press an imprint of Boydell & Brewer Ltd
PO Box 9, Woodbridge, Suffolk IP12 3DF, UK
and of Boydell & Brewer Inc.
PO Box 41026, Rochester, NY 14604–4126, USA

British Library Cataloguing-in-Publication Data
The reckoned expense : Edmund Campion and the early English
Jesuits : essays in celebration of the first centenary of Campion
Hall, Oxford (1896–1996)
1. Campion, Edmund, Saint, 1540–1581   2. Jesuits – England
– History, 16th century   3. Church of England – History
4. Christian biography – England   5. England –
Church history – 1485–
I. McCoog, Thomas M.
271.5'3'02
ISBN 0851155901

Library of Congress Cataloging-in-Publication Data
The reckoned expense : Edmund Campion and the early English Jesuits :
essays in celebration of the first centenary of Campion Hall, Oxford
(1896–1996) / edited by Thomas M. McCoog.
    p.   cm.
Includes bibliographical references and index.
ISBN 0–85115–590–1 (alk. paper)
1. Campion, Edmund, Saint, 1540–1581.   2. Jesuits – England –
History – 16th century.   3. Persecution – England – History –16th
century.   4. England – Church history – 16th century.   I. McCoog,
Thomas M.   II. Campion Hall (University of Oxford)
BX4700.C19R43   1996
272'.7 – dc20   95–54014

This publication is printed on acid-free paper

Printed in Great Britain by
St Edmundsbury Press Ltd, Bury St Edmunds, Suffolk

CONTENTS

ABBREVIATIONS

Add. MS	London, British Library, Additional MSS
AHSI	Archivum Historicum Societatis Iesu
APC	John Roche Dasent, ed., *Acts of the Privy Council of England*, 46 vols (London, 1890–1964)
ARCR	A.F. Allison and D.M. Rogers, *The Contemporary Printed Literature of the English Counter-Reformation between 1558 and 1640*, 2 vols (Aldershot, 1989–94)
ARSI	Archivum Romanum Societatis Jesu
ASV	Archivio segreto vaticano
BL	London, British Library
BM	Biblioteca Marucelliana, Florence
Clancy	Thomas H. Clancy, S.J., *English Catholic Books 1641–1700: A Bibliography* (Chicago, 1974)
CRS	Publications of the Catholic Record Society
CSP Domestic	Robert Lemon *et al.*, *Calendar of State Papers, Domestic Series of the Reigns of Edward VI . . .*, 12 vols (London, 1856–1872)
CSP Foreign	Joseph Stevenson *et al.*, *Calendar of State Papers Foreign Series of the Reign of Elizabeth*, 23 vols in 26 (London, 1863–1950)
CSP Simancas	Martin A.S. Hume, ed., *Calendar of letters and papers . . . preserved principally in the archives of Simancas*, 4 vols (London, 1892–99)
CSP Spanish	Royall Tyler *et al.*, eds, *Calendar of State Papers Spanish*, 15 vols in 20 (London, 1862–1954)
CSP Venetian	Rawdon Brown *et al.*, ed., *Calendar of State Papers and Manuscripts, Relating to English Affairs in the Archives and Collections of Venice*, 38 vols in 40 (London, 1864–1947)
DNB	*Dictionary of National Biography*
Epp. Bobad.	D. Restrepo, S.J., ed., *Bobadillae Monumenta* (Madrid, 1913), MHSI 46

Epp. Nadal	F. Cervós, S.J., and M. Nicolau, S.J., *Epistolae et Monumenta P. Hieronymi Nadal*, 5 vols (Madrid/Rome, 1898–1964), MHSI 13, 15, 21, 27, 90
ERP	A.M. Querini, ed., *Epistolarum Reginaldi Poli*, 5 vols (Brescia, 1744–57)
Lutz	Heinrich Lutz, ed., *Nuntiaturberichte aus Deutschland. Erste Abteilung 1533–1559. 15. Band. Friedenslegation des Reginald Pole zu Kaiser Karl V. und König Heinrich II. (1553–1556)* (Tübingen, 1981)
MHSI	Monumenta Historica Societatis Iesu
MI *Epp. Ign.*	M. Lecina, S.J., V. Agustí, S.J., and D. Restrepo, S.J., eds, *Sancti Ignatii de Loyola Societatis Iesu Fundatoris Epistolae et Instructiones*, 12 vols (Madrid, 1903–11), MHSI 22, 26, 28, 29, 31, 33, 34, 36, 37, 39, 40, 42
Pol. Chron.	J.M. Velez, S.J., and V. Agustí, S.J., eds, *Vita Ignatii Loiolae et rerum Societatis Iesu historia auctore Joanne Alphonso de Polanco* 6 vols (Madrid, 1894–98), MHSI 1, 3, 5, 7, 9, 11
PRO	London, Public Record Office
SP	State Papers
STC	A.W. Pollard and G.R. Redgrave, *A Short Title Catalogue of Books Printed in England, Scotland, & Ireland and of English Books Printed Abroad, 1475–1640*, 2nd edition revised by W.A. Jackson, F.S. Ferguson and K.F. Pantzer, 3 vols (London, 1976–91)
VL	MSS Vaticani latini (Biblioteca apostolica vaticana)
Wing	Donald Wing, *Short-Title Catalogue of Books Printed in England, Scotland, Ireland, Wales, and British America and of English Books Printed in Other Countries 1641–1700*, 2nd edition revised and edited by John J. Morrison, Carolyn W. Nelson, and Matthew Seccombe, 3 vols (New York, 1982–94)

PREFACE

In the summer of 1896 Fr Richard Clarke, acting on behalf of the English Jesuit Provincial, leased No. 40, St Giles, a house easy to recognize because it is the only one in the street with a small garden in front if it. It was to become the first Catholic 'Private Hall' since the Reformation, and was intended for 'scholastics' (Jesuits in formation) who needed to be trained, mainly in classics, in order to staff the many Jesuit schools. As the announcement sent out to the province in 1896 made clear:

> For some time past there has been a feeling existing in our Jesuit Colleges that the examinations of the London University are not altogether suitable for the purposes of large schools. Owing to the number of subjects which the London course requires, it can scarcely form a satisfactory basis for a system of education built upon the classics.
>
> (*Letters and Notices* 23 [1896], p. 541)

The house welcomed its first four students in September. However it soon proved to be too small, and the following year 'Clarke's Hall' moved to the opposite side of the street, No. 11 St Giles, a fine stone-built house belonging to Fr Clarke's former college, St John's. By a happy coincidence this had also been the college of the religious patron of the new hall, Edmund Campion, beatified in 1889. His name replaced that of successive Masters (Fr Richard Clarke, who died after only four years in office, Fr John O'Fallon Pope, 1900–15, and Fr Charles Dominic Plater) in 1918 when the Hall was given permanent status. Then in 1934 a new site was acquired in Brewer Street, the foundation stone solemnly laid in November, and the transfer made in the summer of 1935. The formal opening took place, 26 June 1936, in the presence of the Vice-Chancellor, Mr A.D. Lindsay, the Duke of Berwick and Alba, and other dignitaries invited by Fr Martin D'Arcy, the Master, who had been largely responsible for the erection of the new building. Campion Hall as we know it today was firmly established.

To commemorate the first centenary of the founding of the hall the senior members decided that the publication of a volume of essays devoted to the history of Edmund Campion would be a fitting gesture. The hope was that it would be a lasting academic contribution on a theme that has attracted growing interest among sixteenth century historians – the passage from a Catholic to an Anglican England, and the resistance to this move by the recently founded Jesuit order – while paying homage to our patron in a way befitting a house of Oxford University. We were fortunate in obtaining the support of Fr Thomas M.

McCoog, whose own doctoral thesis (at the University of Warwick under Professor J.J. Scarisbrick) had been on the foundation and early history of the English Province of the Society of Jesus. With his help we invited a number of specialists in the field to collaborate with essays relating to Campion and his times, and received an enthusiastic and effective response. Similarly our publisher (notably Dr Richard Barber) could not have been more helpful.

As the first hundred years of Campion Hall are complete we recall the motto chosen for the hall, *Veritatem facientes in caritate*, which is a bold translation of ἀληθεύοντες ἐν ἀγάπῃ (Eph. 4:15, literally, 'speaking the truth in love'). From the beginning the dynamic of the Christian life carries the believer from speech to action, from saying to doing. It is no mean programme for a house of studies, and for the lives of all who pass through it. We would like the present volume to help in that process.

Joseph A. Munitiz, S.J.

CONTRIBUTORS

John Bossy   is Professor of History, University of York.

Nancy Pollard Brown   is Professor Emeritus, Trinity College, Washington, D.C.

Katherine Duncan-Jones   is a Fellow of Somerville College, Oxford.

Dennis Flynn   is Professor of English, Bentley College, Waltham, Massachusetts.

Victor Houliston   is Senior Lecturer, Department of English, University of Witwatersrand, Johannesburg.

John J. LaRocca, S.J.   is Professor of History, Xavier University, Cincinnati.

Colm Lennon   is Senior Lecturer in Modern History, St Patrick's College, Maynooth.

David Loades   is Professor of History, University of Wales.

James McConica, C.S.B. is a Research Fellow, All Souls College, Oxford.

Thomas M. McCoog, S.J.   is the Archivist of the British Province of the Society of Jesus and a member of the Jesuit Historical Institute, Rome.

Thomas F. Mayer   is an Associate Professor of History, Augustana College, Rock Island, Illinois.

Francisco Borja de Medina, S.J.   is a member of the Jesuit Historical Institute, Rome and on the Faculty of Ecclesiastical History, Pontifical Gregorian University.

Joseph A. Munitiz, S.J.   is Master of Campion Hall.

Michael Questier   is a Post-Doctoral Fellow, British Academy.

Alison Shell   is a Research Fellow, University College, London.

Michael E. Williams   is a Roman Catholic priest of the Archdiocese of Birmingham, and Research Fellow, Trinity and All Saints Colleges, University of Leeds.

INTRODUCTION

After Sir Thomas More was found guilty of treason but before judgement was passed against him, the former chancellor spoke clearly and boldly about the indictment. In a scene made famous by Robert Bolt's successful play and film *A Man for All Seasons*, More argued that the indictment was 'grounded upon an act of parliament directly repugnant to the laws of God and his holy church, the supreme government of which, or any part thereof, may no temporal prince presume by any law to take upon him, as rightfully belonging to the See of Rome, a spiritual preeminence by the mouth of our Saviour himself, personally present upon earth, only to Saint Peter, and his successors, bishops of the same See, by special prerogative granted'. Therefore, he continued, no one part of the Church had the right to pass a law that disagreed with the general law of the Church Universal 'no more than the City of London, being but one poor member in respect of the whole realm, might make a law against an act of parliament to bind the whole realm'.[1]

More's speech and heroic death, however, did nothing to curtail parliamentary involvement in religious matters. For the next twenty-five years the theological content of the faith of the English people would be enacted by parliament. After the Homoean victory in 359, St Jerome wrote that 'the whole world groaned and wondered to find itself Arian'. Between the death of Thomas More in 1535 and the 'definitive' settlement of religion by Queen Elizabeth in 1559, the English people found themselves to be Lutheran, Zwinglian, and Catholic.

In this volume's opening essay, Professor David Loades, historian of the reign of Mary Tudor, surveys the religious changes wrought under King Henry VIII and his son Edward VI. Martin Bucer's complaint that the Reformation in England was largely effected by edicts reluctantly obeyed by the people has been confirmed by the recent historical research of J.J. Scarisbrick, Christopher Haigh, and Eamon Duffy.[2] Yet regardless of their unpopularity, many religious changes, e.g. destruction of the goals of traditional pilgrimages, encouragement of Bible reading, introduction of a new vernacular liturgy, significantly affected the English people. Upon her accession in 1553, Queen Mary could repeal the Henrician and Edwardian legislation and reintroduce traditional Catholic

---

[1] William Roper, *The Life of Sir Thomas More*, ed. S.W. Singer (London, 1822), pp. 86–87.

[2] Respectively, *The Reformation and the English People* (Oxford, 1984); *English Reformations* (Oxford, 1993); *The Stripping of the Altars* (New Haven, 1992).

practices, but she could not erase the experience of twenty years. The spirituality of her Church was thus a 'distinctive hybrid', an 'uneasy mixture of late medieval formalism and humanist intelligence' that owed more to Erasmus and Thomas Cranmer than to Luther or Ignatius Loyola. A spirituality more characteristic of the Counter-Reformation entered England only with the arrival of the seminary priests and the Jesuits during the reign of Mary's successor Elizabeth.

In his unfinished biography of Edmund Campion,[3] Robert Persons[4] placed his birth in context:

> His birth happened in about the year of God 1540, and the thirtieth of K. Henry 8th, which was the year wherein the said K. pulled down and destroyed the greatest religious houses in England and persecuted most violently the Catholic Faith, for defence whereof Fr Campian was afterwards, by God's holy providence, to shed his blood; as also it was the year wherein the religious order, the Society of Jesus, was founded and confirmed in Rome by the See Apostolic, of which order the said Father was to be so worthy a member, as afterwards he proved.[5]

Campion was born on 25 January 1540 in the city of London, probably in the area of St Paul's Cathedral.[6] His father was a bookseller and was probably from the Sawston branch of the Campion family.[7] Upon entering the Society, Campion wrote a short summary of his education: 'First I learned grammer in my native place, then I went to Oxford, where I studied philosophy for seven

---

[3] A word should be added about the biographies of Campion. Richard Simpson's *Edmund Campion: A Biography*, revised edition (London, 1896) remains the best account although it should be updated in light of recent historiography. Subsequent biographies are all derived from Simpson. Evelyn Waugh's *Edmund Campion: Jesuit and Martyr* (London, 1935) is clearly the best written. Although he received assistance from Father Leo Hicks, S.J., there are still a number of irritating historical errors. E.E. Reynolds' *Campion and Parsons* (London, 1980) benefits from the many volumes published by the Catholic Record Society.

[4] Persons has long been – and will probably always remain – a controversial figure. Arguments range from his involvement in plots to the spelling of his name. For the sake of uniformity, we have adopted 'Persons' as opposed to 'Parsons' because it was the form used by a majority of the authors. Unfortunately this volume was completed before the appearance of Francis Edwards, S.J., *Robert Persons: The Biography of an Elizabethan Jesuit 1546–1610* (St. Louis, 1995).

[5] The manuscript can be found at Stonyhurst College, Coll P ff. 76–147. It was published as 'Of the Life and Martyrdom of Father Edmond Campian', *Letters and Notices* 11 (1877), pp. 219–42, 308–39; 12 (1878), pp. 1–68. The manuscript states that the biography was begun on 5 July 1594.

[6] In a letter to Campion from Rome on 28 November 1578, Robert Persons wrote of twenty-four Englishmen who had recently joined the Society, two of whom, he noted, are 'yor countrymen borne in Pater noster row' (Leo Hicks, S.J., ed., *Letters and Memorials of Father Robert Persons, S.J.* [London, 1942], CRS 39, p. 2).

[7] On Campion's family, see Leslie Campion, *The Family of Edmund Campion* (London, 1975).

years and theology for about six – Aristotle, positive theology and the fathers'.[8] Persons specified 'the grammar school of St Paul'[9] as one attended by Campion, and recent research has shown that he spent some time at both Christ's Hospital and St Paul's.[10] On the eve of the feast of St Bartholomew, 23 August 1553, while still a pupil at St Paul's, Campion won a silver pen in a literary contest that involved students from his own school and from Christ's Hospital and St Anthony's. One of his opponents was William Fulke. C.H. Hartshorne, editor of a volume on Fulke for the Parker Society, commented: 'Our aspiring young scholar, being unsuccessful, bore his disappointment with so ill a grace as to shed tears under it, indignantly looking forward to the reprisals of a future competition.'[11] Nearly thirty years later, Fulke and Campion would face each other again, this time in the Tower of London. Presumably because of his success, Campion was selected to deliver a speech before Queen Mary when she stopped at the school on the way to her coronation on 30 September 1553.

During Mary's reign, Ignatius Loyola offered Jesuit assistance for the restoration of Catholicism to Reginald Cardinal Pole. The proposal was consistently ignored. Thomas F. Mayer, author of numerous articles on Pole, is currently writing a biography of the cardinal. Addressing the specific issue of Pole's refusal to take advantage of Loyola's offer, Mayer rejects the explanations presented by Loades in his books on Mary Tudor, and by Thomas M. McCoog, S.J., in his article on the same subject. For Mayer, the reason was neither theological nor nationalist, but personal: Pole resented the way Loyola treated Pole's friend the Jesuit Nicolás Bobadilla, perhaps the least understood of the early followers of Ignatius. Whatever the reason, the Society harboured no resentment, and later English Jesuits extolled Pole while wondering what might have been if the Society had established a college in England.

If Ignatius Loyola had had his way, he anticipated the foundation of a Jesuit college in England. Even without Jesuit assistance, Cardinal Pole sought to strengthen orthodoxy at the English universities. Oxford had been notoriously resistant to religious innovation. Indeed, during the reign of Edward VI, foreign Protestants commented that the university still abounded with Papists. Although Mary Tudor's brief reign confirmed the university's opposition, within a year of Elizabeth's accession, only one college head was allowed to remain from the previous reign. James McConica, historian of Tudor Oxford, investigates the Oxford that Campion would have known, an Oxford where stubborn resistance to Elizabethan religious changes was found in New College, and Corpus, Trinity, Merton, Queen's, Balliol, Exeter, and St John's colleges. Within the first decade

8 Joannes Schmidl, *Historiae Societatis Jesu Provinciae Bohemiae*, 2 vols (Prague, 1747–49), I, p. 338.

9 Persons, 'Life of Campian', p. 220.

10 Michael F.J. McDonnell, 'Edmund Campion, S.J., and St Paul's School', *Notes and Queries* 194 (1949), pp. 46–49, 66–70, 90–92. I shall follow McDonnell's exposition.

11 Cited in McDonnell, 'Campion and St Paul's School', p. 69.

of Elizabeth's reign, over one hundred fellows and senior members left Oxford for religious reasons.

In 1558, a few months before the accession of Elizabeth, Campion entered St John's College, founded barely twelve months earlier by Sir Thomas White, a wealthy merchant, devout Catholic and former Lord Mayor of London.[12] As patron of his foundation White chose St John the Baptist. The founder specified that the College was to work for 'the increase of the orthodox faith and of the Christian profession in so far as it is weakened by the damage of time and the malice of men'.[13] In *Dotatio Collegii*, the second foundation charter of the College, issued on 5 March 1558, 'the Christian profession' was described more precisely as 'not only theology, philosophy and the arts, but also canon and civil law'. Many early members of the College seem to have come from the mercantile and middle classes. The numbers of the College were not specified, but John Bavand was one of three graduate scholars; Edmund Campion and Gregory Martin were among the seven freshmen.[14] John Bavand came to St John's from Christ's College and was appointed tutor to Campion and Martin in their first year. Their friendship endured and was further strengthened when all in turn became priests.[15]

Gregory Martin was Campion's closest friend. They were at St John's together until 1568, when Martin renounced his fellowship in order to become tutor to Philip Howard, Earl of Arundel, son of Thomas, fourth Duke of Norfolk. He went to Douai in 1569 when the Duke was arrested. There he wrote in defence of Catholicism and assisted in the translation of the New Testament published in 1582.

In September 1564 Campion and Martin were elected fellows of the College. Campion was already an eminent member of the University, outstanding as a lecturer and a personality.[16] In March 1565 he was one of eight members of a committee appointed to interpret the new statute *De gratiis concedendis* and to determine whether the obligation to take part in public disputations applied to

---

[12] I am greatly indebted to Philip Caraman's recent article, 'Campion at St John's', *Letters and Notices* 92 (1995), pp. 212–24, for much of the information concerning his stay there.

[13] James McConica, 'The Rise of the Undergraduate College', in James McConica, ed., *The Collegiate University. The History of the University of Oxford* vol. III (Oxford, 1986), p. 46.

[14] W.H. Stevenson and H.E. Salter, *The Early History of St John's College, Oxford* (Oxford, 1939), Oxford Historical Society, p. 119.

[15] On their friendship, see the letters cited in Richard Simpson, *Edmund Campion: A Biography*, revised edition (London, 1896), pp. 121–23, 125–27, and Thomas Francis Knox, ed., *The First and Second Diaries of the English College, Douay* (London, 1878), pp. 308–20. Bavand was back in England during Campion's stay, but we do not know if they met (Godfrey Anstruther, *The Seminary Priests*, 4 vols (Ware/Durham/Great Wakering, 1968–77), I, p. 27.

[16] The traditional claim that in September 1560 Campion delivered his first public oration in Oxford at the reburial of Lady Amy Robsart Dudley, the wife of Sir Robert Dudley future Earl of Leicester, in St Mary's (Persons, 'Life of Campian', pp. 221–22) is disputed by A.F. Vossen (ed. *Two Bokes of the Histories of Ireland compiled by Edmund Campion* [Assen, 1963], p. 3).

lecturers in Greek and Hebrew. Generally the committee was concerned with dispensations from requirements for proceeding to a degree.[17]

Queen Elizabeth visited Oxford at the end of August 1566. Campion was one of four scholars selected for participation in a debate to mark the occasion. He argued that the movement of the tides was governed by the phases of the moon, and that the lower bodies of the universe were ordered by the higher. The University's Chancellor, Robert Dudley, Earl of Leicester, was so impressed by Campion's performance that he invited Campion to visit him privately and promised his patronage.

Three weeks later, on 28 September, Campion was granted one of two exhibitions by the Grocers' Company. There were two conditions: each recipient must have begun his study of divinity, and he must be willing to preach at St Paul's Cross if requested. It was necessary therefore for Campion to receive deacon's orders. He was ordained deacon by Richard Cheyney, Bishop of Gloucester, most likely in late spring of 1569.[18] The precise date is not known; the records at Gloucester have been lost.[19]

On 18 April 1568 a board of six members nominated by Convocation elected Campion junior proctor, then one of the most prestigious and important positions in the University after that of vice-chancellor. Among his many responsibilities Campion handled all public business, summoned Congregations, licensed bachelors, ministered the oath to inceptors, acted as scrutator in the election of officers, and, in addition to the management of the University's finances, took responsibility for good order and the custody of documents.[20] It was during his term of office that Robert Persons, who had moved from St Marys Hall to Balliol in 1566, sought exemption from taking the Oath of Supremacy acknowledging the Queen's headship of the Church. Campion was unable to grant Persons' request. 'Out of juvenile ambition,' Persons was to write later, 'I pronounced the oath with my lips while detesting it within my heart.'[21]

Suspicions about Campion's religious views resulted in a summons on 30 April 1568 from the Grocers' Company. Solidly Protestant like the other city corporations, the Company warned Campion to prepare to preach in St Stephen's Walbrook, the Company's church, on pain of forfeiting his exhibition. On the 9th of July they passed a resolution that Campion, in order to 'utter his mind in favouring the religion now authorised' should 'before Candlemas next preach at St Paul's Cross in London' on receipt of two weeks' notice. A second

[17] Strickland Gibson, ed., *Statuta antiqua Universitatis Oxoniensis* (Oxford, 1931), p. 396.

[18] For the most recent investigation of this perplexing bishop, see Caroline Litzenberger, 'Richard Cheyney, Bishop of Gloucester: An Infidel in Religion?', *Sixteenth Century Journal* 25 (1994), pp. 567–84.

[19] Vossen, *Two Bokes*, pp. 6–7.

[20] Gibson, *Statuta antiqua*, p. lxxv.

[21] Anthony Kenny, 'Reform and Reaction in Elizabethan Balliol', in John Prest, ed., *Balliol Studies* (Oxford, 1982), p. 24; Vossen, *Two Bokes*, p. 4.

resolution five days later declared that Campion was to preach at St Paul's Cross before the second Sunday after Michaelmas. Campion had held the exhibition for two years at Midsummer and, to the Company's knowledge, had not yet preached a single sermon anywhere. In order to clear himself of suspicion, he must do so now. In the meantime his exhibition was to be 'stayed in the renter's hands'.[22]

Campion appeared at the Company's court on 2 August. After having heard the conditions of the grant, Campion pleaded for an extension because his first sermon at St Paul's Cross was a 'thing he would be very wary to presume unto and therefore desired . . . a longer time to prepare himself thereunto'. A compromise was proposed: Campion should preach before the Company at St Stephen's Walbrook on 17 October, a fortnight after Michaelmas. Campion stressed that he was a 'publique person', that is a proctor, and was 'charged with the eduction of divers worshipfull mens children whereof he would, if he might be first discharged'. He asked therefore to be given 'a longer daie'. The court was adamant. Campion acquiesced and asked that he have a copy of the demand in writing. But before the appointed time, Campion resigned his exhibition, setting out in a letter 'divers reasons' why it was not expedient that he comply with the demand. On 25 November at a meeting of the court, Thomas Roe, Lord Mayor of London, asked the Grocers' Company 'to be good to Mr Campion'. In reply Campion was awarded half a year's exhibition (£3 6s 8d).[23]

Campion however was still undecided about his religious conviction. Meanwhile he continued his theological studies. On 19 March 1569 he petitioned the University to be admitted to the degree of Bachelor of Theology on the ground that he had studied theology for five years. To receive the degree, he would have been required to dispute publicly two theological theses, which he would have affixed to the door of the University Church of St Mary the Virgin a fortnight before his defence. It is unlikely that he would have petitioned for the degree unless he was still able to defend the position of the established Church. A month later, however, on 20 April, he completed his year as junior proctor, and in the following weeks he appears to have shifted his religious position. He did not proceed to the Bachelor of Divinity degree in July.

St John's College awarded Campion a travelling scholarship for five years, worth £8 a year. The scholarship, issued on 6 October 1569, took effect from 1 May 1570. Nonetheless Campion did not take advantage of the scholarship. On 7 August 1570 the award was renewed; it was to take effect from 30 September. Moreover the scholarship contained the clause that 'in all the time of his abiding beyond the seas he is not bound to enter into holy orders but may undoubtedly continue a Fellow of the College'. The statute under which Campion was allowed to travel laid down that after five years he was to return to give lectures or

22 Campion, *Family of Campion*, pp. 36–37.
23 Stevenson and Salter, *Early History*, pp. 182–84; Campion, *Family of Campion*, pp. 37–39.

return the money he had received. He also had to give bond of £40 with two friends that he would fulfil these obligations.[24]

A.F. Vossen has thoroughly examined various accounts of Campion's life in order to resolve two important issues: the date of his conversion and the date of his journey to Ireland. His conclusion is this: Campion was definitely a Catholic by 25 August 1570 when he arrived in Ireland.[25] He remained until early summer of 1571.[26] During his final weeks there he composed his *Histories of Ireland*.

Colm Lennon, biographer of Campion's friend Richard Stanihurst, examines Campion's *Histories* in the context of the Earl of Leicester-Sir Henry Sidney faction. Unaware of Campion's true religious sentiments, Leicester remained his patron; Sidney was his protector. During the final weeks of Sidney's viceroyalty, slanderous reports were disseminated throughout Dublin. Campion's *Histories* 'reads as an apologia' for Sidney. Nonetheless it is a significant contribution because it is a 'humanist's vision of a unified English approach to the pacification and civilising of the island's communities at a time when the harmonious coalition of his own "countrymen" and "the Englishe of Ireland" of some thirty years' standing was in danger of breaking down irretrievably'.

By late summer 1571 Campion was in Douai.[27] In 1568 William Allen had founded the English College in Douai, where a university had been established by Philip II in 1560. In 1569 a college in the university would be entrusted to the Belgian Jesuits. From the beginning a number of English Catholic exiles, e.g. Richard Smith and Gregory Martin, would play important roles not just at the English College but throughout the university. Campion studied scholastic theology in Douai for nearly two years and took his B.D. in January 1573.[28] He left for Rome shortly thereafter to join the Society of Jesus. It seems that Campion's motivation was rooted in his abhorrence at having been ordained deacon. According to Persons, Campion

> could not tell what better resolution to take for satisfying both God and man and especially his own conscience, than to break utterly with the world, and with a penitent heart to repair to the holy city of Rome, there to cast himself at the feet of the blessed Apostles St Peter and St Paul, special patrons of that place, and afterwards by their good help and motion to seek to be received (if he might) into the religion of the Society of the B. Name

---

[24] Stevenson and Salter, *Early History*, pp. 186–89; Vossen, *Two Bokes*, pp. 11–13.

[25] Vossen, *Two Bokes*, pp. 10–13.

[26] On the problem of dating his departure, see Vossen, *Two Bokes*, pp. 20–25.

[27] Persons claims that Campion attended the trial of Dr John Storey in London on 26 May 1571 ('Life of Campian', p. 237) and departed for the continent on 1 June. See Vossen's discussion of the problem of precise dates, cited earlier. We do know that Campion purchased a copy of the *Summa*, presumably in Douai, on 13 August 1571.

[28] John Morris, S.J., 'Blessed Edmund Campion at Douay', *The Month* 61 (1887), pp. 30–46.

of Jesus, and therein to lead the rest of his life according to the direction of his Superiors. . . .[29]

Campion arrived in Rome sometime during the spring of 1573 while the Society's third general congregation was in session. The Belgian Everard Mercurian was elected general on 12 April 1573 and the congregation ended on 16 June. Again according to Persons, the various provincials in Rome for the congregation began to 'cast their eyes presently upon him [Campion], and to think with themselves to ask him of the General for their parts. . . .'[30] But why the Austrian province and its novitiate in Prague? Was the decision the General's as Persons stated, a decision that consoled Campion for 'remembering that John Wicklif an Englishman was the first instrument of the devil to infest in times past that noble kingdom with his pestilent heresies'?[31] Or had Campion asked to be sent to that province, perhaps for the same reason?

Campion entered the novitiate at Prague on 26 August 1573. In October he moved to Brno when the new novitiate opened.[32] In 1574 or 1575 Campion returned to Prague to teach rhetoric at the Clementina, the Jesuit college there.[33] In 1577 Sir Philip Sidney, son of Campion's protector in Ireland, arrived in Prague as Queen Elizabeth's ambassador to greet the new Holy Roman Emperor, Rudolph II. During Sidney's visit, he met with Campion. Katherine Duncan-Jones, Sidney's most recent biographer, analyses the effect of this meeting on Sidney and his poetry. Contrary to earlier biographers who prefer to depict Sidney as a consistent champion of Protestantism, Duncan-Jones emphasises his religious wavering and the possibility of his conversion.

In 1578, probably in late summer, Campion was ordained by the Archbishop of Prague. He celebrated his first Mass on 8 September. In October his play *Ambrosia* was first performed. In all Campion wrote three full-length plays, but

---

[29] 'Life of Campian', p. 313. Periodically, Campion was plagued by scruples because of his ordination. See also pp. 318–19. Henry More claimed that Campion decided to enter the Society after his arrival in Rome: 'Perhaps it was the name of Jesus which eventually seized his imagination; or a certain kind of organisation which attracted him more especially; one not only founded to save souls – and how many he saw lost in England! – but to carry out the Pope's will with greater alacrity, and with a vow to that end. . . . Or perhaps it was the very newness of this Order, and the sheer spectacle of its labours, to say nothing of its fresh zeal, which struck him' (*The Elizabethan Jesuits: Historia Missionis Anglicanae Societatis Jesu [1660]*, translated and edited by Francis Edwards, S.J. [London, 1981], p. 46).

[30] 'Life of Campian', p. 316.

[31] 'Life of Campian', p. 317.

[32] Thomas M. McCoog, S.J., ed., *English and Welsh Jesuits 1555–1650*, 2 vols (London, 1994, 1995), CRS 74, 75, II, 186.

[33] Because the Jesuit catalogues for these years are not extant, we do not know the precise year of Campion's return. Dr Simons, in his edition of Campion's *Ambrosia* (Assen, 1969), claims that he returned in 1574 (p. xiii) as does Simpson (*Campion*, p. 113). In Schmidl (*Historiae*, I, p. 366), the first mention of Campion at Prague is dated 1575, at which time he is prefect of the Sodality. He had left Brno by 26 February 1575, the date of his first letter to the novices there (Schmidl, *Historia*, I, pp. 369–71).

this is the most important. Alison Shell completed her doctoral thesis on 'English Catholicism and Drama' at Oxford in 1992. In the light of Campion's fate, his selection of the confrontation between Ambrose and Theodosius is ironic. Working from this play, Dr Shell explores Campion's 'self-fashioning' and his progression from dramatist of Church/State confrontation to victim of such confrontations in later recusant plays.

Campion remained in Prague until spring of 1580. According to Persons, 'he lived in very quiet and contentment of mind all the time he abode in that country . . . [during] which time he applied himself to the labours and functions of his religion with such exceeding charity and zeal and perfect obedience'.[34] Unlike the case of Persons, who worked for the establishment of a Jesuit mission to England, we have no evidence that Campion either volunteered for such a mission or, indeed, concerned himself with its creation. In fact, as Thomas M. McCoog, S.J., points out in his article, the evidence indicates that Campion was a reluctant participant whose involvement was based on obedience. Because the missionary strategy of Allen and Persons involved disputation, they were eager to include in their party a man known for his eloquence.

Robert Persons landed at Dover on 16 June 1580; Campion and the Jesuit laybrother Ralph Emerson followed him on the 24th. In mid-July Persons and Campion met the *incognito* Jesuit Thomas Pounde at Hoxton. There they made their fateful decision to write short *apologiae* in the event of their capture. While Campion was visiting Catholics in Berkshire, Oxfordshire, and Northamptonshire, Pounde's early release of Campion's 'Brag' caused consternation in London. In October, at Uxbridge, the two decided to capitalize on Campion's notoriety with a more sophisticated theological challenge. Campion wrote *Rationes decem* as he travelled throughout Nottinghamshire, Derbyshire, Yorkshire, and Lancashire. Printed at Stonor Park, the book was surreptitiously distributed in the University Church of St Mary in Oxford on 27 June 1581. The site was selected with some irony: candidates were required to debate two theological propositions posted a fortnight in advance on the door of this church in order to gain their B.D. Campion failed to do so in 1569; in 1581 he 'posted' ten! The audacious move intensified the government's search. Less than a month later, on 17 July, he was captured at Lyford Grange. By the 22nd he was in the Tower of London. Because of the publicity generated first by the 'Brag' and then by *Rationes decem*, the government was forced to grant Campion his disputations. The crowds that flocked to the first gradually dissipated as they realised the true nature of events. On 20 November Campion and seven other priests were tried at Westminster Hall. They were found guilty of treason on the charge that they had conspired against the Queen and plotted her death. On 1 December 1581

---

[34] 'Life of Campian', p. 319. In a letter to Persons written from Prague on 25 June 1577, Campion wrote: 'About myself I would only have you know that from the day I arrived here, I have been extremely well, – in a perpetual bloom of health, and that I was never at any age less upset by literary work than now, when I work hardest' (cited in Simpson, *Campion*, p. 120).

Campion, Ralph Sherwin, and Alexander Briant were hanged, drawn, and quartered at Tyburn. Upon his arrival at Tyburn, Campion began to preach on the text 'We are made a spectacle to the world and to angels and men' (1 Cor. 4:9), but he was interrupted by Sir Francis Knollys, who demanded that he simply confess his guilt. Campion replied 'Well, my Lord, I am a Catholic man and a priest. In that faith have I lived, and in that faith do I intend to die; and if you esteem my religion treason, then am I guilty. As for any other treason, I never committed, God is my judge.'[35] Persons meanwhile had escaped to the continent.

Historians often juxtapose Campion and Persons; the former is seen as a chivalrous knight out of the *Morte d'Arthur* and the latter as a ruthless schemer out of Machiavelli's *The Prince*.[36] Professor John Bossy, historian of post-Reformation English Catholicism, begins his contribution to this volume with the recognition that 'Persons was no angel, he got his hands dirty, he was touched with the sin of the world; but if he had kept himself as clean as Campion perhaps nothing would have got done at all'. Persons had the misfortune of surviving. On the continent, he continued to work for the mission by forging alliances whose goal was the restoration of Catholicism generally through the deposition of Elizabeth, and the liberation and accession of Mary Queen of Scots. Persons' involvement with the Guises in their intrigues surrounding Mary and her son James VI is well known. But Professor Bossy, in his detailed exegesis of a rather cryptic letter from Father General Claudio Acquaviva to Persons on 5 June 1583, suggests Persons' support of projects more sinister than invasion.

But Persons did more than intrigue after his arrival in France. Victor Houliston is currently working on a new edition of Persons' popular and enduring spiritual classic *The Book of Resolution*, better known as *The Christian Directory*, a work begun in England and completed in France. So impressed with this book was the Calvinist sub-dean of York, Edward Bunny, that he purged the work of its popish errors and submitted it to an eager public. Persons' consequent anger

---

[35] Cited in E.E. Reynolds, *Campion and Parsons* (London, 1980), p. 200.

[36] E.g. J.B. Black, in *The Reign of Elizabeth*, 2nd edition (Oxford, 1959), wrote of Campion that he 'was the *beau sabreur* of spiritual gladiators – a radiant figure, whose nonchalance in the face of danger won for him imperishable renown among his followers, and a high place in the gallery of great Elizabethans. His saintliness, transparent sincerity, and glowing rhetoric were infectious and it was largely through his ministrations that catholicism in England rose to the heights of heroism it reached during the "eighties" ' (p. 179). Of Persons, he wrote: 'Gifted with a trenchant personality, he had all the qualities – resourcefulness, perseverance, foresight – that show the man of action rather than the saint or the pastor. His mind never ran on small things; and it is more than likely that the general of the order marked him down from the very first as too valuable a man to be "expended" in the narrow field of the English mission. His remarkable talent for organization quickly raised him to the forefront of the counter-reformation. Nevertheless, there is plenty of evidence to show that Persons's sympathy lay with the men who served as the "shock troops" of the church, in the front lines of battle' (p. 180). See also Victor Houliston, 'The Fabrication of the Myth of Father Parsons', *Recusant History* 22 (1994), pp. 141–51.

was not the result of an author's bruised ego, but was outrage at Bunny's distortion of the book's message. In his subsequent battle with Bunny, Persons reworked and revised the book by making explicit the Roman Catholic ramifications of resolution.

According to Ignaz Agricola, the first historian of the Bavarian Jesuit province, Edmund Campion requested that Jasper Heywood be sent on the English mission.[37] Dennis Flynn's interest in John Donne has led him into studying Donne's Jesuit uncles, one of whom was Jasper Heywood. Heywood had been in the Society nearly twenty years when he was withdrawn from Bavaria and sent into England in 1581. Having been raised at court, Heywood knew the Queen and many of the leading nobles. His style and approach were noticeably different from those of Persons, and there was often tension between them. Heywood was 'out of step' and was withdrawn from the mission. After his exile from England in 1585, his Jesuit superiors would not sanction his return. As far as the mission was concerned, Heywood was now a nonentity. From 1586 he worked in Naples, where he died on 19 February 1598.

Among the faculties granted to Campion and Persons was permission to print books anonymously. Even after Persons' departure for France, his Jesuit successors in England, specifically Henry Garnet and Robert Southwell, continued this work. Professor Nancy Pollard Brown, an authority on Southwell and editor of a number of his works, examines his contribution to the mission. Originally rejected when he applied to the Society, Southwell volunteered for the mission; after their initial hesitation, Persons and Allen approved. Now Southwell is famous for his poetry – indeed he was the first commercially successful English Jesuit author – but Professor Brown directs our attention to his spiritual works, books intended to assist the spiritual growth of English Catholic men and women during the troubled times: especially Philip Howard, Earl of Arundel, and Anne Dacre Howard, his Countess.

Of the Jesuit contemporaries included in this volume, it seems likely that William Crichton was the only one not known to Campion. A Scotsman, he entered the Society in Rome in 1561 and spent most of the next twenty years in France, specifically in Aquitaine. His involvement with England began in 1582 with the discussions about invasion of England and liberation of Mary Stuart through Scotland. In 1584 he was intercepted on his way to Scotland and was imprisoned in the Tower of London until May 1587. Crichton assumed a position of authority among the Scottish Catholic refugees comparable to that of Persons – with whom he occasionally clashed – and sought Spanish financial and military assistance to free James VI from his dependence on the Protestants and thus to reinforce his Catholic tendencies. Professor Francisco de Borja Medina, S.J., an authority on the Spanish Jesuits in the sixteenth century, has written an interesting account of Crichton's overlooked involvement in the

---

[37] *Historiae Provinciae Societatis Jesu Germaniae Superioris*, 4 vols (Augsburg, 1727–46), I, p. 244.

mysterious 'Spanish blanks' affair and has published for the first time many pertinent letters.

At the so-called 'Synod of Southwark', held shortly after the arrival of Campion and Persons, some priests already on the mission complained that their appearance threatened the entire mission 'for when upon the said Fathers entrance great stormes begane to rise, and many proclamations were read in every province against them, and many gentlemen and noblemen suspected to be Catholikes were called up to London and comitted to prison upon pretence that they had the doing with Jesuits'.[38] In January 1581 Sir Walter Mildmay harangued Parliament: 'You see how lately he [the Pope] hath sent hither a sort of hypocrites, naming themselves Jesuits, a rabble of vagrant friars newly sprung up and coming through the world to trouble the Church of God; whose principal errand is, by creeping into the houses and familiarities of men of behaviour and reputation, not only to corrupt the realm with false doctrine, but also, under that pretence, to stir sedition.'[39] The arrival of Campion and Persons stirred up the government, and many of the older missionaries feared intensified persecution as a consequence. In his doctoral thesis, John J. LaRocca, S.J., studied the anti-Catholic penal laws during the reigns of Elizabeth I and James I. In his present article he surveys the Elizabethan legislation and addresses the effect of the Jesuit mission on the laws and their implementation.

'My charge', Campion asserted in his 'Brag', 'is, of free cost to preach the Gospel, to minister the sacraments, to instruct the simple, to reforme sinners, to confute errors – in brief, to crie alarme spiritual against foul vice and proud ignorance, wherewith many my dear Countrymen are abused.' A refrain heard often was that this was a spiritual mission. Michael Questier, whose doctoral thesis studied conversions to and from Roman Catholicism between 1580 and 1625, examines the proselytising tactics of the Jesuits in England. With *The Spiritual Exercises* of Ignatius Loyola as their most effective weapon, the Jesuits enjoyed such considerable success that the enemies who derided them, e.g. Edmund Bunny, employed their spiritual works.

Campion claimed that 'Many innocent hands are lifted up to heaven for you daily by those English students, whose posteritie shall never die, which beyond seas, gathering virtue and sufficient knowledge for the purpose, are determined never to give you over, but either to win you heaven, or to die upon your pikes.' Yet, as Michael Williams, historian of the English Colleges in Rome and Valladolid, reminds us, Campion had limited contact with the seminaries founded on the continent. It was through his death that Campion's influence was most keenly felt. As a result of the indictment against Campion, William Allen defended the colleges and their students against the charge of treason. But Campion's martyrdom was a two-edged sword. England needed missioners and

---

[38] John H. Pollen, S.J., ed., 'Memoirs of Father Robert Persons, S.J.', in *Miscellanea II* (London, 1906) CRS 2, p. 177.

[39] J.E. Neale, *Elizabeth I and Her Parliaments, 1559–1581* (London, 1953), pp. 383–84.

not martyrs. The seminarians had to be instructed that they were there to preach the Gospel – and they must be resolute enough to accept death if it were a necessary consequence – but they were not to court martyrdom.

Near the end of his 'Brag', Campion proclaimed 'the expense is reckoned, the enterprise is begun'. With the arrival of Campion, Persons, and Emerson, the Jesuit enterprise had begun, but the expense was high, so high that more than once during its first decade of existence Father General Claudio Acquaviva considered its termination. Nonetheless the mission survived as did the Society's relations with Oxford, scene of the dramatic dispersal of Campion's *Rationes decem* and home of the university that produced many of the Society's English recruits. Brother Henry Foley has traced the Society's presence there from Elizabethan to Victorian times.[40] Occasionally involvement was more intense. In 1633 when William Lord Petre endowed the Jesuit College of the Holy Apostles in East Anglia, he stipulated in the grant that an Oxford college, presumably Exeter, founded by his ancestor, be transferred to the Society upon the restoration of Catholicism.[41] With the accession of James II in 1685, the Society played a significant role in his religious policies. A Jesuit, whose name is not known, received John Massey, dean of Christ Church, into the Roman Church. The Catholic master of University College, Obadiah Walker, named the Jesuit Joseph Wakeman as his chaplain. Wakeman held services in the college's chapel and received the revenues of a fellowship even though he did not have the title. A third Jesuit, Thomas Fairfax (alias Beckett) was appointed professor of philosophy, with a speciality in Oriental languages, at Magdalen College.[42] After the fall of James II in 1688, the Jesuit who served the Catholics in Oxford probably resided at Waterperry. In 1792/93 Charles Leslie, a Jesuit until the suppression of the Society in 1773, moved from Waterperry to Oxford. He built a chapel next to a house he purchased in St Clement's and dedicated it to St Ignatius Loyola. Here both John Henry Newman and Gerald Manley Hopkins worshipped after their reception into the Roman Catholic Church. During Hopkins's time, however, the chapel was administered by a secular priest because in 1859 the Society had ceded its Oxford mission to William Ullathorne, Bishop of Birmingham in 1859. In 1872 Ullathorne asked the Society to resume the administration of the mission. Plans for a new church were formulated almost immediately, and the first stone was laid by Bishop Ullathorne on 20 May 1873. On 23 November 1875 St Aloysius' Church, the first Catholic church built in Oxford since the Reformation, was dedicated by Bishop Ullathorne; Henry

---

[40] *Records of the English Province of the Society of Jesus*, 7 vols in 8 (Roehampton/London, 1875–83), IV, pp. 620–23; V, pp. 953–59.

[41] Thomas M. McCoog, S.J., 'Apostasy and Knavery in Restoration England: The Checkered Career of John Travers', *The Catholic Historical Review* 78 (1992), p. 402, especially n. 27.

[42] Thomas M. McCoog, S.J. 'The Society of Jesus in England, 1623–1688' (unpublished Ph.D. thesis, University of Warwick, 1984), pp. 429–30.

Cardinal Manning, Archbishop of Westminster, preached the sermon. In 1896 the first Catholic private hall since the Reformation, Clarke's Hall, opened close to the church. A third establishment associated with the Society opened in October 1921: the Catholic Workers' College, renamed Plater College in 1965 in honour of Charles Plater, S.J., the driving force behind its foundation. The Society left Plater College in 1964. In 1981 St Aloysius was turned over to the Birmingham archdiocese. It is now the Oxford Oratory. Campion Hall remains an integral part of the Society of Jesus.

PART I

THE CONTEXT

1

The Spirituality of the Restored Catholic Church (1553–1558) in the Context of the Counter Reformation

DAVID LOADES

No serious student of the Reformation would now deny that there was a Catholic reformation in process before Martin Luther made his celebrated protest, and that to see the Counter Reformation simply in terms of a response to that challenge is unacceptable. However, Luther changed the nature of the debate. Before 1517 the issue was mainly about how the undoubted abuses which afflicted the Church could be corrected.[1] How could clergy, and above all bishops, be persuaded to reside upon their cures? How could prelates, and above all popes, be persuaded to give up connoisseurship and politics in favour of spiritual teaching and example? Girolamo Savonarola died a heretic's death for suggesting that uncorrected abuses could nullify the Church's authority, and English Lollards had shared the same fate for over a century making much the same point. If the priest was a sinner, how could his sacraments be valid?[2] However, neither the Lollards nor Savonarola, nor the various spiritual radicals who had assailed the Church in the fifteenth century had proposed a theological solution. Normally the cry was for more discipline, particularly at the top, or for a total separation between spiritual and material concerns. The Lollards were fairly typical in seeing wealth as the root of the Church's problems, and some mystics

---

[1]   This was partly because the whole concept of reformation was based upon the restoration of the true essence of the church, the recovery of its original conformity with the hierarchy of heaven. The preoccupations of the Fifth Lateran Council (1512–17) provide a very good example of this type of reform. Roger Aubenas and Robert Richard, *L'Église et la Renaissance (1449–1517)* (Paris, 1951), vol. 15 in Augustin Fliche and Victor Martin, ed., *Histoire de l'Église depuis les origines jusqu'à nos jours*, 21 vols and Supplément (Paris, 1938–64), pp. 164–65, 187 ff.

[2]   J.A.F. Thomson, *The Later Lollards, 1414–1520* (Oxford, 1965), pp. 237–45.

came close to rejecting the institutional Church altogether in favour of an invisible 'community of the saints'.[3]

In one way and another the debate had been mainly about the Church, its nature and its authority. No one denied that salvation was ultimately an individual matter, but the individual Christian soul outside the context of the Church was a conceptual absurdity. Popular piety was deliberately geared to sacramental observances and ritual acts which were not only very visible and tangible, but also very participatory.[4] In theory both prayer and confession were individual and private acts, but they were carried out within a culture of public awareness. In that culture a failure to attend Easter communion, or to take part in the Corpus Christi plays and processions, could attract social disapprobation, and even ostracism.[5] Nowhere was this context more obvious, or more important, than in the rites of passage, particularly those of death. Death was a crisis, not only in the sense that it marked a radical change of state, but also because it was the point at which the soul's destiny was determined. This was the point at which supernatural beings battled for the custody of the departing spirit, and in that battle not only was the behaviour of the dying person of critical importance, but also the support of the church. The *Ars Moriendi* would have been inconceivable without extreme unction, and the presence of both priest and fellow believers. It was for that reason that lonely or unexpected death was so much dreaded.[6]

Like many other critics of the Church, Luther started from an uneasiness about such priorities, and a keen awareness of the extent to which they were open to abuse. Quite rightly, he identified the type of indulgence which was being sold by the Dominican Johann Tetzel as representative of every misuse to which such a system could be subjected.[7] Unusually, however, the remedy which Luther proposed was theological, not jurisdictional. Justification by faith alone cut the ground from beneath the whole edifice of works salvation upon which much of the practice of the contemporary Church was based. It was not until the very public disagreement between Luther and Erasmus over the question of free will that this issue became apparent, even to well informed observers of the contemporary scene, but once grasped, the implications of Luther's teaching had a wide popular appeal, particularly in Germany.[8] Not only did it provide a

---

[3] For a discussion of these fringe elements in a general context of spiritual extremism, see Norman Cohn, *The Pursuit of the Millennium* (London, 1957).

[4] J.J. Scarisbrick, *The Reformation and the English People* (Oxford, 1984), pp. 1–19; Eamon Duffy, *The Stripping of the Altars* (New Haven, 1992), pp. 109–30.

[5] Duffy, *Stripping of the Altars*, pp. 141–55.

[6] Philippe Aries, *The Hour of Our Death*, trans. H. Weaver (London, 1981), pp. 106–10.

[7] B.J. Kidd, *Documents Illustrative of the Continental Reformation* (Oxford, 1911), pp. 1–11; Euan Cameron, *The European Reformation* (Oxford, 1991), pp. 79–83.

[8] On the debate between Erasmus and Luther on free will, see E. Gordon Rupp, *Luther and Erasmus: Free Will and Salvation* (London, 1969) Library of Christian Classics. On the appeal of Lutheran teaching, see Cameron, *European Reformation*, pp. 111–36; Steven E. Ozment, *The Reformation in the Cities* (New Haven, 1975), pp. 47–53; and R.W. Scribner, *Popular Culture and Popular Movements in Reformation Germany* (London, 1987).

splendid stick with which to beat unsatisfactory clergy, it also proclaimed a degree of independence from institutionalised clerical control. The confessional could be an oppressive, as well as a liberating institution, and many people could feel relieved that their ultimate destiny was in the hands of God, rather than of the Church.[9]

As Luther's followers turned into evangelical congregations between 1525 and 1530, it became apparent that the German doctor had posed fundamental questions, not only about the authority of the pope, and about General Councils, but also about the identity and role of the Church itself. Justification by faith alone challenged generations of received wisdom about the nature and function of the sacraments; and the exclusive authority of Scripture left the whole status of the canon law and of the cumulative authority of tradition in doubt. It was not an adequate response to such fundamental questions to denounce Luther as a fool, in the manner of Thomas Murner,[10] or to demonstrate that some of the same questions had been raised in the past by those later condemned as heretics. Johann Eck's successful elucidation in 1519 of similarities in the teachings of Luther and John Hus encouraged those anxious to secure the former's condemnation, but did nothing to answer his challenge.[11] For several years the Church concentrated upon attempting to silence the troublesome friar, instead of answering him, and that was a grievous tactical mistake, because it created the impression that orthodox theology had no answers to offer.

One of the reasons for this was that opinion among the orthodox was deeply divided. In spite of the climate of popular piety, the Church had always in theory insisted that faith was a prerequisite for salvation. It had never been possible to 'buy' a place in heaven, either literally or metaphorically. Some theologians, who had no sympathy with other aspects of Luther's teaching, nevertheless recognised the Augustinian base of his solifidianism, and respected it. This position was shared by a number of highly placed curial reformers in the 1530s, notably Gasparo Contarini and Reginald Pole.[12] Some of Pole's circle at Viterbo may well have gone beyond that, and Pole himself carefully avoided definitions on so sensitive a subject.[13] This group in Rome were collectively known as the *spirituali*, and they were responsible, among other things, for that embarrassing report known as the *Concilium . . . de emendenda ecclesia*.[14] Very

---

9 Ozment, *Reformation in the Cities*, pp. 49–56.

10 *Von dem grossen Lutherischen Narren*, ed. Paul Merker, in *Thomas Murners Deutsche Schriften mit den Holzschnitten der Erstdrucke*, ed. Franz Schultz *et al.* (Strasbourg, 1918).

11 See the minutes of the disputation, cited from *Lutheri Opera Latina*, III, pp. 23 *et seq.*, in Kidd, *Documents*, pp. 49–51.

12 Dermot Fenlon, *Heresy and Obedience in Tridentine Italy: Cardinal Pole and the Counter-Reformation* (Cambridge, 1972), pp. 7–11, 107–14.

13 On Reginald Pole, the Viterbo circle and the Jesuits, see Thomas F. Mayer's 'A Test of Wills: Cardinal Pole, Ignatius Loyola, and the Jesuits in England' in this volume.

14 *Ibid.*; *Concilium delectorum Cardinalium de emendenda ecclesia*, Josse Le Plat, *Monumentorum ad Historiam Concilii Tridentini*, 7 vols (Louvain, 1781–87), II, pp. 596 *et seq.*

broadly, they sought to deal with what had by then become the Lutheran schism in Germany by a process of negotiation and reconciliation. Unfortunately for the viability of this approach, by the time that it was seriously attempted, at Regensburg in 1541, the opportunity had already passed. Too many vested interests had become involved, and Lutheran theology had evolved too far in its own distinctive direction.[15]

Meanwhile an alternative position had developed within the curia, arising directly out of what might be called the 'disciplinary' aspect of the earlier Catholic reformation. The culture of this group was both rigorous and ascetic, and it was well exemplified by the Theatine community, founded in 1524. Its leader within the College of Cardinals by 1540 was Gian Pietro Carafa, and it was known by the descriptive name of the *zelanti*.[16] The attitude of the *zelanti* to the Lutherans, and to other Protestants both Swiss and Italian can be best described by the use of military metaphors. They sought not reconciliation but conquest. Aware of the fact that abuses of practice and theological imprecision had invited the challenges which had arisen, they sought to counterattack by purging abuses and by defining afresh in a traditional sense those aspects of Catholic doctrine which had come under attack, particularly the role of good works in justification. It was into this intellectual nursery that the Society of Jesus was born in 1540.[17] Consequently, when Paul III eventually succeeded in convening a General Council of the Church at Trent in December 1545, he had at his disposal two radically different strategies, and two radically different groups of advisers, each committed to the Church as they saw it, and to the papal authority, but deeply divided by theological emphasis.

It has been fairly observed that every shade of theological opinion, short of outright Protestantism, was represented at Trent.[18] The strategic problems for the papacy were also compounded by the fact that the Emperor Charles V, who might be described as the 'patron' of the Council, made no secret of the fact that he preferred the programme of the *spirituali*, which was better designed to help him with the intractable political problems presented by the League of Schmalkalden. Consequently the legates appointed by Paul to preside over the Council, Gian Maria del Monte, Marcello Cervini and Reginald Pole, were all of that way of thinking, particularly the latter two. Nevertheless the Council did not go in that direction. In principle it decided to deal with reform and doctrinal definition simultaneously; in fact it concerned itself almost entirely with the latter. As the

---

[15] Kidd, *Documents*, pp. 340–46; Peter Matheson, *Cardinal Contarini at Regensburg* (Oxford, 1972) *passim*.

[16] Fenlon, *Heresy and Obedience*, pp. 32–33.

[17] *The Autobiography of St Ignatius Loyola* ed. John C. Olin, trans. J.F. O'Callahan (New York, 1974); René Fülop-Miller, *The Power and Secret of the Jesuits* (London, 1930); H. Outram Evennett, *The Spirit of the Counter Reformation* (Cambridge, 1968), pp. 43–66. The Jesuits were not part of the *zelanti*, but were a party to the issues.

[18] Remi Taveneaux, 'The Council of Trent and the Catholic Reformation', in Pierre Chaunu, ed., *The Reformation* (Gloucester, 1989), pp. 266–79.

sessions unfolded, the attitude towards Protestantism became increasingly confrontational. Tradition, it was decreed, was of equal authority with scripture. All seven sacraments were instituted by Christ, and were necessary for salvation. The grace conferred by sacraments was *ex opere operato,* and depended solely upon the validity of the celebrant's orders.[19] The primacy of scholastic theology and of the Vulgate text of the Bible over the humanist techniques and interpretations of the previous half century was roundly asserted.[20] Most important of all, solifidianism in all its various manifestations was totally condemned. The legates, particularly Cervini and Pole, fought long and hard against this tide, but failed to stem it, and before the Council collapsed in 1547 the latter had withdrawn having suffered what would now be called a nervous breakdown. The effectual cause of this powerful conservatism was the influence of certain regular theologians, particularly the Dominican Domingo Soto, but the underlying reason was probably the psychological need for battle cries and slogans rather than the uninspiring eirenicism of the legates. When political circumstances allowed del Monte, as Pope Julius III, to reconvene the Council in 1551, it picked up this conservative thread where it had dropped it four years earlier.[21] Neither Pole nor Cervini attended these resumed sessions, and Pole in particular was deeply unsympathetic to the theological climate which was prevailing in the curia by 1552. When Julius called upon him in August 1553 to act as Legate for the redemption of his native land, he may have been the obvious man for the job, but in this very important sense he was not ideally qualified for it.[22]

The English Reformation, unlike its counterpart in Germany or Switzerland, had been political rather than theological in its origins. In its early stages, before 1547, it had been dominated by the personal eccentricities of Henry VIII, and its distinctive spirituality did not correspond to either Catholic or Protestant norms.[23] The regular orders had disappeared, not so much abolished as expropriated, the calendar had been greatly simplified by the removal of many traditional festivals and observations, and an official English Bible had been promulgated. On the other hand it was still a capital offence to preach solifidiansim, or to deny the validity of any of the sacraments. In Rome England was seen as heretical, but Henry insisted to the last on the catholicity of his distinctive Church. The issue was by no means confined to ecclesiastical jurisdiction. By the law of England his only son Edward was his undoubted heir, but by the canon law Edward was illegitimate, having been born while the realm was in schism, and no valid marriages could be contracted. It is not surprising that Henry

---

[19] Hubert Jedin, *A History of the Council of Trent,* trans. E. Graf, 2 vols (London, 1957–61), II, pp. 370–95.

[20] *Ibid.,* pp. 52–124.

[21] Hubert Jedin, *Geschichte des Konzils von Trent,* vol. III (Freiburg-im-Breisgau, 1975).

[22] Fenlon, *Heresy and Obedience,* pp. 220–50.

[23] J.J. Scarisbrick, *Henry VIII* (London, 1968), pp. 384–423; A.G. Dickens, *The English Reformation,* 2nd edn (London, 1989), pp. 216–21; Christopher Haigh, *English Reformations* (Oxford, 1993), pp. 152–68.

entrusted his son, and his realm, to men who were committed to the royal supremacy, even if they were more infected with Protestantism than he might have wished.[24]

No sooner was Henry buried and his son crowned, than the Duke of Somerset, who had secured his own appointment to the twin roles of Lord Protector and Governor of the King's Person in February 1547, began to move the Henrician Church in a Protestant direction. His main guide in this was the Archbishop of Canterbury, Thomas Cranmer, but the motivation was his own, and that of his fellow councillors. It is easy to be cynical about that motivation, and to observe that the first substantive move which affected the normal life of the Church was the destruction of those intercessory foundations known as chantries, and the expropriation of property with a capital value of some £600,000.[25] However, such scepticism would not be entirely justified, because chantries, and other lesser foundations of a similar nature, were intended to maintain prayers for the dead, and this was a devotional area in which the English Church had already strayed into ambiguity. The official manual of orthodoxy was the *Necessary Doctrine and Erudition for any Christen Man*, or *King's Book* of 1543. *The King's Book* declared prayers for the dead to be 'well and profitably done', but had then gone on '. . . it is much necessary that all such abuses as heretofore have been brought in by supporters and maintainers of the Pope in Rome, and their accomplices, concerning this matter, be clearly put away; and that we therefore abstain from the name of purgatory, and no more dispute or reason thereof . . .'[26] Without the concept of posthumous development inspired by purgatory, prayer for the dead lost much of its appeal, and certainly most of its attraction for investors. Recent researches have demonstrated that the *King's Book*, and the campaign against pilgrimage shrines and intercessory practices in general, had seriously undermined traditional piety before Henry's death.[27] The dissolution of the chantries, therefore, was not the body blow it is sometimes represented as being. It was, however, a negative rather than a positive move, and the same could also be said of the withdrawal of the *King's Book*, which happened at the same time, and of the campaigns against images and altars which followed.[28] Martin Bucer, the Strasbourg reformer, was to observe a little later that the Reformation in England was carried out largely by edicts which the majority of people obeyed very reluctantly.[29] To Bucer, Protestant evangelism meant preaching, and he frequently lamented the scarcity of preachers in England; but

[24] David Loades, *Essays on the Reign of Edward VI* (Bangor, 1994), pp. 9–16.

[25] *Ibid.*, pp. 94–100. This was not all profit to the Crown; a substantial proportion was reallocated to religious use by way of continuation certificates.

[26] *A Necessary Doctrine and Erudition for any Christen Man* in *Formularies of the Faith*, edited by Charles Lloyd (Oxford, 1825), pp. 213–337.

[27] Robert Whiting, *The Blind Devotion of the People* (Cambridge, 1989), pp. 17–82.

[28] W.K. Jordan, *Edward VI: The Young King* (London, 1968), pp. 167–85.

[29] Bucer to Brentius, 15 May 1550 in *Original Letters Relative to the English Reformation*, ed. Hastings Robinson, 2 vols (Cambridge, 1846–47), Parker Society, II, p. 542.

there were other ways to inject a positive Protestant spirituality into a Church which had suffered over a decade of debilitating change.

One of these was to encourage the habit of Bible reading, which had become increasingly popular since 1539, and had survived the brief conservative reaction of 1540–42. There was nothing specifically Protestant about vernacular Bibles, but the fact that they had been advocated by the Lollards, and that most of the early translators, such as William Tyndale, had heretical antecedents, made them highly suspect to the orthodox.[30] Bible reading encouraged family worship. Again, there was nothing specifically Protestant about that, but any devotion which took place outside the normal congregational context, and therefore to some extent outside clerical control, was regarded with disfavour. Another way was to create an entirely new liturgy, which would properly reflect the priorities of reformed teaching. Cranmer had been working on such a project since at least 1544, and in 1549 it came to fruition in the *Book of Common Prayer*.[31] Doctrinally the *Book of Common Prayer* was ambiguous, and deliberately so because its main purpose was to establish uniformity of worship, and to reconcile the majority of conservative churchgoers to a rite which was both unfamiliar and sparse. By comparison with the rich diversity of late medieval practice, the Book was limited, and even bleak. The reformers had a different concept of participation. Psalms and responses in the vernacular were designed to give a greater sense of shared experience than mere attendance, which had been the layman's role in most traditional Masses. At the same time the changes of practice reflected in the rubrics, and in the accompanying visitation articles and injunctions, removed the great majority of the corporate acts of devotion which had given the pre-reformation layman his sense of involvement and security.[32] *The Book of Common Prayer*, in spite of its tentative nature, was nearer an end than a beginning. By replacing the Mass, and the other traditional sacraments such as extreme unction, it removed the last landmarks of traditional worship, and completed a revolution which had begun in the 1530s. The rapid simplification of the Prayer Book therefore, between 1549 and 1552, was less significant than is sometimes claimed. It mattered more to genuine Protestants that they now had a satisfactory liturgy, shorn of traditional language, than it did to hostile conservatives, who had already lost everything which they valued.[33] It was not until the summer of 1553, a few weeks before King Edward's death, that the Church of

---

[30] Haigh, *English Reformations*, pp. 51–52, 64–65.

[31] *Two Liturgies . . . of the reign of Edward VI*, ed. Joseph Ketley (Cambridge, 1844), Parker Society, pp. 9–159. F. Procter and W.H. Frere, *A New History of the Book of Common Prayer* (London, 1901), pp. 45–65.

[32] Scarisbrick, *Reformation and the English People*, pp. 61–85; Duffy, *Stripping of the Altars*, pp. 44–77; W.H. Frere and W.M. Kennedy, *Visitation Articles and Injunctions* (London, 1910).

[33] For a typical conservative reaction, see the account by Robert Parkyn, the curate of Adwick-le-Street (Yorks.), 'Robert Parkyn's Narrative of the Reformation', edited by A.G. Dickens in the *English Historical Review* 62 (1947), pp. 58–83.

England acquired a Protestant confession in the form of the Forty-Two Articles, and that the work of the reformers was formally complete.

Given the plentiful evidence of conservative religious sympathies throughout the period from 1530, the degree of conformity achieved by the Edwardian Reformation is remarkable, and it is not surprising that unsympathetic foreign observers, such as imperial ambassador Simon Renard, should have believed that England was a deeply heretical nation.[34] Events were to prove that this was not so, and that most of the conformity was only skin deep, but nevertheless the Church which Mary inherited was far more recalcitrant to her purposes than might have been expected. The Queen herself took the opposite view to Renard. In her eyes Protestantism was merely a political imposition by a handful of wicked and self-interested nobles. The hearts of all true Englishmen were still in the right place.[35] In this perception she was supported, both by her vastly experienced Lord Chancellor, Stephen Gardiner, and by her exiled kinsman, Reginald Cardinal Pole. Unfortunately there was no similar agreement as to where 'the right place' might be. The Queen may have hankered after the faith of her childhood, when everything had appeared to be serene and uncomplicated, and when she had toddled after Dominico Memo, crying 'priest, priest'. However, both Pole and Gardiner knew that the reality had never been quite like that, and that in any case the world had moved on since those days. At first, however, it seemed both sensible and convenient to act as though the Edwardian Reformation had been a mere aberration, quickly corrected and soon forgotten. The Queen's first ecclesiastical proclamation, on the 18th of August, announced a new parliamentary settlement, and in the meantime effectively suspended the ecclesiastical laws of her brother, encouraging the re-establishment of traditional worship.[36] Pole, already on his way to England as Cardinal Legate, but still a long way off, found this deeply offensive. In the first place all English religious legislation was void as *ultra vires* and should not be repealed.[37] Secondly, the Queen should start with a positive affirmation of her allegiance to the Church, not with a kind of negative permissiveness. Both attitudes were to some degree mistaken. Pole did not understand English politics if he believed that the Queen could simply shrug off statutes which she found distasteful. On the other hand if Mary believed that the removal of the Protestant establishment would be sufficient to prompt a spontaneous and universal return to the old ways, she was soon to be disillusioned.

For the first year of the reign, as a result of the Emperor's policy, Pole

---

[34] Renard to the Queen Dowager, 20 August 1553 in CSP Spanish, XI, p. 125.

[35] Mary was much influenced by those who assured her that her accession was a miracle, wrought by God for his own purposes. See David Loades, *The Reign of Mary Tudor: Politics, Government and Religion in England 1553–1558*, 2nd edn (London, 1991), p. 101.

[36] Paul L. Hughes and James F. Larkin, C.S.V., eds, *Tudor Royal Proclamations*, 3 vols (New Haven, 1964–69), II, pp. 5–7.

[37] Pole to Mary, 1 December 1553 in CSP Venetian, V, p. 447.

remained a voice crying in the wilderness, and the direction of ecclesiastical policy was in the hands of Mary and Gardiner. At one level their policy was simple. Edward's religious legislation was repealed in the first parliament of the reign, and those who spoke or demonstrated in favour of the reformed faith were arrested or harried into exile.[38] Married clergy were deprived, and the Prayer Book was banished. More fundamentally, however, there was confusion and uncertainty. The Mass was restored, but not the *King's Book* or the Act of Six Articles. Visitation articles early in 1554 introduced a programme of renovation; altars were to be rebuilt, images replaced, and traditional festivals revived. All this was done by virtue of an ecclesiastical authority which the Queen found deeply distasteful, and the title of which she refused to use.[39] For over a year, from December 1553 to January 1555, the English Church had neither a defined doctrine nor a recognised jurisdiction. The status of the canon law was uncertain, and even heresy was not an offence, except against the Queen's pleasure. Mary deprived the Protestant bishops, and replaced them with sympathetic conservatives, thus ensuring that her policy was properly enforced at the diocesan level, but it was a policy which no orthodox Catholic would have found satisfactory.

The spirituality of the Church at this stage was little more than nostalgia, tinged with an understandable air of jubilation:

> The xxiii day of August (1553) . . . begon the masse at sant Nicolas Colaby, goodly song in laten, and tapers and (set on) the owttwe, and a crosse, in old Fysstrett . . .[40]

> O what joy to hear and see how these carnal priests (which had led their lives in fornication with their whores and harlots) did lour and look down when they were commanded to leave and forsake the concubines and harlots, and to do open penance according to the Cannon law . . . so to be brief, all old ceremonies laudably used beforetime in the holy church was then revived, daily freqented and used . . .[41]

Such sentiments should not, however, be taken as representative of the achievement of the Marian Church. The Queen never intended her 1553 settlement to be more than an interim measure, which is why scarcely any steps were taken at that stage to give the Church a more dynamic or sharply defined faith. All that would come when the *Ecclesia Anglicana* was reconnected to the source of spiritual power and doctrine, the universal Church, and could only come in that way. The notion that the English Church might develop its own distinctive spirituality along traditional lines was unthinkable, both to Mary and to Pole, and if

---

[38] Loades, *Reign of Mary*, pp. 96–128.

[39] *Ibid.*, p. 108.

[40] *The Diary of Henry Machyn*, ed. John Gough Nichols (London, 1848) Camden Society 42, p. 42.

[41] Dickens, 'Robert Parkyn's narrative'.

Gardiner harboured any such thoughts, he suppressed them. Consequently the restoration of papal jurisdiction was fundamental to the Queen's policy from the beginning, not a position which she reached under the pressure of events.[42] Unfortunately her subjects did not see things in the same light. Most of them were perfectly satisfied with 'the Queen's Godly proceedings', and had no desire to re-introduce a distant and alien jurisdiction which would be certain to ask all sorts of uncomfortable questions about what they had been up to over the last twenty years.

Consequently the second stage of Mary's policy was far more controversial, and took far longer, than the first. Gardiner, who was acutely aware of the increasingly obvious connection between the reconciliation and the Queen's forthcoming marriage, tried to smuggle a settlement through parliament in April 1554, but was frustrated.[43] It was eventually Philip, in the autumn of 1554, who persuaded Julius III to write off the Church's claim to its former property in England, and thus open the door to Pole's return and the re-admission of Papal jurisdiction.[44] This was achieved by a second Act of Repeal, which became law in January 1555. The whole apparatus of the royal supremacy was removed, and the early fifteenth century heresy laws were resurrected. Pole then immediately set to work to restore the Church to its former authority, armed with English and Canon law. Most of the story of how he approached that task has to do with jurisdiction and with money. The persecution of dissidents, and the struggle to recover diocesan and parochial resources normally dominate this story, and rightly so in terms of Pole's own priorities, but they are not our concern here.[45] It is sometimes said that the Marian Church was just as negative as its Edwardian predecessor, concentrating its energies on destroying what was dangerous or undesirable, rather than rebuilding a lively and positive Catholic faith. The validity of this view is encapsulated in Professor Dickens' famous observation that Mary 'never discovered the Counter Reformation'.[46] Up to a point that was true, but the implication that this was an omission resulting from ignorance, or shortage of time, will not do. In spite of her Spanish antecedents, Mary never set foot outside England, and her awareness of contemporary Catholic thinking must be largely a matter of conjecture. But Philip was much more a child of the Counter Reformation, even in his early manhood, and Pole, as we have seen, had been deeply involved in the affairs of the curia, at least down to 1547.

Philip, however, was chary of intervening in English affairs, once he had set

[42] CSP Spanish, XI, p. 216.

[43] Loades, *Reign of Mary*, pp. 118–19; Jennifer Loach, *Parliament and the Crown in the Reign of Mary Tudor* (Oxford, 1986), pp. 91–104; Glyn Redworth, *In Defence of the Church Catholic: A Life of Stephen Gardiner* (Oxford, 1990), pp. 311–21.

[44] Philip to Eraso, the Emperor's secretary, 12 October 1553 in CSP Spanish, XIII, pp. 63–64.

[45] R.H. Pogson, 'Reginald Pole and the Priorities of Government in Mary Tudor's Church', *Historical Journal* 18 (1975), pp. 3–21.

[46] Dickens, *English Reformation*, p. 311.

the negotiations in motion, feeling rightly that he did not understand the island-ers, and had no sympathy with their mentality, religious or otherwise. It was therefore Pole and the Queen who endeavoured to re-animate the Catholic faith in England between 1555 and 1558. Stephen Gardiner, who was not a very spiritual animal, was sick and disillusioned by the summer of 1555 and died in November.[47] Mary was extremely conscientious, and cared deeply for the souls of her subjects. This made her a cruel persecutor, but it also gave her a pastoral priority which her kinsman the Legate did not share. When she set down her thoughts in January 1555, she wrote '. . . touching good preaching, I wish that may supply and overcome the evil preaching in time past . . .'[48] Pole did not venture to dissent, but he did nothing to implement her wishes. In his view preaching merely stirred up controversy. What was needed in England was not theological debate, which only played into the hands of heretics, but order, and above all discipline. Ceremonies, which had played such a large part in late medieval piety, were ideal for the purpose of inducing regular and obedient habits:

> Of the observation of ceremonies, begynnethe the very education of the chylderne of God: as the old lawe doyth shewe, that was full of ceremonyes, whiche St. Paul callythe *Pedagogium in Christum* . . .[49]

And in another context:

> . . . this I dare saye, whereunto scrypture doth also agree, that the obser-vatyon of ceremonyes for obedyence sake will gyve more light than all the reddyng of Scrypture can doe, yf the reader have never so good a wytt to understand what he readythe . . .[50]

The laity were 'little children' and the imagery of the nursery and the school-room came readily to his lips. In a sense this was a practical and common sense approach to rebuilding the Church; starting from what was there, and emphasis-ing the familiar and reassuring. Unfortunately, it was based at least as much upon aristocratic and intellectual élitism as it was upon a realistic understanding of what was needed, and that made the Cardinal unable to respond flexibly to more positive developments which had taken place over the last twenty years. Spanish theologians came to England in Philip's train: Pedro de Soto, Juan de Villagarcia, Alonso a Castro, and above all, Bartolomé Carranza. All were active, de Soto and Villagarcia in the universities, a Castro and Carranza at court, but none of them spoke any English, and their impact is hard to assess. Some modern studies

[47] Redworth, *In Defence of the Church Catholic*, pp. 330–32.
[48] BL, Harleian MS 444, f. 27.
[49] John Strype, *Ecclesiastical Memorials*, 3 vols (Oxford, 1721) III/2, p. 502.
[50] *Ibid.*, p. 503. See also David Loades, 'The Piety of the Catholic Restoration in England, 1553–58', in *Humanism and Reform: the Church in Europe, England and Scotland, 1400–1640*, ed. James Kirk (Oxford, 1992) Studies in Church History Subsidia 8, pp. 289–304.

have claimed that Pole was much influenced by Carranza,[51] but the authors of the latter's misfortunes in Spain believed that the influence had worked the other way. None of them succeeded, in stays which varied from two to four years, in injecting the English Church with that rigorous neo-scholasticism which had surfaced so strongly at Trent.

The basic reason for this was not their own limitations, or even the shortness of the time available, but because Pole did not want it. The Cardinal's intellectual background was humanist and whereas he believed fervently that there could be no salvation outside the Roman communion, what he sought from Rome was support for the kind of programme which he had envisaged twenty years before. The key to this programme was clerical education. Pole was appalled by the state of the English clergy, not least by those who professed the warmest enthusiasm for the old ways.[52] It was not only the fabric of parish churches which was in desperate need of repair if parochial life was to recover its old vitality. Clerical behaviour and discipline were just as deficient as that of the laity, and with less excuse. The clergy needed to read their Bibles, both Latin and in English, and to base their lives upon Scriptural precepts. So in spite of pressure from some conservatives, the Great Bible was not withdrawn, although exposition of it was strictly confined to those authorised.[53] As long as the decrees of Trent remained in draft, Julius III was Pope, and his old friend Giovanni Cardinal Morone remained influential in Rome, this kind of support was a reasonable expectation. Moreover the resurgence of traditional piety ended the ordination famine of the previous ten years, and brought forward hundreds of candidates for the priesthood, who could be expected to be willing raw material for the Legate's programme. It had been rightly observed that when he set up his Legatine synod in 1556, Pole modelled it on the Council of Florence, rather than that of Trent,[54] and its most important decree was that for the establishment of diocesan seminaries. A practical and intelligent piety was the ideal. A piety which made the best use of existing attitudes and structures, accepting that, with all its deficiencies and recent perversions, the English Church was still basically sound.

This policy produced a good deal of literature for the guidance of both clergy and laity; works such as Edmund Bonner's *A profitable and necessary doctrine* (London, 1555), and his *Homilies* which were appended to it, or Thomas Watson's

---

[51] J.I. Tellechea Idígoras, 'Bartolomé Carranza y la restauración católica inglesa', *Anthologia Annua* 12 (1964), pp. 159–282.

[52] Strype, *Ecclesiastical Memorials*, III, pp. 484–85. Every visitation showed cures vacant. In 1554 there were only two priests for the eleven parishes of Ipswich (BL, Harleian MS 419, f. 131).

[53] A.F. Bartholomew, 'Lay Piety in the Reign of Mary Tudor' (unpublished M.A. thesis, Manchester University, 1979); Helen C. White, *Tudor Books of Private Devotions* ([Madison], Wisconsin, 1951); Loades, 'Piety of the Catholic Restoration'.

[54] J.P. Marmion, 'The Legatine Synod of Cardinal Pole' (unpublished M.A. thesis, Keele University, 1974); *Reformatio Angliae ex decretis Reginaldi Poli* (Rome, 1562), ARCR I, no. 918.

Holesome and catholyke doctryne (London, 1558).[55] The lineage of this type of homiletics went back through Richard Whitford to John Colet and Thomas Linacre. It was the educated, civil piety of Pole's youth (and Mary's), and in spite of the Cardinal's opportunist insistence upon the importance of ceremonies, it placed much emphasis upon the individual conscience. In insisting upon the centrality of the Mass, for example, Thomas Watson was not interested in the mere attendance which had been the traditional layman's role. He was concerned with the worthy reception of the sacrament, and with the spiritual preparation which that required.[56] Consequently the spirituality of the Marian Church became a distinctive hybrid. Its individualism owed more to Erasmus than it did to Luther or Ignatius Loyola, and the form of its homiletics was more indebted to Thomas Cranmer than to any contemporary Catholic writer.[57] It was not a mission field but an ancient Christian land, and when Loyola offered the assistance of the Society of Jesus in recovering England for the true faith, he was virtually ignored.[58] Pedro Ribadeneira, frustrated by Pole's unwillingness to make use of Jesuit zeal, denounced the Cardinal as a Laodicean, and one of Philip's Spanish nobles declared witheringly: 'I do not believe that the lukewarm go to heaven, even if they are called moderates . . .'[59] A similar ambivalence can be seen over the restoration of the regular orders. Pole had owed much in his youth to the rigorous spirituality of the Carthusians, and their sufferings at the hands of Henry VIII were deeply etched upon his conscience. Both he and Mary expressed enthusiasm for the foundation of new religious houses, but neither took any initiative in that direction.[60] Westminster, the only substantial foundation, was generously funded by the Crown, but only after some delay, and the pressure to re-enter the religious life came from the monks themselves. Pole was

---

[55] STC 3281.5–3285.10; STC 25112–25114.

[56] 'And because a man doth dayley offende, and so decayethe in his spiritual lyfe, therefore aught he often to receive this spiritual medecine, which is called our dayly bread.' *Holesome and Catholyke Doctryne*, sermon 9, f. 48.

[57] On the type of spirituality introduced by the Jesuits, see Nancy Pollard Brown, 'Robert Southwell: The Mission of the Written Word' and Victor Houliston, 'Why Robert Persons Would not be Pacified: Edmund Bunny's Theft of *The Book of Resolution*' in this volume.

[58] Loyola hoped in vain that Philip would take some Jesuits with him to England, although there were none at the time who could speak English. Only one Englishmen joined the order before the founder's death, Thomas Lith, and he was not ordained. Loyola also offered to train young Englishmen in Jesuit schools but his offer was not taken up. Joseph H. Crehan, S.J., 'Saint Ignatius and Cardinal Pole', *Archivum Historicum Societatis Iesu* 25 (1956), 72–98; Bernard Bassett, S.J., *The English Jesuits* (London, 1967), pp. 14–15. For a fuller discussion of this point, see Thomas F. Mayer, 'A Test of Wills: Cardinal Pole, Ignatius Loyola, and the Jesuits in England' in this volume and Thomas M. McCoog, S.J., 'Ignatius Loyola and Reginald Pole: A Reconsideraion', *Journal of Ecclesiastical History* (forthcoming). The best recent study of the order in its early days (although saying very little about England) is John W. O'Malley, S.J., *The First Jesuits* (Cambridge, Mass., 1993).

[59] CSP Spanish, XIII, pp. 370–71.

[60] Loades, *Reign of Mary*, pp. 352–54. Dom David Knowles, *The Religious Orders in England*, 3 vols (Cambridge, 1948–59), III, p. 423.

sufficiently interested to negotiate for two members of the congregation of Monte Cassino to come and inject a little rigour into the new foundation, but they did not come, and the only evidence which we have of the regiment at Westminster under Abbot Feckenham suggests that it was sober and dignified, but not at all ascetic.[61]

The fire of the Counter Reformation was not the only ingredient missing from the Marian Church. Revived monasticism was on too small a scale to make any impact upon the Church as a whole, and one small house of elderly Franciscans could not renew the mendicant tradition of evangelism. More surprisingly, moreover, the great pilgrimage shrines, which had attracted large scale royal and popular patronage in the early sixteenth century, did not reappear at all. St Edward the Confessor was restored to Westminster on the initiative of the monks, but Glastonbury, Walsingham, and Canterbury all remained desolate, nor does any move seem to have been made to revive them.[62] In spite of her apparent enthusiasm for the old ways, Mary never undertook a pilgrimage as Queen, and the place of purgatory in her personal faith must remain an open question. A few chantries were founded, both by royal and private benefaction, but when Mary wanted to give thanks for her victories over the Duke of Northumberland and Sir Thomas Wyatt, she made substantial gifts to the universities.[63] Nor did she patronise any cult, except for that of the Blessed Sacrament. Royal ladies in the past, (and kings as well, if it comes to that) frequently had a favourite devotion, but even in the most stressful moments of her life, Mary does not seem to have called upon any particular saint. Her injunctions were insistent upon the restoration of patronal devotions, but there was no popular demand for saints' lives of the traditional kind. A mere handful were published in her reign, and there was no edition of the *Legenda Aurea* after 1529.[64] Fashions in piety had changed since Mary was a girl, even among the more traditionally minded. The Mass had retained its appeal, and so had the sacraments in general, which was the chief objection to Protestant worship, but intercessory prayer no longer attracted the investment and devotion of the faithful in the way it had once done. Education, Bible reading and private prayer were phenomena of the 'new learning', which both Mary and Pole shared and understood. They did not hanker for the piety of Ceasarius of Heisterbach.[65]

---

[61] 'Fr. Leander Prichard's Life [of Father Baker]' in *Memorials of Father Augustine Baker*, ed. Dom Justin McCann, O.S.B., and Dom Hugh Connolly, O.S.B. (London, 1933) CRS 33, pp. 95–96.

[62] Attempts were made to resurrect the devotion of St Thomas Becket but unconnected with any shrine (Duffy, *Stripping of the Altars*, pp. 543–55; David Loades, *Mary Tudor: A Life* (Oxford, 1989) p. 245).

[63] *Ibid.* Her will, which bequeathed large sums to the religious houses, shows only a conventional concern with intercession (BL, Harleian MS 6949).

[64] STC 24873–24880.

[65] Author of the *Dialogus Miraculorum*, an early thirteenth century Cistercian with a particularly florid line in *exempla*.

Whether their aspirations could have been fulfilled in more favourable circumstances, we do not know. As it was, Mary's death at the age of 43 in 1558, and Pole's a few hours later, doomed their experiment to failure. It might have failed anyway, because although good progress was made in restoring the infrastructure of the old Church, Protestant dissent was not silenced, and positive zeal among the social and political élite was scarce. Marian Catholicism was not a fighting creed; it belonged to an earlier and gentler generation. Moreover it was fatally handicapped by political circumstances. The association between the Catholic restoration and the arrival of an unpopular Spanish king was inevitable, and when this was followed by a persecution of unprecedented scale and severity, it was not only Protestants who began to mutter that the Queen was 'a Spaniard at heart'.[66] Moreover the papacy's own attitude to its prodigal daughter became distinctly ambivalent. Julius III died in March 1555, and after the three week pontificate of Marcellus II, Paul IV was elected in May. Marcellus had been Marcello Cervini, and Pole expected to receive from him the same support that he had received from Julius; but Paul was a different sort of animal. As a Neapolitan he was a bitter enemy of the Habsburgs, and as Gian Pietro Carafa, he had led the *zelanti* in the 1540s. Over 80 by 1555, his memories were bitter and unforgiving. Reginald Pole, whose circle at Viterbo had come under grave suspicion and who was so non-committal on justification, was little better than a heretic. By September 1556 he had forced Philip into open war, and by May 1557 had withdrawn his legates and nuncios from all Habsburg lands.[67] Pole was specifically recalled to Rome to face 'certain charges' and his friend Morone was incarcerated in the castle of Sant' Angelo.[68]

Even though England was not involved in the war, relations with Rome became frosty. Mary refused to allow Pole to leave, and it was believed that the English schism was about to be renewed. That was never a possibility, but the effects of the quarrel were detrimental to the English Church, and disastrous for Pole. English business was endlessly delayed in the curia, and bishoprics vacated after the summer of 1557 remained unfilled at Mary's death.[69] Those who had looked to Rome for spiritual leadership in the wake of the reconciliation were disillusioned, because all that came were administrative demands. At the same time Cardinal Pole, who had become Archbishop of Canterbury in March 1556, was compelled to struggle on using his metropolitan jurisdiction. The papacy occupied a special place in his faith, because its authority supplied the theological certainty which he could not reach by his own efforts, either of thought or

[66] PRO, SP 11/2 no. 10.

[67] Sir Edward Carne, envoy in Rome, to Philip and Mary, 10 April 1557, PRO, SP 69/10 no. 586.

[68] CSP Venetian, VI, pp. 1161, 1166. Paul tried to replace him as legate with the octogenarian friar William Peto but Mary rejected the nomination (PRO, SP 69/11 no. 637); Strype, *Ecclesiastical Memorials*, III/2, p. 37.

[69] W.H. Frere, *The Marian Reaction in its Relation to the English Clergy* (London, 1896), pp. 137–62.

prayer. To be branded as a heretic by the pope was consequently a devastating blow. He protested his innocence in powerful and emotional letters, but he would have obeyed the summons to return, if Mary had not prevented him.[70] In the last year of his life he was deeply uncertain and unhappy, being aware that he had failed to obey the one earthly authority whose supremacy he recognised above all others. The administrative momentum of his reforms was maintained, but the spiritual leadership of the English Church was supplied by lesser men. They were honest and intelligent, but what they were trying to achieve required time, and time was denied by the accidents of politics and mortality.

Consequently Pole's legacy was not the Church of England but the recusant movement. It is now recognised that there was far more vitality in the defeated Catholic Church than was once acknowledged.[71] But nothing could alter the fact of defeat. In 1559 there was no committed Catholic party among the lay peers or parliamentary gentry to offer a determined resistance to the reappearance of the royal supremacy. There were many who would have preferred a Henrician to an Edwardian settlement, but that was not on offer, and only a handful of laymen supported the bishops in their attempt to retain the Roman connection.[72] A substantial number of Catholic intellectuals departed into exile in the early 1560s, when it had become clear that the Elizabethan settlement had struck root, and they were a distinguished tribute to the success of Pole's reform of the universities.[73] But for over a decade, Catholic spirituality consisted mainly of clandestine Masses, conducted for the most part by priests who were also celebrating the Anglican rites. The strength of this 'survivalism' has recently been reappraised, and convincing arguments advanced for its extent and depth.[74] However, cut off from the main stream of Catholic faith and worship, it would inevitably have withered with the passage of time, unless it had been rescued by another political revolution. The mainstream of Catholic spirituality re-entered England with the seminary priests from Douai, and with the first generation of English Jesuits.

These men were not the direct heirs of the Marians. Their training was in an altogether tougher school, and they returned to their homeland prepared to face persecution and death. In many ways they had more in common with the Marian Protestants than they did with the clergy of the last Catholic

[70] London, Inner Temple, Petyt MS 538/46, ff. 391–426 (printed, with commentary, by J.I. Tellechea Idígoras as 'Pole y Paul IV: una celébre Apologia inédita del Cardenal Ingles', *Archivum Historiae Pontificiae* 4 [1966], pp. 105–54).

[71] Haigh, *English Reformations*, pp. 251–67. See also Brown, 'Southwell'.

[72] The fullest account of the debates over the bills of supremacy and uniformity in 1559 is now contained in Norman L. Jones, *Faith by Statute; Parliament and the Settlement of Religion, 1559* (London, 1982), passim.

[73] For more on this, see James McConica, 'The Catholic Experience in Tudor Oxford' in this volume.

[74] Christopher Haigh, 'The Continuity of Catholicism in the English Reformation' in *The English Reformation Revised* (Cambridge, 1987), pp. 176–215.

establishment. Many of their priorities and attitudes were different. Ceremonies and public rituals could hardly feature largely in a clandestine Church, and emphasis upon the sacraments had to be limited when the ministry of a priest might be erratic and occasional. It is not my purpose to discuss the spirituality of the recusants and those who ministered to them, but it is important to realise that the message of the seminarians when they began to arrive after 1570 was something new and largely unfamiliar.[75] The Marian Church had been by law established, and it had relied heavily upon that status to recover its traditional role. That is not to say that it neglected its pastoral responsibilities. Its teaching was sound, orthodox, and conscientiously promoted, but its spirituality was an uneasy mixture of late medieval formalism and humanist intelligence. Nowhere did it reflect the intensity of Domingo Soto or Loyola, the theological rigour of Diego Laínez, nor the mystical passion of St Teresa or St John of the Cross. This was partly because of Pole's own background and of Mary's unwitting insularity, but it was also partly produced by political circumstance. Neither the Pope nor the Spaniards were popular with the governing class in England, and it was very important for the Church to have 'an English face', no matter what its teaching. The Catholics started with an advantage over their rivals because Protestantism was perceived to be German, or in its Edwardian form, Swiss. Cranmer had struggled to domesticate it, by emphasising the English liturgy rather than the Zwinglian theology, but he had only partially succeeded. Unfortunately Mary then levelled the stakes by relying upon Philip to negotiate the reconciliation. By 1557 'the Pope' and 'the Spaniard' had become associated, partly by chance and partly by skilful Protestant propaganda.[76] The fact that Philip and Paul IV were at daggers drawn made no difference to the popular imagery. As a result, Elizabeth was able to anglicise the Protestant image in her own person, and by her durability to fix that image in the public consciousness. It would be hard to argue in these circumstances, that Pole and Mary would have done better to 'discover the Counter-Reformation'. The Counter Reformation did not have an English face, and what they were trying to do was to re-establish the identity between the traditional Church and the realm. It could have been a sensible and enlightened policy, but it would have led to severe friction with the post-Tridentine papacy, and I am not convinced that a more rigorous approach would have solved that problem. Had Mary and Pole been successful, there might have been religious war in England after 1559. That was still a possibility in the 1580s, but in spite of Pole rather than because of him.

---

[75] Philip Hughes, *The Reformation in England* 3 vols (London, 1952–54), III, pp. 257–60; John Bossy, 'The Character of Elizabethan Catholicism', *Past and Present* 21 (1962), pp. 39–59.

[76] Loades, *Reign of Mary*, pp. 236–38.

2

A Test of Wills: Cardinal Pole, Ignatius Loyola, and the Jesuits in England

THOMAS F. MAYER

Despite increasingly broad hints from Ignatius Loyola, Cardinal Pole never agreed to accept Jesuit help in the reconciliation of England.[1] Loyola thought this odd, and he would appear to have had grounds. The Jesuits and the circle of reformers to which Pole belonged, perhaps best still called the *spirituali*, had long-standing and close ties. Pole's mentor Gasparo Contarini had secured the Jesuits' bull of foundation in 1540, and Loyola claimed to have enlisted Pole's ally and fellow labourer in the matter of England, Giovanni Cardinal Morone, to lobby Pole on behalf of the order in 1555. In-between the Jesuits usually regarded Pole as a friend and patron, and he acted the part. Almost from the first Pole's biographers found it difficult to account for his snub of the Jesuits, and recent reinterpretations of the relations between the order and the same currents of reform which shaped Pole – above all humanism – throw into high relief the resemblances between them and make the problem that much harder to resolve.[2]

The few modern efforts to explain Pole's lack of action have emphasised either factors external to him, or disagreements over principle, especially the role of preaching in bringing England back to Rome. Stressing the degree of good-will between Pole and the Jesuits, Joseph Crehan threw out a large number of theories before apparently concluding that it was mainly the (possibly not entirely innocent) bumbling of the last Jesuit agent, Pedro Ribadeneira, coupled with Philip II's resistance, that wrecked the order's prospects.[3] Although not

---

[1]   A note on citations of Pole's letters: In the interest of keeping the notes readily legible, I have given references only to the best text in each case, leaving out citations (often numerous) to other manuscript copies. It should especially be noted that Rawdon Brown took his texts from a manuscript in the Biblioteca Marciana, Venice, which is much inferior to VL 6754.

[2]   See the summary in Thomas M. McCoog, S.J., 'Ignatius Loyola and Reginald Pole: A Reconsideration', *Journal of Ecclesiastical History* (forthcoming), which he very kindly let me read.

[3]   Joseph H. Crehan, S.J., 'Saint Ignatius and Cardinal Pole', *AHSI* 25 (1956), pp. 89–92.

centrally concerned with the question, Dermot Fenlon, Rex Pogson and David Loades all singled out the style of Jesuit preaching as perhaps the biggest stumbling block. It was too 'vigorous' (Pogson) or too full of the 'fire of the counter-reformation' (Loades) to suit Pole.[4] Loades also added theological differences. Most recently, McCoog largely removed the objection about preaching, and engaged with Loades's second point by endorsing Crehan's argument that Pole could no longer have disagreed with the Jesuit view of justification.[5] Instead, McCoog argues that a combination of Pole's agenda with its emphasis on restoring 'the grandeur of Catholicism', a shortage of qualified Jesuits, and the order's identification with Spain prevented Pole from succumbing to Loyola's blandishments.[6]

By shifting the focus away from Pole, these interpretations manifest the effects of what Paolo Simoncelli called Pole's 'myth of sanctity'.[7] Egregious in Crehan's article, less so in Loades' critical reading and McCoog's careful consideration, the same kind of 'teflon' which once protected Ronald Reagan adheres to Pole. We need a more historical reading of Pole's engagement with the Jesuits in general and of why he kept the order out of England in particular. As always with Pole, neither is susceptible of a simple interpretation. Although several of the leading arguments thus far put forward encounter difficulties, elements of nearly all of them retain value. The suggestions I offer here are not meant as alternatives, the more so because any analysis must rest on inference and encounter serious problems of evidence. Nevertheless, two more possibilities deserve attention. First, the complexities of Pole's personality need to be taken

---

[4] Dermot Fenlon, *Heresy and Obedience in Tridentine Italy: Cardinal Pole and the Counter-Reformation* (Cambridge, 1972), p. 257; R.H. Pogson, 'Revival and Reform in Mary Tudor's Church: A Question of Money', in Christopher Haigh, ed., *The English Reformation Revised* (Cambridge, 1987), p. 141 and 'The Legacy of the Schism: Confusion, Continuity and Change in the Marian Clergy', in Jennifer Loach and Robert Tittler, eds, *The Mid-Tudor Polity c. 1540–1560* (London, 1980), p. 134; and David Loades, *The Reign of Mary Tudor: Politics, Government and Religion in England 1553–1558* 2nd edn (London and New York, 1991), pp. 293 and 372. Pogson offers other suggestions in 'Cardinal Pole – Papal Legate to England in Mary Tudor's Reign' (unpublished Ph.D. dissertation, University of Cambridge, 1972), pp. 278 and 335. John W. O'Malley, S.J., *The First Jesuits* (Cambridge, Mass., 1993), p. 274 mentions the problem only in passing and does not raise the question of Pole's involvement.

[5] More could be said about the value Pole placed on preaching and the way he intended to use it in England. For example, a synodal decree ordained that all bishops and curates were to teach and preach. See Pole's letter of 19 February 1556 to Morone, VL 6754, f. 203^r (CSP Venetian VI/1, no. 396; Lutz, p. 310 n. 8). The most thorough treatment is J.P. Marmion, 'The London Synod of Reginald, Cardinal Pole, 1555–56', (unpublished M.A. thesis, University of Keele, 1974). Pole's view of justification is a difficult point and requires separate treatment; suffice it to say that I am very doubtful that the *Treatise of Justification* (ARCR II, no. 650; STC 20088) published under Pole's name in Louvain in 1569 is by him.

[6] McCoog, 'Loyola and Pole'.

[7] Paolo Simoncelli, *Il caso Reginald Pole: eresia e santità nelle polemiche religiose del Cinquecento* (Rome, 1977), pp. 17 and 241.

into account. The constant saint of his first two biographies will no longer do.[8] Two sides of him – one quick to take and remember offence like the high-ranking noble he was, and the other political and therefore subject to change over time – have been almost entirely left out of consideration. Second, the story of his relations with the Jesuits needs to be set in the context of his ties to and attitudes toward other religious orders. The intersection between these two provides a more adequate interpretation of Pole's actions than any previously available.

I shall argue that Crehan's passing suggestion that Pole disliked the way Loyola had treated Nicolás Bobadilla goes very near the heart of the matter.[9] Pole deeply resented Loyola's handling of Bobadilla, not merely within the order as Crehan thought, but more especially how Loyola responded to Pole's attempts to use him. Further, Pole appears to have kept close track of the political winds, above all Paul IV's leanings. Finally, while Pole was perfectly willing to favour the Jesuits at certain times, he preferred the Theatines, the Benedictines, the Dominicans, and even the Knights of St John of Jerusalem, for both personal and political reasons. Throughout, timing proves crucial.

The story begins in 1541 when Pole wrested Bobadilla away from Loyola, Paul III, and Morone. All three had wanted him to go to the Empire, but Pole demanded him for Viterbo, where he went for Advent and may have stayed until the spring.[10] Pole requested him almost certainly at the instance of his 'second mother' Vittoria Colonna, then in Viterbo.[11] She had met Bobadilla in Ferrara in 1539 and invited him to Naples in 1540 to patch up her brother Ascanio's failing marriage.[12] While there he may have frequented the same Valdesian circles as Colonna and as more than a few major future dependants of Pole, above all Marcantonio Flaminio and Apollonio Merenda, with whom Bobadilla visited the Neapolitan diocese of Bisignano.[13] If so, he had some differences with them. According to an anonymous report, Bobadilla attended one meeting

[8] See my 'A Mission Worse than Death: Reginald Pole and the Parisian Theologians', *English Historical Review* 103 (1988), pp. 870–91 and 'A Sticking-plaster Saint? Autobiography and Hagiography in the Making of Reginald Pole', in Thomas F. Mayer and D.R. Woolf, eds, *The Rhetorics of Life-Writing in Early Modern Europe: Forms of Biography from Cassandra Fedele to Louis XIV* (Ann Arbor, 1995), pp. 205–22.

[9] Crehan, 'Ignatius and Pole', p. 93.

[10] *Epp. Bobad.*, pp. 620, 20. According to Bobadilla's autobiography, he left Rome for Germany after the octave of Epiphany (*ibid.*, p. 22) but Loyola announced the news of Bobadilla's legation in March 1542 at which time he said Bobadilla was still with Pole (MI *Epp. Ign.*, I, p. 195, Loyola-Simon Rodriguez, 18 March 1542).

[11] Giuseppe Signorelli, 'Il soggiorno di Vittoria Colonna in Viterbo', *Bolletino storico-archaeologico viterbese* 1:4 (1908), pp. 118–51.

[12] Arthur L. Fisher, 'A Study in Early Jesuit Government: The Nature and Origins of the Dissent of Nicolás Bobadilla', *Viator* 10 (1979), p. 415.

[13] Massimo Firpo, *Tra alumbrados e 'spirituali'. Studi su Juan de Valdés e il Valdesianesimo nella crisi religiosa del '500 italiano* (Florence, 1990), pp. 135 ff., 159–62 and 172–3. For Merenda and Bobadilla in Bisignano and Merenda's actions in Naples, see Massimo Firpo and Dario

at which possibly Juan de Valdés himself (called Paolo Valdes in the text) lectured on Paul. Bobadilla broke up the gathering by shouting that the speaker lied when he called the Pope the Antichrist and then induced the Viceroy and the Archbishop to chase the heretics.[14] Bobadilla's own specialty at the time was reading the epistles of Paul, and that was what he did in Viterbo, along with preaching and hearing confessions. Pole was very pleased on all scores.[15]

This was an especially pivotal moment for Pole and the work he assigned Bobadilla hardly casually chosen, especially not lectures on *Romans*.[16] Pole, in the midst of his tumultuous rupture with Henry VIII, was in the first stages of becoming an Italian and was probably already a believer in justification by faith. According to Massimo Firpo, he had also become one of the targets of a concerted campaign to win cardinal converts to Valdés's ideas. Flaminio was assigned to him for that purpose. Pole and his first biographer would have the story the other way round, that is, Flaminio was welcomed to Pole's household precisely because Pole knew him to be unsound on justification and intended to right that.[17] If Pole's rationale is true, it, combined with all the rest of this, would have made a good confessor (who also happened to be a Paris-trained theologian) a major desideratum. Forty years later Bobadilla claimed that Pole had used him in much that fashion, giving him 'certain suspected books, not his own' to examine before Paul III sent him to Germany.[18] It would only have been human for Pole to be annoyed when Loyola (claiming Paul III's authority) took

---

Marcatto, eds, *Il processo inquisitoriale del Cardinal Giovanni Morone*, 5 vols (Rome, 1981–89), I, pp. 241–43.

[14] *Epp. Bobad.*, pp. 17–21, an anonymous but allegedly contemporary report, sometimes said to be based on materials from Bobadilla, but there is no textual warrant for this. Much of the tale the document tells cannot be true. The mysterious Paolo, for example, is unlikely to have been Valdés who neither taught in public nor could have fled Naples, where he stayed until his death, and he was always very cautious about attacking the institutional church.

[15] Pole-Loyola, Viterbo, 22 December 1541, ARSI, Epistolae Externae 7/I, f. 5 (*Epp. Bobad.*, no. 20 and ERP 5, no. 57).

[16] Is it possible that Bobadilla's success in Viterbo led Pole to recommend to Morone that he bring a Jesuit to Modena to deal with heretics? Morone got Alfonso Salmerón, whom Morone threw out after he caused a major disaster by preaching good works. Massimo Firpo, 'Gli "spirituali", l'Accademia di Modena e il formulario di fede del 1542: controllo del dissenso religioso e nicodemismo', in *Inquisizione romana e controriforma. Studi sul Giovanni Morone e il suo processo d'eresia* (Bologna, 1992), pp. 115–16 and 'Il primo processo inquisitoriale contro il cardinal Giovanni Morone (1552–53)', *ibid.*, pp. 186–87. Could Bobadilla have had more evangelical views than Salmerón? Were there thus differences of opinion within the Jesuits? After all, the report on Bobadilla's actions in Naples says he objected only when the speaker attacked the pope. Was his silence before that a matter of discretion or of tacit agreement? Justification by faith combined with deep loyalty to the institutional church was, of course, Pole's own position.

[17] Firpo, *Allumbrados*, pp. 172–73. Ludovico Becccadelli, 'Vita di Reginaldo Polo' in G.B. Morandi, ed., *Monumenti di varia letteratura*, 2 vols (Bologna, 1797–1804), I/2, pp. 349–50.

[18] 'Ciertos libros sospechosos, no suyos.' *Epp. Bobad.*, p. 560, Bobadilla-Sodali Hispano in Urbe degenti, 17 September 1583.

Bobadilla away. When Pole wrote to Loyola that Bobadilla had just begun to have a positive effect and that 'I would feel great displeasure from it [Bobadilla's withdrawal], when I did not know that, besides obeying our lord [the Pope], it were to the greater glory of God, and the greater benefit of his church', Pole implied that he *was* displeased with Loyola, a fact that a concluding declaration of his 'very ready inclination' to Loyola and the order barely concealed.[19]

Pole never again had Bobadilla at his exclusive disposal, but he did claim his services twice more for others. In 1549 he persuaded Loyola to let Bobadilla visit monasteries in Pisa, probably of the Girolamites, with whom Pole as their protector had been having trouble for several years.[20] There may have been a proposal about then to have Bobadilla join Pole in a projected mission to England.[21] Even more significant, in 1551, against Loyola's wishes, Pole got Bobadilla seconded (as inquisitor, according to Bobadilla's later recollection) to Cardinal Duranti de Durante, who had retired to his bishopric of Brescia.[22] Durante had been Paul III's chamberlain, and was generally held in very low esteem. Pole, however, seems to have done his best to help him, perhaps out of loyalty to the Farnese. In any case, Pole had once more to fight with Loyola over Bobadilla.

By then Bobadilla's relations with Loyola had been severely strained for at least a decade.[23] In 1550–51 Bobadilla delivered blunt criticisms of Loyola's quasi-monarchical government of the order to an assembly called by the general.[24] And although Pole continued to be consulted by the Jesuits, it may not be coincidence that the last contact between them before Edward VI's death sounds fraught. A friend of the Jesuits in Bassano wrote to Loyola that Alvise Priuli, Pole's life-long companion and a principal financial support had ordered ten scudi given to finish a hermitage there. But the writer was not optimistic that he would see the money.[25]

---

[19] 'Io ne [Bobadilla's withdrawal] sentirei gran dispiacere, quando non conoscessi, che, oltra al ubedire alla santità di nostro signore, esso sia a maggior gloria di Dio, et a maggior beneficio della sua chiesa . . . prontissimo animo.' *Epp. Bobad.*, no. 20. See note 13 above.

[20] Pole-Fra Bernardo da Vicenza, provincial of the Congregation of Beato Pietro da Pisa in Venice, 13 January 1541 (ERP, 4, pp. 437–38); Pole (identified as protector) – Santo de Sant' Agatha, Congregation of Beato Pietro da Pisa in Venice, 24 March 1548 (ERP, 4, pp. 440–41); and Pole's undated mandate ordering punishment for Fra Mansueti da Bagnacavallo (ERP, 4, pp. 441–42).

[21] Crehan, 'Ignatius and Pole', p. 83 for the mission. For its background see August von Druffel, 'Die Sendung des Cardinals Sfondrato an den Hof Karls V, 1547–1548', *Abhandlung der historischer Classe der königlicher Bayerischer Akademie der Wissenschaften* 20, Abt. 2 (1893), pp. 312–17.

[22] *Epp. Bobad.*, pp. 167 and 624. MI *Epp. Ign.*, III, pp. 611 and 614.

[23] Fisher, 'Bobadilla', p. 421.

[24] *Ibid.*, p. 427.

[25] Gaspar Gropello-Loyola, Bassano, 10 January 1553, V. Agustí, S.J., ed., *Epistolae Mixtae ex variis Europae locis ab anno 1537 ad 1556*, 5 vols (Madrid, 1898–1901) MHSI 12, 14, 17, 18, 20; III, 58.

In sharp contrast, among the arrangements Pole made before his departure for England in 1553 was the distribution of proceeds from his abbey of Canalnuovo.[26] He instructed the income to be divided between the poor priests of San Nicolò in Venice, and a similar group in Rome. It is most likely that San Nicolò is San Nicolò da Tolentino, the Theatines' Venetian church. The strict new order thus got exactly fifty times as much support directly from Pole as Priuli indirectly gave the Jesuits at almost the same moment, not counting the money which went to Rome. Even if San Nicolò turns out to be the Benedictine house of that name on the Lido, that still reinforces Pole's financial preference for some order other than the Jesuits.[27] Where he chose to put his cash may, of course, be a silly measure of the notoriously 'unworldly' Pole's attitudes, but for a cardinal who always had few resources, a gift equivalent to, for example, two and a half times his principal monthly income from Paul III was no small matter.[28] More important as a sign of Pole's leanings is his notorious interview in April 1553 with Gian Pietro Carafa, founder of the Theatines. Whatever one makes of the sincerity of the reconciliation between the two (I am inclined to give it a degree of credence), Pole emphasized his favour to the Theatines by reminding Carafa early on that he had frequently interceded on behalf of Bernardino Scotti with Carafa.[29] Scotti was one of the earliest Theatines, for many years *praepositus* of its house in Venice, and later right-hand man of Carafa when he became Paul IV.[30]

[26] Pole got the abbey in the distribution of spoils shortly before Paul III's death. Venice, Archivio di Stato, Archivio Proprio Roma, 7 (CSP Venetian, V, no. 586), Matteo Dandolo's report from Rome, 9 November 1549. The abbey, part of Cardinal Benedetto Accolti's rich horde, had been much sought after, with potentates of the stature of Cosimo I involved in its disposition. Beccadelli, 'Vita', p. 323 said Canalnuovo brought in 1000 *scudi* per year. Pole-Pietro Contarini, 22 October 1553 for the dispersal of the income, VL 6754, f. 274ᵛ.

[27] The Benedictine house seems to be excluded as Pole's beneficiary by the specification that the money was to go to 'poor priests'. That phrase instead fits the Theatines perfectly. Then again, Pole was protector of the Benedictine order, and Contarini's nephew Placido, to whom Pole wrote a strongly worded letter about obedience, became prior there by 1557. Bibliothèque publique, Douai, MS 922, vol. 4, pp. 115–21 (?), Pole-Placido Contarini, 16 September 1553 (VL 5967, ff. 330ʳ–37ʳ, fair copy with sigilla, possibly prepared for the press; ERP, 4, no. 12); Biblioteca Palatina, Parma, MS Palatina 1010, f. 174ʳ, Ludovico Beccadelli-Placido Contarini, Priore di San Nicolò a Vinetia, 7 April 1557.

[28] CSP Venetian, V, xiii; and Beccadelli, 'Vita', p. 322 for Pole's basic stipend. Elisabeth Gleason has kindly confirmed that figure from the records of the Datary. Between January 1548 and November 1549 Pole's pension was only 100 *scudi* per month (BAV Vat. lat. 10604 ff. 136ᵛ–75ᵛ).

[29] Morandi, ed., *Monumenti*, I/2, p. 349.

[30] Bartolomé Mas, 'El p. Bernardino Scotti y la legación de Paulo III a Carlos V en 1548', *Regnum Dei* 3 (1947), pp. 181–95 gives Scotti as *praepositus* in 1554, but it is unclear whether he had held the position continuously. Given Inquisitor Scotti's deep interest in Pietro Carnesecchi's abbey of Eboli, it is not impossible that Pole's 'donation' to San Nicolò had something of the character of a bribe. That would make it a partly political and prudential move, but does not lessen its importance as a sign of rapprochement with the Theatines, however motivated. Carnesecchi reported to Giulia Gonzaga on 23 September 1559 that Morone said there had been heavy pressure on him to renounce Eboli to Scotti while he was imprisoned. *Processo*

The nature of Pole's earlier relations with Scotti is unknown, but from then on the rising trajectory of Pole's favour to him traces in reverse the path of Bobadilla's continually sinking star with Loyola.

Similarly, whereas Loyola refused Bobadilla to Pole, Pole's household from at least 1549 included a Theatine who was one of his most important agents. Thomas Goldwell probably met Pole in the late 1530s through the English hospice in Rome of which he was an officer and Pole the *custos*, although they could have met earlier in Padua or Flanders.[31] Goldwell became a Theatine novice in 1548 and was professed in 1550, after serving as one of Pole's attendants in the conclave of Julius III. He thus had an extremely sensitive position in Pole's entourage, and may very well have had much to do with Pole's attitude to his order. Pole gave Goldwell two crucial missions, to Mary in 1553 and, even more significant, to Paul IV during the second half of 1555; he left for Rome at nearly the moment news of Paul's election arrived in England.[32] Goldwell had already been nominated Bishop of St Asaph and would have been translated to Oxford but for Mary's death. He apparently spent a fair amount of time in his diocese, but Pole either continued to consider him such a vital part of his central administration that he deserved permanent accommodation at Lambeth (even if he did not use it) or Goldwell had returned to London by the time of Pole's death. In any case, he had one of the best rooms in Lambeth assigned to him then.[33]

Despite this increasing intimacy with two key Theatines and perhaps with their founder, Pole continued to support the Jesuits, intervening on their behalf in Flanders, for which Loyola warmly thanked him.[34] Loyola had also sent Pole a powerful letter of congratulations on English events in July 1553, but the first explicit offer of help was neatly timed to arrive in February 1555 shortly after Pole returned to England.[35] Loyola probably sent this letter in reply to one from

Morone, 5, p. 537; cf. Giacomo Manzoni, ed., 'Il Processo Carnesecchi', *Miscellanea di storia italiana* 10 (1870), pp. 379–80. When Carnesecchi had been condemned earlier that year, Eboli (worth 1500 *scudi* per year) had gone to Scotti. *Processo Morone*, 5, p. 434n. For the rest of the sordid manoeuvres, see *Processo Carnesecchi*, pp. 342, 353, 407, 411.

[31] A.B. Emden, *A Biographical Register of the University of Oxford A. D. 1501 to 1540* (Oxford, 1974) *s. n.*

[32] Pole's instructions for Goldwell to Mary are in Biblioteca Corsiniana, Rome, MS 33 E 19, 400–10, with other copies in ASV Bolognetti 94, ff. 213^r–18^r, and BL Add. MS 25425, ff. 126^r–29^v. Pole's credentials for Goldwell to Paul IV of 24 June 1555 are in ASV A. A. I–XVIII 6540, f. 154^r, orig.

[33] PRO, SP 12/1, ff. 20^r–29^r. For Goldwell in Wales, see Glanmor Williams, *Renewal and Reformation. Wales c. 1415–1642* (Oxford, 1987), pp. 303–04.

[34] Loyola-Adrian Adriaenssens, 27 February 1554, MI *Epp. Ign.*, VI, p. 391; Loyola-Bernard Olivier, 1 May 1554, *ibid.*, p. 652; Loyola-Pole, 16 October 1554, MI *Epp. Ign.*, VII, p. 665; and *Pol. Chron.*, IV, pp. 285 ff.

[35] Loyola-Pole, 24 January 1555, MI *Epp. Ign.*, VIII, pp. 308–11 (also printed in ERP, 5, no. 59; translated in *Letters of St Ignatius of Loyola*, ed. and trans. William. J. Young, S.J. [Chicago, 1959], pp. 361–62).

Pole full of his hopes for success in England which he apparently sent Loyola before he left Brussels.[36] If so, the letter does not survive. If it did, it seems it would make a marked contrast to Pole's further reaction to Loyola's enthusiasm. He waited nearly four months to reply to the letter which came in February (he was never a quick correspondent) and concluded by asking Loyola especially to greet 'our very dearest Bobadilla'.[37] Pole congratulated Loyola on the election of Marcellus II, but passed over his offer in silence.[38] There could have been more to this exchange than appears on the surface. At almost the moment Loyola's letter arrived, he was alleged to have explicitly excluded Bobadilla (and only him) from consideration in the election for a vicar general of the order, won instead by Jerónimo Nadal.[39] Probably neither Bobadilla (who did not record it years later in his autobiography nor refer to it in his few surviving contemporary letters) nor Pole knew of this slight, if Loyola delivered it, but the mere claim symbolizes the depths Loyola's and Bobadilla's friendship had reached. But it is not impossible that Pole learned what had happened. The moment certainly appears to mark a turning-point in his attitude to the Jesuits.

After Loyola received Pole's possibly not entirely ingenuous letter with its implicit support of Bobadilla, he fired off another offer in reply, but if Pole received it, he ignored it.[40] Instead, he reported to the Pope's nephew his efforts with Philip on behalf of Scotti whom Paul had nominated to the bishopric of Trani in Philip's Italian territory.[41] Undeterred, Loyola gave Goldwell (a possibly ironic bearer!) a short note for Pole in October 1555, designed to prepare the ground for Ribadeneira's proposed mission to England.[42] Pole replied

---

[36] *Ibid.*, p. 222, a news bulletin of 2 January 1555.

[37] 'Nostro carissimo Boadiglia'. Pole-Loyola, 8 May 1555, ARSI, Epistolae Externae 7/II, f. 43ʳ, orig. (ERP, 5, no. 60; also in MI *Epp. Ign.*, XII, p. 508).

[38] For Pole's high opinion of the new pope, see his letter to Marcellus II, 28 April 1555, VL 5967, ff. 402ʳ⁻ᵛ continued on 409ʳ, a minute in Marcantonio Faita's hand with corrections perhaps in Gianbattista Binardi's hand, headed in Binardi's hand (Lutz, no. 94; ERP, 5, no. 3; CSP Venetian, VI/1, no. 66). Cf. William V. Hudon, *Marcello Cervini and Ecclesiastical Government in Tridentine Italy* (DeKalb, Illinois, 1992), p. 154.

[39] Fisher, 'Bobadilla', p. 427. The allegation came from Nadal, one of Bobadilla's strongest detractors, and thus deserves at least some measure of discounting. See Nadal's undated entry for 1555 in *Epp. Nadal*, II, p. 32. The election occurred shortly before 12–13 February when Loyola informed Peter Canisius of the result. MI *Epp. Ign.*, VII, p. 402. Ulderico Parente, 'Nicolás Bobadilla, 1509–1590', *AHSI* 59 (1990), pp. 333–34 does not cite Nadal's entry nor mention this *contre-temps*. He notes for the time in question only that Bobadilla was in Rome in January and had reached Venice by 16 March on his aborted mission to Poland. None of the sources Parente lists for all of 1555 refers to the incident. See also William V. Bangert, S.J., *Jerome Nadal, S. J. 1507–1580. Tracking the First Generation of Jesuits* (Chicago, 1992), pp. 135–36.

[40] 2 July 1555, Loyola-Pole, MI *Epp. Ign.*, IX, pp. 273–75.

[41] Pole-Carlo Carafa, 28–29 August 1555, VL 6754, ff. 179ʳ⁻80ʳ, dated 24 August 1555 (Lutz, no. 106; CSP Venetian, VI/1, no. 196, to Cardinal Carafa, ?28 August 1555).

[42] Loyola-Pole, 25 October 1555, MI *Epp. Ign.*, X, p. 38.

noncommittally in December that he would be happy to see Ribadeneira.[43] By contrast, he enthusiastically took up Scotti's request for advice when Paul nominated him a cardinal, and he continued to pitch hard with Philip about Trani.[44] In January 1556 he offered Scotti any and all services on that score or any other and sent him another much more than cordial letter that spring.[45] Two and a half years later, Priuli, acting as Pole's executor, expected that Scotti would help to fulfil Pole's intentions (and perhaps defend him once more to Paul).[46]

At the turn of 1555–56 Loyola took two new steps at least one of which he explicitly intended to gain the order access to England. First, he claimed to have enlisted Morone's help.[47] If he did, there is no trace of it in the relatively copious Morone-Pole correspondence.[48] The second step is better documented but harder to explain. On 2 February Loyola strongly recommended Francisco Delgado to Pole.[49] This is a little curious on the face of it, since Delgado was a client

---

[43] Pole-Loyola, 15 December 1555, ARSI, Epistolae Externae 7/II, f. 45[r], orig. (*ibid.*, p. 39 and ERP, 5, no. 61).

[44] Scotti-Pole, n. d., in Giuseppe Silos, *Historiarum clericorum regularium*, 3 vols (Rome, 1650–66) I, p. 333; a second letter, *ibid.*; and VL 6754, f. 187[v]. For Trani, VL 6754, ff. 199[v]–200[v] (Lutz, no. 117, text truncated; CSP Venetian, VI/1, no. 361) and ff. 194[v]–95[r] (Lutz, no. 118, text again truncated; CSP Venetian, VI,/1, no. 370). In January 1556 Morone wrote Pole that he thought Scotti a 'vero Israelita, & è tutto affetionato a V. S. R.', (4 January 1556, VL 6404, f. 145[r] auto. orig., no address; ERP, 5, no. 47 and Lutz, 297n), and Pole assured Morone in February that he fully agreed with Paul's high opinion of Scotti (5 February 1556, BM C. 73, f. 169[r], orig.; CSP Venetian, VI/1, no. 378).

[45] 28 January 1556, VL 6754, ff. 195[r]–6[r] (CSP Venetian, VI/1, no. 371) and Spring 1556, ff. 215[v]–16[v] (CSP Venetian, VI/1, no. 530).

[46] Probably after 27 November 1558, Priuli-[Antonio] Giberti, VL 6754, f. 258[v] (English translation in Thomas Duffus Hardy, *Report . . . Upon the Documents in the Archives and Public Libraries of Venice* [London, 1866], pp. 63–67).

[47] Crehan, 'Ignatius and Pole', p. 89.

[48] Pole-Morone, 9 August 1555, VL 6754, ff. 175[v]–77[r] (CSP Venetian, VI/1, no. 179); Pole-Morone, 10 November 1555, *ibid.*, ff. 184[v]–85[v] (CSP Venetian, VI/1, no. 276, dated 11 November); Morone-Pole, 11 December 1555, ASV Armaria 64:32, ff. 210[r]–11[v], orig. (CSP Venetian, VI/1, no. 310; Lutz, no. 111); Morone-Pole, 4 January 1556, VL 6404, f. 145[r], auto. orig., no address (ERP, 5, no. 47; Lutz, 297n); Pole-Morone, 7 January 1556, VL 6754, ff. 188[v]–89[r] (CSP Venetian, VI/1, no. 342; Lutz, no. 114); Pole-Morone, 27 January 1556, ff. 192[v]–93[r] (CSP Venetian, VI/1, no. 369); Pole-Morone, 5 February 1556, BM C. 73, f. 169[r]., orig. (CSP Venetian, VI/1, no. 378); Pole-Morone, 19 February 1556, VL 6754, ff. 201[v]–04[v] (CSP Venetian, VI/1, no. 396; Lutz, 310n8); Morone-Pole, 31 March 1556, VL 6404, ff. 146–47, auto.? (Lutz, no. 124, with mistaken vol. number and incomplete text; ERP, 5, no. 48); Pole-Morone, 18 April 1556? or 3 May 1556?, VL 6754, f. 213[v] (CSP Venetian, VI/1, no. 471, dated 3 May?; cf. ERP, 5, no. 10 for date; Lutz, 318n); Morone-Pole, 9 June 1556, VL 6404, ff. 150[r]–52[r] auto.? (Lutz, no. 126; ERP, 5, no. 50); Pole-Morone, 14 July 1556, BM, Cod. C. 73, ff. 165[r]–66[r] (Lutz, 326n); Morone-Pole, 18 July 1556, VL 6404, ff. 154[r–v], auto.? (Lutz, no. 128; ERP, 5, no. 51); Morone-Pole, 19 August, 1556, VL 6404, f. 156 auto.? (ERP, 5, no. 52; Lutz, 330–31n); Pole-Morone, 14 September 1556, VL 6754, ff. 224[r–v] (CSP Venetian, VI/1, no. 613); Pole-Morone, 12 October 1556, BM C. 73, ff. 170[r–v], orig. (CSP Venetian, VI/1, no. 657); Pole-Morone, 9 November 1556, VL 6407, f. 218, orig. (ERP, 5, no. 53).

[49] Loyola-Pole, 19 February 1556, MI *Epp. Ign.*, XI, p. 26.

of Philip's confessor Bernardo Fresneda.[50] Perhaps Loyola hoped to curry favour with this powerful Franciscan and win him over to a Jesuit mission to England. But there is another, more sinister, interpretation. According to testimony given in Bartolomé Carranza's trial, Fresneda had planted Delgado in Pole's household to spy on Carranza, and everyone knew that as Fresneda's client Delgado was Carranza's enemy.[51] Delgado would indeed testify against him, but he gave at least as damning evidence against Pole and several members of his household.[52] It is plausible to think that Loyola might have helped to 'plant' Delgado since he was said to have had suspicions about members of Pole's household, in particular Flaminio.[53] In Loyola's defence, Delgado seems to have been an effective spy. No one in Pole's household suspected him; rather they expected after Pole's death that he would help in Spain with several of their cases.[54]

Loyola's letter about Delgado was his last to Pole. Within a few months Loyola would be dead, and within a year the order more than ever in need of powerful patrons. Pole was not a likely candidate. Loyola's chosen successor Diego Laínez made a half-hearted approach in late 1556, but Pole rebuffed him.[55] The order encountered a serious problem shortly thereafter. It concerned its constitutions and their confirmation.[56] Bobadilla had his revenge on Loyola by demanding

---

[50] J.I. Tellechea Idígoras, *Fray Bartolomé Carranza y el Cardenal Pole. Un navarro en la restauración católica (1554–1558)* (Pamplona, 1977), p. 176. The relevant part of Diego Jimenez's testimony is edited by Tellechea Idígoras in *Fray Bartolomé Carranza. Documentos historicos* (Madrid, 1966), III, pp. 497–98.

[51] *Ibid.*

[52] J.I. Tellechea Idígoras, *Fray Bartolomé Carranza. Documentos historicos* (Madrid, 1963), II, pp. 944–50.

[53] F. Cervós, S.J., ed., *Epistolae PP. Paschasii Broéti, Claudii Jaji, Joannis Codurii, et Simonis Rodericii, S.I.* (Madrid, 1903) MHSI 24, p. 681, Simon Rodriguez-Ludovico Gonzalez, 29 March 1559.

[54] Biblioteca civica, Bergamo, Archivio Stella in Archivio Silvestri, 40/135 (Giuseppe Bonelli, 'Un archivio privato del Cinquecento: le Carte Stella', *Archivio storico Lombardo* 34 (1907), pp. 332–86, no. 157), Priuli-Nicoló Ormanetto, 27 June 1559; *ibid.*, 40/139 (Bonelli, no. 161), Priuli-Ormanetto, 12 August 1559. If Delgado were really in Spain, this may represent an inconsistency in Jimenez's testimony. He claimed that Fresneda refused Delgado's request to join him there since Delgado was unable to come up with any damaging material about Carranza. *Documentos historicos*, 3, p. 498. Delgado apparently went to Rome after leaving Pole's service, which would square with Jimenez's evidence (BL, Add. MS 35830, f. 30^r, addressed to Francisco Delgado, chaplain in Rome, 30 July 1558), although he still had a room and a servant in Lambeth after Pole's death (PRO, SP 12/1, ff. 20^r–29^r). Jimenez also said that Delgado entered Pole's household in Flanders, which would have to have been before October 1554. If Jimenez was correct, Loyola could not have recommended that Delgado join Pole eighteen months later. Loyola's language is ambiguous ('spero sarà buono et fidele servitor'), and perhaps he meant only to recommend Delgado again. But what was Delgado doing in Rome?

[55] *Pol. Chron.*, VI, p. 452 and Pole's letter of 15 November 1556 to Laínez, ARSI, Epistolae Externae 7/II, f. 52^r, orig. (ERP, 5, no. 62, without place or date).

[56] Mario Scaduto, S.J., *L'Epoca di Giacomo Lainez. Il Governo. 1556–1565. Storia della Compagnia di Gesù in Italia, 3* (Rome, 1964), p. 31.

that Pope Paul, with whom he had a close relationship, pass judgement on the validity of the Jesuits' constitutional structure, in particular whether the order was to be ruled as a monarchy or as an aristocracy, the position Bobadilla favoured.[57] Paul quickly took up Bobadilla's invitation, and assigned the case to two cardinals, Johannes Reuman and Scotti, the second of whom Bobadilla had suggested.[58] Scotti's involvement was one reason the Jesuits could have expected little from Pole. Further, Pole probably sympathized to some degree with Bobadilla's views. The extreme papalist Pole of the hagiographical tradition is a caricature, even in the case of his allegedly most strongly pro-papal work, *Pro ecclesiasticae unitatis defensione*.[59] Instead of endorsing the movement towards papal absolutism in which Paul IV played a crucial role, Pole, both in *De unitate* and even more in *De summo pontifice* (written 1549–50), grounded the papacy not in hierarchical pretensions and power politics, but on the blood of the martyrs, a dangerously charismatic form of legitimacy.[60] He very carefully preserved the role of the rest of the hierarchy, even if he never went as far as his secretary Thomas Starkey who put fully conciliarist views into Pole's mouth.[61] And finally, whatever his conception of the papal office, Pole in early 1556 worked very hard to keep in Paul's good graces in order to avoid a war which would further lacerate 'afflicted Christianity'.[62] For all these reasons, by mid-1556 Pole had lost most of whatever interest he may have had in the Jesuits.

Given Pole's links to the Theatines, the Jesuits may always have been too late to get very far with him. As important and as vibrant as Pole's relations with Goldwell and Scotti were, he had an institutional and spiritual tie to another order which also dampened his enthusiasm for the Jesuits. Since at least 1550, Pole had been protector of the Cassinese congregation of the Benedictines, the reform wing of the order which had its origins in Santa Giustina, Padua.[63] Pole

---

[57] Fisher, 'Bobadilla', *passim*. Bobadilla underscored his intimacy with Paul IV in his 'Autobiography', *Epp. Bobad.*, pp. 38–39. Cf. also Bangert, *Nadal*, pp. 173–92.

[58] March–June 1557, 'Votum de Nicolás Bobadilla', in *Epp. Nadal*, IV, p. 100.

[59] Thomas F. Mayer, 'Nursery of Resistance: Reginald Pole and his Friends', in Paul A. Fideler and Thomas F. Mayer, eds, *The Commonwealth of Tudor England* (London, 1992), pp. 50–74.

[60] For a useful if ahistorical analysis which is also vitiated by its author's failure to find any of the numerous MSS of the work, see Martin Trimpe, 'Macht aus Gehorsam. Grundmotive der Theologie des päpstlichen Primates im Denken Reginald Poles (1500–1558)', Inaugural-Dissertation des Fachbereichs Katholische Theologie der Universität Regensburg, 1972, summarized in Josef Ratzinger, 'The Papal Primacy and the Unity of the People of God', in *Church, Ecumenism and Politics: New Essays in Ecclesiology* (New York, 1988), pp. 36–44.

[61] Thomas Starkey, *A Dialogue between Pole and Lupset*, ed. T.F. Mayer (London, 1989), (Camden Fourth Series, no. 37), pp. 82–3 and 132–33.

[62] For Pole's dread of war within Christendom, see, e.g., his letter to Morone of 14 July 1556, BM, Cod. C. 73, ff. 165^r–66^r.

[63] A letter from Pole to the Prior of San Paolo, Rome, probably written in the early 1550s, showed him deeply involved in the order's affairs, VL 6754, ff. 36^v–37^r (CSP Venetian, V, no. 689, dated December 1550; cf. *Processo Morone*, 2, pp. 567–68, which suggests the early 1550s).

had for years been close to the congregation's piety and Pauline Christianity.[64] When he was appointed legate in 1553 he was in retirement in one of the congregation's houses at Maguzzano. It is unclear whether Pole acted as protector after he returned to England, but he continued to involve himself in the order's affairs.[65] Most important, he tried hard to secure Benedictine visitors for England, including his friend Teofilo Folengo.[66] The peak moment in Pole's efforts coincided with Loyola's strongest push. While Loyola practically implored Pole to accept the Jesuits, Pole was himself begging returning papal envoy Antonio Agustín for help in persuading Charles V's ministers to allow the visitors.[67] Priuli wrote to Pole's agent in Rome at the same time asking him to approach Cardinals Giacomo Puteo and Siguenza (Pedro Pacheco).[68] Agustín thought there would be no problem, but in fact the men Pole wanted went to Spain instead.[69] Visitors or no visitors, Pole went on to help Mary refound the centrally important Benedictine house of Westminster Abbey.

Pole did the same for the Dominican house of Blackfriars. He had manifold and profound links to the order, which could well have interfered in his attitude to the Jesuits. Some of the most powerful Dominicans and some of their most important writers backed Pole strongly. Space precludes a complete discussion, but among these were successive masters of the sacred palace, Egidio Foscarari and even more Girolamo Muzzarelli. Foscarari had a hand in the revision of Pole's works, after suffering imprisonment by Paul IV in 1559.[70] Muzzarelli sacrificed his career in an attempt to forward Pole's peace policy, after having

---

64 Barry Collett, *Italian Benedictine Scholars and the Reformation. The Congregation of Santa Giustina of Padua* (Oxford, 1985), pp. 77–78, 80, 88, 111–12, and *passim*. Cf. also Carlo Ginzburg and Adriano Prosperi, *Giochi di pazienza. Un seminario sul 'Beneficio di Cristo'* (Turin, 1975), which makes much of the similarities between Flaminio's piety and traditional Benedictine forms, and Benedetto da Mantova, *Il Beneficio di Cristo con le versioni del secolo XVI, documenti e testimonianze*, ed. Salvatore Caponetto (DeKalb-Florence, 1972), pp. 469–96.

65 By December 1555 Pole had apparently ceased to act as protector, having been replaced by the Cardinal of Siguenza, his old ally Pedro Pacheco (although it is possible that Priuli meant to refer to Pacheco as the protector of Spain). ASV Armaria 64:28, f. 132^r, Priuli-G. F. Stella, 4 December 1555.

66 The abbot of San Paolo, Rome licensed the visitors in 1557, but they seem never to have come. Pole-Abbot of San Paolo, Rome, 28 May 1557, VL 6754, f. 231^r–v (CSP Venetian, VI/2, no. 904). See also Priuli-Ludovico Beccadelli, 15 December 1556, Bodl. MS. Ital. C. 25, ff. 302^r–304^v (ERP 5, 347). Cf. David Knowles, *The Religious Orders in England*, 3 vols (Cambridge, 1948-59) III, 424–25 and Collett, *Italian Benedictines*, p. 251. In 1546 Folengo had dedicated his *Commentaria in primam D. Ioannis Epistolam* (Venice, Aldus) to Pole. For more on Folengo's career, see Caponetto, ed., *Beneficio*, pp. 486 and 489.

67 ASV Armaria 44:4, ff. 29^r and 32^r–v, 24 November 1555.

68 ASV Armaria 64:28, f. 132^r.

69 ASV Armaria 42:8, ff. 47^r–48^r, 14 July 1556, papal breve to Folengo, the abbot of Santa Maria da Pira and Eutichio de Sant' Angelo.

70 *Processo Carnesecchi*, p. 435; *Processo Morone*, 2, pp. 401–02. Cf. Gigliola Fragnito, 'Aspetti della censura ecclesiastica nell'Europa della controriforma: L'edizione parigina delle opere di Gasparo Contarini', *Rivista di storia e letteratura religiosa* 21 (1985), p. 25.

protected Pole from Carafa and an Inquisition *processo* by strong-arm tactics (at papal orders) in 1552.[71] The respected theologian Reginaldo de' Nerli tried to get Pole to help bring Nerli's fellow Dominican and Cardinal Pietro Bertano back from Lutheranism, and then, like Muzzarelli, if not quite as actively, did his best to wreck the first investigation of Pole and Morone by the Inquisition.[72] Finally, two Spanish Dominicans contributed greatly to Pole's spiritual and probably theological development in the last phase of his career, Pedro de Soto and Bartolomé Carranza.[73] De Soto also acted as Pole's agent at the crucial moment in his negotiations with Charles V over his return to England.[74] It is not a coincidence that de Soto and his brother Dominican Juan de Villagarcia wound up in the two most important English chairs of theology under Pole's regime.

Bishop Burnet closely linked Pole's treatment of the Jesuits and the Benedictines. He claimed that the Jesuits tried to persuade Pole that 'the Benedictine order was become rather a clog than a help to the church', and therefore its property should go to the Jesuits to support 'schools and seminaries'. Further, the Jesuits proposed to get most of the church's expropriated property back through spiritual counsel to the dying.[75] Burnet appeared to allege a source for his story, a manuscript discovered in Venice by his friend Mr Crawford, chaplain to the English ambassador, Sir Thomas Higgins. I have not been able to identify this text. Nevertheless, Burnet's claim seems plausible on three grounds: (1) Pole was

---

[71] Heinrich Lutz, ed., *Nuntiaturberichte aus Deutschland 1533–1559 nebst ergänzenden Aktenstücke*, 14, *Nuntiatur des Girolamo Muzzarelli Sendung des Antonio Agustin Legation des Scipione Rebiba* (Tübingen, 1971) XXIII and *passim*; *Processo Morone*, 1, pp. 285–87 and 2:2, pp. 272–77, 718–22 and 811.

[72] *Processo Morone*, p. 250 for his career and 2, 102 for his role in the *processo*. Nerli was also accounted a friend of the Jesuits (*ibid.*, 300n).

[73] Tellechea Idígoras, *Carranza* and *Sábado espiritual y otros ensayos carrancianos* (Salamanca, 1987); Venancio D. Carro, *El Maestro Fr Pedro de Soto, O. P. y Las controversias politico-teológicas en el siglo XVI*, 2 vols (Salamanca, 1931, 1950). De Soto may have been friendly to the Society; see Bangert, *Nadal*, pp. 141, 142.

[74] See Pole's instructions for de Soto of c. 8 November 1553, PRO, SP 69/1, ff. 150^r–53^v; Lutz, p. 91 n. 3; and their correspondence of 12 December 1553 (*ibid.*, no. 37); 22 December 1553 (*ibid.*, no. 40); 5 August 1554 (Carro, 2, 864–5); 12 August 1554 (Carro, 2, 866); and 2 September 1554 (VL 5967, f. 374^{r-v}; Carro, II, p. 866). Pole may also have recommended de Soto to Scotti. Biblioteca Apostolica Vaticana, MS Ottobonianus 3166, ff. 379^v–80^r, which has a corrupted version of the title which appears without text in VL 6754, f. 187^v as to Don Leonardo [*sic*] che fu poi Cardinal Trani.

[75] Nicholas Pocock, ed., *The History of the Reformation of the Church of England by Gilbert Burnet*, 7 vols (Oxford, 1865), II, pp. 525–26. Burnet's argument was taken over whole by Rasiel de Selva (a pseudonym, according to the British Library catalogue, which proposes to identify him tentatively with Pierre Quesnel, Quesnell of Dieppe, or Charles Gabriel Porée), *The History of the Wonderful Don Ignatius de Loyola*, 2 vols (London, 1754), II, pp. 33–34. I am grateful to Fr McCoog for help with this bibliographical item. At least one of Pole's Anglican detractors also endorsed this argument. Timothy Neve, *Animadversions upon Mr Phillips's History of the Life of Cardinal Pole* (Oxford, 1766), p. 540 with MS notes in part III of Neve's annotated copy in the British Library. Oddly enough, Neve worked from Rasiel de Selva, not Burnet.

undoubtedly concerned about ecclesiastical property and had almost jeopardized the reconciliation by his intransigent demands that it all be returned; (2) he did re-establish the Benedictines; and (3) his synodal legislation of 1556 made provision for establishing seminaries, information he did not report to Loyola.[76]

Burnet's theory might appear little more than a clever inference, except for one point in its favour. On 1 December 1554 the theologians of the University of Paris, following the lead of Cardinal Jean du Bellay, condemned the Jesuits, as 'destructive of monastic life', among other things.[77] This event could well have had particular relevance to Pole's attitude for two reasons, in addition to its strong resonance in Rome. First, he was just then deep in negotiations for peace between France and the Empire, a process in which Mary offered to act as mediator and in which Philip and his court were heavily involved.[78] It would have been difficult for Pole to respond positively to Loyola's approach without risking giving offence to the French. Second, events in Paris might well have had extra signficance to Pole because du Bellay was an old ally, who may even have gone so far as to engineer an opening to him in the conclave of Julius III.[79]

The order's emphasis on education leads to one final reason Pole may not have needed the Jesuits, a reason which further implicates Pole's personality. Not only did he propose to found seminaries in England with which any Jesuit institutions would have competed, but he may also have intended to make the English College, Rome into a seminary.[80] Crehan printed a text which claimed this; the writer apparently hoped entry would be restricted to sons of the nobility.[81] Crehan thought these two points would have made Pole more receptive to Loyola's offers to educate Britons, but the new Jesuit colleges in Rome would again have provided competition for Pole's plan.[82]

I stress competition in both these cases, as I have in examining the triangle

[76] For a brief summary of the controversy over ecclesiastical goods, see Knowles, *Tudor Age*, pp. 421 ff. The most thorough treatment of Pole's legislation is Marmion, 'London Synod', with further discussion in P.V. Brassell, S.J., *Praeformatio reformationis tridentinae de seminario clericorum* (Roehampton, 1938) and Pogson, 'Cardinal Pole', pp. 171 ff., who also points out (p. 352) that Pole neglected to mention his educational legislation in a report to Loyola on the synod.

[77] O'Malley, *First Jesuits*, pp. 288–89.

[78] Lutz, *Friedenslegation*, pp. XLI ff. for a summary.

[79] See Thomas F. Mayer, 'Il fellimento di una candidatura: la "reform tendency", Reginald Pole ed il conclave di Giulio III', *Annali dell'istituto storico italo-germanico in Trento*, forthcoming.

[80] Anthony Kenny, 'From Hospice to College', *The Venerabile* 21 (1962), p. 219.

[81] Crehan, 'Ignatius and Pole' called his anonymous document a letter from Pole's former datary Ormanetto to Gregory XIII, but that description is purely conjectural. Whoever the author was and whatever the status of the text (it seems more likely to be a *consilium* than a letter), it offered Pole's analysis at second-hand.

[82] Crehan, 'Ignatius and Pole', p. 85. McCoog cites a donation from Pole to the *Collegio Germanico*, but it remains to be established whether the entry can be trusted, and whether the payment was ever made. If both prove out, it may also be that the *Germanico* was what attracted Pole rather than the more-or-less official Jesuit sponsorship.

Pole-Bobadilla-Loyola. Pole was a nobleman first last and in-between.[83] As such his honour was very much on his mind, and he could be easily offended. One of the best examples of this is the amusing exchange between him and Carafa at San Paolo fuori le Mura in which both protested that they had only the other's honour at heart, until Pole irritably ended their sallies by offering a hundred witnesses that his conscience was clear.[84] (It was typical of Pole to appeal simultaneously to chivalric and Pauline standards.) Although he had been prepared to sacrifice nearly all of it, Pole took intense pride in his exalted family and rarely missed a chance to tax Henry VIII with his treatment of it. In very dangerous fashion, for example, he stressed its status and its role in Henry's family's succession when delivering an encomium of Princess Mary in *De unitate*, and went on to point to his own right to the throne.[85] Pole's concern for the rest of the nobility was pervasive. As Crehan was the first to point out, the text about Pole's plans for the English Hospice alleged that Pole thought that the English Reformation happened because the bishops – with Fisher's exception – were not gentlemen.[86] At one point in *De unitate*, Pole said the issue at hand was the nature of true nobility, and he later warned Henry both that he could not get a son of a second marriage accepted as his successor 'among such a number of the very noblest families', and also that the nobility would not put up with his tyranny.[87] Both the importance of the nobility in government and its proper education had been major planks in the programme of reform which Starkey put into Pole's mouth – this time probably with good justification.[88] Starkey modelled his English commonwealth on the myth of Venice, the aristocratic republic par excellence. Bobadilla's idea that the Jesuits should be governed by their founding aristocracy much more nearly resembled Starkey's scheme than did Loyola's plans (as Crehan thought). Pole's preference for the Benedictines may have stemmed from his noble identity, and it must have contributed to his forwarding of the interests of the Knights of St John of Jerusalem. Here he was also following Paul IV's orders, but he went much beyond their letter. Paul instructed Pole to do everything in his broad legatine power to help Pedro de Monserrato, the order's *magnus conservator*, on his mission to England in late 1555.[89] In 1557, tacitly rejecting Loyola's offer of a native Irishman, David Wolfe, for a change, Pole instead threw himself into restoring the Hospitallers in Ireland.[90] As in the case

---

[83] *Thomas Starkey and the Commonweal: Humanist Politics and Religion in the Reign of Henry VIII* (Cambridge, 1989), pp. 155–56.

[84] Morandi, *Monumenti*, I/2, p. 350.

[85] *Reginaldi Poli ad Henricum octavum Britanniae regem, pro ecclesiasticae unitatis defensione* (Rome, 1539), ff. LXXXV–LXXXIr.

[86] Crehan, 'Ignatius and Pole', p. 98.

[87] 'In tanto familiarum nobilissimarum numero'. *De unitate*, ff. XLVIIIr, LXXXIr, CXIIr.

[88] Mayer, *Starkey*, chap. 4.

[89] ASV Armaria 44:4, f. 141r–v, Paul IV-Pole, 6 October 1555. Pogson, 'Papal Legate', p. 114, misinterprets this letter as an order to Pole to protect papal interests.

[90] See the certified copies of Pole's letters, taken from the National Archives of Malta, in

of the Cassinese Benedictines, Pole continued to look out for the order, perhaps in part because of his ties to Philip.[91]

It is difficult not to think that politics and even calculation of advantage came into Pole's reasoning about the Jesuits, as it did in the case of these other two orders. McCoog implies the first point when he stresses the role of anti-Spanish prejudice in Pole's decision to exclude the Jesuits, but the case can be pushed further. Could it be that Pole's aversion to the Spanish match and probably to Spaniards helped to draw him (and recommend him) to Paul IV? Paul may have meant to hint as much when he wrote to Pole in December 1555 that although he had rescinded all other legations in Philip's territories, neither Pole's legation to England nor that for peace were included.[92] Is it more than a suspicious coincidence that Paul endorsed in ringing tones Pole's promotion to Canterbury just a month before he appointed Scotti to Trani, intending thereby to establish two especially trusty agents inside Philip's domains?[93] The triumvirate Pole-Scotti-Bobadilla which continued to hold at least until Scotti finally told Bobadilla to submit himself in September 1557 suggests much the same thing.[94] However these two theories may prove out, Pole trimmed his course to fit Scotti's rise and, at least until war broke out, Paul's policies. Neither left much room for the Jesuits in England. Already disinclined to do Loyola any special favours because of their disputes over Bobadilla, Pole solidified his disinterest around

the Library of The Grand Priory of the Most Venerable Order of the Hospital of St John of Jerusalem, St John's Gate, Clerkenwell, London, ref. H 43. There are three letters of 6 May 1557, two to Philip and Mary (English translations in *Six Documents Relating to Queen Mary's Restoration of the Grand Priories of England and Ireland,* by E.J. King [London, n. d.] Order of St John of Jerusalem, Historical Pamphlets, no. 7, pp. 7–10 and 11–13), and a third to the Archbishop of Dublin and the bishops of Meath and Kildare (King, pp. 15–16). On 1 December 1557 Pole wrote both to the brothers themselves (King, pp. 18–20) and also three of his officials, Henry Cole, G.F. Stella (John Francis Steele, according to King) and Maurice Clynog (Clenell in King) (King, pp. 22–3).

91 Pole sent a pair of letters in response to one from the Grand Master, the famous Jean de La Vallette, in March 1558, offering his protection and the services of his agent in Rome, as well as commendations of the Bailly of Aquila and three other knights going to join the order, n. d., but probably 8 March 1558, VL 6754, f. 94^v (CSP Venetian, VI/3, no. 1184) and 8 March 1558, f. 242^v (CSP Venetian, VI/3, no. 1186). La Vallette replied on 7 May 1558 offering his services in return and making it sound as if Pole had been instrumental in acquiring the Baillyship, which the rules of the order obliged the grantee to refuse, BL Add. MS 35830, f. 26^r.

92 ASV Armaria 44:4, ff. 174^v–75^r, 23 December 1555 (Cesare Baroni, *Annales Ecclesiastici,* ed. Oderico Raynaldo and Giov. Laderchi, 37 vols [Paris, 1864–83], XXXIII, pp. 527–28; Lutz, 291n). The Pope wrote another brief on the same day congratulating Pole on the progress of the synod. ASV Armaria 44:4, ff. 175^{r-v} (Raynaldo, XXXIII, p. 527).

93 Bernardo Navagero to Doge and Senate, 14 December 1555, Archivio di Stato, Venice, Archivio Proprio Roma, 8, f. 64^v (CSP Venetian, VI/1, no. 312). Navagero sounded amazed that Pole's enemies (including Paul?) had not even mentioned suspicions about his orthodoxy.

94 Scaduto, p. 45.

political exigencies, personal relations (especially with Goldwell and Scotti, and perhaps even Pope Paul), and spiritual inclinations.

Despite Pole's lack of response, the Jesuit leadership continued to think well of him. Salmerón and Ribadeneira in Brussels were ordered to defend him and Morone against Paul's charges of heresy in early 1558.[95] In March 1558 another mission for Ribadeneira to England was bruited.[96] This time Ribadeneira eventually reached England, but in either case he was probably a bad choice given the heated words he had hurled at Bobadilla during the dispute over the order's constitutions, and one wonders how much good either he or Salmerón (only six months before a prosecution witness against Morone) could have done in Brussels or London; they both urged extreme caution and did very little.[97] The Spanish ambassador in London thought that Pole was too lukewarm to like the Jesuits, in any case, but the ambassador's perspective had been shaped by Pole's enemies in Philip's court led by Fresneda, who would shortly thereafter triumph.[98] Oddly enough, neither Ribadeneira nor other Jesuit historians held Pole's recalcitrance against him, making signal contributions to disseminating his 'myth of sanctity'.[99] But by then past politics and personalities no longer mattered. Pole had transcended them.

---

[95] Firpo, *Inquisizione romana*, pp. 273–75.
[96] Crehan, 'Ignatius and Pole', pp. 90–94.
[97] Scaduto, p. 38. Ribadeneira had gone so far as to call Bobadilla 'Judas'. Firpo, *Inquisizione romana*, pp. 274–75 for Ribadeneira and Salmerón in Brussels. *Processo Morone*, 2, pp. 335 ff. and pp. 623 ff. records Salmerón's depositions against Morone.
[98] Firpo, *Inquisizione romana*, pp. 289 ff.
[99] Mayer, 'Sticking-plaster Saint', *passim*.

3

The Catholic Experience in Tudor Oxford

JAMES McCONICA

On 16 March 1583 William Allen, M.A., sometime fellow of Oriel College and Principal of St Mary Hall and now a doctor in theology of Douai, wrote from the English College at Rheims, 'Great complaints are made to the Queen's councillors about the university of Oxford, because of the numbers who from time to time leave their colleges and are supposed to pass over to us. This torments them exceedingly.'[1]

Allen owed his information to his brother, who had recently spent a month in London whilst waiting for safe passage out of the country. He had not been misled, nor would his brother have found the information at all hard to come by. While both universities supplied recruits for the training of priests at Rouen and in Rome,[2] the government was well aware that the continuing presence of the old religion in the universities was in large part an Oxford problem. In May 1559, lamenting the solidity of the Marian restoration at Oxford, John Jewel had complained to the Swiss reformer Heinrich Bullinger that,

> Our universities are so depressed and ruined, that at Oxford there are scarcely two individuals who think with us; and even they are so dejected and broken in spirit, that they can do nothing. That despicable friar, Soto, and another Spanish monk, I know not who, have so torn up by the roots all that Peter Martyr had so prosperously planted, that they have reduced the vineyard of the Lord into a wilderness.[3]

---

[1] Thomas Francis Knox, ed., *The First and Second Diaries of the English College, Douay* (London, 1878), p. lxx; cf. Appendices 49 and 50, pp. 362–64 for hostile reports of recusancy at Trinity and Balliol Colleges respectively at the same period.

[2] See for example Allen to Alfonso Agazzari, S.J., 3 March 1582 in Thomas Francis Knox, ed., *The Letters and Memorials of William Cardinal Allen* (London, 1882), pp. 120–21.

[3] Rev. John Ayre, ed., *The Works of John Jewel*, 4 vols (Cambridge, 1845–50), Parker Society, IV, 1213. The 'despicable friar' was Pedro de Soto, a distinguished Dominican theologian who had been confessor to Charles V and had held the chair of theology at Dillingen; he was appointed public lecturer in the *Sentences* to re-introduce teaching in

As the Elizabethan authorities were well aware, the universities since the Reformation had come to take a greater role than ever before as the seminaries of the realm. And in the government of the Church, at least up to the time of the Reformation, Oxford had been unmistakably pre-eminent.[4] The rule of the Tudors would change all that, not least because of the tenacious presence in Oxford of Catholics and Catholic practice. To understand this phenomenon it is necessary to know something of the university's earlier experience of the religious policies of Tudor governments, and something as well of the Catholic community both within and outside of Oxford itself.

Looking back with the perspective of the Queen's privy councillors, it would have seemed clear that Oxford had begun badly. The first intimation of the demands that the Tudors would place upon the universities occurred even before the Henrician Act of Supremacy: this was the consultation over the validity of the King's marriage to Catherine of Aragon, the King's 'great matter'.[5] On 3 February 1530 Archbishop William Warham as chancellor wrote to the university asking for a unanimous opinion on the validity of the King's marriage. Since, up to the time of his indictment for *praemunire* in the previous October, Wolsey had been the university's great patron (to the virtual exclusion of its chancellor, the ageing Warham), Oxford stood to be particularly embarrassed by the request. At Cambridge, where the senior members were fairly evenly divided on the issue, their chancellor Stephen Gardiner, Bishop of Winchester, persuaded them to refer the matter to a committee of theologians, and by early March the desired support for the King's position was forthcoming. Not so at Oxford. For whatever reason, in Oxford the issue became entangled – or seemingly so – with resistance by the regent masters to any such delegation of authority. It required a direct command by the King to the 'youth' of the university, and much manipulation by Dr John Longland, the Bishop of Lincoln, as well as by the heads of houses to procure the desired verdict on 8 April. Amidst the opinions prevailing at court this was not a happy augury, and along with other indications of traditionalist and pro-papal opinion in the university led the government to take particular pains to prepare the way for Oxford's repudiation of papal supremacy in 1534. Behind the scenes, the deft manoeuvering of Thomas Cromwell played an indispensable part in achieving that end,

---

scholastic theology. The other 'Spanish monk' was Juan de Villagarcia, D.Th. also a Dominican, praelector in theology at Magdalen College from 1555–57, and holder of the Regius chair in theology from 1556 to 1558. On the quality of these theologians see Jennifer Loach, 'Reformation Controversies', in James McConica, ed., *The Collegiate University. The History of the University of Oxford*, vol. 3 (Oxford, 1986), pp. 347 n. 4, 353, 379.

[4] T.A.R. Evans, 'The Number, Origins and Careers of Scholars', in J.I. Catto and Ralph Evans, eds., *Late Medieval Oxford, The History of the University of Oxford*, vol. 2 (Oxford, 1992), pp. 527–28.

[5] On this see Carl I. Hammer, Jr., 'Oxford Town and Oxford University', and Claire Cross, 'Oxford and the Tudor State from the Accession of Henry VIII to the death of Mary', in *The Collegiate University*, pp. 90–92, 125–26.

and his appointment shortly thereafter as chancellor of Cambridge ensured that, so long as his influence prevailed, the university of Cambridge – and its graduates – would enjoy the access to power, promotion and privilege that had been Oxford's during the long reign of Wolsey and before.[6]

In reflecting on the relatively conservative attitude in Oxford to the religious changes of the time, an attitude which would persist, certain factors suggest themselves. Perhaps the most obvious is geographical. Cambridge was much closer to continental influences, and followers of Protestant opinion were better established there from the beginning, as the reputation of the White Horse Tavern shows. Another element is the powerful recollection, still fresh, of the cost to Oxford in the fourteenth century of the controversy surrounding its brilliant and heterodox theologian, John Wyclif. That experience had brought the university into unprecedented and unwelcome conflict with its historic patrons and protectors, the royal government and the English bishops, and had precipitated (in 1377) the first and only papal intervention into the teaching of the Oxford faculty of theology.[7] The chief legacy of Wycliffism and Lollardy was therefore the memory of an affront to the university's independence, and of the supervision over its masters in the next generation and beyond maintained by the successive archbishops of Canterbury, William Courtenay, Thomas Arundel, and Henry Chichele.

As recently as 1528 the university had had reason to recall those painful years. Ironically enough, the first identifiable adherents of Lutheran opinion at Oxford were discovered in 1527 amongst Cambridge men recruited by Wolsey to staff his newly-founded college.[8] Promptly at Wolsey's direction a search ensued, and by the autumn of 1528 those implicated had either conformed, escaped, or returned to Cambridge. Subsequently, a few Lutheran books continued to be circulated and read, and some members of the university were converted to the new doctrines, among them such notable representatives of reformed opinion later on as John Philpot, John Foxe and Alexander Nowell; yet there is no evidence of anything resembling a substantial community of Protestant opinion at Oxford through the rest of Henry VIII's reign.

Finally, it is just conceivable that the dissolution of the religious houses in Oxford may have left lingering resentments more deep-seated than those at Cambridge.[9] The number of monks and friars in residence had always been greater at Oxford where indeed, their foundations were among the most im-

---

[6] See Hammer, 'Oxford Town', and Cross, 'Oxford and the Tudor State', pp. 126–30 for details.

[7] See the discussion by J.I. Catto, 'Wyclif and Wycliffism at Oxford 1356–1430', and 'Theology after Wycliffism', in *Late Medieval Oxford*, chapters 5 and 6, pp. 175–261 and 263–80 respectively.

[8] See Cross, 'Oxford and the Tudor State', p. 123; on the foundation of Cardinal College, see James McConica, 'The Rise of the Undergraduate College', in *The Collegiate University*, pp. 29 ff.

[9] See R.B. Dobson, 'The Religious Orders 1370–1540', in *Late Medieval Oxford*, pp. 539 ff.

posing and academically significant within the ambience of the university. As recent study has shown, the members of both the monastic and mendicant orders attached greater importance to a university degree in the decades immediately prior to the dissolution than at any time previous, so that (quite apart from the value to the university of their excellent libraries) they could not have been thought of by contemporaries as languishing facilities, marginal to the life of the academic community, and the blow against them was one felt by the university itself as well as the local populace.[10]

The declaration of the royal supremacy had affected Catholics in the university no differently than Catholics throughout the kingdom. The first direct challenge to them as such came with the accession of Edward VI. Henry VIII died on 27 January 1547. The death of the chancellor, Dr John Longland[11] on 15 May following virtually coincided with the new reign, leaving this key post vacant for the government's nominee. He was a convinced Protestant, Richard Cox. Cox was a Cambridge man and one of those suspect appointees to Christ Church who had removed themselves during the investigation of Lutheran opinion there. He had been tutor to Prince Edward from 1540 to 1547, was a member of the Privy Council, and had played a prominent part in the evolution of the Prayer Book and the composition of the King's Book of 1543. Such critical responsibilities in the court undoubtedly marked him for advancement, and in November 1546 he had already been appointed dean of Christ Church. Within days of the death of Longland, on 21 May 1547, he was made chancellor as well. He was clearly selected to play a key part in the Edwardine government's plans for Oxford, and in the words of one historian, he 'soon revealed himself to be a committed Protestant and co-operated closely with Cranmer in the uphill task of transforming Oxford into a Protestant university'.[12]

That story has been told elsewhere.[13] For Catholics the implications were revealed at once with the deprivation in 1547 of the first holder of the Regius chair of theology, Dr Richard Smith, and his replacement with the continental theologian Peter Martyr. Martyr was followed by other continental scholars of like persuasion, and their presence in Oxford was intended, like the new communion service and the royal visitation from May to July 1549, to convert the

for a recent examination of the size, vitality and commitment to university training of the monks and friars in the years prior to the dissolution.

[10] 'For those not positively antipathetic to the desirability of university learning on the part of the Christian religious orders, the dissolution of the monastic and mendicant houses in the late 1530s is accordingly one of the greater academic as well as architectural misfortunes in the history of Oxford', Dobson, 'Religious Orders', p. 540.

[11] Upon the death of Warham on 22 August 1532, he had been elected chancellor by the regent masters at the king's direction, had been a firm upholder of the royal supremacy, and had been sent to Oxford in 1530 to organize support for the king's divorce; see above.

[12] Cross, 'Oxford and the Tudor State', p. 133.

[13] See Cross, 'Oxford and the Tudor State', pp. 133–40, and Loach, 'Reformation Controversies', pp. 368–74.

university and colleges away from the old opinions and observances. A new set of statutes presented by the visitors on 4 June 1549 was issued in the name of '*Edwardus sextus, Dei gratia . . . fidei defensor, et in terra ecclesiae Anglicanae et Hibernicae supremum caput*'. It abrogated all previous statutes implying traditional doctrine and worship, and thus associated the university effectively with Protestantism.[14] It was now mandatory for all members of the university to attend the new prayer book communion service at the beginning of each term, and to participate in the approved prayers in college chapels.

Coinciding with the visitation, and adding to its urgency, was the western 'Prayer-Book' rebellion of 1549.[15] The immediate occasion was the introduction of the new prayer book service on Whitsun of that year. Despite the west-country origins of this uprising, it moved with speed alarming to the government and by July had inspired sympathetic risings in Berkshire, Buckinghamshire, Northampton and Oxfordshire. While the motivation of the rising varied from place to place with other concerns connected with enclosures, there is no doubt about its religious significance in Buckinghamshire and Oxford. While little is known of the actual events of the uprising and its suppression, it was sufficiently serious to disturb the council and justify the dispatch of a professional soldier, Lord Grey of Wilton, with a band of some 1,500 mercenary (German and Swiss) horse and foot who were otherwise destined to help the government's efforts in the west. The head of government in the royal minority, Edward Seymour, Duke of Somerset and Lord Protector, wrote to Lord Russell on 12 July about the 'sturr [sic] here in Bucks. and Oxfordshire by instigacion of sundery priests (kepe it to your self), for these matyers of religion'. On 18 July Somerset reported that the rising had been crushed and some two hundred prisoners taken with a dozen of the ring leaders. King Edward noted in his journal that Grey 'did so abash the rebels, that more then hauf of them rann ther wayes, and other that tarried were some slain, some taken and some hanged'.

The rising was put down ruthlessly indeed. The number executed is not known, but Lord Grey left instructions for the *further* summary execution in various towns of fourteen individuals, priests and yeomen whom he deemed to be traitorous, 'and after execution done, the heads of every of them in the same towns to be set up in the highest place for the more terror of the said evil people'. The towns chosen are a partial gazetteer of later recusant activity in the region

---

[14] Cf. Strickland Gibson, ed., *Statuta antiqua universitatis oxoniensis* (Oxford, 1931), pp. 342: 33–40, 343: 1–3, and 350: 11–15: '*Pridie uniuscuiusque termini fractio panis et sacrosancta Communio sit in singulis collegiis, aliisque scholasticis edibus, et preces ad Deum generales, et brevis preterea exhortatio ad scholasticos, a prelectoribus aut magistro collegii facta, ut se studiis literarum et pietati dedant*', On the policies of the government under Edward VI, see Cross, 'Oxford and the Tudor State', pp. 133–39.

[15] For what follows see A. Vere Woodman, 'The Buckinghamshire and Oxfordshire Rising of 1549', *Oxoniensia* 22 (1957), pp. 79–82; Frances Rose-Troup, *The Western Rebellion of 1549* (London, 1913), pp. 234, 242, 262; W.R.D. Jones, *The Mid-Tudor Crisis 1539–1563* (London, 1973), p. 46.

around Oxford: Banbury, Dedington, Islip, Watlington, Thame, Bicester, Chipping Norton, Bloxham, Haseley and Oxford itself. Some victims were hanged, drawn and quartered; the vicar of Chipping Norton and the parish priest of Bloxham were to be hanged from the steeples of their churches. Local sentiment will have prevailed in some cases since it appears that not all of those listed were put to death. Another priest, James Webbe, who was vicar of Barford St Michael, seems to have been a special case and was tried in London, then sent to Aylesbury to be hanged, drawn and quartered. In the wake of Lord Grey's ferocious descent on the county, Johann Ulmer, a Swiss student of medicine, wrote with satisfaction from Christ Church to his patron, the Zurich reformer Heinrich Bullinger, 'The Oxfordshire papists are at last reduced to order, many of them having been apprehended, and some gibbeted, and their heads fastened to the walls.'[16]

When we take into consideration the importance of the county network of Catholic families to the adherents of the old faith in the university (a phenomenon unmistakably clear by the reign of Elizabeth) it is perhaps not surprising that the subsequent fall of Somerset from power was greeted with joyful demonstrations in Oxford. On 14 January 1550, Somerset was deposed from the Protectorate by act of Parliament and deprived of all his offices, the first stage in a process which would conclude with his execution on 22 January 1552. On 6 February 1550, however, Somerset was set at liberty, temporarily as it proved, and on the 28th Johann Stumphius, one of the community of foreign Protestants in Oxford, wrote to Bullinger about the initial reactions in Oxford to the first event:

> those cruel beasts the Romanists, with which Oxford abounds, were now beginning to triumph over the downfall of our duke, the overthrow of our gospel now at its last gasp, and the restoration of their darling mass, as though they had already obtained a complete victory. They had begun to revive the celebration of their abominable mass in their conventicles, to practise their ancient mummeries at funerals and other offices of that kind, and to inundate themselves with wine, as became the champions of such a religion as theirs.[17]

From 1550 under the new Protector, John Dudley, Duke of Northumberland, the government moved firmly against individuals in the university, among them some of considerable prominence.[18] At New College the conservative Warden

---

[16] Hastings Robinson, ed., *Original Letters Relative to the English Reformation*, 2 vols (Cambridge, 1846–47) Parker Society, II, letter 188 (7 August 1549), p. 391; cf. also letter 189. Cf. Penry Williams, *The Tudor Regime* (Oxford, 1979), p. 325: '. . . the Oxfordshire rebels seem to have been mainly concerned with religion'.

[17] Robinson, *Original Letters*, II, p. 464.

[18] On this and the following, cf. APC, III, pp. 287, 305, 307; G.D. Duncan, 'The Heads of Houses and Religious Change in Tudor Oxford 1547–1558', *Oxoniensia* 45 (1980), pp. 226–34. On matters at Corpus, see Thomas Fowler, *The History of Corpus Christi College* (Oxford, 1898),

Henry Cole was displaced in April 1551 in favour of a committed Protestant, Ralph Skinner (a former fellow who had resigned to marry), a victory for pressure from the Privy Council combined with that of a vocal Protestant faction in the college. The Dean of Corpus Christi College, William Chedsey, was called before the Privy Council for seditious preaching and was later imprisoned in the Marshalsea. The president of Corpus too, the scholarly Robert Morwyn or Morwent was detained in the Fleet with two of the fellows for a month in 1552 for having used the old form of service on the preceding Corpus Christi Day. John Jewel, the pupil of Peter Martyr whose career was to flourish in the Elizabethan Church, was appointed by the Privy Council as acting-president during the absence of Morwyn. In the same year Dr Owen Oglethorpe, the president of Magdalen College and former vice-chancellor, was compelled by pressure of the King's council working again with a sympathetic minority in the college to resign in favour of a Protestant candidate, Walter Haddon.

The purging of distinguished Catholics from the university had the unforeseen effect of establishing what was to become the chief centre of scholarly opposition to the policies of the government of Elizabeth, in a community of learned Catholics in exile at Louvain. Richard Smith left his chair at Oxford to become professor of theology there, and later ended his career at Douai as the first chancellor and professor of theology. He was joined at Louvain in 1549 by John Clement, who had been appointed by Wolsey the first reader in humanity at Cardinal College in the autumn of 1518. Clement had entered Wolsey's service from a position as tutor in the household of Thomas More where he had met his wife, Margaret Giggs. In 1520 he had left Oxford for Louvain and Italy to study medicine, and in Venice had assisted in the completion of the Aldine edition of Galen. He also studied medicine at Padua where he probably took his M.D., and in 1528 was admitted to the Royal College of Physicians, of which he became president in 1544. With the accession of Edward VI, however, he removed once again to the Low Countries. His son Thomas had already enrolled at Louvain in July, 1547 along with More's grandson, Thomas Roper. In due course, with the assistance of More's old associate Antonio Bonvisi, the Rastells and the biographer of Thomas More, Nicholas Harpesfield,[19] were also enabled to join this

Oxford Historical Society 25, p. 97; Morwyn was not formally deprived of office, and the date of his return to the college is unknown; Duncan, p. 231, cf. Fowler, p. 97. On 1 June 1550 Stumphius, reporting the arrest and confinement of a massing priest, reported to Bullinger that, 'A certain sacrilegious mass-priest, the head of the papists of whom a great number still remain, . . . having often acted the fable of the mass in the popish conventicles, was at last caught in the fact during these holidays, and thrown into prison . . .', Robinson, *Original Letters*, II, p. 467. In November he complained that, 'The Oxford men . . . are still pertinaciously sticking in the mud of popery, and master Cox, in his opposition to them, seems to me rather too fond of the Fabian tactics . . .', *ibid.*, pp. 457–58.

[19] A Wykehamist and fellow (1537) of New College, admitted BCL in 1543, he was principal of White and Laurence Halls on the site of Jesus College. He matriculated at Louvain in January, 1551 and remained there for the rest of the reign. In addition to his life of

group, as was John Christopherson of St John's College, Cambridge. Yet another Oxford associate was a future martyr, John Story, D.C.L., the first Regius professor of civil law, who was deprived of his chair by the Edwardine government about 1549 and who then removed to Louvain.[20] John Harpesfield, D.Th., the older brother of Nicholas and like him a Wykehamist and fellow of New College, was the first holder of the Regius chair of Greek at Oxford. He seems to have vacated it by 1545 to take orders,[21] and following the accession of Edward VI had made his own way to Louvain by 1551.

There were others of prominence who left the university apart from the exiles in Louvain. Among them were George Etheridge, B.M., a fellow of Corpus who had succeeded John Harpesfield in the Regius chair of Greek. As a junior in the college Etheridge seems to have supported the Protestant party. He evidently changed his views, and was deprived of his chair in late 1550 or early 1551. He turned to the practice of medicine in Oxford, ran an academic hall in Kybald Street and was still living there in the year of the Armada, a prominent link with pre-Reformation Oxford in the heartland of the university.[22]

Thomas Harding, another product of Winchester and New College, was the first Regius praelector in Hebrew and the second university reader in that subject, succeeding John Shepreve in 1544. He vacated his chair in 1547 and apparently withdrew from the university for a time as chaplain to Henry Grey, Marquis of Dorset. He would reappear later on as a leading Catholic controversialist in the 1560s.[23] John Morwen, a fellow of Corpus who was appointed lector in Greek in 1545, seems to have shared Etheridge's distinction as a foremost Grecian in the college, as he also shared Etheridge's early sympathy with the reforming party there. Like Etheridge too he changed his views, and with the accession of Edward VI withdrew from an active role in teaching to turn to the study of medicine. Immediately on the accession of Queen Mary he sought holy orders and was ordained to the sub-diaconate in September 1554. In February

Thomas More, he was the author of the important *Historia Anglicana Eccelesiastica* and several other scholarly works; see A.B. Emden, *A Biographical Register of the University of Oxford A.D. 1501–1540* (Oxford, 1974), pp. 268–69.

[20] See G.D. Duncan, 'Public Lectures and Professorial Chairs', in *The Collegiate University*, pp. 52 ff *sub nomine;* Cross, 'Oxford and the Tudor State', pp. 138–39; on the Louvain circle, James Kelsey McConica, *English Humanists and Reformation Politics* (Oxford, 1965), pp. 266–71; on Clement, see also Emden, *Biographical Register*, pp. 121–22; Germain Marc'hadour, *L'Univers de Thomas More* (Paris, 1963), p. 535; on Story, see Emden, *Biographical Register*, pp. 544–45, John Barton, 'The Faculty of Law', in *The Collegiate University*, pp. 262–64, 285–87.

[21] Emden, *Biographical Register*, p. 268.

[22] Emden, *Biographical Register*, p. 194; Gillian Lewis, 'The Faculty of Medicine', in *The Collegiate University* (*sub nomine* 'Edrych'), pp. 238–39, 242, 248. On the complaints to Cranmer at Corpus in 1535, see J.G. Milne, *The Early History of Corpus Christi College Oxford* (Oxford, 1946), pp. 29–33.

[23] Duncan, 'Heads of Houses', p. 357; Emden, *Biographical Register*, pp. 265–66.

1556 he was priested to the title of his fellowship. He became a chaplain to Bishop Edward Bonner, and was deprived in the next reign early in 1560.[24]

The government's more positive initiatives in Oxford, for which Peter Martyr furnished the theological spearhead, had their successes. Other Protestant scholars were attracted from abroad and in Oxford, Martyr won a particularly distinguished disciple in John Jewel. As a fellow of Corpus (1544), Jewel was reader in humanity there from 1548 to 1554 and for a time, as we have seen, acting president. Yet despite the fact that there were some other prominent converts, notably in Magdalen, New College and Corpus Christi, the ethos of the university was slow to change, and many of the conservative heads of house remained in place.[25] Martin Bucer, Peter Martyr's opposite number at Cambridge, died in February 1551, and another Swiss Protestant, Johann Burcher, in writing to Bullinger the following August about finding a successor for him remarked, 'Nor will he find the Cambridge men so perversely learned as Master Peter found those at Oxford. For the scholars of that university [i.e.Cambridge] have always been suspected of 'heresy', as they call it . . . by which you will judge that their studies have always been of a purer character than those at Oxford'.[26] As a direct reflection of the general mood of uncertainty, particularly about the prospects for a career in the Church, the numbers attending Oxford also plummeted during the reign of Edward VI.[27] All things considered, the ensuing response of Oxford to the accession of Queen Mary is scarcely surprising.

Mary came to the throne in July, 1553. Almost at once, both universities were ordered to rescind any statutes or ordinances adopted since the death of her father, restoring at a stroke all of the traditional observances in religion as in other matters purely academic. The study of canon law and of scholastic philosophy was revived, and a Dominican house was re-established in the university. After the comparatively brief and uncertain interlude of official Protestantism, the return of a Catholic monarch was greeted by most in Oxford with a sense of relief. Exiles returned to take up new careers. John Clement, M.D., returned from the Low Countries and set up a medical practice in Essex. John

---

[24] Milne, *Early History*; McConica, *English Humanists*, p. 267; DNB (W.A.J. Archbold). Morwen was bursar of Corpus from 1541–46, and numbered among his pupils John Jewel. He had connections with the Roper family, and was tutor to Mary, the daughter of Margaret More and William Roper. After his deprivation he migrated to the north-west of England where he was harboured by recusant families and continued his priestly work.

[25] Cross, 'Oxford and the Tudor State', pp. 134–35, 'compared with Cambridge, . . . the acceptance of Protestantism seems to have been slow', p. 139. For a full account of the theological debates in Oxford at the time of Peter Martyr, see Loach, 'Reformation Controversies', pp. 368–74. On the limitations of the Edwardine policies in Oxford, see also Duncan, 'Heads of Houses', pp. 230–31.

[26] Robinson, *Original Letters*, II, p. 680.

[27] Cf. Cross, 'Oxford and the Tudor State', p. 140: 'The government's efforts to attract students to study civil law had no demonstrable result, and it seems that in Edward's reign the number of students at Oxford may have reached its lowest ebb for the entire century'. Cf. James McConica, 'Studies and Faculties: Introduction' in *The Collegiate University*, p. 153.

Harpesfield, who had been ordained to the priesthood in April 1547, returned to England to take up a clerical career and became chaplain to Bishop Bonner (like John Morwen) and archdeacon of London. His brother Nicholas likewise returned to be made within a year archdeacon of Canterbury and a canon of St Paul's, London. In Oxford itself, Dr Richard Smith was restored to the chair he had been forced to vacate for Peter Martyr, as Dr John Story was to the Regius chair in civil law.[28] Peter Martyr and the other foreign Protestants hastily left the scene. Warden Ralph Skinner of New College was deprived of office, along with the Rector of Exeter, William More, and Richard Cox of Christ Church. At Magdalen, Walter Haddon, Oglethorpe's successor, resigned from the presidency and saw the restoration of his predecessor, deposed by the previous government, in his place. Beyond these measures, the government appears to have been able henceforth to rely on the fellows to choose acceptable heads of college from their own number without further intervention in elections. At Corpus, Robert Morwyn, who had survived disfavour and temporary displacement in the reign of Edward VI, stayed on as president until his death on 16 August 1558, three months before that of Queen Mary. Restored to office at her accession, he produced from their hiding place the college chapel vestments, plate and altar furniture for Mass.[29]

Morwyn's actions seem to symbolize the transition in Oxford from the rule of Edward VI to that of his successor. For the university as a whole, the reign of Mary Tudor was restorative. Unlike her predecessor she was not faced with a largely indifferent or actively hostile university population, and the university seems to have resumed without much ado to its traditional observances.[30] Numbers rose again in a mood of greater confidence. The Queen associated her policy of restoration with an endowment of unprecedented generosity to the university itself, a gift of rectories the income from which tripled the university's revenue and allowed, among other things, the repair of public buildings such as the schools.[31] She assisted colleges that had fallen victim to the rapacity of

[28] It should be noted that not all of the university posts changed occupants at each change of régime. The Lady Margaret Professorship, the oldest in the university, was evacuated by its Edwardine holder, Christopher Goodman, in 1553, and was filled by the provost of Oriel, John Smith, whose career extended well into the reign of Elizabeth. He had become provost in 1550 and remained in office until 1565, having been treasurer of Chichester cathedral also from 1555 to 1562. Richard Bruerne, a canon of Christ Church from 1553–1565, occupied the Regius chair in Hebrew through three reigns from 1547 to 1569. See Duncan, 'Public Lectures and Professorial Chairs', pp. 351, 357.

[29] Fowler, *History*, pp. 97–98; Duncan, 'Heads of Houses', p. 233. Senior members of the colleges, apart from foreign scholars who returned to the continent, were scrutinized in a series of episcopal visitations in the autumn of 1553 and a number of Protestant fellows were expelled, many to become Marian exiles; see Cross, 'Oxford and the Tudor State', p. 142.

[30] Cf. Duncan, 'Heads of Houses', p. 234: 'Mary's government had benefitted signally from the abject failure of Edward's to convert the university in heads and members to Protestantism'.

[31] Cross, 'Oxford and the Tudor State', p. 141; Loach, 'Reformation Controversies', pp.

Somerset's régime by restoring appropriated livings, and in a particularly notable gesture, made up a deficiency in her father's provision for Christ Church.[32] Even more striking for the population at large was the foundation with royal encouragement of two new colleges on the deserted sites of earlier religious houses. Both Trinity College and St John's College were established by wealthy Catholic laymen, Trinity by Sir Thomas Pope in 1555, and St John's in 1557 by Sir Thomas White. Their statutes reflected not only a commitment to the promotion of the orthodox faith and of good learning (those at St John's included provision for the teaching of canon law), but a forward-looking understanding of the social function emerging in the university, with statutory provision for the first time for numbers of undergraduate commoners to join foundation-scholars as integral members of these new collegiate societies.[33]

Nothing about Marian Oxford is so well remembered, of course, as the trial and execution of the three bishops, Thomas Cranmer, Hugh Latimer, and Nicholas Ridley. They were imprisoned in the Tower in the autumn of 1553, and were removed in March of the next year to Oxford for their state trial. In part the decision indicates the government's wish to underscore in an academic setting the issues of doctrinal heresy: the disputations which began the public proceedings were simply the latest in a long series at Oxford begun by Peter Martyr which would continue into the reign of Elizabeth. What effect the outcome had upon Catholic opinion in Oxford must be conjectural, but the prolonged presence in the city of the future Protestant martyrs was clearly the doing of the government rather than of the university as such.[34]

By the time Elizabeth I succeeded to the throne on 17 November 1558, the universities of the realm had felt the force of successive religious changes as directly as had any institution in Church or state. They had known no less than three official investigations by visitation, that of Thomas Cromwell under Henry VIII in 1535, that of Somerset's government under Edward VI in 1549, and under Mary, the legatine visitation of Cardinal Pole in 1556. Each of these visitations had brought its own set of inquiries and injunctions, and each of the last two had imposed a new set of statutes. Never before in their history had Oxford and Cambridge seen their autonomy and their internal democracy of masters so subverted from outside as they had under these Tudor monarchs. Under Elizabeth that tendency was to be consolidated, not reversed.

377–78. See also Gerald Aylmer, 'The Economics and Finances of the Colleges and University c. 1530–1640', in *The Collegiate University*, p. 550.

[32] Loach, 'Reformation Controversies', p. 377.

[33] James McConica, 'The Rise of the Undergraduate College', pp. 42–46. Pope's college was founded on the site of Durham College, the house of studies of the Benedictines of Durham Priory; St John's on the site of the Cistercian foundation of St Bernard's College.

[34] Cross, 'Oxford and the Tudor State', pp. 144–45; 'The university . . . had been given a salutary and very recent warning the fate of heretics'. See also the account of Jennifer Loach, 'Oxford could afford to shrug aside the fortitude of the martyrs', 'Reformation Controversies', pp. 374–77.

It is generally agreed that, in the first few years of the reign of Elizabeth the life of Catholics for the most part was little troubled, provided they were peaceable and made accommodations of outward conformity with the religious settlement. Rather, it was Protestant radicals who drew attention as disturbers of the peace.[35] The universities, however, as the chief hope for the provision of an educated Protestant clergy, were not the ordinary case. In the summer of 1559 the Acts of Supremacy and of Uniformity once again abolished all papal jurisdiction in England, and restored the second (1552) Prayer Book of Edward VI with some minor changes, prohibiting all other forms of worship. The former act required every person proceeding to a university degree, along with all ecclesiastical persons, justices, mayors and other officers of the state, to take an oath renouncing papal authority and acknowledging the royal supremacy. It also laid down penalties for upholding the papal jurisdiction, a second offence incurring those of *praemunire*, and a third, those of high treason. The Act of Uniformity required all over the age of sixteen years to attend church on Sundays and holy days. Failure to do so incurred a fine of one shilling for each offence to be levied by the churchwarden to help the poor. Communion was required on three occasions a year, although no penalty was attached for failure to participate.

While these provisions were open to widely varying degrees of observance, particularly in the country at large,[36] in Oxford and Cambridge the government was not slow to make its wishes unmistakably clear. In Oxford at least it would prove remarkably difficult to unmake the Marian achievement and something much more than outward conformity was sought.[37] The records of the royal visitation of 1559, like those of all its predecessors in Tudor Oxford, have inexplicably disappeared, but the toll of college heads is eloquent. Indeed, within two years of Elizabeth's accession, only one survived from the preceding

---

35 Norman L. Jones, *The Birth of the Elizabethan Age* (Oxford, 1993), pp. 66–69.

36 It would be inappropriate here to attempt to summarize the vast literature on 'occasional conformity', 'church papists', and the variety and general ambiguity of a strictly 'Catholic' allegiance in this period. For important contributions see: Alan Davidson, 'Roman Catholics in Oxfordshire from the Late Elizabethan Period to the Civil War (c. 1580–1640)', (unpublished PhD thesis, University of Bristol, 1970), ch. 1 and *passim*; John Bossy, *The English Catholic Community, 1570–1850* (London, 1975), 'The Character of Elizabethan Catholicism' in *Past and Present* 21 (1962), 39–59, and the critique by Christopher Haigh, 'The Continuity of Catholicism in the English Reformation' in *The English Reformation Revised* (Cambridge, 1987), pp. 176–215; Eamon Duffy, *The Stripping of the Altars* (New Haven, 1992), especially Part 2; Alexandra Walsham, *Church Papists* (London, 1993); C.M.J.F. Swan, 'The Question of Dissimulation among Elizabethan Catholics', *Report of the Canadian Catholic Historical Association* (Ottawa, 1957), pp. 105–19; W.R. Trimble, *The Catholic Laity in Elizabethan England 1558–1603* (Cambridge, Mass. 1964); Elliot E. Rose, *Cases of Conscience* (Cambridge, 1975) and discussions in other works cited here.

37 Loach, 'Reformation Controversies', p. 381: 'Catholicism was . . . to prove more difficult to eradicate than Protestantism had been'. See also Penry Williams, 'Elizabethan Oxford: State, Church and University', in *The Collegiate University*, p. 405.

reign, Thomas Whyte of New College.[38] Bishop Robert Horne of Winchester, who was visitor of New College as of Trinity, Corpus and Magdalen, found that the first three were so hostile to the new religious settlement that he decided not to press its acceptance too strongly.[39] In May of 1560 the Spanish ambassador, Alvaro de la Quadra, Bishop of Aquila, reported that as part of an intensification in the persecution of Catholics, great numbers of students at Oxford and in the Inns of Court had been taken into custody; and in November, 1561, that six Oxford students who resisted removal of the crucifix in their college chapel were imprisoned in the Tower and taken before the Privy Council, where they boldly offered to dispute in public or in private the Catholic doctrine of the sacrament.[40] The mayor of Oxford informed the scandalized council that such views were typical of Oxford, and that there were not three houses in it free of papists.[41]

This then was the background to that steady stream of Oxford men who made their way throughout the 1560s and 1570s to the seminaries of Louvain, Rheims and Douai. The purge continued, most evidently at New College, whence at least thirty-three fellows left in the first decade after the accession of Elizabeth. Among them were important publicists: Thomas Dorman (twice an exile and by now a fellow of All Souls) and Nicholas Sanders, who followed their predecessors from New College – John Rastell, Thomas Harding and the Harpesfields – into exile and debate. From such talent there came, inevitably, a flood-tide of controversial literature: here Harding, Thomas Stapleton, Sanders, and Dorman were outstanding, with Robert Persons of Balliol and Gregory Martin, a founding fellow of Edmund Campion's college, St John's.[42] For although New College was the most conspicuously Catholic of the Oxford colleges in the reign of Elizabeth as it had been in that of Edward VI, stubborn resistance to the prescribed religion was found elsewhere, in Corpus, Trinity, Merton, Queen's, Balliol, Exeter, St John's – indeed, for special reasons in each case, in all but Magdalen, Oriel and Christ Church. Oriel however had produced in William Allen an exile of unusual and enduring importance.[43] All told, some-

---

[38] Williams, 'State, Church and University', p. 406; cf. Duncan, 'Heads of Houses', p. 234.

[39] Williams, 'State, Church and University', p. 406; Loach, 'Reformation Controversies', p. 381; Trimble, *Catholic Laity*, p. 12.

[40] CSP Simancas, I, nos 106, 143.

[41] *Ibid.* I, nos 143, 218.

[42] Williams, 'State, Church and University', pp. 407–08; Loach, 'Reformation Controversies', pp. 385–7. For the influence of these men on the direction taken by religious apologetics in Oxford see Loach, pp. 387–90, 394–95 and S.L. Greenslade, 'The Faculty of Theology', *The Collegiate University*, pp. 329 ff.

[43] Allen, a former principal of St Mary's Hall, established the first English seminary abroad at Douai in 1568. It removed to Rheims a decade later because of turmoil in Flanders, and was moved back to Douai in 1593. The English College at Rome was established in 1579; two further seminaries in Spain at Valladolid and Seville were added before the end of the century through the work of Robert Persons S.J. of Balliol College.

thing over a hundred fellows and other senior members left Oxford during the first decade of the reign of Elizabeth, a great percentage of them into the priesthood and the work of the English mission.[44]

A purge of college headships and fellowships was a substantial and evident gain for the government; the halls, lacking statutes and visible establishment, were another matter. Gloucester Hall, in the buildings of the former Benedictine house of studies, Gloucester College, was particularly suspect as a leading refuge of recusants who, if they pursued their studies privately and took no degree, need not come to the university's attention at all.[45] Another example of a private hall where recusant undergraduates almost certainly met with sympathetic supervision was that of Dr George Etheridge, the former fellow of Corpus and Edwardine exile, referred to above. The halls accommodated a substantial portion of the university's undergraduate population, since the decline in the number of independent halls was accompanied by a rise in the size of the halls remaining.[46] They were the last bastion of the university's medieval democracy, and while the principal of each hall had to be a regent master and was made to register his hall each year in the vice-chancellor's court, the choice of the principal rested in theory with the members of the hall. By the time of Elizabeth, many of the halls had fallen informally under the jurisdiction of a college, a process of annexation by which, earlier, some in effect had been absorbed. While annexation to a college could provide some degree of control it was an uncertain solution, and it was one of Leicester's changes, a very characteristic one, that during his chancellorship the rights of nomination to the principalships came to be vested in the chancellor and his successors.[47]

The elusive activity of the halls in contributing to the remarkable persistence of Catholic loyalty in the university brings us directly to the influence of the native Catholicism of the region. As H.E. Salter observed many years ago,[48] its strength is an outstanding feature of the ecclesiastical history of the period, a strength derived not only from numbers but from the prominence and wealth of the leading families. Salter estimated that one-third of the manors of the county

---

[44] Williams, 'Church, State and University', pp. 408–12; John Bossy, *English Catholic Community*, pp. 12–13.

[45] See Michael Foster, 'Thomas Allen, Gloucester Hall and the Survival of Catholicism in Post-Reformation Oxford', *Oxoniensia* 46 (1981), pp. 99–128; Loach, 'Reformation Controversies', pp. 381–2; on the manuscripts collected by Thomas Allen, see Andrew G. Watson, 'Thomas Allen of Oxford and his Manuscripts', in M.B. Parkes and A.G. Watson, eds., *Medieval Scribes, Manuscripts and Libraries: Essays presented to N.R. Ker* (London, 1978), pp. 279–314.

[46] In a census of the colleges and halls in 1552, the number reported in the eight surviving halls was some 260 scholars, about a quarter of the total recorded; see Duncan, 'Heads of Houses', p. 231.

[47] A.B. Emden, *An Oxford Hall in Medieval Times* (Oxford, 1927), p. 262; the exception was St Edmund Hall, owned by Queen's.

[48] Rev. H.E. Salter, 'Ecclesiastical History', in William Page, ed., *The Victoria History of the County of Oxford* (London, 1907), II, p. 43. For what follows I am chiefly indebted to the doctoral dissertation of Alan Davidson (note 36 above).

of Oxford were in recusant ownership, particularly in the south. As we have seen already, the local response to the 'Prayer-Book' rebellion of 1549 revealed a deeply-rooted resistance to the religious changes of the government of the Protector Somerset, and that in a region – the Thames valley – where Lollardy had once flourished, and which in its proximity to London differed profoundly from the remoter regions of Lancashire and Yorkshire where recusancy was also well-entrenched. Nevertheless, Catholic families can be identified in all parts of Oxfordshire and in the parts of Buckinghamshire adjacent. The heartland, however, was in the southern sector, dominated by the powerful Stonors who with related families – the Chamberlaines of Shirburn and Clare, and the Symeons of Chilworth, Brightwell and Britwell, – owned a tract of land fifteen miles long by five miles wide. Adjacent manors were also in recusant hands: the Belsons (Stokenchurch and Kingston Blount), the Fettiplaces (Swyncombe), the Cursons (Waterperry), the Lenthalls (the Haseleys, where the Huddlestons and Horsemans were also to be found), and hidden in a densely wooded bend of the river, the Blounts at Mapledurham.[49]

The recusant rolls reveal an invisible network of support in the vicinity of Oxford itself. Starting with locations as nearby as Nuneham Courtenay, Dorchester, Sandford on Thames, Cowley, Culham, Cuddesdon, Garsington, Godstow and Wolvercote, a second division would include Islip, Merton and Bicester, Charlbury, Chipping Norton and Brize Norton, Minster Lovell, the Bartons, Britwell Salome, Bampton, Kidlington, Cassington, Nettlebed, Eynsham, Stanton Harcourt, East Ilsley and Waterperry. This is not to mention Holywell, just outside the city wall, where the manor (with a house in Temple Cowley) was owned by the Nappers, a family three of whose members were ordained to the priesthood, and who would furnish Oxford with a martyr in the next reign.

By its very nature, recusant activity was recorded officially only when it was discovered by the government, and it is reasonable to assume that the known activity was only a portion of the whole, even if a considerable portion. Notoriously, Catholic families sustained the activity of missionary priests, and at one time or another, these were reported in the vicinity of Oxford at many of the centres mentioned above: at Garsington protected by the Fords and Spencers; at Temple Cowley and Holywell Manor by the Nappers; by Richard Owen at Godstow, at Bicester by John Hart, by William Hart at Eynsham, the Rainolds family at Cassington, the Horseman family at Cuddesdon, at Aston by the Belsons, at Dorchester by a whole group of yeoman families, the Princes, Days

---

[49] Salter, 'Ecclesiastical History', pp. 43–44, 'The great majority of the middle and lower classes accepted the reformed religion, but showed no enthusiasm for it, and if in Oxfordshire a poll of the gentry had been taken at any time during the reign of Queen Elizabeth, it is likely that the decision would have been to return to the unreformed religion'. Cf. Davidson, 'Roman Catholics in Oxfordshire', p. 6.

and Daveys. At Eynsham, too, there appears to have been a varied and substantial Catholic community including local gentry, farmers and tradesmen.[50]

There were similar discoveries within the city itself, several indeed within All Saints parish in the centre of the city, the accused being both gentlemen and tradesmen.[51] In general there seems to have been no shortage of priests, who ministered both to the university and to the townspeople.[52] Some of these were Marian priests who had not conformed or had half-conformed, a virtually anonymous group; others after 1574 were from the first arrivals of the mission from the continent. Mass was celebrated in some inns in Oxford and in its immediate vicinity, including the Mitre, the Swan, the Star and the Catherine Wheel, at tradesmen's premises or houses as well as at the houses of more prominent citizens such as the Nappers. In 1577 a return of recusants in the town of Oxford listed 14 esquires and gentlemen, 25 'inferior men', 10 women and a priest, and in the university 23 recusants including two priests.[53] Books too were supplied. A papist stationer, Rowland Jenks, was arrested by order of the Privy Council in May 1577, his house was searched and all his goods were seized. He was examined in London, then returned to Oxford prison to await trial at the next assizes. This was on 4 July, when he was condemned to lose his ears. A plague at once arose which gave the name of the 'Black Assize' to the trial. As it was described by Anthony Wood, 'Judgment being passed and the prisoner taken away, there arose such infectious damp or breath among the people that many there present, to the apprehensions of most men, were then smothered, and others so deeply infected that they lived not many hours after'. Among those that were infected and died, 'were Sir Robert Bell, Baron of the Exchequer, [and] Sir Nich. Barham, Serjeant at Law, both stiff enemies to the R. Cath. Religion'. Whatever the cause, there is no doubt of the virulence of the plague, which lasted over a month and carried off the judges, the clerk of assize, the lord lieutenant and sheriff, the coroner and some four hundred other victims from Oxford and its neighbourhood, and bestowed upon the unfortunate Jenks and his enterprise a quite unlooked-for celebrity.[54]

In fostering the recusant community in Oxford and elsewhere it is now clear that women were notably instrumental, married women in particular being a

[50] Davidson, 'Roman Catholicism in Oxfordshire', cap. 3, and pp. 289, 293–95.

[51] *Ibid.*, pp. 330–31.

[52] Davidson, 'Roman Catholicism in Oxfordshire', cap. 4 and pp. 665 ff; a summary of Davidson's findings appears in Foster, 'Thomas Allen', p. 117. See also Christina Colvin, 'Roman Catholicism', in Alan Crossley, ed., *A History of the County of Oxford* (Oxford, 1979) IV, pp. 412–13.

[53] Colvin, 'Roman Catholicism', p. 412.

[54] *Ibid.*, pp. 412–13; cf. William H. Turner, ed., *Selections from the Records of the City of Oxford Henry VIII to Elizabeth I [1509–1583]* (Oxford, 1880), pp. 389, 391–92; Margaret Gosling, 'Berkshire and Oxfordshire Catholics and the Lenten Assize of 1588', *Oxoniensia* 58 (1993), p. 256.

cause of continuing vexation to the authorities.[55] Whilst spinsters and widows were held responsible for their own actions and could be fined and if necessary (but rarely) imprisoned, married women by virtue of their legal subordination to their husbands were largely immune from the penalties of the law. Everywhere they were prominent among those who refused to attend the appointed prayer book services (while their husbands might conform), and prominent also in the highly illegal and dangerous activity of harbouring priests. Under the statute of 1585 all priests ordained abroad were liable to prosecution when they returned to England, and all who harboured them were liable to indictment for a capital felony.[56] Among those who were prepared to take the risk was Mrs Williams of the Swan in Oxford, to the certain discomfiture of her husband, a J.P. and an alderman.[57] It was this network of allegiances that, in the absence of bishops or of the support that had been provided in medieval Oxford so lavishly by the numerous parishes and religious orders, sustained the Catholic population within the university and without. During the reign of Elizabeth it produced from the county some thirty secular priests, and a further twelve Jesuits before the Civil War.[58]

On 1 June 1571, Dr John Story, the first Regius praelector of civil law in the University of Oxford, a former Member of Parliament under Edward VI and Elizabeth, twice an exile for religion, was executed at Tyburn for treason.[59] As well as any single event his death symbolizes the drawing in of the boundaries of the Elizabethan settlement through the second half of the 1560s, and the mounting cost of Catholic dissent. Among those who witnessed the execution, it seems, was a brilliant fellow of St John's College, an Anglican deacon, a former university orator and junior proctor, Edmund Campion. It is said that the execution of Story was the event that precipitated his decision to leave England and its established religion and to make his fateful journey to Douai.[60] A decade later on 1 December, having been taken at Lyford in the recusant countryside west of Oxford, he was racked and executed at Tyburn as a Jesuit.[61]

---

[55] Marie B. Rowlands, 'Recusant Women 1560–1640', in Mary Prior, ed., *Women in English Society 1500–1800* (London and New York, 1985), pp. 149–66.

[56] Rowlands, 'Recusant Women', p. 156.

[57] *Ibid.*, p. 157.

[58] Foster, 'Thomas Allen', p. 117, citing Davidson. It is an interesting footnote to the history of Marian Oxford that Cardinal Pole declined to admit Jesuit teachers to England, despite the fact that Loyola was receiving young Englishmen in the Flemish College as early as 1554. See in this volume, Thomas F. Mayer, 'A Test of Wills: Cardinal Pole, Ignatius Loyola, and the Jesuits in England', and A.C.F. Beales, *Education Under Penalty* (London, 1963), p. 25.

[59] Emden, *Biographical Register*, pp. 544–45; John Barton, 'The King's Readers', in *The Collegiate University*, pp. 285–87.

[60] Jones, *Birth of the Elizabethan Age*, p. 77.

[61] By 23 Eliz. c. 1 all Jesuits and seminary priests were to be 'holden, esteemed, and taken for traitors', an act which confirmed a proclamation of 1582. See Williams, *Tudor Regime*, pp. 278, 376; and John LaRocca, S.J.'s 'Popery and Pounds: The Effect of the Jesuit Mission on Penal Legislation' in this volume.

Although the evidence was mounting through the 1560s that the government's tolerance of Catholic dissent was fading, it was the conjunction of three fatally intertwined events at the end of the decade that shattered the uneasy peace: the flight of Mary Queen of Scots to England, the ensuing rebellion of the northern earls, and the bull *Regnans in excelsis* of 25 February 1570, excommunicating the Queen and calling upon her faithful Catholic subjects to depose her. The government responded with a series of measures in 1571 and 1572 intended to combat a subversive minority within the country, and to identify those who were refusing to conform to the religious settlement.[62] The first seminary priests, instilled with zeal, arrived from Douai in 1574, and in 1575 the Privy Council began a campaign of sustained coercion against leading Catholic laymen in the counties. The predicament of English Catholics had entered a new phase.

At Oxford, the change is marked by the chancellorship of Robert Dudley, Earl of Leicester lasting from 1564 until his death in 1588. As recent study has shown, he took a 'close and constant interest' in the affairs of the university, using it in part as a source of beneficial leases and other forms of patronage for his friends, but also attending closely to its internal affairs, often in detail.[63] One lasting effect of his governance was further to enhance royal control over policy and appointments. From 1570 the chancellor's commissary or local deputy, once chosen by the regent masters, was filled annually by the nominee of the chancellor.[64] So too, as we have seen, were the headships of halls. Inevitably, the government's concern about religious conformity was no small part of Leicester's preoccupation. In 1577 the Privy Council directed all bishops to compile lists of recusants in their dioceses, and the survey in Oxford showed a substantial advance in Protestant adherence, although with significant Catholic presence still.[65] In the university it was only at All Souls, Exeter, Balliol and Queen's that there were thought to be recusants, Exeter (with its strong west country connections) having the highest proportion. It was in the halls, then, that the Catholic presence was most noticeable, and the continuing arrival of Jesuits and seminar priests only intensified the government's anxiety.[66]

Leicester pressed repeatedly for the university to take action against the threat of popery. In June 1581 copies of Edmund Campion's *Rationes decem* were left in each place at the university Act – its graduation ceremony in St Mary's. In October 1581, Leicester warned that 'many papists have heretofore and may

---

62 Beales, *Education Under Penalty*, pp. 37–39; for the coercive measures taken through the 1580s and 1590s, see Williams, *Tudor Regime*, pp. 275–77; Rose, *Cases of Conscience*, pp. 36 ff.; also on the wider background, see Jones, *Birth of the Elizabethan Age*, pp. 80–86.

63 Williams, 'State, Church and University', pp. 423–31.

64 The title 'vice-chancellor' summarizes the change; *ibid.*, pp. 423, 425.

65 *Ibid.*, p. 413; see above n. 53.

66 *Ibid.*

hereafter lurk among you, and be brought up by corrupt tutors'.[67] The result was the university's matriculation statute of 14 November 1581,[68] which insisted that any matriculand aged sixteen years or over subscribe both to the articles of religion and to the royal supremacy within a week of admission to any hall or college. Its regulations applied only in Oxford; Cambridge was made to follow suit only in the reign of James I. The next year Leicester, complaining still of Catholicism in Oxford and noting that 'the other [university] is untouched with it', warned of 'secret and lurking Papists amongst you, which seduce your youth and carry them over by flocks to the Seminaries beyond Seas'.[69] In this atmosphere a concerted effort was made to detect and extirpate the stubborn Catholic presence.

The problem of keeping track of the undergraduate members of the university was one of very long standing. The medieval university had kept no record of its membership, although early statutes required all students to be on the rolls of a regent master.[70] In 1420 a royal ordinance declared that within a month of arrival at the university, scholars and their servants were to take an oath to observe the statutes, to be under the government of the principal of a hall (then almost the only place of undergraduate residence), and not to lodge privately with townsmen. In 1552, for reasons that remain obscure, the commissary's deputy revived this ordinance and entered it in his register along with the names of scholars in the various colleges and halls, thus creating the first list of those in residence in the university. There was no sequel to this action under Mary, and by the time of Elizabeth it was the Catholics chiefly who posed the problem that before had been raised by unruly undergraduates living in the town as 'chamber-deacons' without adequate supervision. Equally suspect for the same reason were unlicensed tutors, and in 1562 the bedell of civil law summoned all scholars living with townsmen to state the name of the tutor under whom they had placed themselves, recording almost one hundred names.

In 1565 came the first major achievement of Leicester's chancellorship, the new statutes – *nova statuta*[71] – which concluded a fitful quest by the university from the time of Wolsey and before. These provided, at least in theory, that a register of matriculation should be kept by the university to record for each college and hall the name, age, place of origin and social status of each member, scholar, servant or other person 'privileged' by the university (such as tradesmen). All – if at least sixteen years of age – were to take the oath to observe the university's statutes in the presence of the chancellor or his deputy. It was the responsibility of heads of houses and halls to see that all new arrivals were

[67] *Ibid.*

[68] Andrew Clark, ed., *Register of the University of Oxford* (Oxford, 1887), II/1, Oxford Historical Society x, pp. 167–69; Strickland Gibson, *Statuta antiqua*, pp. 421–23. See also McConica, 'Rise of the Undergraduate College', pp. 50–51.

[69] Loach, 'Reformation Controversies', p. 393; Williams, *Tudor Regime*, pp. 389, 413.

[70] For the background, see McConica, 'Rise of the Undergraduate College', pp. 48 ff.

[71] Strickland Gibson, *Statuta antiqua*, pp. 378 ff. The matriculation statute is pp. 391–95.

presented for this ceremony within a week of admission – a rule in force at the present day. Unattached scholars were to be placed under the supervision of some master or tutor who was a member of a college or hall. As might be assumed from the detailed provisions of the enactment, it was administered only casually. Regular listings began only in 1572 and for a decade the records remained very imperfect.

Continuing concern about the presence of Catholics was the principal incentive to tighten the system further. In December 1579, following the survey of recusants in 1577, all students living with townsmen were ordered to move into colleges and halls – as indeed was required already by the statutes. The next February the oath of supremacy was introduced into the statutes,[72] and the matriculation statute the following year which required the oath to be administered to every new student added the further requirement of subscription to the articles of religion. The statute was also retroactive, in that every student of the age of sixteen or upward who had not already matriculated in a college or hall was to leave the university within a fortnight unless he could show that he had made the required subscriptions, and was to be registered in the matriculations-book. Scholars between the ages of twelve and sixteen were required only to subscribe; under the age of twelve they need only matriculate until they were 'of years sufficient to performs the rest'.[73] The penalty for omission was a fine of 20 shillings for the head of a college or hall, and for the scholar 40 shillings for every week in default, '*toties quoties*'. No tutor or reader in the university, 'that is or shall be by othe detected of vehement suspicion of poperye shall after the Nativitye of Christ next insuinge retaine any pupill or scholler', unless he purge himself before the vice-chancellor and proctors and three preachers of the university.

The system thus established placed the onus of responsibility effectively on the heads of the colleges and halls to see that their junior members had conformed to the religious settlement. By this time as well, every head of college or hall was required to appoint a catechist, and to provide for termly religious examinations in the house with professors of theology present. A regulation of June 1580 provided that permission to supplicate for graces and promotion to any degree was made contingent not only on membership of a recognized academic body but on entry of the candidate's hall or college in the register with every grace. Those proposing the candidate were to be members of the scholar's own house, who could be presumed to vouch for him. It was this series of developments, culminating in the matriculation statute of November 1581, which gave the colleges and halls virtual control over admission to the university, and which finally brought into being a Protestant, undergraduate, collegiate university.[74] Leicester's persistence was at last rewarded, and the passing of the

72 *Ibid.*, pp. 416–17.
73 Clark, *Registers*, p. 167; Strickland Gibson, *Statuta antiqua*, p. 421.
74 McConica, 'Rise of the Undergraduate College', p. 50.

matriculation statute was accompanied by an energetic search for unregistered undergraduates that brought the total of matriculands that year to over eight hundred.[75]

The special problem posed by the halls was addressed by the university itself in made-to-order visitations. Records of these aularian visitations do not appear in the university register, but the surviving records must have been kept by the registrar or vice-chancellor.[76] Early inquiries record the concerns of the university officials about studies and discipline in the halls, which as we have seen, did not fit comfortably into the more authoritarian and disciplined Tudor university; they were correspondingly thought to require the direct supervision of the university itself. New Inn Hall was visited in 1575, and the inquiry consisted of six articles only dealing, for the most part, with lectures and the neglected responsibilities of the principal.[77] Earlier, about 1565–66, Balliol College had experienced a similar visitation, when the master was accused, *inter alia*, of placing 'all his scolars with the godsall, a masemounging papist', and six fellows were reported by name never to have received communion in the chapel.[78]

As the decade progressed, the articles reflect increasingly the government's apprehension about the Catholic presence at Oxford. Broadgates Hall and Gloucester Hall were visited in 1580-81, and the inquiries by then were far more comprehensive and detailed.[79] It was asked for example about the catechism, by whom is it given and for what stipend? Who does not attend, or does so negligently? Are the offenders punished? Grace is to be said before and after meals; by whom is it said? Do any sit down before grace or depart before the concluding grace? Is there any laughter or talk during grace? By whom? Are they punished? Do the members of the house resort every sabbath and festival day to the parish church in mornings and evenings? Do they remain there devoutly? If not, who fails to do so? Are they punished? Is communion provided for those over the age of sixteen? Are there any who refuse it or refuse to go to church? Are there any who have in their possession popish prohibited books? Have any delayed matriculation for a month or more? Are any scrupulously observing feasts or fish days now abolished?

Of course, no system is perfect. Sympathetic authorities might fail to administer at least a part of the oath, or unacknowledged attendance – the more likely solution – was still possible especially in the halls. Moreover some Catholic families saw to it that their sons came up to the university while still under age. If

---

[75] *Ibid.*, p. 51.

[76] *Ibid.*, p. 54; Oxford University Archives, NEP/supra/45.

[77] *Ibid.*

[78] NEP/supra/45, f. 3. That Balliol should have been treated in this respect as a hall may be related to the fact that under Richard Fox's statutes of 1507, the college was given the right to elect its own visitor; see John Jones, *Balliol College: A History 1263–1939* (Oxford, 1988), p. 42.

[79] *Ibid.*, f. 15, with variants from f. 19. I am indebted to W.T. Mitchell for allowing me to make use of the typed transcripts in the University Archives.

they were disinclined to take a degree, as was by no means unusual among commoners in general, they might spend two or three years in effective study with a sympathetic tutor before leaving and without the need for perjury or dissimulation, provided that they also escaped scrutiny about their church attendance or, at least, attendance at communion three times a year. Of the comparatively few undergraduates who did matriculate under the age of sixteen, their names provide some grounds for thinking that the background frequently was Catholic. A clear example is that of the future Jesuit, John Gerard. By his own account, he came of staunchly Catholic parentage and was sent to Oxford at the age of twelve, to Exeter, a college known for its Catholic sympathies. He matriculated on 3 December 1575 without the need for subscription, but left within a year when, at Easter, there was an attempt to force him to attend church and receive the 'Protestant sacrament'.[80]

Under Leicester's successors the scrutiny was intensified. Sir Christopher Hatton was elected chancellor in September 1588. Doubtless with the recent and presumed future threat of Spanish invasion in mind, he prescribed the strict enforcement of all religious tests, insisting that all who were required to subscribe must also confess that the prayer book and the articles of religion contained nothing contrary to the word of God.[81] In January 1589 it was decided that promotion to B.A. and M.A. was to be made conditional on the candidate's ability to recite the articles of faith and religion by heart, and to give an account of them in a scriptural sense – '*secundum sensum scripturarum rationem sufficientem reddere*' – and this before the vice-chancellor, proctors and regent masters. Moreover, no grace was to be asked unless the candidate was personally present in St Mary's, ready to submit himself to the questioning of these senior members, and not only in the articles of the faith.[82] In the event, it appears that these clumsy additions were ignored, to Hatton's fury.[83]

Hatton would seem to have been responsible for yet bolder initiatives in seeking out Catholics, one of which coincided with the foregoing measures and resulted in a spectacular act of terror and quadruple martyrdom within Oxford.[84]

On 18 May 1589, just before the hour of midnight, four men were arrested at the Catherine Wheel Inn by officers of the university.[85] Two were seminary

---

[80] *The Autobiography of an Elizabethan*, edited by Philip Caraman, S.J. (London, 1951), p. 1.

[81] Williams, 'Church, State and University', p. 432.

[82] Clark, *Register*, p. 169.

[83] Williams, 'Church, State, and University'.

[84] The principal sources for this account are: John Hungerford Pollen, S.J., ed., *Unpublished Documents Relating to the English Martyrs (1584–1603)* (London, 1908), CRS 5, pp. 168–69; John Hungerford Pollen, S.J., ed, Richard Challoner DD, *Memoirs of Missionary Priests* (London, 1924), pp. 153–59; APC XVII, pp. 205, 329. See also Christine Kelly, *Blessed Thomas Belson, His Life and Times 1563–1589* (London, 1987), which prints from an account entitled the *Breve relatione*, published in Rome in 1590, pp. 85–100. On this account, see ARCR I, nos. 897, 898.

[85] Assisted most likely by a pursuivant, Richard Ellesworth, from London; see Kelly,

priests – Father George Nichols and Father Richard Yaxley (also called 'Tankard') – and two were laymen. One of the laymen was a gentleman, Thomas Belson (also called 'Bolster') of the Aston Rowant and Brill connection, the other the Welsh servant of the inn, Humphrey ap Richard ('Prichard'). The next day they were taken for questioning in the presence of the vice-chancellor and other university officers, where all confessed to being Catholics. After a second interrogation concerned particularly with their Catholic contacts in and about Oxford, they were sent up to London for further examination by the Privy Council and by Secretary Francis Walsingham. Nichols had confessed to being a priest, and Yaxley's true status was revealed by the testimony of two apostate priests. The priests especially were then tortured severely in Bridewell prison and subsequently in the Tower. After a month the four were returned to Oxford where they were condemned at the assize and executed on 5 July, the two priests for high treason, the laymen for felony. The laymen were hanged, and the priests hanged, drawn and quartered, their heads displayed on the castle walls, and their quarters impaled over the four gates of the city. The widow who owned the Catherine Wheel was convicted in a *praemunire*, all of her goods were confiscated and she herself was condemned to perpetual imprisonment.

It is certain that these measures were intended specifically to intimidate the recusant community in and around Oxford. A Catholic report of the assize sent to Sir Francis Englefield the following October concluded with the observation that, 'Since this execution they began to execute their wicked statute more strictly and severely.'[86] Sir Francis Knollys, a member of the Privy Council who had travelled to Oxford to oversee the trial, reported to Burghley on 5 July that the proceedings had worked 'to the dawntinge of all the papistes, that before this proceedings here did prowdly advaunce them selves, as though they ought to be taken for good subjects'.[87]

The victims were well-chosen for the purpose, since at least three of the four must have been well-known to the recusant community in Oxford. Nichols had been born in Oxford and had attended Brasenose in the mid-1560s[88] where he supplicated for the B.A. in 1571. He had taught at St Paul's school for several years afterwards before departing for seminary training abroad. He was ordained to the priesthood at Douai in 1583. Thomas Belson, from the local recusant gentry family, was another Oxford man and had matriculated at Exeter College on 3 December 1575 at the age of seventeen. Like Nichols, he had left the university after supplicating for his B.A. without taking the degree, thus

---

Belson, p. 102. The inn was located on the site of the Bristol Buildings of modern Balliol College. By 27 Elizabeth cap. 2 (1585) it was high treason to be a priest in England who had been ordained beyond the seas; cf. note 61 above.

[86] Valladolid MSS, printed by Pollen in *Unpublished Manuscripts*, p. 169; cf. Kelly, *Belson*, pp. 102–03.

[87] Kelly, *Belson*, p. 101.

[88] Clark, *Register*, II/2, p. 27.

avoiding the oath. Although a layman, he had studied at Rheims in 1584 where he may well have met Nichols, and had resumed to England with Father Francis Ingolby who was martyred at York in 1586. On his fateful visit to Oxford he was going to see his 'ghostly father', which tends to confirm the tradition that Nichols was a familiar figure, much in and about Oxford. Thomas Belson had been committed to the Tower before, on 24 June 1585, apparently for acting as a courier between English Catholics and the continent. On 6 November 1586 he had been released under bond to leave the realm.[89] He was therefore much in jeopardy when he was arrested once again. Of Yaxley, less is known, except that he came from a gentry family in Boston, Lincolnshire, and after ordination at Rheims, had joined the English mission in 1586, a man much younger than Nichols, who looked to the older priest 'as a father'. While all died with arresting courage and integrity, it was left to the servant, of whom least is known, to leave the most memorable testimony.[90] As the last to mount the scaffold, Humphrey ap Richard had been in a position to observe the behaviour of his three predecessors, and, possibly in emulation, asked the bystanders to witness that he 'died Catholic'. Challenged by a 'minister' that he could not know what that meant, the Welshman replied, 'What I cannot say in words, I will seal with my blood'.

When Chancellor Hatton died in 1591 he was succeeded by Thomas Sackville, Lord Buckhurst, who held the office until his death in 1608. An anti-Puritan, Buckhurst was no less anxious than his predecessor to seek out the Catholics in the university, and urged repeatedly that they and all recusants be hunted down. Thus on 10 December 1594 he urged the university to enforce existing laws so that, 'the universitie may be purged from all Jesuits, Seminaries and notorious recusants which have secretly crept in amongst you and may happelie lye still lurking there in corners'.[91] Despite all the measures taken, the most worrying aspect of recusancy in Oxford – the steady stream of men leaving to be trained as seminary priests or Jesuits abroad – was extraordinarily difficult to staunch. Campion's death may have had the opposite effect on some, as that of John Story seems to have had upon him; ten Oxford men left for Rheims in 1583.[92] Apart from those who escaped with their lives, the list of Oxford men who are claimed as martyrs in Tudor and Stuart times commands respect from any point of view. Of the nearly seventy listed who are known to have belonged to the university of Oxford, more than fifty left the university in the reign of

[89] John Hungerford Pollen, S.J. and William MacMahon, S.J., eds, *The Venerable Philip Howard Earl of Arundel 1557–1595* (London, 1919), CRS 21, 'Tower Records', p. 132.

[90] All of the descriptive accounts are Catholic, with a predictable hagiographic stance more notable in the *Breve relatione* published in Rome in 1590, than in the account dated 19 October 1589, surviving in the Valladolid MSS. As the latter, more concise version lacks much of the rhetorical elaboration intended for the wider audience of the printed account, I have drawn upon it in preference as the more reliable. Challoner's account, written two centuries later, is again more economical; his sources are listed in the cited edition, p. 153n.

[91] Oxford University Archives, Reg. Cong. 1582–95, f. 272[r–v].

[92] Loach, 'Reformation Controversies', p. 381.

Elizabeth.[93] Of these, most were secular priests; seven were laymen, including John Story, D.C.L., M.P.; four were Jesuits, two were Benedictines and another a Franciscan. Five of these were actually born in Oxford – William Filby, Edward Stransham, George Nichols, George Napper and Thomas Reynolds – and the rest, including seventeen executed at Tyburn, were martyred away from the university. Nevertheless as the Catholic records show, their ministry and fate was well known to those they had left behind in Oxford.

The memory and example of these graduates, most of them young men who had been, often enough, close friends or associates at Oxford, will have made an indelible impression upon their co-religionists in the university, something about which we can only conjecture. What is clear is that despite the effective triumph of the government's policy by the end of Elizabeth's reign, the Catholicism of the place was tenacious still. Even a decade after the public execution in Oxford of Father George Napper of the Holywell family in 1610, Catholic priests could be thought still to enjoy remarkable freedom in the community. Recusant rolls of the period record a total of sixty-six papists in Oxford, mostly amongst small tradespeople,[94] and it is clear that Catholic recusancy maintained at least a tenuous life to the time of the Restoration. Even thereafter in the countryside, beyond the walls of Oxford and its suburbs, the recusant families among the gentry maintained their traditions with discreet observance, until Catholic emancipation and the Oxford Movement signalled a new entitlement for some of the university's most ancient traditions.

---

[93] The list specifically of Elizabethan martyrs following is based upon the 1928 Report of the Oxford University Catholic Association in the Bodleian Library, the official calendar of the Diocese of Birmingham, and Patrick McGrath, *Brasenose Priests and Martyrs under Elizabeth I* (Oxford, 1985). Thomas Pilchard, fellow of **Balliol**; Ralph Sherwin and John Cornelius S.J. of **Exeter**; William Marsden, Stephen Rowsham and John Sugar of **Oriel** (or St Mary Hall); Richard Thirkeld and John Boste of **Queen's**; John Slade, John Bodey and John Munden of **New College**; William Filby and William Hart of **Lincoln**; William Freeman, Anthony Brorby O.F.M. and John Travers of **Magdalen**; there were six from **Brasenose**, including George Nichols mentioned already – John Shert, Laurence Johnson *alias* Richardson, Thomas Cottam S.J., Robert Anderton and Francis Ingleby; of **Corpus**, Thomas Plumtree, James Fenn and Edward Burden in addition to George Napper, who was martyed in Oxford itself in 1610; Robert Sutton and Anthony Page of **Christ Church**; Thomas Ford, William Spenser, George Errington (a layman) and Christopher Wharton of **Trinity**; seven of **St John's** – in addition to Edmund Campion S.J. – Cuthbert Mayne, Edward Stransham, Robert Ludlam, Edward James, William Hartley and John Roberts O.S.B.; from Broadgates Hall, now **Pembroke** College, John Storey, Hugh More and Richard Martin, all laymen; Edward Campion (Edwards) of **Jesus**; Nicholas Garlick, Richard or Robert Simpson, Robert Widmerpool and Ralph Crockett of Gloucester Hall, now **Worcester College**; and from Hart Hall, now **Hertford College**, Alexander Briant S.J. and Thomas Hemerford. A further seven of uncertain affiliation raises the total for the Elizabethan period to 56 – Richard White, Richard Sergeant, John Adams, Edmund Sykes, Robert Sutton, William Davies, Mark Barkworth O.S.B.

[94] See Colvin, 'Roman Catholicism', p. 413 for the continuation of this story.

PART II

CAMPION AND HIS CONTEMPORARIES

4

Edmund Campion's *Histories of Ireland* and Reform in Tudor Ireland

COLM LENNON

Edmund Campion composed his *Histories of Ireland* in a period of ten weeks in the late spring of 1571 while on a visit to the country.[1] The work, which was prefaced by dedicatory letters to his patron, Robert Dudley Earl of Leicester, and the 'loving' reader, was later decried by its author as an 'immature' production and not worthy of publication.[2] Nevertheless the unpublished manuscript, heavily revised by Campion's friend, Richard Stanihurst (whose family were his Dublin hosts), was incorporated by the Irishman in his contribution to Holinshed's *Chronicles of England, Scotland and Ireland,* first published in 1577. Stanihurst was aware that the work of his 'fast friend and inward companion' was imperfect (in Campion's own eyes), saying that it 'twitled more tales out of school and drowned weightier matters in silence, than the author, upon better view and larger search, would have permitted'.[3] Indeed Campion, according to Stanihurst, had intended to prepare a more complete version, but was 'crossed in the nick of this determination'.[4] Although not published in its own right until 1633 when edited by Sir James Ware,[5] the manuscript history was known to writers in Ireland in the early seventeenth century. The opinion of Barnaby Rich, a

---

[1] A.F. Vossen, ed., *Two Bokes of the Histories of Ireland compiled by Edmund Campion* (Assen, 1963), introduction, p. 1.

[2] John H. Pollen, S.J., 'Edmund Campion's History of Ireland', *The Month* 107 (1906), p. 158.

[3] Richard Stanihurst, 'Description of Ireland' in *Holinshed's Irish Chronicle 1577*, ed. Liam Miller and Eileen Power (Dublin, 1979), pp. 7–8.

[4] *Ibid.*, p. 7.

[5] *The historie of Ireland, collected by three learned authors, viz. Meredith Hanmer, Edmund Campion and Edmund Spenser*, ed. James Ware (Dublin, 1633). Hanmer gathered materials for his 'Chronicle of Ireland' while serving as a churchman there from 1591 to 1604, but he made little use of Campion's history. Hanmer had controverted Campion's 'Brag' in 1581: for Hanmer, see DNB; see also Andrew Hadfield, 'Briton and Scythian: Tudor Representations of Irish Origins', *Irish Historical Studies* 28 (1993), pp. 395, 397.

puritanical soldier living in retirement in Ireland, who adduced the evidence of Campion's execution as proof of his unreliability[6] was counterpointed by that of Geoffrey Keating who castigated English historians including Campion as being congenitally impervious to the merits of Ireland and its inhabitants.[7] The reprinting of Ware's edition of Campion and other writers in the early nineteenth century under the auspices of the Dublin Society advanced the claim of the *Histories* to historiographical substantiality.[8] At the turn of the century favourable reassessments of the *Histories* emerged in articles by two historians who wished to reconcile the colonial and humanistic strains in the work of one who was to become a martyr for the Catholic faith.[9]

The enhancement of Campion's reputation as commentator on Elizabethan Ireland had its culmination in the scholarly edition of the *Histories* by A.F. Vossen in 1963.[10] The editor who applied exacting standards of historical research to the text set his examination of the work in the context of Campion's visit to Ireland and the intellectual milieu which fostered its production. In doing so he provided fairly conclusive solutions to puzzles in relation to dates and circumstances which had thitherto exercised Campion's biographers. Vossen consistently pointed up the veracity of the earliest, near-contemporary biographers. Having examined the question of Campion's private convictions at the time by reference to the accounts by Robert Persons and Pietro Bombino[11] (who were informed by Richard Stanihurst), Vossen concluded that he was definitely a Catholic at the time of his arrival in Ireland.[12] The date of Campion's coming to Ireland for the visit during which he wrote the *Histories* is given as 25 August 1570, although the editor concedes that this might have been his second trip.[13] As to its purpose, no firm evidence of Campion's connection with the scheme for the foundation of an Irish university can be adduced.[14] Vossen argues that the date of Campion's departure from Drogheda in the early summer of 1571 is

[6] See Edmund Hogan, S.J., 'The Blessed Edmund Campion's "History of Ireland" and its Critics', *Irish Ecclesiastical Record*, 3rd series, 12 (1891), p. 631.

[7] *Ibid.*, p. 632.

[8] *Ancient Irish Histories: the works of Spencer, Campion, Hanmer and Marleburrough*, 2 vols (Dublin, 1809).

[9] Hogan, 'Campion's "History"' and Pollen, 'Campion's History', *The Month* 106 (1905), pp. 561–76; 107 (1906), pp. 156–69.

[10] See full bibliographical reference in Note 1, above; hereafter all references to the *Histories* are to this edition which will be cited as Campion, *Histories*, ed. Vossen.

[11] Robert Persons, 'Vita' is in Stonyhurst College Collectanea, P.1. ff. 76–146, 147–59 and published as 'Of the Life and Martyrdom of Father Edmond Campian', *Letters and Notices* 11 (1977), pp. 219–42, 308–39; 12 (1878), pp. 1–68; Pietro Bombino, *Vita et martyrium Edmundi Campiani* (Antwerp, 1618), ARCR I, no. 194.

[12] Campion, *Histories*, ed. Vossen, introduction, pp. 2–11.

[13] *Ibid.*, introduction, pp. 11–13.

[14] *Ibid.*, introduction, pp. 13–14, 16–20; but see R. Dudley Edwards, 'Ireland, Elizabeth I and the Counter-Reformation', in S.T. Bindoff, Joel Hurstfield, and C.H. Williams, ed., *Elizabethan Government and Society: Essays Presented to Sir John Neale* (London, 1961), pp. 323–26.

uncertain because of a clash of events, each supposed to have involved Campion. But serious doubts are cast on the story of the confiscation of the manuscript of the *Histories*, there being no evidence from the contemporary sources that the document was taken from its author by searchers at Drogheda.[15]

In his balanced assessment of Campion's technique and method as a historian, Vossen emphasised his subject's strengths and weaknesses as a Renaissance writer.[16] While Campion attempted to harmonise beauty with truth and to establish the antiquity of national roots, the critical sense as applied especially through auxiliary sciences was lacking. Within the overall purposive framework of providing edifying lessons for statesmen and others, Campion aimed at enlightening Leicester, his patron, on Irish history and affairs, and at giving a lead for Irish antiquaries to follow. As he tried to apply critical scholarly standards to the myths and chronicling of early Irish history, Campion was motivated by his desire to show the antiquity of the English claim to Ireland. As well as being a pioneer in writing the first extended history of Ireland since the twelfth century, Campion was an innovator in his use of documentary evidence in his study. Although forced into this course because of the lack of information in existing chronicles and annals, his researching of original records is perhaps a facet of which Vossen could have been more commendatory. Many of the sources were to hand in the library of James Stanihurst, Richard's father, whom Campion praises fulsomely in the preface to the 'loving reader'. Among those which he made use of were statute rolls, official letters and urban chronicles, as well as versions of Giraldus Cambrensis and Philip Flatsbury's compilations. While criticism of Campion's deficiencies in his analysis of documentation may be anachronistic, more valid may be the charge that the work is enervated, having a 'dead kernel',[17] by virtue of the strict contrariety of English and Irish in his history to the detriment of rational explanation for historical events. Nevertheless the *Histories* are seen to have been rightly praised for the rich quality of some of the prose, the vividness and succinctness of much of the narrative, and the effective presentation of set-piece events.[18]

The objectives which Campion set himself in the prefaces to his work evidently serve to shape the nature of the text and the methodology which he employed. He stated in his dedicatory letter to the Earl of Leicester that he was anxious to show that his time in Ireland had been well spent, and that he wished to provide his English patron with an honorific tribute as well as an informative account of Ireland and its history to guide him in his policy-making. On a professional level, the author hoped to furnish the learned antiquaries 'of this country birth' with a model in terms of research and method which they could

---

[15] Campion, *Histories*, ed. Vossen, introduction, pp. 20–25.
[16] *Ibid.*, introduction, pp. 61–85.
[17] *Ibid.*, introduction, p. 70.
[18] *Ibid.*, introduction, pp. 70–85; cf. Pollen, 'Campion's History', pp. 165–66.

'polish' by their own studies.[19] While these motives are seen by Vossen to have impelled Campion's writing of the *Histories*, it is instructive to explore the circumstances of the composition of the work in the light of the recent historiography of Tudor Ireland. For example, the Leicester-Sir Henry Sidney-Campion nexus may be charged with added significance due to the critical part which faction has been shown to have played in shaping events in Ireland and England. Thus Campion's dedication of the *Histories* to the earl may have had more importance than the gesture of a grateful client. Also the investigation in recent writings of the methods of reform by persuasive means casts Campion's rôle as exemplary historian for native antiquaries in a slightly different light, and indeed raises questions about the reasons for his presence in Ireland. In order to justify a reassessment of the purpose and nature of Campion's *Histories*, it may be useful to sketch very briefly the main lines of the latest interpretative framework for Tudor Irish history.

The theme of constitutional and institutional reform in the mid-Tudor decades has informed the work of scholars of early modern Ireland in the last twenty-five years. The calling off of the conquest begun in 1169 was betokened by the kingship of Ireland act of 1541 and the contemporaneous reception of the non-indentured, sovereign Gaelic and gaelicised political leaders into the newly-unified body politic ruled by the English monarch as king of Ireland. The strategy employed to bring about this latter aim was conciliatory, comprising negotiation, education and pacification through demilitarisation. In the discrete lordships of Ireland, reform meant the abolition of the arbitrary and oppressive forms of taxation known as coign and livery and the dismantling of the pan-provincial networks of factional alliances which loosely bound the fragmented Irish polity. Instead the English administration with its council and courts, modelled on those of the mother-country, was being revitalised and the range of its activities slowly expanded from the mid-sixteenth century onwards. This expansion was to be fostered by the erection of provincial presidencies and councils, and its agents were newcomers from England as well as government-favoured officials of long-settled families of English origin (the Old English). The reforms were to be financed ultimately by the loyalist community which was being taxed more heavily by the 1560s, much to its chagrin. Within the remit of the central and regional agencies was the task of religious reform, aiming at asserting royal ecclesiastical supremacy and the substitution of the new doctrinal and liturgical regime for traditional rites. The rôle of the older colonials in this reforming activity was ambivalent, some wholeheartedly backing ethno-cultural integration by peaceful means and others prepared only to support the safe-guarding of the old Pale area in eastern Ireland. At the time of Campion's visit to Ireland, the weaknesses of the first phase of reform were manifest and a reassessment of aims and methods was in progress within both newly-arrived

---

[19] Campion, *Histories*, ed. Vossen, 'To the loving reader'.

and Old English circles. The alienation of the Old English from state policy was evident as was the dissatisfaction of many Gaelic lords. As Sir Henry Sidney prepared to relinquish the governorship in 1571 after his first spell as Lord Deputy, the mood was one of retrospection as well as of anticipation.[20]

It was at this juncture that Edmund Campion hastily researched and wrote his *Histories of Ireland*. Besides the explicit motives as stated in the prefaces, he was undoubtedly concerned to justify the actions of his patron's protégé in Ireland, Sir Henry Sidney. Campion also expressed his indebtedness to his Dublin hosts, the Stanihursts, and their perspective and that of their fellow-Old English on events in Irish history are incorporated in the *Histories*. Of critical importance is the perception of Gaelic Ireland which had experienced the thrust of political and social reforms for almost three decades. In this context the depiction of Gaelic customs is particularly interesting, as is the version of the origins of the Gaelic race in Ireland, given the stress on the upholding of the claims of the English monarch to sovereignty over the island. By studying the text of the *Histories* against the backdrop of the revised accounts of the period we may come to a deeper comprehension of Campion's purpose and also gain valuable perceptions of the early successes and failures of English reform policies from one who was eminently well-connected and well placed to comment.

Perhaps a key to understanding the creative design of Edmund Campion when penning his *Histories of Ireland* is given to us in the climactic exchange between Lord Deputy Henry Sidney and Speaker James Stanihurst.[21] The occasion of the speeches which Campion heard and reconstructed in the work was the final session of the Irish parliament in 1571 at which Stanihurst sat as M.P. for Dublin city as well as presiding in the House of Commons.[22] In the conventional address of thanks to the governor, Stanihurst took the opportunity to dwell on the theme of education which was of great personal interest to him as well as being of national importance. The Lord Deputy's reply in acknowledgement of the work of the parliamentarians took up the theme of Stanihurst's oration and also expatiated on his own principal concerns in his last months in office. This telling set piece embraces Old and New English ideas about reform, being framed by the word, 'reformation',[23] and represents Campion's effort to

---

[20] Among the major recent contributions to the advancement of an understanding of Tudor Ireland are the following: Brendan Bradshaw, *The Irish Constitutional Revolution of the Sixteenth Century* (Cambridge, 1979); Ciaran Brady, *The Chief Governors: The Rise and Fall of Reform Government in Ireland* (Cambridge, 1995); Nicholas Canny, *From Reformation to Restoration: Ireland, 1534–1660* (Dublin, 1987) and *The Elizabethan Conquest of Ireland: A Pattern Established, 1565–76* (Hassocks, 1976); Steven Ellis, *Tudor Ireland: Crown and Community and the Conflict of Cultures, 1470–1603* (London, 1985) and *Reform and Renewal: English Government in Ireland, 1470–1534* (London, 1985).

[21] Campion, *Histories*, ed. Vossen, pp. 182–95.

[22] For an account of this parliament, see Victor Treadwell, 'The Irish Parliament of 1569–71', *Proceedings of the Royal Irish Academy* lxv, sect. C (1966), pp. 55–89.

[23] The phrase occurs near the beginning Stanihurst's oration when he proclaims 'the zeal

reconcile the two perspectives. The speeches, unlike other orations in the *Histories* which are largely apocryphal, are authentic in that Campion worked from notes made by him as observer of the parliamentary proceedings, and their genuineness is attested by the reiteration of sentiments known to be of abiding concern to the interlocutors. In seeking to synthesise the manifestly deviating positions of natives and newcomers Campion was not only rendering obeisance to those to whom he was indebted for his pleasant Irish stay but also teasing out the implications of the historical process which he had thereunto described.

James Stanihurst's concentration on education as a vehicle for reform is characteristic of one who was renowned for his learning and liberality. In fact the *Histories* could not have been written without Stanihurst's 'familiar societie', 'daly table talk', and 'thowsand loving turnes' supplemented by the Speaker's own library and documents.[24] In extolling the beneficial effects of educational migration for the sons of Irish 'noble men and worshipful, with others of ability', Stanihurst could be seen to have practised what he preached: his son, Richard, had attended University College, Oxford, where he first encountered Campion.[25] The speaker advocated that action be taken on foot of the passage of the statute for the setting up of diocesan grammar schools. Stanihurst regarded this as vital for anglicisation ('the breeding of stout English hearts') and the vitiation of the insidious influences of the Palespeople's 'unbroken borderers' – the Gaelic and gaelicised inhabitants. The measure had been opposed by the Irish bishops who feared the diminution of their incomes but was agreed after amendments were made in relation to funding and patronage. The benefits would include not just the furthering of learning and religion but also the eliciting of 'pure English tongue, habit, fashion and discipline' for the advancement of political obedience and civic order. James Stanihurst makes reference to the failure of the scheme for the foundation of a university, mentioning the governor's involvement as potential benefactor, and sees the schools act as prelusive to a future academic foundation. In rehearsing Stanihurst's eloquent words so carefully Campion is conveying the mentality of a scholarly advocate who was representative of a humanistic, reforming élite of the Pale, and also bearing witness to his own enthusiasm for the advancement of education in Ireland.

Lord Deputy Sidney's reply to the speaker's address as relayed by Campion is at once an exhortation of the assembled political community and a defence of his own administration which was about to end.[26] His theme was the health of the Irish commonwealth which had been advanced to some extent by the parliamentary legislation but which was being threatened by extra-constitutional

which I have to the reformation of this realm' as a motive for pressing the adoption of a statute for establishing grammar schools; in Sidney's concluding sentence, he exhorts his hearers to 'good and substantial reformation' of the country according to the principles he has enunciated (Campion, *Histories*, ed. Vossen, pp. 182, 195).

24 *Ibid.*, 'To the loving reader'.

25 See Colm Lennon, *Richard Stanihurst the Dubliner* (Dublin, 1981), pp. 22–23, 26–27.

26 Campion, *Histories*, ed. Vossen, pp. 185–96.

forces. He welcomed the 'godly statute' for providing diocesan grammar schools but bemoaned the lack of opportunity for second-level students to proceed to an Irish university college given the failure of the scheme for such an academy which he had championed. Despite this reverse which he ascribed to a failure of self-confidence in the Irish political nation, Sidney commended the lords and commons on passing many bills which would benefit both crown and commonwealth. Although about to be removed from the country, the Lord Deputy envisaged himself being a constant advocate of the interests of Ireland which he defined as 'a nation derived from our ancestors, ingraffed and incorporate into one body with us', 'yoked together under one obedience, English bloods and English hearts'. Because of his commitment to the constitutional nexus bodied forth by this relationship, Sidney's defence of the garrison and his own unpopular victualling policies was all the more fervent. He argued that the English army was necessary to cow the 'barbarous people that lap your blood as greedily as ours'. While the presence of a properly-victualled garrison was a necessary evil which the English government countenanced only for the gravest of reasons, Sidney claimed that his own administration had attempted to alleviate the burdensomeness of the military establishment and its camp-followers for the loyal population. Rejecting spurious comparisons with other countries which allegedly managed with local militias, Sir Henry pointed to the greater security of the eastern Pale and the more commodious lifestyle of its inhabitants in his time as governor as evidence of the efficacy of a strong, well-supported English garrison.

The two speeches taken together form a crescendo for the *Histories of Ireland*, and help us to understand the English author's purpose and perspective. His own personal debts are repaid in some measure by the flattering portraits of his host and patron's protégé which are contained in this last section. The encomiastic words of Sidney in respect of Stanihurst form a suitable tribute to one whom the writer saw as the inspiration behind his work: the Lord Deputy confirms 'the opinion which my self and the general voyce long since retained of your rare virtues, devotion, wisdom, learning and modestie'.[27] Sidney's words here seem to go beyond mere dutiful acknowledgement of the speaker's rôle. Sidney himself emerges as a hero in the *Histories*. Scattered throughout the earlier chapters are references to his deeds – the reconciliation of gaelicised lords with the crown, the reclaiming of the earldom of Ulster for Queen Elizabeth and the rebuilding of Christ Church cathedral in Dublin.[28] Not only are his principles of governance clearly outlined in his valedictory speech but the very last sentence is an extended pen-portrait, enumerating conventional humanistic traits but all the more powerful for being the concluding passage: Sidney was

---

[27] *Ibid.*, pp. 190–91.
[28] *Ibid.*, pp. 7, 11, 54, 102.

stately without disdaine, familiar without contempt, very continent and chaste of body, no more than enough liberal, learned in many languages, and a great lover of learning, perfect in blazoning of arms, skilful of antiquities, of wit fresh and lively, in consultations very temperate, in utterance happy, which his experience and wisdom hath made artificial, a preferrer of many, a father to his servants, both in war and peace of commendable courage.[29]

According to Campion, Sir Henry Sidney's greatest success in that first viceroyalty was the overthrow of Shane O'Neill, the paramount chieftain of Ulster, with whose 'rebellion' the Lord Deputy had found the realm of Ireland 'distempered' in 1565.[30] Indeed failure to defeat O'Neill had ruined the career in Ireland of an illustrious predecessor as governor, the Earl of Sussex Thomas Radcliffe. The version of the killing of Shane O'Neill in 1567 contained in the *Histories* is based very closely on the account in the preamble to the statute which attainted O'Neill as traitor in the parliament of 1569–71.[31] The English visitor had access to parliamentary rolls in the household of the parliamentary speaker, and it is quite possible that James Stanihurst may have been involved in drafting the long narrative of occurrences which formed a background to O'Neill's attainder.[32] The nub of this official version as retailed by Campion is that, having been routed by the O'Donnells at Farsetmore, Shane sought refuge with the Mac-Donnells whom he had defeated two years previously at Glenshesk. Having been welcomed at a banquet, Shane was engaged in a drunken brawl by the avenging Scots and hacked to pieces. As has been convincingly shown the real circumstances in which Shane O'Neill met his violent death were much more complicated.[33] Although weakened by defeat, O'Neill was gambling on reaching an accord with the Scots who were also apparently being courted by Lord Deputy Sidney through his agent, Captain William Piers. By the late 1560s evidence of such contacts would prove embarrassing for the government which now aimed at extirpating the Scots from the north-east and initiating English settlements there. The story of the fatal stabbing at a drunkards' fight was 'an imaginative piece of late Renaissance historiography' which served to cover up the traces of English negotiations with the Scots and present both Gaelic clans in a most unflattering light. Whether Campion was aware of the fabrication as he adapted the story in

---

[29] *Ibid.*, p. 196.

[30] *Ibid.*, p. 173.

[31] 11 Eliz. I, sess. 3, cap. 1, *Irish Statutes*, I, pp. 322–38.

[32] Stanihurst took his responsibilities for the keeping of parliamentary records very seriously and was the prime mover in having the Irish statutes printed in 1573. See D.B. Quinn, 'Government Printing and the Publication of the Irish Statutes in the Sixteenth Century', *Proceedings of the Royal Irish Academy* xlix, sect. C (1943), pp. 54–55.

[33] Ciaran Brady, 'The Killing of Shane O'Neill: Some New Evidence', *The Irish Sword* 15 (1982), pp. 116–23.

the statutory preamble is uncertain but that version certainly aided his vaunting of Sir Henry Sidney's reputation.[34]

It was not just in the presentation of his achievements that Campion was jealous of the 'blessed memory'[35] of Sidney being preserved but also in providing a medium for the venting of the governor's frustration at the difficulties placed in the way of his administration. In the Parliament of 1569–71 there was much opposition to government measures, including the original draft of the diocesan schools bill.[36] Sidney's favoured scheme for a university in Ireland never even reached the stage of parliamentary proposal. His disappointment is voiced in the cry contained in his speech to Parliament as conveyed by Campion, 'shall we be so curious or so testy that nothing will please us?' and in his warning to the Members not to let previous advances in political and civic life 'be utterly lost and frustrate'.[37] It is clear, however, that Sidney was most exercised by the circulation shortly before the last session of the Parliament of a seditious document signed by 'Tom Troth'. Campion's reference to this incident is important as it does not occur elsewhere.[38] He says that the document was 'let fall in the streets of Dublin' and that it 'nipped by name divers honourable and worshipfull of the realm and certain officers of the deputyes household for greeving the land with impositions of cesse'. The response of the government was the issuing of a proclamation on 28 January 1571 to 'cut off many such murmures'.[39] Over half of Sidney's valedictory speech is devoted to answering the criticisms expressed by the 'brokers of lible' in 'Tom, a loodles rime'.[40] In his vigorous defence of the garrison policy, the lord deputy realises that he is 'perhaps out of all order' but his points are rendered faithfully by Campion.

Although the libellous paper does not appear to be extant, there is among the Irish state papers a similar document, perhaps from the same source.[41] Its tone, if not the content, enables us to judge the reasons for Sidney's anger at the original. This flysheet which was signed by 'Thom Troth' and 'John Justifier' was transmitted with a covering note to the Privy Council in London on 31 January 1572 by Sidney's successor in the deputyship, Sir William Fitzwilliam, and the Irish council.[42] It had been handed in at the office of John Thomas, chief remembrancer of the exchequer in Dublin, and erstwhile supplier of information to Campion for the *Histories*. Accusations of extortion and bribery were levelled at Thomas who was described as 'rankest knave', 'cutthroat villain', 'vilest briber', 'extortioner' and 'bloodsucker'. Thomas had allegedly embezzled

34 *Ibid.*, p. 121.
35 Campion, *Histories*, ed. Vossen, p. 181.
36 See Treadwell, 'Parliament of 1569–71'.
37 Campion, *Histories*, ed. Vossen, p. 187.
38 38 *Ibid.*, p. 181.
39 *Ibid.*
40 *Ibid.*, pp. 189–92.
41 PRO, SP 63/35/11(i).
42 PRO, SP 63/35/11.

the sum of £10,000 from the 'poor subjects' of the Queen under the 'noble cloak' of Sir Henry Sidney while he was in office. Dark warnings such as 'look to thyself' ended the bill, but most disconcerting for the Irish councillors was the aspiration that 'all offices will come to be exercised only by men of this nation (as secluding therein the English)'. In fact the writers of the bill merely expressed the hope that the Queen would preserve the position of the Old English, who educated their children to 'great charges', rather than replace them with newly-arrived English. The alienation of the older English community of which Thom Troth and John Justifier were self-appointed spokespersons overshadowed the last phase of Sir Henry Sidney's administration down to his departure from Ireland on 25 March 1571. Indeed the 'blessed memorie' of his positive achievements was threatened with occlusion due to a welter of controversy and revolt. Adverse reactions to tentative administrative advances into the provinces elicited the 'tumults' among the descendants of the Anglo-Norman aristocrats in the late 1560s referred to by Campion, including those of the Butler brothers of Ormond and James Fitzmaurice of the Desmond Geraldines.[43] In many ways the last half-chapter of the *Histories of Ireland* reads as an apologia for the viceroyalty of Sir Henry Sidney, hurriedly researched and written in ten weeks as his governance ended, to counter the damaging effects of slanderous pamphlets. But the contentious issue of the cess, the combined set of government demands upon the local community to maintain the military establishment and the Lord Deputy's household, is shown by Campion to have predated Sidney's regime. In the time of his immediate predecessor, Sir Nicholas Arnold, the 'abuses . . . of cesse and soldyors' did 'so impoverisshe and alienate the nedie fermors from us' that 'thei saye they might as easlie beare the Irish oppressions of quoynes and codies, from which wee pretend to deliver them'.[44] Certainly the authors of the later of the two scurrilous pamphlets exempted Sir Henry from responsibility for injustice, referring to him as the most 'curtuouse governor that ever rayned, full of pittie and mercy to every man'.[45] The question of the origins of factionalism and disillusionment among the older English population of Ireland is thrown into relief by these occurrences, and a brief survey of Campion's depiction of their historical rôle may be appropriate at this point.

At the outset the author gives notice of wishing to help the English of Ireland to 'favour the memorie of their noble auncestors'.[46] In order to achieve this, he traces the origins of direct English involvement in Ireland from the twelfth century onwards[47] though he is careful to reserve for the English monarchy a much more ancient title to the island. He makes a firm distinction between the

---

[43] Campion, *Histories*, ed. Vossen, pp. 180–81.

[44] *Ibid.*, p. 172; for a discussion of the controversy, see Ciaran Brady, ' "Conservative Subversives": The Community of the Pale and the Dublin Administration, 1556–86' in P.J. Corish, ed., *Radicals, Rebels and Establishments: Historical Studies XV* (Belfast, 1985), pp. 11–32.

[45] PRO, SP 63/35/11(i).

[46] Campion, *Histories*, ed. Vossen, 'To the loving reader'.

[47] *Ibid.*, pp. 21–22.

'simple Irish' and 'oure Englishe of Ireland'[48] who have retained their identity apart down to the present and the core community of whom are to be found in the English Pale. The heroic age of the Anglo-Norman barons is duly recorded after Giraldus Cambrensis but within a century of the conquest inter-settler factions are shown to have become endemic. Indeed to factionalism ('thus fell the English lords at variance among themselves'; 'the English of birth and the English of bloud falling to words, and divided in factions about it')[49] is attributed the degeneration of the Anglo-Normans who 'became Irish' such as the Cork families of Roche and Courcy. Rivalries among the descendants of the invaders also allowed the Irish to recover ground lost at the conquest ('the Irish lay wayting for the contention, so as the Realme was even on point to give over all and rebell').[50] Most seriously the occurrence of splits among those of English descent was detrimental to the flourishing of municipal life, as in the case of Cork, for example, to the decay of which Campion devotes much attention. An original letter from the mayor and corporation of the southern city was given to the scholar by Francis Agard, a member of the Irish council and confidant of Sidney, to exemplify 'the decay of those partes and the state of the Realme in times past'.[51] This early fifteenth-century letter he reproduced *in toto*.[52] As the English presence contracted in the later middle ages, centres such as Cork found it difficult to survive but Dublin on the other hand is presented as a centre of municipal thriving, the 'bountiful hospitality' of the mayoralty of which 'exceeded any English city, except London'.[53] Campion had access (no doubt among the papers of James Stanihurst) to a mayoral chronicle of the principal city.[54] Another major contribution of the English of Ireland, details of which interlace the military and political highlights, is the benefaction of the Church: many references are made to the foundations of abbeys by aristocratic families.[55]

The continuity in the political and cultural traditions of the older English was stressed by Campion, especially as maintained by the aristocracy and gentry.[56] At the apex of their society the heads of the great families of Ormond Butlers and Kildare Fitzgeralds, Earls Thomas and Gerald respectively, represented for him the best hope for healing factional rifts, as they attempted to 'put up' their 'quarrels' and to 'love unfainedly'.[57] Practically, the greatest contribution of the Old English families to the state within the recent past is seen to have been their assistance in military expeditions against restive clans to the south, west and

---

48 *Ibid.*, p. 21.
49 *Ibid.*, pp. 111, 118.
50 *Ibid.*, p. 111.
51 *Ibid.*, p. 116.
52 *Ibid.*, pp. 116–18.
53 *Ibid.*, p. 119.
54 *Ibid.*, p. 134.
55 *Ibid.*, pp 91, 93, 94, 97, for example.
56 See *ibid.*, Book One, cap. ii, 'The temporall nobilitie', and p. 113.
57 *Ibid.*, p. 134.

north of the Pale.[58] Individual citizen-servitors are recalled by name for their bravery in these sorties, including Alderman William Sarsfield of Dublin who in his mayoral year of 1566 campaigned in defence of Drogheda against Shane O'Neill and was knighted for his exploits in the field.[59] The defence of remoter areas of English civility such as Cork from 'unquiet neighbours', both Gaelic and gaelicised, was as yet beyond the compass of central government but there is a reference to the possibility of alleviation in the implementation of one of Sidney's most cherished reforms. Campion expressed the hope that 'the late sent over Lord President of Mounster', Sir John Perrot, who had appointed Cork as his seat of administration, would 'ease the inhabitants' of 'feare' and 'scourge the Irish outlawes that annoy the whole region of Mounster'.[60]

It is in his approval for the programme of anglicisation principally through educational reform that Campion's views and those of an influential élite of Old English in the inner Pale converged. Among the reasons for his indebtedness to James and Richard Stanihurst was their provision of a relaxed, scholarly and hospitable ambience in their Dublin home. In a letter to James he wrote:

> You sated me with every pleasure of place, season and company. You set me up a library selected from your own and provided so admirably that I should have ease and opportunity for study, that may I perish if ever I conversed so sweetly with the Muses outside of Oxford's walls.[61]

Through the Stanihursts, Campion met other patrician and gentry family-members including Sir Christopher Barnewall of Turvey with whom he stayed for his last three months in Ireland, Patrick Plunket, the baron of Dunsany, and Sir Christopher St Lawrence, the baron of Howth. These Old Englishmen supplied him with materials for his research on Irish history.[62] They were among the 'noble men and worshipfull, with others of ability' who had helped the country to become 'halfe deale more civill then it was' by sending their sons 'into England to the Law, to Universities, or to schooles'.[63] It was among them perhaps that Campion hoped to find employment as educator for, notwithstanding the lack of direct evidence to connect him to the university scheme of the late 1560s, it is clear that the English scholar took a great interest in the general progress of education in Ireland, and in the particular circumstances of a former academic foundation. This was the fourteenth-century papally-sponsored university which had flourished for a brief period before being discontinued. It was hoped to revitalise this institution under Sir Henry Sidney's patronage but

---

58 *Ibid.*, pp. 165, 170, 171.

59 *Ibid.*, p. 177.

60 *Ibid.*, p. 119.

61 Edmund Campion, *Opuscula omnia*, ed. Robert Turner (Cologne, 1625), ARCR I, no. 1269, p. 208. For the various editions of Campion's *Opuscula*, see ARCR I, nos. 130–34, nos. 1263–70.

62 Campion, *Histories*, ed. Vossen, introduction, chapter 3.

63 *Ibid.*, pp. 183–84.

disputes over the location and 'other cicumstances' caused the plans to be dropped.[64]

The view of the Old English which is presented by Campion in his *Histories* is understandably based on his perceptions gleaned from living close to the heart of the English region of Ireland for seven months. There is little attention given to English areas outside of eastern Leinster, and even the society of the heartland is sketched in an impressionistic and inchoate manner. By contrast the description of Ireland by Campion's disciple, Richard Stanihurst, contains a coherent representation of the long-settled colonial community which celebrates the members' political and cultural achievements and establishes for them an identity apart both from the Gaelic Irish and the English by birth.[65] For Campion (and for Sir Henry Sidney) the Old English people whom he admired for their civility and liberality could have fitted in as well in Oxford and London. Their interests were conjoined under a blanket assumption of loyalty ('yoked together under one obedience, English blouds and English hearts'),[66] and hence the air of injured bewilderment on the Lord Deputy's part at the signs of dissidence and disaffection in the late 1560s. But while this familiarity with his host society caused Campion to take their Englishness for granted, he admitted that he was disadvantaged in being at a second remove from Gaelic civilisation. For its depiction he was completely reliant on those of long standing in Ireland, as a knowledge of the Irish language 'asketh continuance in the land of more years than I had moneths to spare about this business'.[67] With the information on Gaelic customs and institutions it was natural that he would imbibe the prejudices and predilections of his informants who were predominantly Old English.

An entire chapter in Book One of the *Histories* is devoted to the 'meere Irish'. Campion was anxious therein to make distinctions between the outlandish behaviour and customs of their ancestors as portrayed by Cambrensis and others and the modern-day Gaelic Irish, and between the best of the latter who 'excell' and the 'vitious' who were 'worse then too badde'.[68] Among the many positive character traits of the general populace were their charitableness, religiosity, patience, hospitality and sharpwittedness. Besides the unflattering description of some minor groups such as the professional gamblers or 'carrowes', Campion

---

[64] *Ibid.*, p. 108.

[65] Cf. Colm Lennon, 'Richard Stanihurst (1547–1618) and Old English identity', *Irish Historical Studies* 21 (1978), pp. 121–43.

[66] Campion, *Histories*, ed. Vossen, p. 189.

[67] *Ibid.*, 'To the loving reader'.

[68] *Ibid.*, p. 20; many of Campion's complaints about the Gaelic world had been foreshadowed in the reports of the first Jesuit missioners in Ireland in 1542, Paschase Broët and Alfonso Salmerón: see Edmund Hogan, S.J., ed., *Ibernia Ignatiana, seu Ibernorum Societatis Iesu Patrum Monumenta* (Dublin, 1880), pp. 6–7. An English summary of the documents published in various volumes of the Monumenta series can be found in William V. Bangert, S.J., *Claude Jay and Alfonso Salmerón* (Chicago, 1985), pp. 167–72.

reserved his substantial criticisms for aspects of the Gaelic world which made for instability and intellectual superficiality. The 'faithless and periured' nature of Gaelic political relations had long undermined intra- and inter-clan covenants and indentures, and was proving to be detrimental to the programme of assimilation of the mid-Tudor reform. The inheritance custom by descent through the agnatic family group 'breedeth among them continuall warres and treasons'. Gaelic attitudes to marriage and sexuality 'where the cleargie is faint' fostered 'divorcementes at pleasure', weddings within the forbidden degrees, clandestine marriages and extra-matrimonial liaisons which encouraged noblemen to bring as many of their name 'into the field, base or other'. And those whom he considered to be charlatans such as taletellers and poets could play upon a general love of learning and deference to scholarship to induce gullibility and vainglory. But Campion was quick to point to the malleability of the Gaelic population. Given the right kind of conditions, 'soone they bee reclaymed' and they can aspire to 'rare gifts of grace and wisdom'.[69]

As was seen at times in the past, the hope for the redeemability of the 'meere' Irish from their 'enormities' lay in the conquest of the island by the English for which Ireland 'is beholding to God'.[70] In order to invest the Tudor claim to Ireland, upon which the reform programme turned, with greater antiquity than the granting of the lordship of the island to Henry II by Pope Adrian IV by the bull, *Laudabiliter*, Campion rehearsed the origin-legends of British and Scythian settlement there.[71] While narrating the story of the migration of the Greek prince, Gathelus, husband of Pharaoh Amenophis's daughter, Scota, to Ireland, the author identified the arrival of descendants of Gathelus, including Hiberus, as crucial for establishing the British right by conquest. These later migrants had lived in the region of Galicia in Spain 'whereof Bayon was the chief imperiall citie' in the possession of the British King Gurguntius.[72] It was he who had directed this party of his subjects to reside in Ireland and subdue the Irish, the descendants of waves of Scythian invaders. It is suggested by Campion that Gurguntius had had a foothold in Ireland even before the settlement of the group from Spain, thus providing an anterior British claim.[73] The 'Bayonne title' had been dusted down for the Angevin kings by Giraldus Cambrensis in the late twelfth century and had been canvassed in the period just before Campion's visit when included in the list of Queen Elizabeth's claims to Ireland in the statute of attainder of Shane O'Neill in 1569.[74] Campion explicitly rejected the

---

[69] *Ibid.*, pp 21, 23.

[70] *Ibid.*, p. 23.

[71] *Ibid.*, caps. vii–ix.

[72] *Ibid.*, pp. 42–44.

[73] *Ibid.*, p. 40: for a recent discussion of the use of mythology and origin-legends by Tudor historians, see Hadfield, 'Briton and Scythian', pp. 390–408.

[74] Campion, *Histories*, ed. Vossen, introduction, pp. 98–101; Richard Bolton, ed., *The Statutes of Ireland, beginning the third year of King Edward the Second* (Dublin, 1621), pp. 315–17.

contention of Hector Boece, the Scottish historian, that Hiberus and his company were of the next generation to Gathelus, thus allowing for the absorption of the Scythian ancestors of the Irish within the island before the advent of the true conquerors.[75] This mythological history of the peoples of Ireland (which was copied by Richard Stanihurst in Holinshed's *Chronicles*)[76] affirmed the contemporary English claim to Ireland and showed the subsidiarity of the Gaelic inhabitants to those whose origin was British, the Old English.

The political implications of the Tudors' right to the sovereignty of Ireland, buttressed by nine separate claims to the land as rehearsed by Campion, were of far-reaching significance. The declaration during the deputyship of Sir Anthony St Leger of Henry VIII as king of Ireland in 1541 'because he recognised no longer to hold it of the pope' focused attention on alternative supports for the title.[77] The practical value of historical research into the sources is attested by the recital of these bases for authority in the statutory underpinning of Queen Elizabeth's right to the province of Ulster in the wake of Shane O'Neill's attainder. Certainly Campion hoped in 1571 to assist in the publicising of the title. Under its aegis the reforming deputies during the previous three decades had conducted vigorous administrations although there is little or no pattern to be divined in the narrative presented by Edmund Campion. The religious Reformation is not mentioned, apart from the dissolution of abbeys and the demeanour of two governors, Sir Edward Bellingham who was 'an exceeding fervent Protestant', and St Leger who fell foul of Queen Mary by composing a 'noble sonnet' 'against the Reall Presence'.[78] Besides the impression given of Parliament being used more frequently as an agency of reform,[79] the other tangible benefit of this increased administrative activity was the extension of the Pale into the midlands and south Leinster by the incorporation of 'the countreys of Leix, Slewmargie [Slievemargy], Ofalie, Irrye [Iregan] and Glinmalire [Glenmalure]' under Sussex.[80] Thus Sidney could claim that the Palespeople were enabled to 'dwell neately' and 'sleepe on featherbeds' in 'wealthe and prosperity' by contrast with their forebears whose living conditions were more straitened.[81] As yet there was little progress to be reported in the extension of English institutions into the other provinces as the presidency system was only getting under way in 1569. Indeed the most serious 'tumult' occasioned by the government's policies was the revolt of Edmund Butler, to some of whose lands the Devon adventurer, Sir Peter Carew, had laid claim. Campion made it clear that

---

[75] Campion, *Histories*, ed. Vossen, pp. 42–43.
[76] *Holinshed's Irish Chronicle*, ed. Miller and Power, pp. 117–26.
[77] Campion, *Histories*, ed. Vossen, p. 165.
[78] *Ibid.*, pp. 165, 168, 169–70.
[79] *Ibid.*, pp. 165, 171, 181 ff.
[80] *Ibid.*, p. 170.
[81] *Ibid.*, pp. 194–95.

he supported Carew's 'very direct and manifest claime' to these possessions and others in the Pale which Sidney promoted much to the resentment of the Old English gentry.[82] This was one of the most notable episodes to date of English colonisers laying claim to territory in Ireland on the basis of defective titles of the occupiers of English or Gaelic descent.[83]

While Edmund Campion loyally backed the position of Sir Henry Sidney in relation to the Carew land claims, there is no real evidence elsewhere of his favouring colonial schemes which would extirpate the sitting inhabitants. His belief in the superiority of the English claim to Ireland through the British inheritance endows his writings with a surety that the English of Ireland had the right to establish their ascendancy through a cultural conquest of the Gaelic and gaelicised populations. Pedagogy was to be used to anglicise and turn the tide of gaelicisation, a phenomenon which was caused by the force of education to 'marre' as well as 'make' in cases of degeneration of English settlers through intercourse with 'the brutish sorte of that people'.[84] The Gaelic Irish might be 'brutish' or 'barbarous'[85] but there is no suggestion that they were incorrigibly savage. The barrier erected by the Irish language, a tongue of such complexity and mongrel nature that 'scarce one among five score can either write, read, or understand it',[86] could be surmounted by the teaching of English in newly-provided diocesan grammar-schools. Likewise the impermanence and fluidity of Gaelic society could be countered by the inurement in 'a pure English tongue, habite, fashion and discipline'. Those who would not conform were to be deprived of the opportunity to 'infect others,' and were to be contained by 'the terrour and feare' of 'oure Bande,' the English army.

Before he completed his *Histories*, Campion's official protector while in Dublin, Sir Henry Sidney, had returned to England. The influence of his factional support at court headed by the Earl of Leicester was on the wane, and the expenses and failings of his Irish regime were being used by his enemies to secure his discomfiture.[87] Campion had performed a service for his patron and protector by writing up the account of the Sidney administration in as flattering a way as possible. His own career development had perhaps been stunted temporarily with the failure to found a university in which he could have hoped to obtain a senior position. He also attempted to paper over the cracks which had begun to open up between Old English and newcomers from England over substantial matters of policy as well as strategy. Edmund Campion's major contribution in terms of reform in later Tudor Ireland was to present a

---

82 *Ibid.*, p. 180.
83 See Canny, *Elizabethan Conquest*, pp. 66–92.
84 Campion, *Histories*, ed. Vossen, p. 21.
85 *Ibid.*, p. 191.
86 *Ibid.*, p. 18; see also Hadfield, 'Briton and Scythian', pp. 404–05.
87 Brady, 'Government of Ireland', pp. 205–08.

humanist's vision of a unified English approach to the pacification and civilising of the island's communities at a time when the harmonious coalition of his own 'countrymen' and 'the Englishe of Ireland' of some thirty years' standing was in danger of breaking down irretrievably.

5

Sir Philip Sidney's Debt to Edmund Campion

KATHERINE DUNCAN-JONES

A few months ago Philip Sidney came from England to Prague as ambassador, magnificently provided. He had much conversation with me, –
I hope not in vain, for to all appearance he was most eager. I commend
him to your sacrifices, for he asked the prayers of all good men, and at
the same time put into my hands some alms to be distributed to the poor
for him, which I have done. Tell this to Dr Nicholas Sanders, because if
any one of the labourers sent into the vineyard from the Douai seminary
has an opportunity of watering this plant, he may watch the occasion for
helping a poor wavering soul. If this young man, so wonderfully beloved
and admired by his countrymen, chances to be converted, he will
astonish his noble father, the Deputy of Ireland, his uncles the Dudleys,
and all the young courtiers, and Cecil himself. Let it be kept secret.[1]

Since the appearance of Richard Simpson's great biography of Campion in
1867, in which the above passage first appeared in print, it has been known that
Sidney visited Campion in April 1577, when he led a delegation from Elizabeth
I to greet the newly acceded Emperor Rudolph II. However, most of Sidney's
twentieth-century biographers have been committed to sustaining, or even rein-
forcing, the posthumously-fashioned icon of Sidney as a Protestant hero, whose
whole life – as most clearly signalled by his death, fighting the Spanish in the
Netherlands – supposedly declared his commitment to the reformed faith.
Sidney's meetings with Campion could not be explained away, for they were
attested at the time by Campion himself, in the letter to his old tutor John
Bavand quoted above, and later by Fr Robert Persons, and later still by Fr
Thomas Fitzherbert.[2] But while Simpson saw the meetings as the probable cause

---

[1]   Richard Simpson, *Edmund Campion: A Biography*, revised edition (London, 1896), p. 123.
The original Latin letter from Campion to John Bavand can be found in Stonyhurst College,
Anglia I/4a.
[2]   Simpson, *Campion*, pp. 114–23. Sir Thomas Tresham's allusion to Campion's high
repute among 'Protestants of good account that returned from the Emperor's court', Add. MS
139830, ff. 47–49, may be yet another allusion to Sidney's conferences with Campion.

of Sidney's disappointing lack of career development in the late 1570s – and therefore, though Simpson did not point this out, possibly crucial to Sidney's decision to undertake the major literary works for which he is now remembered – later scholars have played down their importance.

Malcolm Wallace, who completed his extremely well-researched biography of Sidney days before the outbreak of the First World War, treated Sidney's meetings with Campion in a reasonably balanced way. Though he dismissed Campion's claim that Sidney was on the verge of conversion as 'absurd',[3] he pointed out quite rightly that both Sidney and his father, Sir Henry Sidney, 'always deprecated harsh measures' against Catholics, and were sympathetic towards many individual recusants. John Buxton in 1964 also quoted Campion's account of his meetings with Sidney, but polarized the roles of the two men, treating Sidney as cool and cunning, Campion as muddled and gullible. According to Buxton, Campion's judgement was 'clouded by his conversion', and his admired prose style had been corrupted by it, collapsing into 'second-hand verbiage'. If Campion had not been in such a regrettable state of intellectual confusion, says Buxton,

> he might . . . have recognized in Sidney a leader of the Puritans, using all his tact and charm to learn from Campion's own lips how far conversion had led him on the path of disloyalty.[4]

According to Buxton, then, the twenty-two-year-old Sidney was too crafty for the thirty-six-year-old Jesuit, practised orator and academic, and led Campion into a trap. This picture is extremely disagreeable and surely unconvincing; yet it has set the tone for some later writers on Sidney. Roger Howell in 1968 handled the episode cautiously. He suggested, plausibly, that Sidney may have been interested in talking to Campion 'because of the undoubted powers of his intellect',[5] and claimed that 'Sidney was a firm Protestant more in a political sense than in a theological one'. However, he held back from examining the subject-matter of Sidney's meetings with Campion, or from considering what these may have offered apart from general intellectual stimulation. In particular, Howell failed to ask why Campion might have thought Sidney 'most eager' to embrace Catholicism. Perhaps he was embarrassed, or could not make up his mind what to think. J.M. Osborn in 1972 had no such scruples, but strongly supported John Buxton's view of Sidney as so hypocritical and crafty that Campion was deceived by him:

> Apparently Sidney was so tactful that Campion did not realize that, though enthralled by his performance, his listener was unconvinced by it.[6]

---

3   M.W. Wallace, *The Life of Sir Philip Sidney* (Cambridge, 1915), p. 178.
4   John Buxton, *Sir Philip Sidney and the English Renaissance*, 2nd edn (London, 1964), p. 88.
5   Roger Howell, *Sir Philip Sidney: The Shepherd Knight* (London, 1968), p. 39.
6   James M. Osborn, *Young Philip Sidney 1572–77* (New Haven, 1972), p. 467.

Osborn impugned Simpson's scholarship, as well as Campion's discernment, by suggesting that the account of the meetings by 'Father Parson' [sic] was 'fiction-alized' by Richard Simpson, who would supposedly go to any lengths to tell his Catholic readers what they wanted to hear. Osborn also claimed, rather over-protestingly, that Sidney and Campion 'lived in quite different worlds', and that Sidney therefore cannot have taken much interest in him. In a particularly muddled passage Osborn suggested that on his first visit to Oxford Sidney was 'swathed with the attention of the dons', and therefore would not have encoun-tered Campion – apparently forgetting that one of Oxford's most celebrated 'dons' at that time was Campion. I would like to challenge both parts of Osborn's claim, and to suggest, instead, that Sidney and Campion had a good deal of contact, and had much in common. In addition, Simpson's claim that their meetings in Prague were of great importance to Sidney may well be correct, not only with reference to his dismally un-prosperous career at Court, but also in terms of the context in which the *Arcadia* was written.

It was probably in late August 1566 that Sidney, aged eleven, first encoun-tered Campion, during his well-documented participation in the Queen's visit to Oxford. The detailed accounts which survive of Sidney's expenses during this vacation from Shrewsbury School make it clear that he was in attendance on his uncle, the Earl of Leicester, who was Chancellor of the University. Young Edmund Campion had already demonstrated his exceptional skill in oratory in 1560 when he was given the extremely tricky job of making an oration on the occasion of the re-burial of Leicester's wife, Amy Robsart, in the University Church. Some of those present had heard, or even disseminated, rumours that Leicester had arranged to have Amy Robsart murdered in order to be free to marry the Queen. It may be assumed that Campion did much better on this occasion than did Dr Francis Babington, one of Leicester's chaplains, who is said to have slipped into referring to Amy Robsart as 'pitifully murdered'.[7] Campion was again chosen for a high-profile oration in 1564, at the funeral of Sir Thomas White, founder of St John's. In 1566 Campion performed publicly at least twice, first in making a speech of welcome to the Queen, and again six days later when he engaged in a public disputation on two cosmological questions: 'Whether the tides are caused by the moon's motion?' and 'Whether the lower bodies of the universe are regulated by the higher?' Rather as in a tournament, he faced four challengers, whom he overcame. But Campion was a courtly orator, not an astronomer. Both propositions presumably had a fairly transparent political sub-text, for the Queen was already beginning to be celebrated as Cynthia, the moon-goddess, who ruled the waves and reigned over all merely mortal 'lower bodies'. For the schoolboy Sidney, who was being trained at Shrewsbury in rhetoric and declamation, his uncle's protégé, the 'champion' Campion, must

---

[7]   Dwight C. Peck, ed., *Leicester's Commonwealth: 'The Copy of a Letter Written by a Master of Art of Cambridge' (1584) and Related Documents* (Athens, Ohio, 1985), p. 91.

have served as a model of how a training in rhetoric, closely akin to poetry, could equip a talented man to serve his monarch.

When Sidney came to Christ Church as an undergraduate, early in 1568,[8] he was probably eager to hear Campion once more. He may even have been a late recruit to the ranks of student 'Campionists', who imitated the speech, gait and diet of the charismatic Fellow of St John's, Junior Proctor and newly-ordained deacon. Certainly he cannot have been unaware of Campion's increasing troubles, caused by his refusal to satisfy his sponsors the Grocers' Company as to his reformed faith by preaching publicly in London. When Campion left Oxford for Ireland in August 1570 he came under the patronage of Sir Henry Sidney, as well as that of James Stanihurst, Speaker of the Irish House of Commons.[9] It was Sir Henry Sidney who saved Campion's life by warning Stanihurst, in the spring of 1571, that Campion was in danger, following the posting of Pius V's excommunication of Elizabeth, and should flee the country. Campion's aborted studies, during his too brief period of refuge in Ireland, concerned two topics of great interest also to the younger Sidney: the career of a gentleman scholar (*De Homine Academico*), and the history and topography of Ireland. It could even have been from Campion's hastily-penned *Two Bokes of the Histories of Ireland* that Sidney gleaned some of his knowledge of the high regard in which the Irish held their vernacular poets:

> they esteeme theire poetes who wright Irishe learnedly, and penne therein sonettes heroicall, for the which they are bountefully rewarded.[10]

As Sidney was to write a decade or so later,

> In our neighbour country Ireland, where truly learning goeth very bare, yet are their poets held in a devout reverence.[11]

It may have been partly from Campion, too, that Sidney learned of the danger of provoking the Irish bards' disapproval:

> yf not [praised], they sende out lybells in dispraise, whereof the gentlemen, specially the meere Irishe, stande in great awe.[12]

---

[8] Katherine Duncan-Jones, *Sir Philip Sidney: Courtier Poet* (New Haven/London 1991), p. 39.

[9] On the Stanihurst family, see Colm Lennon, 'Recusancy and the Dublin Stanyhursts,' *Archivium Hibernicum* 33 (1975), pp. 101–10 and 'Edmund Campion's *Histories of Ireland* and Reform in Tudor Ireland' in this volume.

[10] A.F. Vossen, ed., *Two Bokes of the Histories of Ireland compiled by Edmund Campion* (Assen, 1963), pp. 11–19. There is some disagreement over the date of Campion's departure for Ireland. We follow Vossen's dating. See his discussion of the problem in the pages cited above.

[11] Katherine Duncan-Jones and J.A. van Dorsten, eds, *Miscellaneous Prose of Sir Philip Sidney* (Oxford, 1973), pp. 75–76.

[12] Vossen, *Two Bokes, ibid.*

Sidney was to make a joke of this in the peroration to his *Defence of Poesy*:

> I will not wish unto you . . . to be rhymed to death, as is said to be done in Ireland.[13]

However, when he travelled to the West of Ireland with his father in the summer of 1576 he probably discovered how dangerously misleading was Campion's account of the physical configuration of Ireland:

> In proportion it resembleth an egg blont and playne, on the sydes not reaching forthe to sea nookes and elbows of land as Brytan.[14]

Campion was no more a cartographer than he was an astronomer. (In one of the more baffling passages in his conferences in the Tower in 1581 Campion offered 'to prove that the heavens are as hard as crystal'.[15]) If any of the pilots of the 1588 Armada used his *Two Bokes* as their guide to the Irish coast, it is scarcely surprising that so few returned safely to Spain.

Whether or not Sidney was directly influenced by Campion's *Two Bokes*, he surely knew it, written as it was under the immediate patronage of his father and his uncle. The two men embrace the work, Leicester being its dedicatee and Sir Henry Sidney its hero. To both men, Campion addressed himself in terms which can only be called obsequious. That already much-hated man the Earl of Leicester is praised as a morally faultless royal favourite, who has added to his many social virtues by showing particular favour to the writer:

> . . . your severall courtesies toward me, how oft at Oxford, how oft at the court, how at Ricot. how at Wynsore, how by letters, how by reportes you have not ceassed to further . . . me, a single student.[16]

The *Two Bokes* ends with an extravagant tribute to Sir Henry Sidney as a Lord Deputy Governor of Ireland who was a true 'Renaissance man':

> . . . learned in manie languages, and a great lover of learninge, perfitt in blasinge armes, scilfull of antiquities, of witt freshe and livelie, in consultations very temperate, in utterance happie which his experience and wisedome hath made artificiall, a preferrer of many, a father to his servantes, both in war and peace of commendable courage.[17]

Sidney shared Campion's view of Ireland as a half-conquered country which needed to be subdued by severe discipline, but also required to be civilized by the formation of a national university. It is striking that Sidney's secretary, William

---

13 Duncan-Jones and van Dorsten, *Misc. Prose*, p. 121.
14 Vossen, *Two Bokes*, p. 7.
15 Simpson, *Campion*, p. 334.
16 Vossen, *Two Bokes*, p. 3.
17 *Ibid.*, p. 151.

Temple, was to be the first Provost of Trinity College, Dublin, helping to enact the project which neither Campion nor Sidney lived to see realized.

From 1571 to 1577 it is for the most part perfectly true that, as Osborn claimed, Campion and Sidney 'lived in quite different worlds'. Campion was training as a Jesuit in Bohemia; Sidney was completing his Grand Tour and initiating his career at Court. This is not the place for a full review of Sidney's continental travels and his acquisition of an astonishingly wide-ranging network of friends among statesmen, academics, diplomats and theologians all over Central Europe. These connections have been amply chronicled by Osborn. However, it may be worth pointing out here that neither his passport – which explicitly forbade him to 'haunt or keep company with' any unlicensed English exile[18] – nor repeated pleas from his Protestant mentor Hubert Languet, inhibited Sidney from forming numerous friendships with Catholic Englishmen. The horrific experience of the St Bartholomew's Day massacre which he witnessed in Paris in August 1572 appears to have left Sidney anti-Valois rather than anti-Catholic. Perhaps above all, it left him deeply hostile to the French Queen Mother, Catherine de' Medici, whom he referred to as 'the Jezebel of our age',[19] and on whom he may have based the scheming Cecropia, engineer of forced marriage and torture, in his 'New' *Arcadia*. It was in Venice, where Sidney spent nearly a year, that he formed his closest Catholic friendships. In March 1575 Languet warned him that Walsingham and others at Court 'have begun to suspect you on the score of religion because at Venice you were so intimate with those who profess a different creed from your own'.[20] These Venetian friends included Edward, third Baron Windsor, a devout Catholic, and also Sidney's kinsman Richard Shelley. nephew of the titular Grand Prior of the Knights of St John. Though Sidney felt obliged, in writing to Languet, to point out that young Shelley 'was very much devoted to papist superstition', he also made it clear that he liked him very much and esteemed his learning.[21] Sidney's strong devotion to Lord Windsor – who died in January 1575, and was splendidly interred in SS Giovanni e Paolo – is confirmed by the fact that his son and heir, the fourth Baron Windsor, took part alongside Sidney as one of the 'Four Foster Children of Desire' in the splendid two-day tournament of April 1581.[22] Yet another exiled Englishman whom Sidney may have encountered during his Grand Tour is Campion himself. In February 1575 Sidney spent nine days in Prague. Since Campion, recently appointed as Professor of Rhetoric at the Jesuit College, was beginning to be as valued an orator at Maximilian's court as he had been at Elizabeth's,[23] it is quite possible that he addressed the English visitors

---

[18] Duncan-Jones, *Sidney*, p. 55.

[19] Duncan-Jones and van Dorsten, *Misc. Prose*, p. 48.

[20] Steuart A. Pears, ed., *The Correspondence of Sir Philip Sidney and Hubert Languet* (London, 1845), p. 92.

[21] Osborn, *Young Sidney*, p. 165.

[22] Duncan-Jones, *Sidney*, pp. 204–12.

when Sidney had an audience with the Emperor. Alternatively, Sidney, whose habitual practice was to look up old friends wherever he went, may have visited him privately. However, unlike the 1577 encounters, the 1575 ones are 'not proven'.

The 1577 meetings between Sidney and Campion should be placed in their context. The immediate occasion of Sidney's trip to Prague was his leadership of a diplomatic mission from Elizabeth to the newly acceded Emperor Rudolph II, whose own religious allegiance was something of a mystery. The twenty-two-year-old Sidney was qualified for this important diplomatic posting by his skill in languages, his wide and recent acquaintance with the courts of central Europe, and his position of double expectation as nephew and heir to Elizabeth's favourite Leicester, and son and heir to the Lord Deputy Governor, or 'Pro-Rex', of Ireland. The fact that Sidney took his Christian name from his godfather, Philip II, another Hapsburg monarch, may also have had a fortuitous appropriateness. However, his youthful energy and impulsiveness was moderated by the inclusion in the delegation of several old and seasoned courtiers of proven loyalty to Elizabeth, such as the Queen's Champion, Sir Henry Lee, aged forty-five, and Sir Jerome Bowes, a committed Protestant. When in 1583 Bowes was appointed ambassador to Muscovy he was credited with many feats of pugnacious devotion to Elizabeth and claims for her superiority to the Tsar (who happened to be Ivan the Terrible), such as 'flinging down his gauntlet before the emperor and challenging all the nobility to take it up, in defence of the emperor against his queen'.[24] With companions like these, it is not surprising that, as Persons was to report, it was difficult for Sidney to arrange his meetings with Campion because 'he was afraid of so many spies set and sent about him by the English Council': however, according to Persons,

> he managed to have divers large and secret conferences with his old friend. After much argument, he professed himself convinced, but said that it was necessary for him to hold on the course which he had hitherto followed; yet he promised never to hurt or injure any Catholic, which for the most part he performed; and for Father Campion himself he assured him that where-insoever he could stand him in stead, he should find him a trusty friend, which he performed not, for afterwards, Campion being condemned to death, and the other in most high favour, when he might have done him favour he denied to do it, for fear not to offend.[25]

This important account by Persons supplements the letter from Campion himself quoted at the head of this essay. Using both accounts, we can reconstruct the character of Sidney's meetings. They were private and furtive; Sidney must have had to find some feigned pretext for breaking away from the rest of the party,

---

23 Simpson, *Campion*, p. 113.
24 Samuel Pepys quoted in the DNB article on Bowes.
25 Simpson, *Campion*, p. 115.

especially from its senior members. Possibly he had his friend Fulke Greville with him, but if so, there is no hint of this. There was more than one meeting – perhaps as many as three or four – and they were prolonged. Campion referred to 'much conversation', Persons to 'large . . . conferences'. Sidney's demeanour towards the man Persons called 'his old friend', was warm, attentive and generous. He gave Campion alms for the poor, which was his normal practice when meeting clerics, whether Catholic or Protestant. But most important, according to Persons, he declared himself 'convinced' of the truth of the old religion, though even in the excitement of the moment he realized that he would not be able to practise it openly – 'it was necessary for him to hold on the course which he had hitherto followed'. This is consistent with Campion's account of Sidney as 'most eager', but not as yet ready to make a public profession of his beliefs at the English Court.

Persons' damaging claim that Sidney made no attempt to save Campion's life will be dealt with in a moment. First I will examine Campion's claim that if Sidney at some point makes a full conversion, it 'will astonish his noble father'. Perhaps what would have astonished Sir Henry would have been the suicidal rashness of a public profession of conversion, not the private belief that such a profession would reflect, for considerable uncertainty attaches to Sir Henry Sidney's own commitment to the reformed faith. Unlike the most committed Protestants of the Edwardian court, such as Francis Walsingham, Henry Sidney was not a Marian exile. Indeed, despite his connection by marriage with the Duke of Northumberland and the ill-fated attempt to enthrone Lady Jane Grey, as well as his intimate association with the boy-king Edward VI,[26] his career flourished during the reign of Mary Tudor. He was one of the delegates sent to escort Philip II from Spain to England for his marriage to Mary, and the Spanish king's role as godfather to Sir Henry's first-born son helped to cement this association. The younger Sidney's Christian name must have provided a continual, and irritating, reminder to Elizabeth of Sir Henry Sidney's high profile at Court during the Marian years. Wallace plausibly suggested that Sir Henry owed his surprisingly easy transition from favour in Edward's Protestant reign to favour in Mary's Catholic one to the fact that two of his sisters, Mabell and Elizabeth, were members of Mary's household, and were unshakably devoted both to her and to the Catholic faith.[27] It is odd that nothing is heard of these ladies after 1558, and though it has been assumed that both of them conveniently died within Mary's reign, there is no record of their dates of death. If either or both survived into Elizabeth's reign, perhaps they lived tucked away in a remote corner of some Catholic household, possibly under changed names, or as nuns. A Catholic kinswoman who certainly did survive was his niece, Lady Jane Dormer, Duchess of Feria, who formed a powerful leader of English

---

[26] Wallace, *Life of Sidney*, pp. 7–8.
[27] *Ibid.*, p. 11.

Catholic exiles in Spain.[28] At several points in his career as Lord President of the Marches of Wales it seems that Sir Henry was suspected of being lukewarm in his implementation of measures against recusants.[29] It is difficult to know how to interpret what appears to be some sort of brotherly banter between Sir Henry Sidney and the Earl of Leicester in 1568, when Sidney offered to design a chapel for the latter's newly-acquired Kenilworth Castle.[30] Sir Henry Sidney's innermost beliefs are no more accessible to us than are those of most Elizabethans. But in order to be a durably successful courtier, who held responsible offices in three reigns, the middle one Catholic, he must at least have been adept in outward conformity. As a practised wind-watcher, he no doubt realized, after the savage judicial measures against the Jesuit mission of 1581, that any lingering sympathy with Catholicism would have to be thoroughly hidden. From this point of view, marrying his eldest son to the daughter of the Puritan Walsingham in 1583 was surely an astute move.

As for the younger Sidney: there is a good deal of further evidence of his friendship with Catholics. Even when writing a semi-public piece of propaganda at the end of 1579, his *Letter . . . to Queen Elizabeth, touching her marriage with Monsieur*, he gave an account of the Catholic faction at Court which revealed a surprising degree of sympathy for their fearful dilemmas, while ostensibly warning the queen of the threat they would offer her if they had a leader in her consort. He called the Papists

> men whose spirits are full of anguish; some being forced to oaths they account damnable; some having their ambition stopped, because they are not in the way of advancement; some in prison and disgrace; some whose best friends are banished practisers . . . all burdened with the weight of their consciences; men of great number, of great riches (because the affairs of the state have not lain on them).[31]

As we have seen, Sidney's own 'best friends' included some 'banished practisers'. Nor did he avoid the company of Catholics when he was back in England. For instance, in the splendid 'Four Foster Children of Desire' tournament already mentioned, he not only had the Catholic Lord Windsor as a fellow-challenger, but also Philip Howard, Earl of Arundel. The political significance of the 'Foster Children' piece is very hard to interpret. It is possible that part of its propaganda purpose was to demonstrate to the large French delegation for whose benefit it was performed, that Elizabeth's Catholic courtiers were just as devoted to her as her Protestant ones. Nevertheless, it is striking that this

---

[28] See Joseph Stevenson, S.J., ed., *Henry Clifford: The Life of Jane Dormer, Duchess of Feria* (London, 1887) and Duncan-Jones, *Sidney*, p. 3.

[29] Duncan-Jones, *Sidney*, p. 129; Wallace, *Life of Sidney*, p. 223.

[30] Historical Manuscripts Commission, *Report on the Manuscripts of Lord De L'Isle and Dudley, preserved at Penshurst Place*, 6 vols (London, 1925–1966), II, p. 8.

[31] Duncan-Jones and van Dorsten, *Misc. Prose*, p. 48.

'Triumph', which Sidney played a major role in devising, required Sidney and his friend Greville to display themselves in close alliance with two known Catholic sympathizers.

There is more explicit evidence of Sidney's tender feelings towards Catholics elsewhere, especially in his correspondence. One document, a letter to the Catholic Lady Kytson, is so revealing that it should be quoted in its entirety:

> Madame,
>
> I have, according to your Ladyship's comandment, by lettre and by my cousin Grivel, delivered unto me, dealt with Mr Secretarie, for his favour toward Sir Thomas Cornwallies. Truly, madam, hitherunto I can obtain no furdre than this, that there is a present intention of a general mitigation, to be used in respect of recusants; so as he may not, he saith, prevent her Majesties dealing therein, in any particular case, and would not put himself in subjection to the tonges of such kind of men with whom he should deal, but assures me that there is ment a speedy easing of the greatnes of your burdne. I assure you, Madam, upon my faithe, I dealt carefully and earnestlie, owing a particular duti unto Sir Thomas, which I will never fail to shewe to my uttermost, and if otherwise have been thought, I have been mistaken, and if said, the more wronged. But do your Ladyship hold your good opinion of me, and I will deserve it, with bearing you much honor, as your favourable courtesies toward me, and long acquaintance bind me, and so I take my leave, praying to God for your long and happy life. At Court, this 28th of March,1581.
>
> Your Ladyship's fellow and frend
to do you service,
Ph. Sidnei.[32]

This seems to provide powerful confirmation of Sidney's good faith in promising to Campion that he would 'never hurt or injure any catholic'. Indeed, it suggests that Sidney saw himself as obliged to act as a spokesman at Court for beleaguered recusants. Lady Kytson's father, Sir Thomas Cornwallis, perfectly fits Sidney's description of the Catholic aristocracy as men 'of great riches' who are 'not in the way of advancement'. Cornwallis, who had been Controller of the Household to Mary Tudor, was banished to his Suffolk estates throughout Elizabeth's reign, where he devoted much of his wealth to rebuilding Brome Hall. Sidney's information, apparently from Walsingham, 'that there is a present intention of a general mitigation' towards recusants, and that therefore no special relief from fines could be allowed to Cornwallis, seems to have been quite wrong. But presumably the message was passed on in good faith. Sidney's anxiety about what people are thinking or saying about him is very characteristic. It would be good to know in what respect Sidney owed 'a particular duti unto Sir Thomas' – had he lent him money? It would also be nice to know more about his

---

[32] Albert Feuillerat, ed., *The Complete Works of Sir Philip Sidney*, 4 vols (Cambridge, 1912–26, repr. 1962), III, pp. 134–35.

'long acquaintance' with Elizabeth Kytson, née Cornwallis, whose splendid 1573 portrait by George Gower suggests a woman of strong character.[33] But most of all, it would be good to know whether the phrase 'upon my faithe' amounts here to something more than a formula, and what exactly Sidney meant in signing himself 'Your Ladyship's fellow and frend'. It is difficult to conjecture what, other than shared faith, could have characterized Sidney as a 'fellow' of this Catholic noblewoman.

Only eight months after his kindly, if misinformed, letter to Lady Kytson Sidney's career reached a point of crisis. Displaced from major inheritance by the birth of a legitimate son to his uncle in April 1581,[34] alienated from Court and in retirement with his sister in Wiltshire, he appeared to have a chance of shoring up his fortunes with the help of a grant of money confiscated from Catholics. His response to this possibility was uncomfortable and embarrassed. To Sir Christopher Hatton he wrote in some confusion, not sure whether to accept the grant, if firmly offered, but confessing that 'my necessitie is greate'.[35] Ten days later, writing to Leicester, he was more revealing:

> . . . I know not truly what to sai since her Majestie is pleased so to answer, for as well mai her Majestie refuse the matter of the papistes and then have I both shame and skorne. I beseech yowr Lordeshippe resolve of it with Mr Vichamberlain, for I find my self in deed much bownd unto him, and then if yowr Lordeshippe determin of it that I may know it before yowr Lordeshippe take furdre paines in it. But this I beseech yowr Lordeshipe without it be 3000[li] never to trouble yowr self in it, for my cace is not so desperate , that I wold gett clamor for less. Truly I lyke not their persons and much worse their religions, but I think my fortune very hard that my reward must be built uppon other mens punishmentes. Well my Lord yowr Lordeshippe made me a cowrtier do yow thinke of it as seemes best unto yow.[36]

This is extraordinarily revealing. Despite Sidney's obligatory assertion that he dislikes both the 'persons' and 'religions' of the penalized recusants, he makes it clear that he does not want to be thought of as willing to receive recusant fines – 'for then have I both shame and skorne', presumably from the many Catholic aristocrats who were his personal friends, and to whom, as the letter to Lady Kytson shows, he felt closely attached. However, if the price was right, and the offer firm, he could after all perhaps see his way to accepting money derived from 'other mens punishmentes'. Finally, he abandons moral responsibility to

---

[33] This portrait is reproduced in Roy Strong, *The English Icon* (London, 1969), p. 169, alongside that of her husband Sir Thomas Kytson. For a detailed study of Sir Thomas Cornwallis, see Patrick McGrath and Joy Rowe, 'The Recusancy of Sir Thomas Cornwallis,' *Proceedings of the Suffolk Institute of Archaeology* 28 (1961), pp. 226–71, esp. p. 244.

[34] Grateful thanks to Dr Simon Adams, who has discovered the christening date of Baron Denbigh, Leicester's son.

[35] Feuillerat, *Complete Works*, III, p. 139.

[36] *Ibid.*, III, p. 140.

Leicester, who has made his nephew a courtier, with the consequent vast expenses that entailed. If the only way that his courtiership can be sustained is through money confiscated from some of his best friends, let the betrayal be one forced on him by his uncle, not one for which he is personally responsible. This is consistent, just about, with Persons's report that Sidney told Campion 'that it was necessary for him to hold on the course which he had hitherto followed'. But back in 1577 Sidney probably did not foresee how excruciatingly painful his commitment to a double life was to become. Still, the money eventually materialized, and he took it. By 1583 it seems that Sidney, along with Leicester and Sir Thomas Cecil, was receiving sums of £1000 from recusant fines.[37] The expense he reckoned was that of a landless courtier with a career still to make.

1581, a critical year in Sidney's life, was of course even more critical in that of Campion. At the end of June his *Rationes decem* were distributed in the University Church at the time of Commencement, presided over by Sidney's uncle Leicester. Sidney himself may have been present, and a personal recipient of the treatise; but whether or no, he cannot have failed to learn speedily of this bold propaganda ploy by his 'old friend'. Although E.E. Reynolds has observed that 'there may seem something naive, even pathetic, in Campion's belief that a well-conducted disputation according to academic practice could gain a victory for Catholicism',[38] analogous strategies were used by Sidney on several occasions, such as his attempt to prevent the Queen's marriage to Alençon by writing a semi-public treatise against it, or his later attempt to defend his uncle against libel by publicly deploying both his pen and his sword.[39] Challenge and disputation, conducted on lines partly academic, partly chivalric, which may now seem a quixotic and haphazard method of enforcing public assent to an important proposition, were then normal procedures. For Sidney, such debate was conducted in council chambers, in Parliament, and in the tiltyard; for Campion in his Jesuit years, in debating schools, churches, and finally in Westminster Hall, the scene of his trial. This is not the place to tell in full the painful story of Campion's arrest at Lyford Grange. But it is worth noting that Sidney must have learned of it, if not at once, then surely at the time of Campion's interview with Leicester, the Earl of Bedford, Hatton and others at the end of July, which has now been shown to have taken place at York House.[40] Likewise, Sidney was surely well aware of Campion's four public conferences in the Tower in September, in the course of which, though weakened by torture and close confinement, and deprived of access to books, he showed that he had lost none of his old skill in public speaking and debate.[41] Among the eminent courtiers and privy

---

[37] Wallace, *Life of Sidney*, p. 272.

[38] E.E. Reynolds, *Campion and Parsons* (London, 1980), p. 105.

[39] Duncan-Jones and van Dorsten, *Misc. Prose*, pp. 33–57, 123–41.

[40] Marion Colthorpe, 'Edmund Campion's Alleged Interview with Queen Elizabeth in 1581', *Recusant History* 17 (1985), pp. 197–200.

[41] On these disputations, see Thomas M. McCoog, S.J., ' "Playing the Champion": The Role of Disputation in the Jesuit Mission' in this volume.

councillors present at the conferences in the chapel of St Peter ad Vincula in the Tower was Sidney's friend and recent fellow-tilter Philip Howard, Earl of Arundel. He is said to have made a private decision at that time, convinced by Campion, to commit himself to Catholicism, though he did not make a public profession until a couple of years later.[42] It is unlikely that Sidney himself attended any of the conferences, since for most of September he was hanging around at Dover and elsewhere on the Kent coast preparing to escort the Portuguese pretender, Dom Antonio, off English soil. Perhaps in any case a recollection of the promise he had made – if Persons reports correctly – to 'stand him in stead' if Campion were ever in trouble weighed heavily upon him, and he decided not to expose himself to further anguish of conscience by getting involved. Likewise, it is unlikely that Sidney attended Campion's trial on 20 November, though he was certainly in London six days earlier, when he wrote an obsequious begging letter to Sir Christopher Hatton.[43] Yet, as I hope to show, there is some reason to think that Sidney was either deeply affected by the outrageous injustice of Campion's trial, or had extraordinarily prophetic powers of imagination.

Probably Sidney knew that he could not save Campion. The powerful Leicester had tried and failed: all he had managed to do was to improve the physical conditions of his imprisonment.[44] And though, from Persons's viewpoint, Sidney appeared to be 'in most high favour' at the time of Campion's arrest and trial, this was certainly not how it seemed to Sidney. Probably Persons took his view of Sidney's career as a courtier from the legation to Prague in 1577, which was its high point. During the later part of 1581 Sidney was desperately short of money, and lacked any court office apart from the inherited sinecure of Royal Cupbearer. Though he was among the courtiers deputed to see Dom Antonio off, and at one point was used as a messenger to him by the Queen,[45] this gave him no special privilege or power, but was, as he saw it, simply a tedious errand which he resented: 'having divers busynesses of myne own and my fathers, that some thinge importe me, and to deale playnly with you being growen almost to the bottome of my pursse', as he wrote to Hatton from Dover on 26 September.[46] A fortnight later he described himself to Burghley as 'holy out of comfort', and desperate for an income of £100 a year 'in impropriations' – presumably recusant fines.[47] Yet against this depressing evidence of Sidney's compromised position, in which such money as he had was derived entirely from 'other mens punishmentes', and those men in some cases his personal friends, should be set some indications that, even after the crackdown on Catholics that followed

[42] F.W. Steen, ed., *The Life of St Philip Howard* (London, 1857, revised edn 1971), pp. 9–10.
[43] Feuillerat, *Complete Works*, III, p. 138.
[44] Reynolds, *Campion and Parsons*, p. 131.
[45] CSP Simancas, III, p. 178.
[46] Feuillerat, *Complete Works*, III, pp. 135–36.
[47] *Ibid.*, pp. 136–37.

Campion's execution, Sidney did take some trouble to help the Catholic nobility. For instance, in the summer of 1582 a scheme was devised to allow Catholic gentlemen life, liberty and religious freedom on condition that they settled in the New World. Two such gentlemen, Sir George Peckham and Sir Thomas Gerard, both of whom had endured a spell of imprisonment, were encouraged to travel to America with Sir Humphrey Gilbert, 'for which purpose they might avail themselves of the intercession of Philip Sidney'.[48] Notionally, Sidney had purchased three million acres of (as yet undiscovered) territory, and had liberty to colonize yet more. Though he almost immediately sold his 'land' to Sir George Peckham, he was again considering departure for Florida according to Sir Humphrey Gilbert's scheme in July 1584.[49] At that year's Accession Day Tilt he tilted alongside Thomas Gerard.[50] The following summer, in August 1585, Sidney, accompanied by his friend Fulke Greville, made his most serious attempt to travel (or escape?) to the New World by joining Drake's fleet at Plymouth. Had the Queen not peremptorily summoned him back, he would have travelled with Drake to the West Indies and Florida – but might not have returned with him. Since Sidney's 1583 involvement in New World ventures was definitely associated with the quest by recusants for religious freedom, it is difficult not to suspect that Sidney, too, had a notion that if only he could get to Florida he might be longer among those 'forced to oaths they account damnable', as he had described the Catholic nobility.

Of course, Sidney's New World visions did no good to Campion. There is no getting round the fact that while Campion was undergoing torture and martyrdom, Sidney was suffering from nothing worse than poverty and a bad conscience as he braced himself to shore up his fortunes by accepting recusant fines. But there was one area of his life – other than that dreamed of but unreachable Florida – where he could still enjoy considerable freedom. If his writing-plan was on schedule, he should have completed the first version of his *Arcadia* before the summer of Campion's arrest, for he promised his brother Robert a copy of his 'toyfull book' by February 1581.[51] However, as the 'Old' *Arcadia*'s Oxford editor has pointed out, there is good reason to think that 'Sidney continued to tinker with his transcript during 1581–2'.[52] Thomas Howell, a servant of the Countess of Pembroke, complains in a poem published in 1581, apparently referring to the *Arcadia*, that 'all too long thou hid'st so perfect work'.[53] Though it seems from his promise of his 'toyfull book' to his brother Robert that Sidney had told some of his immediate circle about the *Arcadia*, it is

48 CSP Simancas, III, p. 384.
49 Feuillerat, *Complete Works*, III, p. 145.
50 Duncan-Jones, *Sidney*, p. 271.
51 Feuillerat, *Complete Works*, III, p. 132.
52 Jean Robertson, *Sir Philip Sidney: The Countess of Pembroke's Arcadia (The Old Arcadia)* (London, 1973), p. xvii.
53 *Ibid.*, p. xvi.

possible that during 1581 he was still 'hiding' it for the very good reason that it was not yet finished. A plausible period for its completion would be the Christmas holiday of 1581–82, which Sidney spent with his sister in Wiltshire. We know that at this time he was deeply depressed about his poverty and lack of preferment; it may be that this externally-articulated depression was compounded by a more secret misery at the execution of his friend Edmund Campion on 1 December.

What follows is speculative. I would like to suggest that Campion's trial and execution gave a sudden jolt to Sidney when he was in the final stages of writing the *Arcadia*, and had some direct influence on its fifth and final book, especially the final scene in which the two young princes who are the book's heroes are charged with conspiracy to assassinate the monarch and are put on trial. Most first-time readers of the 'Old' *Arcadia* are startled by the abrupt change of register which occurs between the end of the Third Eclogues and the beginning of the Fourth Book or Act. A playful amorous romance is suddenly overshadowed by themes of political chaos, grief, confusion, and divine retribution for human errors. No doubt this change of tone and viewpoint is part of the *Arcadia*'s design – that 'orderly disposition' for which Edmund Molyneux, Sir Henry Sidney's secretary, especially praised it. However, the fifth and final book is more shocking still. Arcadia, previously a country celebrated for 'the moderate and well tempered minds of the people', where a little civil disturbance can easily be quelled by a fine oration, and even the monarch's sudden death initially serves only to prove that 'men are loving creatures', becomes alarmingly confused, with 'The dangerous division of men's minds' and 'the ruinous renting of all estates'. Most grimly, in this final book, apparent virtues mutate in their new environment into vices. The princes' Ciceronian friendship with each other becomes a narcissistic mutual admiration society: they close ranks to protect each other from an acknowledgement of their sins. The loyalty to the monarch which is the distinctive virtue of the aptly-named Philanax, associated in Book 1 with prudence and moderation, is transmuted into vindictive savagery against the monarch's supposed killers. Euarchus, apparently a *deus ex machina* figure, presides over the trial of the two princes and the widowed Duchess, and seems at first to offer an admirable model of undeviating justice. But in the light of fuller knowledge this seems to be a chillingly cold-hearted legalism. In his devotion to a single virtue, justice, untempered by mercy, Euarchus himself is drawn into the crime of infanticide, in persisting in condemning his own son and nephew to death – and after a most perfunctory collection of evidence.

A closing trial scene may always have been part of Sidney's plan for the *Arcadia*, though the earliest version of the oracle does not make this clear.[54] If we accept the hypothesis that Sidney was delayed in completing the *Arcadia*, not

---

[54] *Ibid.*, p. 5.

finishing the final book until the winter of 1581–82, it seems possible that some of Sidney's shock and indignation at the monstrously unjust trial of Campion (and others) may have fed into his treatment of this final section. On the face of it, it may seem that Sidney's amorous young princes have little in common with the learned and mature Jesuit martyr. Yet, like Campion, Sidney's princes are put on trial for a capital offence – conspiracy to murder the monarch, in both cases – of which it is grotesquely unlikely that they are guilty. Like Campion, they are condemned under an old and sleeping piece of legislation which has not been enforced for many years (Campion was indicted under Edward III's 'Act of Treason' of 1351). Like Campion, Sidney's princes are rightly accused of disguising themselves, of degrading their status and changing their names. Campion, on leaving Ireland, had disguised himself as 'Mr. Patrick', a lackey; later, as one 'Hastings', who wore a velvet hat and velvet venetians. Sidney's Pyrocles transformed himself, first, into the splendidly-arrayed Amazon Cleophila, then into 'Timopyrus'; Musidorus first reduced himself into the drably-dressed shepherd 'Dorus', then became the aristocratic 'Palladius'. Like Campion, Sidney's princes have travelled far beyond the bounds of their native cities and countries, making strangely circuitous journeys, often at great speed. Like Campion, the princes are exceptionally gifted with the arts of language, and charm all whom they encounter, even in situations in which they are apparently at a disadvantage.

But the closest parallel between Sidney's fictitious princes and his real-life friend Edmund Campion lies in the manner of their trial. They are found guilty on the basis not of evidence, but of abuse and character-assassination by the prosecuting counsel. While this may have been how many Tudor state trials were conducted, it is at least a possibility – if the suggested period of the completion of the 'Old' *Arcadia* is right – that in his account of the princes' trial Sidney was venting some of his indignation at the unjust and vindictive manner in which Campion had been condemned. As long ago as 1947 it was suggested that Sidney's Philanax, in his self-appointed role as prosecutor, has something in common with Edmund Anderson, Q.C., who prosecuted Campion.[55] Most of the similarities are general rather than particular, but the passage in which Anderson laid Campion's 'disguising in apparel' against him does seem to parallel Philanax's attack on Pyrocles's disguise – which, unlike Campion's, entailed a change of gender. While Campion is accused of disguisings unbecoming to a priest, Pyrocles is accused of those unfit for a prince. Anderson:

> Your name being Campion, why were you called Hastings? You a priest and dead to the world, what pleasure had you to roist it? A velvet hat and a feather, a buff leather jerkin, velvet venetians, are they weeds for dead men?

[55] K.T. Rowe, 'Romantic Love and Parental Authority in Sidney's *Arcadia*', *University of Michigan Contributions in Modern Philology* 1–12 (1947–49), pp. 18–19.

... No, there was a further matter intended; your lurking and lying hid in secret places concludeth with the rest a mischievous meaning.[56]

Philanax:

Why alone, if he be a prince? How so richly jewelled, if he be not a prince? Why then a woman, if now a man? Why now Timopyrus, if then Cleophila? Was all this play for nothing? Or if it had an end, what end but the end of my dear master?[57]

In his *Defence of Poesy*, Sidney celebrated fiction for the scope it offered to the writer to show 'what may be and should be', not confined by the 'bare *Was*' of historical narrative, in which all too often virtue suffers and the wicked flourish:

For see we not valiant Miltiades rot in his fetters? The just Phocion and the accomplished Socrates put to death like traitors? The cruel Severus live prosperously? The excellent Severus miserably murdered? Sulla and Marius dying in their beds?[58]

Only in the golden world of poetry could human beings be reliably preserved from the unjust sufferings so often endured by the virtuous in this fallen world. At the end of the *Arcadia* three major characters are unjustly condemned. The Duchess Gynecia, on the basis of a false confession, is to be buried alive; Pyrocles is to be thrown from a high tower; Musidorus to be executed. But with the unforeseen recovery of the supposedly dead Duke, Basilius, everyone is forgiven and all ends happily; that is what fiction can do. Though the news of Campion's trial and execution cannot be claimed as a major influence on the construction of the *Arcadia*, whose narrative outline must have been worked out long before the summer of 1581, these events may have given an extra boost to Sidney's imagination when he came to write the trial scene. For himself, as well as for his readers, the adventitious happy ending may have provided a brief emotional release.

Sidney began work on his *Arcadia*, according to Edmund Molyneux, 'Not long after his journey [to Prague], and before his further employment by her Majesty'.[59] He began to immerse himself in it, therefore, soon after his secret meetings with Campion. By the time he finished it – probably – Campion was dead. When he began to re-cast the *Arcadia*, on a much more ample scale, he made it clear from the outset that the world of his characters was a tragic one, from which 'Urania', traditionally identified as the Muse of Divine poetry, had

---

[56] Reynolds, *Campion and Persons*, p. 178.

[57] Robertson, *Old Arcadia*, p. 389.

[58] Duncan-Jones and van Dorsten, *Misc. Prose*, pp. 81, 89, 90.

[59] Edmund Molyneux, *Historical Remembrance of the Sidneys, the father and the son (1588)* in Katherine Duncan-Jones, ed., *The Oxford Authors: Sir Philip Sidney* (Oxford, 1989), p. 311.

disappeared.[60] There are many possible reasons why Sidney, in the early 1580s, felt that 'I now must change/Those notes to tragic'.[61] The martyrdom of his old friend Campion, with all that it implied for Catholics and Catholic sympathizers in England, may have been one of them.

[60] Victor Skretkowicz, ed., *The Countess of Pembroke's Arcadia (The New Arcadia)* (Oxford, 1987), pp. 3–5.
[61] John Milton, *Paradise Lost*, Book X, ll. 5–6.

6

'We are Made a Spectacle':
Campion's Dramas

ALISON SHELL[1]

Edmund Campion was the rhetorician among the Elizabethan Catholic martyrs; and, as is less well-known, he was also the dramatist. During his stay at the Jesuit College in Prague from 1574 to 1580, as a member of the Austrian Province of the Society of Jesus, he wrote a number of plays and dramatic exercises for the boys under his care. Being school dramas, they are all to some extent didactic.[2] The didactic themes have a double significance: in the general context of Jesuit educational philosophy, and more particularly in the context of Campion's own continuous self-fashioning. At a time before English Jesuits had founded colleges on the continent, and consequently before English Jesuit dramas became common, he promulgated the cause of the Counter Reformation by imaginative means. He may well have bequeathed a prototype to some later dramatists from his own country; but he certainly left them a personality which came to be incorporated into their own propagandist plays to celebrate and advance the Catholic cause.

The Renaissance made considerable use of the dialogue-form in education: both as a straightforward means of imparting knowledge, and, more subtly, to promote mental training by offering different points of view and giving them superficially equal weight.[3] Three educational dialogues attributed to Campion survive.[4] Two out of three, though amusing in a classroom context, manifest

---

[1]   I would like to thank T.A. Birrell, Henry Harvey, Arnold Hunt, Michelle Lāstōvičková and Michael Questier for their generous scholarly and practical help in the writing of this article.
[2]   For discussion of the ways in which Jesuit educational ideals affected their drama, see William H. McCabe, S.J., *An Introduction to the Jesuit Theater* (St Louis, 1983).
[3]   General studies addressing the genre include Anthony Grafton and Lisa Jardine, *From Humanism to the Humanities* (London, 1986) and Virginia Cox, *Renaissance Dialogue* (Cambridge, 1992).
[4]   Stonyhurst College, A.V.1 (N11) (Grene, Collectanea). Stonyhurst MS A.V.3,

nothing more than the inkhorn jocularity of Renaissance Latinists at play; but the third exhibits a greater didactic seriousness. Entitled *Dialogus mutus (Silent Colloquy)*, it falls into four miniature acts with five choruses. Its title – perhaps deliberately – is misleading: it is no dialogue, but a series of tableaux which, if performed, would have lent themselves to dumb show, commentary and chorus.

In Act 1, two young men hold up the cups of death and life, the first cup made from rich gold but concealing poison under the rim, and the second from chaste translucent glass. Act 2 compares the properties of the ball and the square, asserting that the square is morally superior because it remains steadfast in response to whatever external impetuses befall it. A boy in Act 3 demonstrates the impossibility of breaking a bundle, even though the sticks contained in it are frangible individually, and draws from this the lesson of divinely sanctioned *esprit de corps*. The chorus sings:

> Charity recovered the high heavens.
> The charity of Christ invites the faithful,
> soldering the blessed chains
> of our common and personal salvation.[5]

The message is reinforced in Act 4 by a lame man and a blind man who help each other along the road, and finally, in Act 5, a water-clock (*clepsydra*) stands as emblem of the fleeting and fragile nature of life, and the consequent necessity to use time well. The whole small piece, in fact, is a *catena* of living emblems: but emblems selected for an end conducive to the ultimate aims of Jesuit education.[6] They stress above all the merits of solidarity with one's brethren in religion, and of stoicism as a means of withstanding the trials of a largely hostile world.

The manner in which the dialogues were preserved is suggestive. They may well have been considered too slight for editors to include in the posthumously published editions of Campion's writings; but in the manuscript 'Collectanea' surviving at Stonyhurst College, undertaken by Christopher Grene (1629–1697) to collect evidence to justify the canonisation of English martyrs, they are recorded and in part transcribed.[7] There is nothing in the dialogue that could

---

containing occasional writings by Campion, also includes a very rough draft of a Latin dramatic poem *Pro die Corporis Christi*, perhaps designed for an *auto sacramental*.

[5] Charitas Caelos reparauit altos
Charitas Christi sociat fideles
Sancta communis propriaeque firmans
    vincla salutis.

[6] See Alison Shell, 'English Catholicism and Drama, 1578–1688' (unpublished D.Phil., University of Oxford, 1992), ch. 4.

[7] Grene, Collectanea, *loc. cit.* A photocopy also exists in the Jesuit archives at Farm Street. I am grateful to Fr F.J. Turner (at Stonyhurst) and Fr Geoffrey Holt (at Farm Street) for their scholarly advice and assistance.

Richard Simpson, *Edmund Campion: a Biography* (London, 1867; a second revised edition appeared in 1896), pp. 504–05, identifies two of them (though not, apparently, the *Dialogus mutus*) and gives a translation of the opening monologue from the dialogue between Stratocles

not have been found in almost any emblem-book, but to save it because it demonstrated literary originality would perhaps have been redundant or even harmful; Grene was preserving evidence not of originality, but of orthodoxy.

I *Ambrosia*

School plays to celebrate prize days, church festivals or the visits of dignitaries figured prominently on the Jesuit curriculum; and from the surviving evidence, Prague seems to have been fairly typical in mingling allegorical themes with stories from the Bible and from saints' lives.[8] As a teaching-aid these dramas trained the boys in fluent Latinity, poise and memory skills; and as didactic instruments they inculcated the capacity to make moral judgements, though always within a framework conditioning the boys in characteristically Jesuit mental habits of resourceful obedience. At Prague, Campion composed three full-length dramas. The first is lost, but seems to have been a reworking of a very popular theme in Jesuit drama, Abraham's interrupted sacrifice of Isaac: popular because of the opportunity it gave for a boy's part, and also because its message of youthful sacrifice was appropriate to an order which gave high priority to both teaching and missionary work. Jesuits who faced spectacular dangers abroad, in the Far East and in America as well as in England, were constantly commended to the pupils' admiration and possible emulation. Campion's second play, on the subject of Saul, is also lost; but the third, which survives, tells the story of St Ambrose, Bishop of Milan.[9] A fascinating forerunner of many themes that were to assume a central importance to the genre later on, it nevertheless stands apart from the main tradition of English Jesuit drama: partly through its chronological precedence, and partly because the dramatic impetus that finds expression in the plays of the early seventeenth century was founded on a consciousness of recent martyrs, of whom Campion was one.

and Eubulus. For Christopher Grene, see Henry Foley, S.J., *Records of the English Province of the Society of Jesus*, 7 vols in 8 (Roehampton/London, 1875–83), III, pp. 499–500; VI, p. 369; VII, p. 317; and for an account of his MS collections, see John Morris, S.J., *Troubles of our Catholic Forefathers* 3 vols (London, 1872–77), III, pp. 2–7, and archival records at Stonyhurst.

8 See Jean-Marie Valentin, *Le théâtre des Jésuites dans les pays de langue allemande*, 2 vols (Stuttgart, 1983–84), nos. 6, 9, 13, 18–19, 23, 27, 33, 40, 50–52, 61, 66, 76–77, 86–87 (for titles of plays performed prior to Campion's arrival).

9 Joannes Schmidl, *Historiae Societatis Jesu Provinciae Bohemiae*, 2 vols (Prague, 1747), I, p. 369 (Abraham), p. 419 (*Ambrosia*); Valentin, *Théâtre de Jésuites*, under titles. *Ambrosia* has been translated and edited by Jos. Simons (Assen, 1969): all page-references, quotations and translations, sometimes slightly adjusted, are taken from this edition. For non-English plays about St Ambrose, see Valentin, *Théâtre des Jésuites*, subject-index. For contemporaneous plays about Abraham & Isaac, see Valentin, *Théâtre des Jésuites*, 62 (Vienna, 1567), 170 (Treves, 1581), 292 (Dillingen, 1590); and about Saul, 23 (Prague, 1562), 141 (Vienna, 1578).

Narrating all the dramatically significant episodes of Ambrose's life, the play begins with his quarrel with the Empress-regent Justina. In A.D. 386, she demanded a basilica in Milan, where Ambrose was Bishop, for the use of an heretical Arian sect. Ambrose and his congregation occupied the basilica, eventually dissuading Justina's soldiers from taking possession of it. Though the Empress was forced to give in on that occasion, Ambrose was later sentenced to go into banishment and again barricaded himself in a basilica where his followers kept vigil with him; for the second time, the Empress's troops dared not attack him, and the court had eventually to capitulate, to avoid riots between the soldiers and the citizens.

The first part of *Ambrosia* is taken up with this sequence of events; and its double theme, the triumph of orthodoxy over heresy and the relative rights of Church and state, becomes fissured in the second part. In a slight but significant subplot, St Augustine of Hippo is saved from heresy by the prayers of his mother Monica and is baptised by Ambrose. The main plot narrates Ambrose's encounter with Theodosius. Theodosius, the ruler of the eastern Roman Empire, had ordered a massacre at Thessalonica in 390 after rioters had killed the Roman governor of the province; the carnage was such that Ambrose wrote to warn Theodosius that it was a crime expiable only by public penance, and was obliged to excommunicate him. The conflict is resolved by Theodosius submitting to Ambrose's ruling. He drives out idolaters from his kingdom, and the play ends with a celebration of divinely appointed kingship.

In the two halves of the play, the reigns of Justina and of Theodosius, Campion is constructing two models: the first of how a pious priest should behave when threatened by an heretical state, and the second of how that same priest can move a monarch to repentance. The King is appointed by God, but so is the priest; and if kingship is glorified, it is seen to be most glorious in its submission to the Church. The action of *Ambrosia* closes with a joyous extract from Psalm 21:

> In thy strength the king shall joy, most excellent Father of all saints; under thy protection he shall be safe, under thy guidance he shall be steadfast. How quickly, what great things, what favours hast Thou heaped upon him! A splendid crown shalt Thou set upon his head.[10]

As the song of the clerics dies away, Ambrose and Theodosius engage in a brief and formal dialogue that definitively settles the balance of power:

> AMB: Shall we embrace?
> THEO: If you first bless me with your mouth.

---

10   Rex virtute tuo exsiliet, Pater optime divûm;
       Auspice te sospes, te duce firmus erit.
       Quam cito, quanta illi quamque accumulata dedisti!
       Eximium pones in diadema caput. (V x, 1393–96 [Psalm 21:1–2])

> AMB: From high heaven may the bountiful Lord grant you his grace.
> THEO: How good it is to obey! Truly, how have I been longing for this pleasure!
> AMB: Glory and praise be to God!
> Theo: Let us enter the Church and offer our souls and ourselves as a sacrifice to the highest Sovereign.[11]

It is within the territorial bounds of the church that an earlier encounter, related by the courtier Sosticus in Act V Scene vii, has already made explicit the King's subservient status. The abject Theodosius, eager to receive the Eucharist from Ambrose, is rebuked for trespassing in the sanctuary where only priests have the right to tread:

> After he had made for the sanctuary, his face wet with tears and without any suspicion since he deemed lawful what had been tolerated by a less stringent usage, he asked for the bread of life, because he was free from sins. Ambrose began to speak: 'O Caesar, you drape this purple over a king, not over a priest. So leave this space to us, stay behind your curtains.' When the good prince had acknowledged his error, he left the sacred place and remained, in a dignified manner, behind the holy sanctuary.[12]

In his submission to Ambrose's ruling, the King illustrates Ambrose's maxim: 'The emperor is within the church: he is not above it.' Campion borrowed this incident from the Byzantine historian Theodoret, who adds that in Constantinople it was the usual custom for the Emperor to stand within the altar-rail, and that on his return there Theodosius told the local bishop, Nectarius, that he no longer wanted to sit near the altar because Ambrose had taught him the difference between an emperor and a priest.[13]

---

11   AMB: Imus in amplexum?   THEO: Si me prius ore sacraris.
      AMB: Dives ab aethereo tibi gratiam devotet axe.
      THEO: Quam parere bonum! Quam enim sperata voluptas!
      AMB: Gloria lausque Deo!   THEO: Subeamus templa, supremo
      Regnatori animas et nos in vota feramus.   (V x, 1403–07)

12   Postquam fletibus vultum rigans
      Adyta petisset inscius, licita ratus
      Quae tulerat usus iniquior, vitae cibum
      Purgatus expetit. Ambrosius infit loqui:
      'O Caesar, isthac purpura regem tegis,
      Non ordines sacros. Sinito nostra spatia,
      Aulaea vestra posside.' Princeps bonus
      Errata fassus deserit penetralia,
      Sublime residens dia post sacraria.   (V vii, 1282–90)

13 Simons, *Ambrosia*, p. 104.

II *Initial approaches*

It would be misinterpreting Campion to read *Ambrosia* as a play belittling monarchy; the play was, indeed, performed to the court at Prague.[14] But its main message is unambiguous: heresy leads to internecine conflict and evil action, and princes, to rule wisely, must be accountable to the Church in a way that only Catholic monarchs can claim to be. The plot of *Ambrosia* is designed to illustrate this in a neat, almost schematic manner: the two monarchs, Justina and Theodosius, respectively demonstrate obdurate heresy and pride brought to shame through evil deeds. England was Campion's most obvious model for a heretical country, but the plot is not especially susceptible to a point-by-point comparison with English history; nor need it have been, given that Campion was based in the centre of Europe at the time the play was written. The plight of Bohemia itself was perhaps a more obvious inspiration, since it was in the Jesuits' interests to encourage a Catholic court and largely Catholic nobility to remain steadfast in the faith, though surrounded by Protestant subjects. But it draws from patristic precedent an ideal for future action from which any heretical country might benefit, including England.

Similarly, one should beware of identifying playwright too readily with protagonist. A strong autodidactic element is characteristic of Jesuit drama, with boys often participating in composition, and masters on occasion writing roles more didactically appropriate to themselves than to their pupils.[15] The saintly Ambrose would therefore seem to be an appropriate role-model for Campion, but certain important provisos need to be made. Firstly, the roles of a bishop and a Jesuit are different. The first – when not *in partibus infidelium* – has official status within a country, and contributes to the legislation and organisation of a Church. The second, in contrast, belongs to a missionary order, professing obedience to the Pope but operating to a large extent independently from the Church hierarchy within a country: a situation which, as the Appellant controversy was to demonstrate in early seventeenth-century England, could lead to fatal ambiguity and conflict. The Jesuit-General, Everard Mercurian, only acceded to William Allen's request for a Jesuit presence in England on condition that they gave the English government no cause to accuse the Jesuits of treason; and Campion, when sent on the English mission, was not authorised to deal in politics. As he wrote:

> I never had mynde and am straightly forbidden by our fathers that sent me
> to deale in any respects with matters of state or policye of this realme, as

---

[14] Schmidl, *Historia*, I, p. 419. For a discussion of the religious tensions in Prague at the time that the Jesuit College was founded, see James Brodrick, S.J., *Saint Peter Canisius* (London, 1963 edn), chap. VII.

[15] See Shell, 'English Catholicism', ch. 3.

those things wch. appertaine not to my vocation, and from wch. I do gladly estrange and sequester my thoughts.[16]

His instructions stipulated that English Jesuits should not interfere in matters of state 'except it were in such cases, as the one should be soe ioyned & intangled with the other, as it were not possible to deale in the later without touching in the former, of wch. cases there be store at this day in England . . .'[17]

Nevertheless, high claims are made for the priest's role. Persons' *The Jesuits' Memorial*, written long after Campion's death but highly reminiscent of *Ambrosia*, makes explicit the complementary but separate duties of Church and state.[18] Distinguishing between spiritual and temporal power, Persons writes that the state of the clergy exceeds that of the laity insofar as the soul is more important than the body; that this spiritual jurisdiction can be traced to Christ's institution of the apostles; and this has the effect of confirming temporal power, not denying it. The ideal is the peaceful hegemony of the Church over the state, but the implications are of tension; in Persons' pure form, there is allowed to the clergy an autonomy that any monarchy would find a threat. As Persons admits, the spiritual government of Christ and his apostles was established at a time when 'all Temporal Princes of the World were Infidels and Enemies' (p. 196); but apostolic evangelism resulted in princes becoming Christians, and subjecting themselves to 'Jurisdiction of Souls' (p. 197). From this, it is only a short step to reconverting princely heretics. The Jesuits are cast in an apostolic role, concerned with spiritual government only; but one of the aims of that spiritual government is to guide the King.

Persons deliberately underplays the subversive implications by stressing the importance and dignity of temporal power, but he is unambiguous about its inferiority to spiritual power on the Divine scale. 'All Kings and Emperors that would be saved' must subject themselves to it,

> as our Great Constantine . . . and after him the most renowned of the rest, as Valentinian, the two Theodosius's, Justinian, Charles the great, and others . . . and yet by this did they not lose, or diminish one jot of Temporal authority . . . but rather did greatly confirm and increase the same; for that

---

[16] 'Copy of a letter sent . . . to the councell of England', Stonyhurst College, MS A.IV.2, ff. 593–94 (foliated by openings). This, 'Campion's Brag', has often been reprinted, e.g. Evelyn Waugh, *Edmund Campion* (London, 1935), pp. 219–23.

[17] See Thomas M. McCoog, S.J., ed., *English and Welsh Jesuits, 1555–1650. Part I: A–F* (London, 1994), CRS 74, pp. 9–10, and 'The Establishment of the English Province of the Society of Jesus', *Recusant History* 17 (1984), pp. 121–39. The instructions are reprinted in Leo Hicks, S.J., ed., *Letters and Memorials of Father Robert Persons, S.J.* (London, 1942), CRS 39, pp. 316–19.

[18] Though written in 1596, it was only published in 1690. For discussion of the theoretical importance of *The Jesuits' Memorial*, see John Bossy, *The English Catholic Community, 1570–1850* (London, 1975), pp. 20–24; Peter Holmes, *Resistance and Compromise: The Political Thought of the Elizabethan Catholics* (Cambridge, 1982), ch. 14.

Spiritual Pastors and Governors of Souls do teach, and command all due reverence, and obedience to be done in Temporal matters to Temporal Princes, and do exhibit the same also themselves . . . (pp. 199–200)

Persons and Campion may have discussed the ideal relationship between Church and state, but this must remain speculative; and even allowing for the latter's early death, Persons seems to have been a more political creature than Campion. Nevertheless, Campion's exploration of the relationship between Ambrose and Theodosius reveals a conception of politics as moral persuasion: directing the head of state in paths appropriate to a professed Christian monarch, and leaving the state to deal with details.

An Ambrosian perspective on the ideal relationship between Church and state was by no means exclusively Catholic, though opinions differed on how to interpret the story. Elizabeth understood the royal supremacy as allowing the acceptance of advice from those best qualified to give it, and Ambrosian exemplars were often employed by her advisers when she was perceived as stepping out of line.[19] It was seen to be Theodosius' greatest glory that he submitted to ecclesiastical admonishment, but Ambrose's chiefest merit that he did not coerce him. The balance here is delicate, downplaying Ambrose's excommunication of Theodosius, and it is hardly surprising that some found the incident too problematic for use. Richard Hooker regarded it as a case outside ordinary ecclesiastical jurisdiction, from which he held that kings were exempt. Though Constantine is joined with Theodosius in Persons' roll-call of godly princes, it was Constantine and not Theodosius who was the preferred model for Protestant monarchs; in John Foxe's *Actes and monuments* the former is central to both argument and iconography, and the latter scarcely gets a mention. Theodosius' excommunication, in particular, was seen as allowing too much power to the Church. Thomas Bilson complained that 'The Jesuites helpe this storie with their admixtions', to justify insurrection against princes: the example he cites is how the historical Theodosius voluntarily left off his imperial robes after Ambrose's reproof and excommunication, while in Jesuit versions of the story Ambrose orders him to take them off.[20]

III   *Self-fashioning*

Ambrose possesses the acknowledged authority which Campion lacked, but *Ambrosia* is still an arena for anticipatory role-playing. It explores the various ways in which Church and state can collude and collide: in particular, the means by

[19] For the arguments contained in this paragraph, cf. 'If Constantine, then also Theodosius: St Ambrose and the Integrity of the Elizabethan *Ecclesia Anglicana*', in Patrick Collinson, *Godly People: Essays on English Protestantism and Puritanism* (London, 1983), pp. 109–33.

[20] *The true difference betweene christian subiection and unchristian rebellion* (Oxford, 1585), STC 3071, p. 373 (sidenote). This is not borne out by *Ambrosia*, V iii, 1103.

which a priest can assert ecclesiastical power and retain spiritual integrity when the state is against him. Even in 1578, Campion seems to have had no specific knowledge of his future role within the Jesuit order. Though Persons was certainly campaigning for a mission to England at that date, final details had not been agreed; and Campion might instead have envisaged a future for himself on the European stage, and a fate more analogous to Ambrose's. *Ambrosia* is not merely a historical drama, but a compellingly imaginative and profoundly practical preparation for a possible future.

The possibility of *Ambrosia* being an autodidactic model for Campion – in a sense limited by circumstance – is further suggested by Campion's own use of disguises and pseudonyms. Perhaps as a means of sacralising the surface dishonesty of pretence, possibly even as a deliberate riposte to Protestant criticism of Catholic deceit, these were assumed with emulatory purpose. When disguised as an Irishman on his travel to England he assumed the name of Ireland's patron Saint Patrick, being 'Apte of yt Country'; and later, on arriving in England, he called himself Edmonds 'in remembrance of S. Edmond king & martyr of England whome he desired to imitate'.[21] Role-playing, disguises and multiple names, all the stock anti-Jesuit accusations familiar from Protestant propaganda, here seem designed as a kind of moral memento tending towards veneration and emulation of the saints. Assuming the name of a saint would also, in Catholic terms, have constituted a claim to his especial protection. In a very short time, this claim was to be made on Campion himself. The brothers Richard, Robert and William Wigmore all adopted the alias of Campion, as did John Poyntz and Charles Wilkinson; and an 'Edwd. Campion' is listed in the 1587 return of names of priests and Jesuits in London prisons.[22] Given that the name would have been instantly conspicuous to pursuivants, its commonness is quiet testimony to the inspiration of Campion's life and the efficacy of his death.

Campion's delight in role-playing shines through biographical anecdote. An account by Ralph Sherwin, Campion's companion on his journey to England and later his fellow-martyr, gives a spirited account of Campion's character-acting as an Irish servant while the party of Jesuits was passing through Geneva: 'if you had seen how naturally he played his parte, the remembrance of it would have made you merrie'. When the party attracted hostile interest, 'one would need be doinge with Mr Campion . . . and in Latin asked him (*cuius es*) which he . . . answered '*senior no*' and the fellow therewith amazed sayed (*Potesne loqui Latine*) and Mr Campion gave a shrink with his Shoulders and soe choked off the Knave'.[23] On this occasion, and later while the priests talked with Theodore

[21] Quotations taken from Persons' 'Life of Campion', Stonyhurst College MS A.IV.2 (PI), f. 109 and published *Letters and Notices* 12 (1878), p. 2. Simpson, *Campion*, comments on the highly dramatised nature of Campion's *History of Ireland* (p. 50); cf. Colm Lennon, 'Edmund Campion's *Histories of Ireland* and Reform in Tudor Ireland' in the present volume.

[22] Foley, *Records*, I, p. 481; VI, p. 298; VII, pp. 842–43.

[23] Ralph Sherwin to Mr Ralph Bickley, Paris 11 June 1580: Foley transcript, Stonyhurst MS A.IV.7, item 10.

Beza, Campion's ultimate quick-wittedness was to feign inarticulacy; and this renders devastating his last piece of doctrinal horseplay. When the party was leaving Geneva, Campion went on ahead out of the city gates:

> and there, by chance, met with one of the 9 Ministers of Geneva and by & by buckled with him in questions about their Church until he had almost made the fellow mad, for when we came in sight, Mr Campion went his way, & left the heretic, & when we came to him, he seemed to be in desparcation [desperation] & toulde us that there was a fellow held a strong opinion, & had mocked him about his Church, then all our Companie fell upon him, & shooke up the poor Shackerell [vagabond] before the Soldiers just by the gate . . .

Campion's mischievous use of Geneva's boundaries marks off the pretence of an actor from real identity, and doctrinal truth from Calvinist lies.

Comedy, in all its senses, was perhaps easier for the first generation of Jesuits. *Ambrosia* is classified on the manuscript as a *comoedia*, and the play's ending is, in worldly terms, brilliantly optimistic; this in itself is enough to sever it from the Jesuit plays that were to follow in the 1590s and later. Optimism about the effects of Campion's brilliance on Europe prompted Archbishop Antonius Brus to tell him, on his departure from Prague, that as the Englishman John Wyclif had brought evil upon Bohemia, so God had provided another Englishman to heal Bohemia's wounds. Joannes Schmidl also suggests that at least one of Campion's contemporaries earmarked him for a different exemplary part: on the night before Campion's departure from Prague to England, Jacobus Gallus of Silesia is said to have written on the wall of Campion's bedroom 'P. Edmundus Campianus Martyr'.[24] A pious anecdote of this kind is not necessarily false, but should always be used with caution by the historian; it represents, at the very least, the end of a rigorous teleological process by which the storyteller purges out irrelevant material from the brief life of a saint. Nevertheless these two anecdotes, pointing different ways, may demonstrate that Campion's contemporaries imagined at least two futures for him, or rather two different exemplary roles to fulfil: the voice of Catholic authority, and the martyr.

IV   *Prophecy and history*

It is a commonplace among historians of early modern Europe to talk of the scaffold as a theatre of death.[25] But the text chosen by Campion at his execution makes it clear that he was conscious of one enormous obligation: for a martyr's

[24] Schmidl, *Historia*, I, p. 437.
[25] See John R. Knott, *Discourses on Martyrdom in English Literature, 1563–1694* (Cambridge, 1993); and David Nicholls, 'The Theatre of Martyrdom in the French Reformation', *Past and Present* 121 (1988), pp. 49–73.

death not to be a private matter alone, but one which fulfilled the expectations of his audience. He began his scaffold-speech with the words 'We are made a spectacle, or a sight, unto God, unto his Angels, and unto men,' an adaptation of 1 Corinthians 4:9, where the original reads 'a spectacle to the world, to angels and to men'.[26] This slight but significant expository alteration seems intended to shift the attention of the audience: not away from public display, as the omission of 'to the world' would seem to imply, but towards the greater and more terrible arena of God's final judgement. The *spectaculum*, or spectacle, has many exemplary nuances. Some are obvious: a public display, a sight, a means of seeing. Others are peculiarly applicable to martyrdom: a person or thing exhibited to the public as an object either of curiosity and contempt, or of wonder and admiration; a mirror, model, pattern and standard; or, figuratively, a means or medium through which something is regarded. Protestants might come to mock at Campion's shame, and Catholics to marvel. Campion's behaviour served not only as a standard for steadfastness but as a means of rendering transparent, by sacrifice, the division between earthly and heavenly things: in the most literal sense possible, a sight unto God and His angels. Campion's speech would perhaps have expounded the more modest of these meanings, had it not been cut short by the executioner.

Many 'good catholike gentlemen' were 'desirous to be eye witnesses of that which might happen in the speach, demeinor, & passage' of Campion, Sherwin and Alexander Briant, 'those three rare patterns of piety, vertue, and innocencie', while two others, disputing on the motion of the sun at the beginning of the execution, were 'by the end of [the] pageant . . . charitably moued and affected with compassion' (A 4a, B 2b). Theatrical metaphor is integral to the language used by the Catholic witness Thomas Alfield, contrasting suggestively with his heavily ironical criticism of Anthony Munday for mountebankery: Munday's profession of player, for instance, is 'no doubt a calling of some creditt' (D 4b–E 1a). It would be hard to find better demonstrated the moral ambiguity of the dramatic metaphor.

In Campion hagiography, drama is seen as only one manifestation of his copious rhetorical gifts. The pun transmuting St Ambrose's name into the food of the gods must have suggested itself to contemporary panegyrists of Campion's rhetorical skill, even before his execution gave it a new and poignant meaning.[27] The only manuscript of *Ambrosia* to survive is inscribed 'By the most holy martyr Edmund Campion', and as epigraph has an epigram on him:

> When Edmund presented the nation and its leaders with the translation in great triumph of the relics of Gervasius, this augured the time when he

[26] A detailed eye-witness account can be found in Thomas Alfield, *A true reporte of the death and martyrdome of M. Campion jesuite* (npd [London, 1582]), ARCR II, no. 4; STC 4537, A 4–B 4, from which the above quotations are taken.

[27] Simpson, *Campion*, p. 127 (though without giving any specific reference).

himself would be a martyr wreathed with a purple crown. And it was not a false prophecy, for as a martyr amongst martyrs he passes never-ending eternity with gladness and rejoicing. Sing of the martyrs therefore, O most holy martyr. For is it not a swan who can best praise other hymning swans?[28]

The epigram's pious augury is anachronistic: *Ambrosia* is a play about martyrdom, but martyrdom either exhumed, as with the bones of Gervase and Protase, or risked and averted, in the case of Ambrose himself. But the crucial link is between martyrdom and rhetoric: martyrdom as an action more powerful than any word, and rhetoric as a duty to the dead. Just as Ambrose in the play exhumes the early Christian martyr Gervase, Campion popularises Ambrose, and in turn the anonymous epigrammatist urges other Jesuit writers to do the same for Campion. The swan sings only at its death; and so in the act of hymning it, other swans commit themselves to the same death.

The dynamic of sweet rhetoric also dominates a more famous lament for Campion, 'Why do I use my paper, ink and pen?'[29] Since rhetoric is futile if not persuasive, it stresses the inseparability of speaker, deed and word in presenting the act of persuasion. Campion's martyrdom has given him a wider audience than he ever enjoyed in life, and is its own best rhetorical testimony to that which he died to defend:

> You thought perhaps when learned Campion dyes,
> his pen must cease, his sugred tong be still,
> but you forgot how lowde his death it cryes,
> how farre beyond the sound of tongue and quil . . .
> Liuing he spake to them that present were,
> his writings tooke their censure [judgement] of the viewe,
> Now fame reports his lerning farre and nere,
> and now his death confirmes his doctrine true . . .   (E 4a)

Anthony Munday's systematic parody of the poem fastens on the potential

---

28   Lipsana Gervasii magno translata triumpho
        Cum populo Edmundus principibusque daret,
        Portendebatur tempus fore quando corona
        Cinctus purpurea martyr et ipse foret.
        Nec vanum augurium, martyr nam martyras inter
        Immortale aevum laetus ovansque agitat.
        Martyras ergo cane, o martyr sanctissime. Nam quis
        Hymnidicos melius pangat olore cygnos?   (Ambrosia, p. 2)

[29] Quoted below from the version given in Alfield, with contractions silently expanded. Full bibliographical details of known printed and MS copies and versions can be found in *The Arundel Harington Manuscript of Tudor Poetry*, ed. Ruth Hughey, 2 vols (Columbus, Ohio, 1960), I, No. 66; II, pp. 57–66. See also Thomas M. McCoog, S.J., ' "The Flower of Oxford": The Role of Edmund Campion in Early Recusant Polemics', *Sixteenth Century Journal* 24 (1993), pp. 899–913.

deceptions of rhetoric: Campion's 'sugred tongue' disguised a 'vicious will', and when writing, 'the trueth he did suppres, / Stopping the way that Christians did desire.'[30] In Protestant drama, Campion's rhetorical facility is again seen to have brought about his undoing; as in Holinshed's *Chronicles*, he was thought to have been 'so fine in his quirks and fantasticall coniectures, that the ignorant he woon by his smooth deuises, some other affecting his pleasant imaginations he charmed with subtiltie and choked with sophistrie'.[31] Thomas Dekker's *The Whore of Babylon* is a dramatisation of mythologies borrowed from Edmund Spenser's *The Faerie Queene*, apparently written in response to the Gunpowder Plot and cast in chronicle form to celebrate Elizabeth I's deliverance from nefarious Catholic plotters.[32] Campion, or Campeius, figures among these.[33] The Fairy Queen – Elizabeth I – though admitting that he is 'Deeply learnd', qualifies her praise by saying that 'he caries, / A soul within him framde of a thousand wheeles: / Yet not one steddy' (II i, lines 186, 188–90): rhetorical facility, which presupposes an ability to argue a myriad of cases with equal conviction, signifies a shameful infirmity of purpose. This is demonstrated immediately in Act II Scene ii, when Campeius is seduced into Catholicism by the evil Third King, or Philip II. Cross-questioning Campeius about his scholarly credentials, he tries to elicit disloyalty from him by remarking on England's reluctance to give scholars any just financial reward. Campeius, brusque at first, eventually succumbs to avarice: 'Ile write in gall and poyson gainst my nurce / This Fairie land, for not rewarding merit . . .' (lines 126–27).

Some commentators have claimed that Campeius is portrayed in a pronouncedly sympathetic manner.[34] But this is, perhaps, no more than saying that, in a play populated by two-dimensional moving caricatures, the development of his character is crucial to the play's didactic message. The audience witnesses his temptation, change and apostasy, and his final intellectual hubris. Paying obeisance to the Empress of Babylon before travelling back to England, he promises

---

30 'Verses in the Libell, made in prayse of the death of Maister Campion . . . heere chaunged to the reproofe of him . . .,' in *A breefe answer made unto two seditious pamphlets* (London, 1582), STC 18262, ff. D 7–E 4a (quotation f. D7b). In 'An other upon the same', ff. E 2b–4a, he parodies the text of Campion's scaffold-speech:

> An yrksome spectacle was presented then:
> In sight of God, of Angels, Saints and men.   (f. E 3b)

31 Raphael Holinshed, *The first and second volumes of chronicles* (London, 1586), STC 13569, p. 1327, column 2, ll. 39–44.

32 See Fredson Bowers, ed., *The Dramatic Works of Thomas Dekker*, 4 vols (Cambridge, 1953–61), II, introduction to 'The Whore of Babylon'. All quotations are taken from this edition. See also the most recent scholarly discussion of the play, contained in Jean E. Howard, *The Stage and Social Struggle in Early Modern England* (London, 1994), pp. 49–57.

33 A subsidiary reference to Cardinal Campeggio, called Campeus in Samuel Rowley's 'When You See Me You Know Me' (1604), and Shakespeare's 'Henry VIII' (1613), may be incorporated.

34 Cyrus Hoy, 'Introductions, Notes, and Commentaries', in Bowers, *Dekker*, II, p. 303; Mary Leland Hunt, *Thomas Dekker: A Study* (New York, 1911), p. 41.

her that he will try and win apocalyptic honours by all the scholarly skill at his command:

> If all the Spels
> That wit, or eloquence, or arts can set:
> If all the sleights that bookemen vse in schooles
> Be powrefull in such happinesse, 'tis mine.   (III i, lines 172–75)

Campeius's 'sleights' refer back to the Empress's injunctions to her followers, to

> Haue change of haires, of eie-brows, halt with soldiers,
> Be shauen and be old women, take all shapes
> To escape taking.   (lines 162–64)

Disguise and deceit invalidate Catholic cleverness; but Campeius's final appearance reveals his hypocrisy and dehumanises him utterly. In the allegorical dumb show of Act IV Scene 1, Falshood strikes the ground to summon Campeius and a number of other anti-Catholic icons: a friar, a gentleman with a drawn sword, another with poisoned gloves in a box, and another with a bridle. Truth, Time and Plain-Dealing – the latter a Protestant riposte to Catholic intellectual virtuosity – identify these iconographical figures as the various 'conduit-heads of treason' (1.8), and Time expounds Campeius thus:

> See Truth, see sonne, the snake slips off his skinne,
> A scholler makes a ruffian . . .
> And see, that shape which earst shew'd reuerend,
> And wore, the outward badge of sanctitie,
> Is cloath'd in garments of hypocrisie.   (lines 12–13, 15–17)

Dekker was not the only writer to introduce Campion into English drama. Campion's death may have been part of the plot in such Jesuit plays as the lost *Anglia Lapsa Resurgens*,[35] performed at Seville in 1595 and depicting the events of Elizabeth's reign; and he figures prominently in the roll-call of recent Catholic martyrs that was a standard feature of many plays. To give one example, he is mentioned in Act IV Scene ii of *S. Thomas Cantuar*, performed at Rome in 1613. The dramatic occasion is the appearance of an angel to Becket, to warn him of his impending martyrdom; Becket asks the apparition what will happen to the Church when he is gone, and he is given a panoramic, processional view of the future to the Reformation and beyond. The heretic Wyclif and the Teutonic Luther are invoked and condemned, and their invasion of England is foretold:

> See that Religion arms against her foes: she summons to the fight, and the palm admits the joyous to the chorus of heaven. Here unconquered More encourages, and Fisher as well. The Carthusian Order sees her offspring in

---

[35] For information on this, cf. Martin Murphy, *St. Gregory's College, Seville, 1592–1767* (London, 1992), CRS 73, pp. 19–20.

heaven. The majority of bishops deviated in the first crisis, and in the end none is captured so that in the second conflict the noble band may expiate the error by a rain of their blood.[36]

The second and third generation of Catholic martyrs is hymned, and a fourth prophesied, in the conclusion to the Angel's speech:

Great dangers crown the pious with eternal leafy garlands. Do you see how great a band, defended on all sides by the flower of virtues, rises up against the enemy? Robert Persons leads with the banner; spreading the name JESUS, he shields the cares of the standard-bearer with a sacred cover. See the labours of the uphill struggle. Edmund Campion will accord you a great and famous triumph, and Robert Southwell in equal measure, Henry Walpole on a false charge, and Henry Garnet, hurt very little: happily and innocently he approaches the stars, and the miracles of his countenance remain on the earth . . . Given these preludes, you, Thomas, seize the fragrant crowns that holy liberty weaves and displays.[37]

Catholic veneration of martyrs, combined with a conscious anticipation of martyrdom – individual with Campion, collective with the seminarians – has the effect of an apostolic succession: martyrs are quickly made, quickly recognised and quickly emulated.[38]

English Jesuit drama began in earnest from the 1590s and beyond, after the brief hopes raised by the Spanish invasion. The Jesuits' task had now to be seen as lengthy, difficult and bloody; and to imitate the optimism of Campion would

36   Vide ut contra suos
      Religio pugiles armet; ad pugnam ciet
      Palmaque laetos inserit Caeli choris.
      His Morus invictus pariter Roffensis adurget . . .
      Polo cerent Carthusia prolem.
      Plurimus in primo discrimine Praesul aberrat
      Nullus in extremo capitur: quo sanguinis imbre
      Expiat errorem congressu turma secundo
      Nobilis . . .   (Liber 321(2), Venerable English College, Rome, n.p.)
37   Magna pios discrimina fronde coronant
      Aeterna, cernis quantus consurgit in hostem
      Undique virtutum munitus flore manip[u]lus?
      Vexillum (?) praefert Personius, illud Jesu
      Diffundens nomen sacrato tegmine obumbrat
      Signiferi curas; successus, cerne labores.
      Campianus clarum dedit tibi magne triumphum
      Southwellusque suum, Walpolus, crimine falso,
      Garnettus minime laesus, faeliciter insons
      Astra subit, vultus remanent miracula terris . . .
      His tu praeludis, libertas sancta coronas
      Nectit odoriferas, quas exhibet arripe Thoma.   (*Loc. cit.* [Note 34])
   38 Cf. Michael E. Williams, 'Campion and the English Continental Seminaries', in this volume.

have been impossible in the context of his martyrdom. Robert Persons moved from demands for reconversion to requests for toleration. There were to be no more endings where Church and state were reconciled after a brief conflict; the saints triumph, but triumph in death. Though all questions relating to the Pope's power of excommunicating and deposing princes were omitted from courses in English Jesuit colleges overseas, martyrdom, in *Ambrosia* merely a subject of bones and visions, assumed centre stage in the plays. It has been suggested that Jesuit plays throughout Europe during the early 1600s saw a shift in emphasis from dramatising the triumph of the Church over heresy to exploring conflicts between the Church and heretical kings.[39] If this is true – and generalisation is perhaps dangerous in the present state of rapidly evolving scholarship on Jesuit drama – then Campion can be seen as working within one theme while anticipating the other. His nationality, and the stimulus of autodidacticism, empowered him to do this.

---

[39] See James A. Parente, Jr., 'Tyranny and Revolution on the Baroque Stage: The Dramas of Joseph Simons', *Humanistica Lovaniensia* 32 (1983), pp. 309–24.

7

'Playing the Champion': The Role of Disputation in the Jesuit Mission

THOMAS M. McCOOG, S.J.

Delivered in London on 26 November 1559 for the first time, John Jewel's famous 'challenge' sermon was based on 1 Cor. 11:23: 'I have received of the Lord that thing which I also have delivered unto you; that is, that the Lord Jesus, in the night that he was betrayed, took bread, etc.'[1] Focusing on Christianity's principal act of worship, he maintained that the communion service as established by the Elizabethan Church was in fact a restoration of the practice of the primitive Church. What Paul had received from Christ and had passed on to his converts, what had been the norm for the first six hundred years of the Church's history was now once again available with the elimination of the corruptions that had distorted the service into the Mass. Not content to establish continuity between primitive and Elizabethan liturgical practices, Jewel argued that the use of the Latin language, communion under one kind, the canon of the Mass, 'the adoration of the sacrament', and the practice of private Mass were abuses not found in the early Church. The sermon ended with the challenge:

> If any one of all our adversaries be able clearly and plainly to prove, by such authority of the scriptures, the old doctors, and councils . . . I am content to yield unto him, and to subscribe. But I am well assured that they shall never be able truly to allege one sentence. And because I know it, therefore I speak it, lest ye happily [sic] should be deceived'.[2]

Jewel was not the first to challenge the opposition. Indeed Martin Luther's '95 Theses' in 1517 heralded an era of religious turmoil punctuated with demands for disputations. After Johann Eck accepted the challenge and Luther was given

---

[1]   This translation and the excerpts from the sermon itself come from John Ayre, ed., *The Works of John Jewel*, 4 vols (Cambridge, 1845–50), Parker Society, I, pp. 1–25.

[2]   *Ibid.*, pp. 21–22.

a guarantee of safe passage, he travelled to Leipzig, where he and Eck debated in July of 1519.[3] Luther later defended this use of debates:

> We theologians, more even than lawyers and doctors, are bound to labour in the Lord's vineyard. We are a *spectaculum* to all the world and we are accused of heresy and of being authors of new doctrine. So we must defend ourselves in public disputation. Indeed, the civil authorities require us to do so.[4]

As the Reformation progressed however, 'disinterested' academic disputations diminished. Unless the minority church had strong enough political support to obtain a colloquy such as those held at Regensburg (1541) and Poissy (1561), public disputations were theological trials held to demonstrate the wicked errors of a convicted heretic or to destroy religious opposition.[5] At both, examiners tried to get an opponent to admit or deny a premise that would ultimately lead to the contradiction of his original position.[6]

In England the Protestant Peter Martyr Vermigli was challenged by Richard Smith, former Regius Professor of Theology, in theologically conservative Oxford. By the time the disputation started in May 1549, Smith had fled Oxford and was replaced by William Tresham of Christ Church, William Chedsey of Corpus Christi, and Morgan Phillips of St Mary Hall. Martyr was dissatisfied with the result and later dissuaded his friends from participating in formal debates. Further debates were postponed by a royal edict that forbade such exercises because of the disruption they caused. In September 1550, after the edict's expiration, a second debate was scheduled. It was, however, cancelled by the Vice-Chancellor for fear of a disturbance. Formal disputations with Archbishop Thomas Cranmer and Bishops Hugh Latimer and Nicholas Ridley were held in April 1554 as part of the proceedings against them.[7]

At the start of Elizabeth's reign, a public disputation between Protestant and

---

[3] See Roland Bainton, *Here I Stand: Martin Luther* (Tring, 1983 edn), pp. 102–20 for a presentation of the debate.

[4] Cited in G.R. Evans, *Problems of Authority in the Reformation Debates* (Cambridge, 1992), p. 103. Compare Luther's comment to the bishop of Leipzig in 1519 cited in Bainton, *Here I Stand*, p. 108.

[5] Peter Matheson reminds us that a 'purely theological Reformation never existed, and by the time of the Diet of Regensburg in 1541 doctrinal and socio-political questions were inextricably bound up with one another' (*Cardinal Contarini at Regensburg* [Oxford, 1972], p. 5). For more detailed information on Regensburg and Poissy, see Elisabeth G. Gleason, *Gasparo Contarini: Venice, Rome, and Reform* (Berkeley, 1993), pp. 186–256, and Donald Nugent, *Ecumenism in the Age of the Reformation: The Colloquy of Poissy* (Cambridge, Mass., 1974).

[6] On the nature of debates, see Evans, *Problems of Authority*, pp. 94–112.

[7] For more on these debates, see Jennifer Loach, 'Reformation Controversies' in James McConica, ed., *The Collegiate University. The History of the University of Oxford* vol. III (Oxford, 1986), pp. 369–77.

Catholic ecclesiastics was staged at Westminster in late March 1559 as part of a campaign to gain parliamentary approval for the re-introduction of Protestant worship with an Act of Uniformity. The debate settled nothing but it did eliminate opposition to the religious legislation and thus guaranteed passage of Acts of Supremacy and Uniformity.[8] A few months later royal injunctions forbade further religious debates and required a licence for the publication of any book.[9]

Dr Henry Cole, the deposed dean of St Paul's and a participant in the Westminster disputation, replied to Jewel's challenge on 20 March 1560, three days after Jewel delivered the sermon for the second time. Cole had to proceed carefully because he could be punished for defending Catholicism. In the ensuing correspondence, later published, Jewel repeated his challenge and extended it to include other doctrinal claims, such as authority of the Bishop of Rome.

The subsequent battle, called the 'Great Controversy' by A.C. Southern,[10] involved many of the best English theologians. The Catholic position was upheld by Thomas Harding, formerly Regius Professor of Hebrew and Warden-elect of New College, Oxford, and his fellow Wykehamists Thomas Dorman, John Rastell, Thomas Stapleton, and Nicolas Sander, all then based in Louvain.[11] Jewel was ably assisted by Thomas Cooper, future Bishop of Lincoln and later of Winchester; Puritan minister Edward Dering; William Fulke, Master of Pembroke Hall, Cambridge; Alexander Nowell, Dean of St Paul's, and Robert Horne, Bishop of Winchester.[12] The Catholics operated at a considerable disadvantage: their books were written and printed on the continent. On 1 March 1569 a royal proclamation forbade imported books that would stir up sedition and lead the Queen's subjects into religious error.[13] Although the controversy lost its fervour with the deaths of Jewel in 1571 and Harding in 1572, its influence on the formation of the English Catholic clergy remained strong.

With the foundation of an English seminary at Douai in 1568, William Allen hoped, as he explained to Jean de Vendeville, to produce a Church-in-exile ready to return once the heretics were no longer in control.[14] Allen, however, soon

---

[8] Norman L. Jones, *Faith By Statute: Parliament and the Settlement of Religion, 1559* (London, 1982), pp. 123–27, and *The Birth of the Elizabethan Age* (Oxford, 1993), pp. 23–24.

[9] Henry Gee, *The Elizabethan Clergy and the Settlement of Religion* (Oxford, 1898), pp. 43, 60–62.

[10] *Elizabethan Recusant Prose, 1559–1582* (London, nd [1950]), pp. 60–119.

[11] For the religious background of these men, see James McConica, 'The Catholic Experience in Tudor Oxford' in this volume.

[12] For specific information on the books and their authors, see Peter Milward, S.J., *Religious Controversies of the Elizabethan Age: A Survey of Printed Sources* (London, 1977), pp. 1–16.

[13] Paul L. Hughes and James F. Larkin, C.S.V., eds, *Tudor Royal Proclamations*, 3 vols (New Haven, 1964–69), II, p. 312. Similar proclamations were issued 1 July 1570, 14 November 1570, 28 September 1573, 26 March 1576, and 12 October 1584 (*Tudor Royal Proclamations*, II, pp. 341–43, 347–48, 376–79, 400–01, 506–08).

[14] William Allen to Jean de Vendeville, Rheims 16 September 1578, in Thomas Francis

realized that Catholicism's full restoration would be impossible unless missionary priests were sent to England to sustain and encourage believers.[15] Therefore the seminarians were trained for the problems that they would encounter in England. To be successful, the priests required sophisticated knowledge of Scripture and controversial theology.

The seminarians were trained for disputations. With an eye on current controversial issues, they studied Scriptural passages that either confirmed the truths of Catholicism or were favoured by Protestants in their arguments. Replies to the latter were clearly formulated. Once a week there was a public disputation in which selected students would not only defend Catholic doctrine against Protestant assault but also sharpen their skills by maintaining Protestant views against their colleagues. To augment their knowledge of Scripture, the students learned Greek and Hebrew so that they could read both Testaments in the original languages and avoid 'the sophisms which heretics extract from the properties and meanings of words'. A second weekly disputation involved chosen articles from the *Summa*. For private study, the decrees of the Council of Trent; English church history, specifically the works of the Venerable Bede and Bishop William Lyndewode's collection of provincial councils, and selected works of Augustine, Cyprian, and Jerome were recommended. Finally the students were acquainted 'with the chief impieties, blasphemies, absurdities, cheats and trickeries of the English heretics, as well as their ridiculous writings, sayings and doings'.[16]

Allen's attempts to interest Everard Mercurian, the Superior General of the Society of Jesus, in a Jesuit mission to England were frustrated.[17] In late 1575 or

---

Knox, ed., *The Letters and Memorials of William Cardinal Allen* (London, 1882), p. 54. I have used the translation found in Thomas Francis Knox, ed., *The First and Second Diaries of the English College, Douay* (London, 1878), p. xxvi.

[15] Is this change a sign of Vendeville's influence? In a letter written to the city fathers in 1568, Vendeville explained that the new English College would '. . . exercise them [the students] in controversial questions, and give them, over and above a general acquaintance with the whole of theology which many of them already possess, a more than ordinary knowledge of ecclesiastical history and antiquities, in order that after having been trained and practised in this manner during two years or thereabouts they may be employed in promoting the catholic cause in England even at the peril of their lives . . .' (cited in Knox, *Douai Diaries*, p. xxviii). On Allen and Vendeville, see Michael E. Williams, 'William Allen: The Sixteenth Century Spanish Connection,' *Recusant History* 22 (1994), p. 127. Recently Eamon Duffy has claimed that too much has been made of Vendeville's influence in the transformation of Douai College into a missionary enterprise ('William, Cardinal Allen, 1532–1594', *Recusant History* 22 [1995], pp. 272–74).

[16] Allen to Vendeville, Rheims 16 September 1578, in Knox, *Letters and Memorials*, pp. 62–67. Again I have used the translation from Knox, *Douai Diaries*, pp. xxxviii–xliii.

[17] One reason for Mercurian's refusal was the problem of the Jesuit mission to Ireland in general and of the Irish Jesuit David Wolfe in particular. For more on this see Manuel da Costa, S.J., 'The Last Years of a Confessor of the Faith: Father David Wolf,' *AHSI* 15 (1946), pp. 127–43.

early 1576 Allen drafted a memorandum for a forthcoming meeting with Mercurian in which he explained the English situation. There were, Allen pointed out, certain Englishmen within the Society who were extremely well qualified for the mission. Even their own countrymen judged them to be very skilful and learned. He named the Rastell brothers, Edward and John, who had earlier written against Jewel, and the Heywood brothers, Jasper and Ellis.[18] The fifth Englishman named by Allen was Edmund Campion. Allen knew not where he was currently working, but Campion was commonly acknowledged 'a most brilliant orator and of most ready wit'. Although Allen conceded that Jesuits were the best judges of how their men should be employed, he insinuated that their talents would be best used in England.[19] The talents that appealed to Allen were literary and intellectual.

With assistance from Robert Persons and support from the General's consultors, Allen finally persuaded Mercurian to approve a Jesuit mission to England. On 5 December 1579 Allen wrote from Rome to inform Campion of his selection as missioner. Father General, Allen explained, had 'acceded to the prayers of many people' and assigned Campion to the new mission.[20] The 'many people' included Allen, Gregory Martin, and Henry Holland. Allen probably selected Campion because of the Jesuit's erudition and eloquence. Perhaps that was the reason for the selection of Ralph Sherwin, a secular priest with wide philosophical and theological knowledge and facility with Latin, Greek, and Hebrew.[21] The inclusion of priests such as Campion and Sherwin testifies to

[18] Dennis Flynn in both 'The English Mission of Jasper Heywood, S.J.,' *AHSI* 54 (1985), pp. 49–50, and his contribution to this volume, ' "Out of Step:" Six Supplementary Notes on Jasper Heywood' draws attention to this request and to a rumour according to which a petition was to be addressed to Elizabeth, through the mediation of Philip of Spain, that sought permission for William Allen, Nicholas Sander, and Jasper and Ellis Heywood to preach freely in England. Flynn suggests that this rumour may be behind Allen's request for specific Jesuits noted in England for their learning. For biographical information on all four Jesuits, see Thomas M. McCoog, S.J., ed., *Monumenta Angliae*, 2 vols (Rome, 1992), MHSI 142, 143, II, pp. 351–52, 450–51.

[19] 'Some Correspondence of Cardinal Allen, 1579–85', ed. Patrick Ryan, S.J., in *Miscellanea VII* (London, 1911), CRS 9, pp. 62–69.

[20] Knox, *Letters and Memorials*, pp. 84–85. I use the translation provided in Henry More, S.J., *The Elizabethan Jesuits: Historia Missionis Anglicanae Societatis Jesu (1660)*, translated and edited by Francis Edwards, S.J. (London, 1981), pp. 72–73. Interestingly the letter written by Mercurian to Campion a day earlier, on 4 December 1579, ordered him to depart for Padua as soon as possible. There he would find friends to explain the mission. Mercurian did not mention England. Apparently this letter never reached Campion, and Mercurian wrote two more times, on 6 February and 18 March 1580. In the letter of the 6th of February, Mercurian ordered Campion to come directly to Rome (ARSI, Austr. I/1a, pp. 240–41, 244, 255–56).

[21] More, *Elizabethan Jesuits*, pp. 128–29.

Allen's concern that the mission include priests qualified to defend the truth of Catholicism against Protestant attack.

II

Unlike Robert Persons, who agitated in favour of a Jesuit mission to England,[22] Campion seems to have given little thought to returning to his country.[23] In a letter to Persons written from Prague on 25 June 1577, Campion congratulated him on the increasing number of English within the Society and hoped that their number would continue to grow. On the state of the realm itself, Campion's judgement was non-committal:

> Your reflections on the tears of our orthodox countrymen are quite true; wavering minds, mischievous attachments, cowardly tempers, illogical intellects. But these things will carry them into port when our Lord gives a good wind. I have used up all my paper so I will end.[24]

---

22 From Rome, Persons kept track of the various Englishmen who entered the Society, and hoped that Jesuits would eventually collaborate with the secular clergy within the kingdom. See his letters to Campion written from Rome on 28 November 1578 and to Allen from Rome on 30 March 1579, both of which were published in Leo Hicks, S.J., ed., *Letters and Memorials of Father Robert Persons, S.J.* (London, 1942), CRS 39, pp. 1–5. In a letter to William Good written sometime after 19 March 1579, Persons blamed him for the lack of Jesuit involvement in England: 'But now you will say, heere are Missions for all Contryes but only for England which seemeth to be abandoned above all others. To this I answere that you perhaps are much in falt of this, who had not solicited the cause, when you were heere and had more help than I now have, or can looke for' (*ibid.*, pp. 6–7).

23 On his activities in Prague, see Alison Shell, ' "We Are Made a Spectacle:" Campion's Dramas' in this volume.

24 Quoted in Richard Simpson, *Edmund Campion*, rev. edn (London, 1896), p. 120. In his unpublished life of Campion, Persons claimed that Campion insinuated in various letters that he was ready to return to England 'when His divine Majesty should like thereof'. He was in the meantime well content in Prague, where his efforts were 'not altogether unprofitable also for England', viz. his conversation with certain English gentlemen at the imperial court on matters of religion ('Of the Life and Martyrdom of Father Edmond Campian', *Letters and Notices* 11 [1887], pp. 320–21). Sir Philip Sidney was one of these gentlemen. See Katherine Duncan-Jones, 'Sir Philip Sidney's Debt to Edmund Campion' in this volume.

Yet Campion left Prague, albeit reluctantly,[25] in early March.[26] He arrived in Rome on Easter Saturday, 9 April 1580.[27]

Mercurian's instructions for the Jesuit missionaries challenged Allen's understanding of a mission that involved the discussion of controversial theological issues. Fearful that the venture would be interpreted by the English government as a political venture, Father General stressed that the objects of the mission were 'to advance in the faith and in our Catholic religion all who are found to be Catholics in England; and, secondly, to bring back to it whoever may have strayed from it either through ignorance or at the instigation of others'. The mission, as interpreted by Mercurian, was aimed at Catholics, either faithful or lapsed. There was to be no direct dealing with heretics. The Jesuits were to behave cautiously and prudently. Immoderate fervour, such as concern for the heretics (or, indeed, public disputations), could hinder their work. Mercurian specifically forbade disputations with Protestants unless 'necessity force them'. Debates were ineffective because 'it is a characteristic of heretics, when they are clearly beaten in argument, to be unwilling to give in to anybody'. Yet, if there were a debate, the Jesuits were to avoid 'bitter wrangling' and to advance solid arguments. Mercurian wanted the Jesuits to give witness in any debate not just to learning but also to modesty and charity by refraining 'from biting and intemperate words'.[28]

---

25 In his letter of 9 December 1579, Allen made a cryptic comment: '. . . your brothers according to the flesh also urge you [to come to England]. Even if you cannot hear their voices, God himself has heard their prayers . . .' (ARSI, Fondo Gesuitico 651/594 published in Knox, *Letters and Memorials*, pp. 84–85, and translated in More, *Elizabethan Jesuits*, pp. 72–73). Is Allen insinuating that Campion refused to heed their pleas? In a letter written from Rheims on 14 February [1579?], Henry Holland reprimanded Campion for his silence. Most of the letter is an exaltation of the delights of contemplation, and an admonition that Campion was so captivated by these that he has forgotten his friends. One cannot remain on the mountain top permanently: 'the eagle flies aloft and with his sharp eye, said to be the most powerful, scans everything more carefully in all directions; yet at times, whether from some sense of pity towards its young or from some need of nature, it is compelled to come down for food' (ARSI, Fondo Gesuitico 651/628). Is this simply a plea to write more frequently or a veiled reference to Campion's current life in Prague, oblivious of the demands of England?

26 Understandably the Austrian province was reluctant to lose Campion. This is especially true of the Jesuits at the college in Prague, where Campion was the ordinary professor of physics (Henry Blyssem to Father General, Prague 18 January 1580 and from Graz 12 February 1580, ARSI, Germ. 158, ff. 31^v–32^r; 47^v). On 8 March John Paul Companus, the rector of the college, wrote that Campion had departed a few days earlier: 'All are affected with the loss who knew his virtue, his powerful eloquence, and his other talents. But obedience is as strong as death so we submit with equanimity, considering that God wills it so' (ARSI, Germ. 158, f. 84^v).

27 On 9 April Mercurian complained to the Austrian provincial Henry Blyssem that Campion still had not arrived and that the delay was causing some problems (ARSI, Austr. I/1a, pp. 257–59).

28 These instructions can be found in Hicks, *Letters of Persons*, pp. 316–21.

Twice in Persons' account of the journey from Rome to England he drew attention to Sherwin's and Campion's rhetorical skills. In Bologna Archbishop Gabriel Cardinal Paleotto asked the missionaries to deliver an extemporaneous speech in Latin. Other members of the mission spoke, but Persons specifically cited the efforts of Sherwin and Campion. The former spoke well but the latter was outstanding with his application of Pythagorean/Ciceronian insights to the Christian life.[29] Sherwin and Campion later were the leaders in a confrontation with Theodore Beza. Passing through Geneva, they and John Paschal decided to visit Beza 'to enter some speech with him if they might, either about the Catholic religion or about the controversy between the Protestants and Puritans . . .'. Although the uninvited visitors were not asked into Beza's house, they wished to hear his reasons for asserting that Catholicism was not the legitimate descendant of the Apostolic Church. Beza pleaded that he was too busy with other affairs to discuss the matter. But Campion pushed on: he wanted to know how Beza could claim that the Queen of England was of his religion when he defended the Puritans whom Elizabeth despised. When Beza dismissed the differences between Puritans and more moderate supporters of the Elizabethan settlement, Campion offered to demonstrate that the differences 'were many and very important and essential'.

Candida, Beza's wife, intervened with more work for her husband, but he promised that he would send an English student to discuss the matter with them. A group of English Protestants duly appeared at their lodgings. The ensuing debate grew so heated that a Mr Powell, one of the Englishmen who knew Sherwin and Persons from Oxford, feared for the safety of the Catholics, especially if the municipal authorities were to learn of the challenge levelled at Beza by Sherwin and others. A few of the English priests had proposed to debate with Beza and his supporters before an impartial judge and offered their lives if they were not successful. Fearing possible recriminations, the English Catholics departed the next morning, but not before another clash over the visible head of the Church between Campion and a Protestant minister. Again their Oxford friend intervened to quell the dispute.[30]

Despite his eagerness to debate Beza, Campion was still not enthusiastic about the mission. Prompted by news of the papal-Spanish invasion of Ireland, Campion protested to Allen in Rheims:

> Well, sir, here now I am; you have desired my going to England, and I am come a long journey, as you see, – from Prague to Rome, and from Rome hither. Do you think that my labours in England will countervail all this

29 'Life of Campian', *Letters and Notices* 12 (1878), pp. 3–4.

30 Persons, 'Life of Campian', pp. 6–9. Sherwin's contemporary account of the sojourn adds that Powell asked Campion why he did not remain in Geneva to debate with Beza. The Jesuit replied that they would return if their safety were guaranteed (Sherwin to Ralph Bickley, Paris 11 June 1580, Stonyhurst College, Anglia I, 8 [printed in Dom Bede Camm, O.S.B., ed., *Lives of the English Martyrs*, 2 vols (London, 1904–5), II, pp. 366–73]).

travail, as well as my absence from Bohemia, where, though I did not much, yet I was not idle nor unemployed, and that also against heretics?

After Allen explained that Campion's talents could be best employed in England, Campion replied: 'As for me, all is one; and I hope I am and shall be ever indifferent for all nations and functions whereinsoever my superiors under God shall employ me.'[31] On 7 June Campion, Persons, and Emerson left Rheims for St Omer.[32] There they heard that the English government was aware of their approach and that all ports had been alerted.

In his first letter to Mercurian after Persons' departure for England, Campion confessed that he was worried not 'by mere rumours but by something positively like a clamour that heralds our approach. Only divine Providence can counteract this kind of publicity, and we fully acquiesce in its dispositions.' Nonetheless, he followed orders and was prepared to do what he could 'even if it means death'. Often the first troops of a conquering army were defeated but, Campion continued, '*if* our Society pushes on with this campaign, it will be necessary to overcome much ignorance and sheer wickedness'.[33] The Society did push on with the campaign: Campion followed Persons across the channel on 24 June.

In mid-July Campion and Persons evaded governmental surveillance in London by withdrawing to a village, probably Hoxton, outside the city. On a visit Thomas Pounde persuaded them to refute sundry libels disseminated by the government. These libels, Pounde feared, would increase if the Jesuits were

---

[31] Cited in Simpson, *Campion*, p. 167. John Hungerford Pollen, S.J., attributes Campion's misgiving to scruples ('Blessed Edmund Campion's Journey from Rome to England', *The Month* 90 [1897], p. 262). Simpson thinks that Campion's hesitation resulted from the complication introduced by the Irish invasion. But it is equally possible that this invasion simply aggravated his earlier doubts. At his trial Campion insisted that he had come to England out of obedience to his religious superior 'who . . . according to my vow (which, by the grace of God, I will in no case violate) appointed me to undertake this journey to England, the which I accordingly I [sic] enterprised, being commanded thereto, not as a traitor to conspire the subversion of my country, but as a priest to minister the sacraments and to hear confessions; the which ambassage I protest before God I would as gladly have executed and was as ready and willing to discharge, had I been sent to the Indians or uttermost regions of the world, as I was being sent into my native country (cited in E.E. Reynolds, *Campion and Parsons* [London, 1980], p. 177).

[32] It is interesting to note how the departure of Campion and Persons was described in the *Douai Diary*: 'June 7. Mr Edmund Campion and Mr Robert Persons left us, on their way to England. Both are excellent dialecticians, more than ordinarily skilled in Greek and Latin classics, and good theologians. Mr Campion in speech so polished and eloquent as to have few equals, Mr Persons in act so prudent as to have few betters among men of his years. Our hopes regarding them are high as they well can be, not only because of their gifts and accomplishments, but even more so for the alacrity with which they accepted their task, thinking themselves fortunate to be selected first to break through the ice, since there is hardly a man of that Society, now so numerous and so widely spread, who would not gladly have faced the same dangers. Large indeed is the debt that our afflicted nation owes to this great and truly holy Society' (Knox, *Douai Diaries*, p. 166).

[33] Campion to Mercurian, 20 June 1580, published in More, *Elizabethan Jesuits*, pp. 77–79.

captured. As a precaution, Pounde suggested that each draft a statement to explain the Society's mission. These statements would later be released to contradict any propaganda spread by the government after their capture. Both agreed.[34]

A comparison between Persons' statement and Campion's more familiar 'Brag' reveals that the two followed the same format and addressed the same questions. Persons' statement is the longer, more personal, and indeed the better of the two. But the Brag, bold and impassioned, a work of great bravura, is more effective. It has an urgency the other lacks. Not until the spectre of communism arose would a literary image so haunt a country as Campion's enterprise did England.[35] Both men offered to debate religious issues. If a zeal for truth were not a sufficient motive for acknowledging his petition, Persons would provide a more basic reason: to dispel forever the persistent rumour 'that your ignorant Ministers have never dared to submit to the test of any disputation'. Campion was willing to demonstrate the truth of Catholicism 'by proofs innumerable, Scriptures, Councils, Fathers, History, natural and moral reasons' before selected doctors and masters from Oxford and Cambridge. Echoing Persons, Campion asserted that his confidence was not insolence but resulted from his 'impregnable' evidence:

> I know perfectly that no one Protestant, nor all the Protestants living, nor any sect of our adversaries, (howsoever they face men down in pulpits and overrule us in their kingdom of grammarians and unlearned ears) can maintain their doctrine in disputation.

Once a 'few small withered flowers of oratory' had been lopped off, both were sure that Protestant errors would be manifest to all.

By 10 November 1580 William Allen had copies of both statements in Rheims and he wrote to Agazzari that 'these written fly-leaves pass from hand to hand everywhere among people in England and are a source of strength to many . . .'.[36] Allen was clearly pleased by the incident. The General's reaction

---

[34] Persons' declaration can be found in Hicks, *Letters of Persons*, pp. 28–41. Campion's has been reprinted often, e.g. Bernard Basset, S.J., *The English Jesuits* (London, 1967), pp. 454–56.

[35] Compare Campion's 'And touching our Society be it known to you that we have made a league – all the Jesuits in the world, whose succession and multitude must overreach all the practices of England – cheerfully to carry the cross you shall lay on us, and never to despair your recovery, while we have a man left to enjoy your Tyburn, or to be racked with your torments, or consumed with your prisons. The expense is reckoned, the enterprise is begun, it is of God, it cannot be withstood. So the faith is planted, so it must be restored' with Persons' 'if your intentions are bloodthirsty (from which evil may God defend you) there will be no lack of scope for them. For you are persecuting a corporation that will never die, and sooner will your hearts and hands, sated with blood, fail you, than will there be lacking men, eminent for virtue and learning, who will be sent by this Society and allow their blood to be shed by you for this cause'.

[36] Ryan, 'Correspondence of Allen', p. 31. Since Allen had copies of both statements, Persons' also must have been opened and read. Was it judged too tame for wider circulation? Or was the reputation of Campion the deciding factor?

was another matter. In a letter presumably written to the General in November, Campion explained the situation carefully and cautiously:

> I had put in writing in the form of propositions some very reasonable postulates and demands. I admitted that I was a priest of the Society who had come with the purpose of spreading Catholic faith, teaching the Gospel and administering the Sacraments. I begged audience with the Queen and the principal men of the kingdom, and I challenged my adversaries to a contest. I decided to keep one copy by me for when I should be taken before the magistrates. The other I gave to a friend, so that if they should lay hold of me and my possessions, the other might be passed around indefinitely. My friend, far from concealing it, had it printed and published.[37]

According to Campion, many Anglican theologians claimed that they were ready to accept the challenge but were unable to do so because the Queen had forbidden further disputations on matters that had long been settled.

In the uproar the Jesuits were called 'seditious, hypocritical, even heretical'. Yet, Campion reasoned, this 'mistake has served our cause' because the government would be obliged to grant the requested disputation – and that is something that they would not be eager to do! The whole affair, according to Campion, was a mistake but one that could be wonderfully exploited by the Catholics. We know not whether Mercurian would have accepted his explanation or, indeed, whether he would have had second thoughts regarding the mission's future because of the mistake. Perhaps it was fortunate for Campion and Persons that Mercurian had died on 1 August and the Society's Vicar-General was Oliver Mannaerts, then a strong supporter of the mission.

III

Two rejoinders quickly greeted the sudden appearance of a well-known champion: the Puritan William Charke's *An answere to a seditious pamphlet lately cast abroade by a jesuite, with a discoverie of that blasphemous sect*[38] and Meredith Hanmer's *The great bragge and challenge of M. Champion a jesuite.*[39] The second contributed to the wider circulation of Campion's 'Brag' because its full text was published for refutation. Both authors claimed that the time for religious debates had passed. The religious issue had been settled. According to Charke it was silly to answer

---

[37] ARSI, Fondo Gesuitico 651/612. Henry More included the letter in his *Historia Provinciae Anglicanae Societatis Jesu* (St Omers, 1660), pp. 74–76. In Edwards's translation, *Elizabethan Jesuits*, it can be found on pp. 88–91. The letter lacks both an address and a date. Because of Campion's statement that he had been in the kingdom for five months, it must have been written in November. Compare Persons' account in his letter of 17 November to Agazzari, in Hicks, *Letters of Persons*, pp. 57–58.

[38] (London, 1580) STC 5005.

[39] (London, 1581) STC 12745.

every vain challenge after so many years of religious peace. Moreover a response was not needed since true Christians were 'so assured of the manifest trueth'. As for those who sought conferences, they were so vowed to error and their minds were so closed to truth that there was nothing to be gained from a debate.

Hanmer wondered if in his eagerness to 'play the champion', Campion really thought that he could add anything to the arguments advanced by Harding, Sanders, and the other Catholic theologians? What new insight could he contribute to a debate that was long over? Or had Campion forgotten how his colleagues had been vanquished, how all their accusations had been answered, how all their arguments had been destroyed and all their proofs shown to be untenable? Yet both were willing to participate in a debate if it were absolutely necessary. Both however insisted that any contest must be rooted in Scripture alone; the use of 'naturall and morall reason . . . two great nourses of Atheisme and heresie', and of conciliar decrees, canons, and constitutions was unacceptable.[40]

Under the assumed name of John Howlet, Robert Persons entered the battle with *A brief discours contayning certayne reasons why Catholiques refuse to goe to Church.*[41] In the opening dedication to the Queen, duly acknowledged 'Most Highe & Mightie Princesse Elizabeth by the grace of God, Quene of England France and Irland &c', Persons reminded Her Majesty that the Catholics, although first challenged at Paul's Cross, had been prevented from acceptance. Indeed, Protestant challengers later had obtained a proclamation from the Queen that prohibited Catholic books. Persons urged that some form of public disputation be held so that 'mens doubtes might be resolved'. Many were eager to accept the challenge; therefore Persons, 'in their names, most humblie on my knees, even for God's cause and the love of his truth', pleaded that some form of trial be arranged. He suggested either scholastic debates, speeches, or sermons. The Catholic party asked nothing more than a promise of safe conduct.

Persons' *A brief censure vppon two bookes written in answere to M. Edmonde Campions offer of disputation*[42] was more pugnacious. Protestant rebuttals had been ineffective. The challenge had been made and it could not be explained away. It must be either accepted or rejected. If the authors were serious in their desire to establish Protestantism firmly and permanently within the kingdom, a victory at a disputation was the most secure way. The Catholics could and did continue the battle with their pens, as Hanmer had suggested, but the distribution of their books remained a major problem. Yet Persons marvelled that, instead of taking advantage of the opportunity offered, the Protestant writers asserted that all English subjects not members of the established Church were traitors and the Queen's enemies. Would Charke, Persons wondered, then agree that his

---

40 *An answere to a seditious pamphlet*, A iii^r, iiii^{r–v}, [v^r], v^v, vi^r, C iii^{r–v}, v^{r–v}; *The great bragge*, A 3^v, 8^v, 18^v, 19^v, 20^r, 21^v.

41 (Doway [*vere* London], 1580), STC 19394, ARCR II, no. 613.

42 (Doway [*vere* London], 1581), STC 19393, ARCR II, no. 612.

so-called martyrs during the reign of Queen Mary were also traitors because they refused to accept the Church as then established?

Regardless of Charke's reply to this rhetorical question, the very topic was a smokescreen to obscure the real issue. Contrary to Charke's dismissal of the challenge because the religious question had already been answered and the new contenders had nothing new to merit a re-examination, a victory would benefit the Protestant cause 'for they shal gayne al the Catholiques in England to their side, and us that are abrode also, if they can shew the truthe to be with them'. Because both Charke and Hanmer insisted that any disputation be based solely on Scripture, Persons defended the value of ecclesiastical history, conciliar pronouncements, the fathers of the Church, and reason:

> For by Councelles, Fathers, and Stories, we come to knowe not onlie which is the worde of God, and whiche is not: but also, which is the righte meaning of the same, among soe infinite wrong interpretations, which so manye hereticks from time to time have invented upon the same. . . . And albeit these thinges may be abused, as also Scripture may: yet is it grosse ignorance, for an abuse that may be, to condemne the thinges which are excellent giftes of God, and sparkes of his most high and infinite wisdome. To deprive us therfor of al these helpes, and to turne us over onely to a bare letter of Scripture, the which eche man may ether deny to be Scripture, or wrangle at his pleasure uppon the sense, it is as much to saye, as that controversies in religion, shall never be ended: as both reason teacheth us, and experience, not only of al ages past, but also of our times, sheweth.

Heretics have always insisted that Scripture alone be the rule of Christian faith. It is therefore no surprise that sixteen distinct sects have developed out of the movement started by Luther.[43]

IV

Campion's follow-up to the 'Brag', *Rationes decem*,[44] was secretly distributed in the University Church of St Mary's in Oxford on 27 June 1581. In it Campion repeated his challenge and chided his critics for personal attacks and slanders about the Society instead of consent to a debate. The only honest answer, Campion contended, was the one they refused to give: 'We embrace the conditions, the Queen pledges her word, come at once.' Instead they shouted 'Conspirator!' 'Traitor!' and accused him of arrogance.[45] Because other works, e.g. Persons' *Brief Censure*, had exonerated the reputation of the Society from the

---

[43] *Ibid.*, A ii^r, [D viii^r], E i^r, E ii^v–[E vii^r], F ii^r.

[44] *Rationes decem* (np [Stonor Park], nd [1581]) STC 4536.5, ARCR I, no. 135.1. It was translated and edited by John H. Pollen, S.J. and published as *Campion's Ten Reasons* (London, 1914). All citations will be from this edition.

[45] *Campion's Ten Reasons*, p. 90.

libels of Charke and Hanmer, Campion's task was a simple one: to explicate ten reasons for his confidence.

The first two reasons concerned Scripture. Protestants either had eliminated passages that contradicted their doctrines, or twisted the meaning of such passages to conform to their heresy. Having dismissed the fathers of the Church, having discarded ecclesiastical traditions, having destroyed liturgical practices, Protestants continued their devastation with the dissection of Scripture. If asked on whose authority such decisions are made, the Protestants always reply 'the Spirit'. As a result, 'in believing all things every man in the faith of his own spirit, they horribly belie and blaspheme the name of the Holy Ghost'.[46] Whenever there is a disagreement over proper interpretation of a Scriptural passage, Catholics appeal to the authority of the Church, the fathers, the saints; Protestants seek refuge in Luther and Calvin and their followers.

Protestants – the third reason – have destroyed the nature of the Church. Because of an inability to trace their theological pedigree, they claimed a Church 'all hidden away'. As a result the Church has ceased to be a visible, historical entity and has become an invisible community perceived by only a few. Fourthly, Campion appealed to the ecumenical councils. If, and here Campion apparently had John Jewel in mind, 'England' approved the teachings of the early councils as she claimed, why did she not accept their decrees on the primacy of Rome and the sacrifice of the Mass? Campion was willing to demonstrate that other councils, including the Council of Trent, possessed the same authority. From his consideration of councils, Campion concluded 'the man who refuses consideration and weight to a Plenary Council, brought to a conclusion in due and orderly fashion, seems to me witless, brainless, a dullard in theology, and a fool in politics'.[47]

The fifth and sixth reasons were the testimonies of the fathers of the Church. If appeal to the fathers was permitted, the battle was won for the Catholics; for 'they are as thoroughly ours as is Gregory XIII. himself, the loving Father of the children of the Church'.[48] In fact no contemporary recusant theologian could repudiate Protestant arguments as vigorously as the fathers. Campion recalled Jewel's 'incredible arrogance' when he cited the fathers as witnesses in his infamous challenge. From the consequent controversy all came 'to understand that the Fathers were Catholics, that is to say ours'.[49] The fathers were not the only witnesses to the legitimacy of the Roman Church: the entire history of the Church – the seventh reason – attested to it. Protestants granted that the Roman Church was once holy, Catholic, and Apostolic. When, Campion asked, did it cease to be so? When did Rome cease to be what she was?

The inherent weaknesses in the writings of the Protestants and their fallacious

[46] *Ibid.*, p. 96.
[47] *Ibid.*, p. 105.
[48] *Ibid.*, p. 109.
[49] *Ibid.*, p. 115.

logic were the eighth and ninth reasons. Regardless of a person's knowledge, eloquence, and rhetorical skills, 'his thought must dry up and his utterance fail him when he shall have to maintain such impossible positions'.[50] Citing specific passages such as Calvin's statement 'God is the author and cause of evil, willing it, suggesting it, effecting it, commanding it, working it out, and guiding the guilty counsels of the wicked to this end', Campion judges such views to be 'so odious, so tasteless, so stupid' that he would do battle against them. Moreover their argumentation was fallacious, but Campion preferred to unravel it before a university audience.

Finally, the truth of the Roman Catholic position has been affirmed by all manner of witnesses throughout the ages: saints and sinners, bishops and heretics, kings and serfs. Whose company do you prefer? asked Campion in his conclusion: Luther and Calvin or the witnesses of the ages? Borrowing the Ignatian image of the two standards, Campion exhorted his readers to renounce heresy, the means by which the devil extended his kingdom, and to rally round the true King with whom they 'may gain triumphs, and show [themselves] men truly most learned, truly most illustrious'.[51]

The impact of *Rationes decem* was felt well beyond the walls of the University Church. Sometime in July William Cecil, Lord Burghley, wrote to John Aylmer, Bishop of London, about the book. All attempts to obtain a copy, the bishop replied, had been in vain. By the 27th Aylmer received a copy from Burghley. He read it with interest and suggested that a counter-attack could focus on Campion's use of the Septuagint instead of the Hebrew Bible. Moreover the passages from Luther, Calvin, and Beza selected by Campion for ridicule meant nothing to the established Church and could be ignored. Nonetheless Aylmer excused himself from entering the contest for reasons of health. He did, however, ask the Regius Professors at both Oxford and Cambridge to write a rebuttal.[52] William Whitaker, professor at Cambridge, quickly published a Latin rejoinder, *Ad rationes decem Edmundi Campiani Iesuitae responsio*.[53] In September Aylmer informed Burghley that he intended to have Whitaker's booklet translated, but an English translation did not appear until 1606.[54]

Meanwhile the Scottish Jesuit John Dury joined the fray with a reply to Whitaker.[55] Laurence Humphrey, Regius Professor at Oxford, wrote a longer

---

50 *Ibid.*, p. 122.

51 *Ibid.*, p. 145.

52 Probably unsolicited, Sir William Herbert wrote a brief rejoinder that was never published. The manuscript can be found in British Library, Lansdowne MS 97, no. 7. Herbert had been Laurence Humphrey's student at Oxford and was knighted by the queen on 21 December 1578. See DNB.

53 (London, 1581), STC 25358.

54 Aylmer's letters can be found in British Library, Lansdowne MS 33, nos. 17, 18, 19, 23, and 24. They are discussed in Simpson, *Campion*, pp. 357–60. The translation is *An answere to the ten reasons of E. Campion the Iesuit* (London, 1606), STC 25360.

55 *Confutatio responsionis Gulielmi Whitakeri . . . ad Rationes decem . . .* (Paris, 1582), ARCR I, no.

reply, the first volume of which appeared in 1582 and the second in 1584.[56] Campion, however, played no further role: on 17 July, less than a month after the distribution of *Rationes decem*, he was betrayed by a lapsed Catholic and captured at Lyford Grange in Berkshire. By the 22nd he was in the Tower of London, imprisoned in the narrow dungeon, Little Ease, and twice tortured.[57] On the 25th he was taken to the house of his former patron Robert Dudley, Earl of Leicester. Special favours and rapid promotions were promised to him if he would only disown *Rationes decem* and conform to the established Church. Having failed to seduce Campion, the government sought to discredit him.

V

By the end of July rumours circulated throughout London that Campion was yielding to government pressure and would shortly conform to the established Church. It was claimed that Campion's confessions revealed the names of Catholics who had housed him on his travels. In early August the Privy Council issued warrants for officials to search the houses of his hosts. The examination of many known Catholics and the reports that their names had been given to the government by Campion alarmed many, one of whom was Thomas Pounde. From prison Pounde wrote to Campion secretly to inform him of the reports being spread about his confession and to encourage him 'to play the man'. In his reply Campion admitted that he had named a few houses out of frailty but that he had revealed nothing that the government had not already known, nor would he 'come rack, come rope'.[58]

---

334. Whitaker's reply was *Responsionis ad decem illas rationes . . . Defensio contra Confutationem Ioannis Duraei Scoti, Presbyteri Iesuitae . . .* (London, 1583), STC 23562. In a letter probably to Claudio Acquaviva in the first half of 1588 (ARSI, Fondo Gesuitico 651/648 and printed in Thomas M. McCoog, S.J., ed., 'The Letters of Robert Southwell, S.J.', *AHSI* 63 (1994), p. 111), Robert Southwell called Whitaker a 'famous and notable manufacturer of lies.' Nonetheless Whitaker was respected by Robert Bellarmine. See Robert W. Richgels, 'The Pattern of Controversy in a Counter-Reformation Classic: The *Controversies* of Robert Bellarmine', *Sixteenth Century Journal* 11 (1980), pp. 3–15.

56 *Iesuitismi pars prima: sive de praxi Romanae curiae contra respublicas et principes, et de nova legatione Iesuitarum in Angliam . . . praemonitio* (London, 1582), STC 13961; *Iesuitismi pars secunda: Puritanopapismi, seu doctrinae iesuiticae . . . confutatio* (London, 1584), STC 13962.

57 Persons' account of the events leading up to Campion's capture and ending with Campion's arrival at the Tower can be found in his letter to Acquaviva, London 30 August [1581], ARSI, Fondo Gesuitico 651/640. On the use of torture to extract 'truth' from Campion, see Elizabeth Hanson, 'Torture and Truth in Renaissance England', *Representations* 34 (1991), pp. 53–84. Because of alarm about the presence of Jesuits, authorization for the use of torture was given by the Privy Council on 1 December 1580 'to make some example of them by punishement, to the terrour of others . . .' (APC, XII, pp. 271, 294–95. See also Michael A.R. Graves, *Thomas Norton: The Parliament Man* [Oxford, 1994], pp. 249–50).

58 Neither Pounde's letter nor Campion's reply is extant. Historians have reconstructed their contents from various reports. For more details, see Simpson, *Campion*, pp. 348–49;

Despite the protests of the Bishop of London, it was decided by a higher authority that the popularity of *Rationes decem* demanded a public disputation to demonstrate that the government was not afraid of a discussion. Bishop Aylmer complied: he ordered Alexander Nowell, Dean of St Paul's, and William Day, Dean of Windsor, to prepare for a debate on 31 August.[59] In the guidelines drawn up before the first debate by either the disputants or the Bishop of London, it was agreed that they would abstain from angry words and *ad hominem* arguments, ground their case firmly in Scripture, and insist that Campion's was rooted only in human tradition.[60]

The conferences were held on 31 August and 18, 23, and 27 September.[61] The first three were in the parish church of St Peter ad Vincula within the Tower; the fourth, in the hall within the lieutenant's house. Each debate was divided into two sessions, from 8:00 until 11:00 and then from 2:00 to 5:00. Every effort was made to insure that the right side won the contest. The Anglicans had time and assistance for preparation; Campion, on the other hand, was not informed of either the event or the topics until a few hours before the start. In the conferences Nowell and Day were succeeded by William Fulke; Roger Goade, former Vice-Chancellor of Cambridge University; William Charke, and John Walker, Archdeacon of Essex.

The topics included justification by faith, the nature of the Church, real presence in the Eucharist, and the canon of Scripture. Throughout Campion was on the defensive and allowed only to answer the points raised. Books were provided for the Anglicans; Campion was given a Bible and the assistance of

---

Henry Foley, S.J., *Records of the English Province of the Society of Jesus*, 7 vols in 8 (Roehampton/London, 1875–83), III, pp. 650–52. On the authenticity of the confessions, compare Simpson, who argues that they are forgeries (*Campion*, pp. 351–56), and John H. Pollen, S.J., 'Blessed Edmund Campion's Confessions', *The Month* 134 (1919), pp. 258–61. Although Pollen grants their authenticity, he argues that 'it was not cowardice which led Campion to make his grave mistake, but that exaggerated deference to authority which was the common failing of his age'. A copy of the confessions can be found in British Library, Lansdowne MS 30, no. 78.

59 Simpson, *Campion*, pp. 362–63.

60 London, Inner Temple Petyt MS 538, vol. 47, f. 18. This illustrates G.R. Evans' claim that in the Reformation debates there had developed a ' "power-struggle" between the divine gift of Scripture and the rival authorities of human scholarship, human fancy, human reasoning, human opinion, human tradition, and above all a "human" Church authority' and 'the Bible was being set over against this "merely human" Church as though they were rival authorities' (*Problems of Authority*, pp. 241, 281).

61 The Protestant account is Alexander Nowell and William Day, *A true report of the Disputation or rather private Conference had in the Tower of London, with Ed. Campion Iesuite, the last of August 1581* and *The three last dayes conferences had in the Tower with Edmund Campion Iesuite, the 18: 23 and 27 of September 1581* published together in London in 1583 (STC 18744). The Catholic accounts can be found in British Library, Harleian MS 422, ff. 132ʳ–33ʳ; 136ʳ–72ᵛ; Add. MS 39828, f. 38 (printed in Historical Manuscripts Commission, *Various Collections*, 8 vols [London, 1901–1914], III, pp. 8–16); Add. MS 11055, f. 188ʳ–92ᵛ; Oxford, Bodleian Library, Rawlinson MS D 353, ff. 1–35. Before the debates can be studied in detail, the different versions must be correlated.

Ralph Sherwin. From the beginning, the author of the *Rationes decem* was the centre of attention and the object of attack. The crowds that flocked to the first debate quietly dwindled as it became clear that the intention was not the pursuit of truth but the humiliation of the Jesuit.

Despite the control exercised over topics and format, the government was not satisfied with the debates' progress. On 27 September Bishop Aylmer complained to Burghley that he did not approve allowing so many to attend the debates, presumably because Campion was doing well. Opposed to the conferences from the start, Aylmer argued that they should now be aborted.[62] Thomas Norton, Campion's 'rackmaster', echoed Aylmer's concern. In late September he drafted a list of recommendations for future conferences. He advocated fewer Anglican disputants, greater control over the topics, stricter observance of rules for debates, and tighter restrictions on observers.[63] Despite government efforts, tales circulated that Campion was holding his own. A certain Cawood was thrown into the Clink for declaring Campion victor. Oliver Pluckett of Holborn was questioned because he praised Campion's learning.[64]

As a consequence of Aylmer's anxieties, Norton's suggestions, and popular rumors, a fifth debate scheduled for 13 October was cancelled. Laurence Humphrey admitted that he had been summoned by Aylmer to that debate and that, as he was preparing to travel up to London, a second letter informed him that the debate had been cancelled:

> It was then, perhaps, smelt out that a different course was to be taken with the Jesuits, and that they would have to plead not for religion, but for life, and be accused not of heresy, but of treason.[65]

On 20 November Campion was tried at Westminster Hall. It was claimed that he and seven other priests had plotted treason and conspired against the life of the Queen. He was charged under Edward III's Act of Treason (1351) and found guilty. On 1 December Campion, his debating partner Ralph Sherwin, and Alexander Briant were martyred at Tyburn. In the translator's preface to Pollen's edition of the *Rationes decem*, J.R. [Joseph Rickaby, S.J.] observed that the 'Protestant answer to the Ten Reasons was not given in the Divinity School at Oxford. It was the rack in the Tower, and the gibbet at Tyburn; and that answer was returned ere the year was out.'[66]

[62] British Library, Lansdowne MS 33, no. 24.
[63] Graves, *Thomas Norton*, pp. 263–65.
[64] Simpson, *Campion*, p. 379. See also Reynolds, *Campion and Parsons*, pp. 144–48.
[65] Quoted in Simpson, *Campion*, p. 360.
[66] *Campion's Ten Reasons*, p. 88.

VI

Father Pollen placed the blame for the early release of Campion's 'Brag' entirely on Pounde, who circulated the unsealed statement. Indeed, according to Pollen,

> it is clear that Pounde set up an ideal which was distinctly different from that contemplated by Father Mercurian. Instead of the Jesuits being expected to confine their ministrations more or less exclusively to their co-religionists, the great public began to look for disputations and challenges to disputation as an integral, perhaps a leading feature in the Jesuits' missionary work.[67]

In fact, one wonders if Pollen does not have it backwards. The stress on disputation did not originate with Pounde. Indeed, Pounde began his agitation for a debate only after his meeting with Campion and Persons. Had they convinced him of its value? It seems that Persons' understanding of the mission was more harmonious with Allen's than with Mercurian's because of the emphasis on eloquence and disputation in his account of the journey to England. The General allowed them to debate only if they were forced to do so. Even then, as we have seen, the General warned them that heretics would never concede defeat. Allen, on the other hand, valued eloquence and intelligence and, as we have seen, requested the assistance of English Jesuits who possessed either or both. Had Allen and Persons won over a reluctant Campion by demonstrating the importance of his reputation and abilities for the encounters foreseen?

The early release of Campion's profession – whether accidental or calculated – provided the justification the two Jesuits needed to abandon Mercurian's instructions. Thomas Harding and others had earlier rebutted Bishop Jewel through their books; now Campion and Persons came in person to pick up the thrown gauntlet and to prove the truth of the Catholic faith. All things considered, Pollen concluded, the premature publication of the 'Brag' was a *felix culpa*. Perhaps, but culpability must not rest solely on Pounde.

Campion's and Persons' Protestant contemporaries accused them of insolence. Many since have thought them naive. Did they honestly think that a successful disputation would undo the religious settlement established twenty years earlier? Did they expect the walls of Jericho to fall? Nowhere does either state that as a goal. Their design was much more moderate. Commenting on Campion's *Rationes decem*, Persons claimed:

> And truly I can affirm of my knowledge that it was Fr Campian's perpetual opinion that heresy was desperate and that few or no men of judgment did think in their consciences that doctrine to be true and defensible that was commonly taught and practised, the absurdities thereof being so many and

---

[67] 'Blessed Edmund Campion's "Challenge" ', *The Month* 115 (1910), p. 64.

manifest as they were; but that some, of policy, some for present government, others for ease, others for gain, honour, and preferment, and all commonly for some temporal interest or other did stretch out a hand to hold it up for a time by force and violence.[68]

Both believed that many supported the established Church half-heartedly or out of self-interest.[69] A public demonstration of the truth of Catholicism would confirm the faith of Catholics and weaken the commitment of waverers by exposing the sophistry of Protestantism and the threat that it posed to their salvation.

Their efforts at embarrassing the government finally gained a disputation, but not the type that they had hoped. Both had asked that the Catholic participants be granted immunity from the penal laws so that they could engage in the debates. But the Catholic participants were prisoners and the content and style of the debates were controlled. Charke and Hanmer were right: the time for discussion had passed. New anti-Catholic, anti-Jesuit legislation was the official response.[70] Allen's strategy had failed: Catholicism may have had the most articulate spokesmen, but the government was not willing to provide a platform from which they could attack the established Church. Moreover the new legislation had altered the situation. Orthodoxy and heresy were replaced with loyalty and treason. In 1581 and 1582 Allen and Persons issued new challenges, but this strategy was gradually abandoned.[71] Events had confirmed Mercurian's evaluation. In 1583 George Gilbert claimed that 'the heretical spirit is so much given to pride that few of them are converted by argument, because they object to being beaten'.[72] In a way Persons returned to a policy that had been the norm in the Society. Ignatius Loyola believed that gentle preaching was more effective than direct confrontation. Diatribes were unnecessary. The careful exposition of

---

[68] 'Life of Campian', p. 65.

[69] On the opposition to occasional conformity or Church papistry, see Alexandra Walsham, *Church Papists* (London, 1993).

[70] On this see John J. LaRocca, S.J., 'Popery and Pounds: The Effect of the Jesuit Mission on Penal Legislation' in this volume.

[71] William Allen asked for a disputation in *An apologie and true declaration of the institution and endevours of the two English colleges* (Mons, 1581), STC 369, ARCR II, no. 6. He contended that the Westminster conference of 1559 was 'without al order and indifferencie, and at that time when there was such a greedy desire of novelty and change, that wil and affection forcibly overruled al the matter' (ff. 65ᵛ, 66ʳ). Persons renewed the challenge in *A defence of the Censure, gyven upon two bookes of William Charke and Meredith Hanmer, mynysters* (np [Rouen], 1582), STC 19401, ARCR II, no. 624), p. 9.

[72] 'A Way to Deal with Persons of All Sorts', in Hicks, *Letters of Persons*, p. 334. In an undated but clearly Elizabethan 'Some Instructions for Members of the Society Living in England in These Times', the author, presumably Persons, stated 'it is characteristic of heretics never to be willing to give in to any man – even the most learned – in the presence of others. Hence, as a general rule, at table or in other groups where a heretic might be present, there must be no talk about controversial matters, unless one should judge from other circumstances that this would be very useful for the glory of God . . .' (ARSI, Rom. 156/II, f. 167ᵛ).

Catholicism was more persuasive than controversy.[73] Spiritual works were more effective.[74]

The triumphal procession that left Rome in April 1580 was in ruins sixteen months later. By the end of August 1581 Campion was in the Tower and Persons was a fugitive in France. There, as he explained to the General, he hoped to establish a press to publish the books needed for the mission. Moreover, as a result of political developments, 'the greatest hope we have lies in Scotland, on which country depends the conversion not only of England but of all the lands in the North'.[75] Persons may have lost the first battle, but now in France, with new friends and new strategies, he would continue his work for the conversion of England.[76]

---

[73] For more on this approach to Protestants, see Thomas M. McCoog, S.J., 'Ignatius Loyola and Reginald Pole: A Reconsideration', *Journal of Ecclesiastical History*, forthcoming.

[74] On this, see Michael Questier, ' "Like Locusts over all the World": Conversion, Indoctrination and the Society of Jesus in late Elizabethan and Jacobean England' in this volume.

[75] Persons to Acquaviva, 21 October 1581, in Hicks, *Letters of Persons*, p. 109. Contrary to Michael L. Carrafiello's assertion that Persons focussed on Scotland from the start of the mission ('English Catholicism and the Jesuit Mission of 1580–1581', *Historical Journal* 37 [1994] pp. 761–74), Persons first became interested in Scotland as a refuge for English Catholics and only gradually as a base for a more militant type of conversion of England.

[76] See John Bossy, 'The Heart of Robert Persons' in this volume.

8

The Heart of Robert Persons[1]

JOHN BOSSY

For a long time I have felt unhappy about Edmund Campion. His angelism, his rhetorical mode, his way of turning a mission into a melodrama, all seem unattractive; sometimes I think that it was only after his partial collapse under interrogation that he turned out to be human after all. This is probably very unfair; besides, in so far as I have in mind his doings during his mission in England, I may only be repeating what he had implied to William Allen as he came through Rheims from Rome on the way, that he would have been better suited if he had been allowed to remain in Prague.[2] Still, whenever I have met the classic twin portrait of himself and his companion Robert Persons, painted in contrasting white and black, I have felt like protesting. Yes, Persons was no angel, he got his hands dirty, he was touched with the sin of the world; but if he had kept himself as clean as Campion perhaps nothing would have got done at all. I have also admired what I took, rightly or wrongly, to be Persons' understanding that the English mission was a difficult operation and might be an unrewarding one, and that the walls of Jericho were not going to fall down at the first blast of the Jesuit trumpet.[3] There was surely a romanticism here, perhaps as much as in the usual portrait of Campion: a version of the political romanticism or counter-romanticism which has flourished in the world during the past fifty years, and has been used to justify various kinds of terrorism.[4] There *was*

---

[1]   An earlier version of this piece appeared, under the title 'The Society of Jesus in the Wars of Religion', in *Monastic Studies: The Continuity of Tradition*, ed. Judith Loades (Bangor, 1990), pp. 229–44. I have now completely rewritten it.

[2]   Robert Persons, 'Of the Life and Martyrdom of Fr Edmond Campian', *Letters and Notices* 11 (1877), pp. 219–42, 308–39; 12 (1878), pp. 1–68, at 12, p. 11. I am grateful to Dr Munitiz for providing me with a copy of the 'Life'.

[3]   Cf. my *English Catholic Community, 1570–1850* (London, 1976), p. 19.

[4]   I discuss the point in my 'Unrethinking the Sixteenth-Century Wars of Religion', in Thomas Kselman, ed., *Belief in History: Innovative Approaches to European and American Religion* (Notre Dame/London, 1991), pp. 273–75.

141

something the matter with the conventional twin portrait; but it will emerge that turning it back to front was not the way to make it more lifelike.

I have nothing to say about Campion; but a source of new knowledge about Persons has recently been inching into view. It is a correspondence between him and the General of the Society, Claudio Acquaviva, beginning in August 1581 just after Campion's arrest, about the time when Persons left England for France, and ending four years later. It is not complete, but it contains some forty letters.[5] Some of Persons' were published by Leo Hicks in his edition of Persons' letters; Hicks also cited Acquaviva's side of the correspondence, and some of it has been used by A. Lynn Martin in his *Henry III and the Jesuit Politicians*, the most recent addition to public information on the subject.[6] But a number of them were not known to either Hicks or Martin when they published. I shall now try to give an outline of the correspondence as a whole, keeping particularly in mind what its partners had to say about two things: the politics of the Wars of Religion during their most aggressive period; and the implications of these for the history of the Jesuit 'institute' as a mode of religious life.

On each of these matters there is something to be said before we start. The Jesuit ethos committed members of the Society to a life of external activity with the purpose of assisting the salvation of souls; it also embraced the doctrine of 'finding God in all things'. Did this doctrine allow or encourage Jesuits to engage in political activity? Ignatius had been laconic on the subject, but it seems reasonably clear that he had no objection, where he thought the general interest

---

[5]   The main source is ARSI, Fondo Gesuitico 651 (*Epistolae Selectae ex Anglia*). This contains files of letters from Englishmen, arranged alphabetically by author; the one containing Persons' letters is numbered 640. Other files from it have been used by Christopher Devlin, S.J., *The Life of Robert Southwell: Poet and Martyr* (London, 1956), see viii; Philip Caraman, S.J., *Henry Garnet (1565–1606) and the Gunpowder Plot* (London, 1964); and Penelope Renold, *Letters of William Allen and Richard Barret, 1572–1598* (London, 1967), CRS 58, who gives references to some of Persons' letters. One of these is quoted in Leo Hicks, S.J., *An Elizabethan Problem: Some Aspects of the Careers of Two Exile Adventurers* (London, 1964), pp. 117 ff. Southwell's letters have now been published by Thomas M. McCoog, S.J., ed., 'The Letters of Robert Southwell, S.J.', *AHSI* 63 (1994), pp. 101–24; Father McCoog is also preparing an edition of those of Persons. The other sources I have used from the same archive, mainly for Acquaviva's letters to Persons, are the volumes Francia I/1, and Gallia 44 and 91. I refer to these as described, and to the main source as FG 651 (the items in the file are not numbered). I should like to record my gratitude to Fr Edmond Lamalle, S.J., the then archivist, for the exceptional kindness and generosity he showed me when I was working in the archive in 1986, and for permission to quote.

[6]   Leo Hicks, S.J., ed., *Letters and Memorials of Fr Robert Persons, S.J.* (London, 1942) CRS 39; A. Lynn Martin, *Henry III and the Jesuit Politicians* (Geneva, 1973). Hicks published eight letters and three extracts of letters from Persons to Acquaviva; three letters from Gallia 91; one short extract, via a secondary source, from FG 651; and five letters and two extracts from elsewhere. To these we may now add from FG 651 ten to Acquaviva, including the full version of the one extracted and the one noticed in n. 5; and five more to Alfonso Agazzari, the rector of the English College in Rome, all from 1585 and part of a parallel correspondence much of which was published by Fr Hicks.

of Catholicism was at stake, to the sending of Jesuits on missions which an impartial observer would regard as political. It appears that Acquaviva understood him differently.[7]

The burning question in Catholic politics during the 1580s was, whether Catholics were entitled, or perhaps obliged, to organize, collaborate in or encourage civil or military action aimed at the overthrow of Protestant governments or of Catholic governments thought to be in collusion with them. The question arose in England and in France, both of whose governments were the object of Catholic political hostilities: in the English case, from a series of invasion schemes which preceded the Armada of 1588; and in the French, from the forces of Catholic zeal which organized themselves into the Catholic League of 1585 and precipitated a civil war and the assassination of King Henri III in 1589. The two cases were closely entangled with each other; in both, more or less of the responsibility has been attributed to Jesuits, in the English case to Persons. A word about the French case, which will probably be the less familiar. In France the 'black legend', as we may call it, had roots almost as strong as it had in England; but towards the end of the nineteenth century it was vigorously opposed by the official historian of the French Jesuits, Henri Fouqueray, who produced quite a lot of evidence to show that Acquaviva was very hostile to the Catholic League, and disciplined Jesuits whom he thought too closely connected with it. It has recently been revived in a modified form by Martin, who has indicated that Acquaviva's protestations of hostility to Catholic politics were not always candid, and in particular that he concealed from King Henri III that several of his subjects in France were actively engaged in Catholic politics in respect of England. The best authority at present on the French wars of religion takes the statesmanlike view that the Jesuits in France 'were by no means united in the Leaguer cause'.[8] Hence a correspondence between Acquaviva and Persons during the years 1581 to 1585 is likely to shed a good deal of light on controverted questions. Acquaviva, I should say, had been elected General of the Society in February 1581, in the middle of Campion's and Persons' mission to England; our correspondence took place at the very beginning of a distinguished generalship which was to last for thirty-four years.[9] I shall try, a little artificially,

---

[7] My favourite guides to the ethos of the Society are Thomas H. Clancy, S.J., *An Introduction to Jesuit Life* (St Louis, 1976) and H.O. Evennett, *The Spirit of the Counter Reformation* (Cambridge, 1968). On the political question, Paul de Chastonay, S.J., *Les Constitutions de l'ordre des Jésuites* (Paris, 1941), pp. 123, 149, 188–91; for Acquaviva, Martin, *Henry III*, pp. 98 ff., 139 ff., 160 n. 22, 203 ff.

[8] Henri Fouqueray, S.J., *Histoire de la Compagnie de Jésus en France*, 5 vols (Paris, 1910–25), II, pp. 120–81; Martin, *Henry III*, chaps. iv, vii–xv; J.H.M. Salmon, *Society in Crisis: France in the Sixteenth Century* (London, 1975), p. 237.

[9] The exterior facts of Acquaviva's generalship are recounted in William V. Bangert, S.J., *A History of the Society of Jesus* (St. Louis, 1972), pp. 97–176; interior matters in Joseph de Guibert, S.J. *The Jesuits: Their Spiritual Doctrine and Practice*, trans. William J. Young (St Louis, 1972 edn), pp. 230–81; also Clancy, *Introduction*, pp. 138–42.

to see it first from Persons' angle, where the matters at issue are relatively well known, then from Acquaviva's.

The political side of Persons' work was carried out in the context of a number of other activities which I shall only touch on: in particular, missionary operations and the writing and publishing of books, including his spiritual guide the *Book of Resolution*.[10] It had probably started in England, through his connections with the Spanish ambassador, Bernardino de Mendoza; for our purposes, the first relevant question was where he was to live: *mansio* seems to be the technical term. When he escaped from England, via the Sussex coast, he had come to Rouen in Normandy, and there he had been given houseroom by one of the more powerful clerical figures in the city, Michel de Monchy. De Monchy was a member of an important Norman noble family, a canon of the cathedral, Archdeacon of Rouen, and vicar-general of the non-resident archbishop, Cardinal Bourbon. The arrangement was made in secret, for good reason, and the secret was fairly successfully preserved as long as Persons remained there. The question between him and Acquaviva was whether he ought to be living more conventionally in a Jesuit house, and whether it was proper to keep his whereabouts secret. On both points Acquaviva deferred to Persons' judgement, though he eventually concluded that Persons was keeping up this mode of life longer than was good for himself or for the Society.[11] De Monchy's house was not a politically innocent situation, since he was the principal local figure in the semi-underground Catholic mafia which came out into the open in 1585 as the Catholic League. We do not know how Persons had made contact with him: a message from Mendoza to the future leader of the League, the Duke of Guise, and from him via Cardinal Bourbon, seems the likely channel. For political purposes Persons was from his arrival in France a Leaguer *avant la lettre*. I do not see how he could have avoided this. He needed political protection. But there was a price to pay, and he would shortly have to pay it.[12]

The cheque was cashed in May 1582, when he was summoned to Paris to attend a meeting between the Duke of Guise, the ambassadors in France of Spain, the Pope and Mary Queen of Scots, and William Allen, head of the

---

[10] The story is best followed in Hicks, *Letters of Persons*, pp. xxxix–lxxii; and in Persons' memoir, 'Notes Concerning the English Mission', ed. John H. Pollen, S.J. in *Miscellanea IV* (London, 1907), CRS 4, pp. 1–161). On the *Book of Resolution*, see Victor Houliston's 'Why Robert Persons Would not be Pacified: Edmund Bunny's Theft of *The Book of Resolution*', in this volume.

[11] Acquaviva to Persons, 17 February, 19 March, and 5 December 1582, 11 August 1583 (Francia I/1, ff. 121ᵛ, 130ᵛ, 144ᵛ, 170ᵛ).

[12] On De Monchy, Philip Benedict, *Rouen during the Wars of Religion* (Cambridge, 1981), index under name; and my Ph.D. thesis, 'Elizabethan Catholicism: The Link with France' (Unpublished D.Phil. thesis, University of Cambridge, 1961), pp. 78–91. There is a lot about De Monchy's relations with the Jesuits, which were close, in Acquaviva's correspondence; in 1584 Persons wrote recommending him for the bishopric of Verdun: to Acquaviva, 10 July 1584 (FG 651).

English College at Rheims and of the English mission as a whole. Guise was interested in direct action in Scotland and England. What the meeting recommended was a scheme for the invasion of Scotland in support of Guise's friend the Duke of Lennox, who was temporarily in control of the country, and for a subsequent invasion of England from the north which was intended to overthrow Elizabeth. After it, Persons and the Scottish Jesuit William Crichton were despatched to Lisbon and to Rome to deal with Philip II and Gregory XIII.[13] In Lisbon Persons found Philip, who was engaged in defending the Azores against an expedition supported by the French, none too keen on the idea. On his way back he fell seriously ill in northern Spain, and did not return to France until the following spring. Meanwhile the Duke of Lennox had been overthrown in Scotland, returned to France, and died. In August 1583 another meeting was called in Paris, which took the view that there should now be a two-pronged attack on England only, a force under Guise attacking Sussex and a Spanish force landing in the north-west. Although Philip was still unconvinced, and was shortly to wash his hands of the scheme, Francis Throckmorton was recruited as an agent in England to work in conjunction with Mendoza, and Persons sent on another mission, this time to Rome. He returned with a promise of money and with bulls renewing the excommunication of Elizabeth and appointing Allen Bishop of Durham in preparation for the enterprise; he was back by the middle of October. A month later the scheme was aborted by the arrest of Francis Throckmorton in London, and no further effort of the kind was attempted. Guise's interest in an expedition across the Channel faded with the death in June 1584 of King Henri III's brother and heir, the Duke of Anjou, which obliged Guise to fix his attention on an impending civil war in France.[14]

After his lightning trip to Rome, Persons went back to Rouen and resumed his interrupted missionary, logistical and literary work; but he was not able to keep out of politics, whether he wanted to or not. He was sent to the Netherlands with a brief to discover whether the enterprise of England, or some more modest version of it, could be taken up by Philip II's commander, the Duke of Parma. He had to attend to a movement of rising hostility against his role from English Catholic exiles in France and from his French colleagues in the Society. In the summer of 1585, when Allen appeared to be dying, he used his influence with the Guise family to plan a coup which would protect the college at Rheims from falling into what he considered the wrong hands.[15] Perhaps most remarkably, he

---

[13] Father de Medina's article treats Crichton's ongoing involvement in Scottish political affairs. See 'Intrigues of a Scottish Jesuit at the Spanish Court: Unpublished Letters of William Crichton to Claudio Acquaviva (Madrid 1590–1592)'.

[14] Philip Hughes, *The Reformation in England*, 3 vols (London, 1952–54), III, pp. 315–34; Hicks, *Letters of Persons*, pp. liii–lxii, 348–55.

[15] Persons and Parma: Persons to Mary, 10 October [?] 1585 (Hicks, *Letters of Persons*, pp. 246–52) and to Acquaviva, 12 February 1585 (below); Persons and the seminary: Persons to Agazzari, 12 August 1585 (FG 651); Richard Barret to Agazzari, 8 & 22 August 1585 (Renold, *Letters of Allen and Barret*, pp. 168, 172–75, where Persons' letter to Agazzari is cited).

avenged the failure of the invasion scheme by publishing and distributing in England and France the scurrilous, occasionally obscene, and highly successful polemic against Elizabeth's favourite the Earl of Leicester generally known as *Leicester's Commonwealth*. Whether he had written it himself is a debated question: I am now inclined to think that he had.[16] He left France in September 1585.

In the light of Acquaviva's record of antagonism to Catholic politics, we can expect his attitude to much of this to be fairly hostile, as indeed it was. But there could be no question of hostility on Acquaviva's part to Persons himself, for whom he had a fund of respect and admiration. They had met in Rome, when Persons had been negotiating the despatch of the Jesuit mission to England; Acquaviva knew his way around the Curia, and helped him. He is credibly reported to have wanted to go on the mission himself. For a time I think he regarded Persons as a model of what a Jesuit ought to be, a sort of Francis Xavier updated for the 1580s; taken as a whole, their correspondence indicates intimacy and warmth, and rather more of both on Acquaviva's side than on Persons'.[17] We may consider him as feeling towards Persons like a staff officer towards someone who has a history of bravery, tactical skill and organizational genius on the battlefield.

Nevertheless, there were issues between them, and not only about politics. There was a question about the mission which, like everything else, had political implications, but was really about a different aspect of the interpretation of the Jesuit institute. I shall say a little about it, because it helps to show the character of the relationship, and is something of a model for their exchanges on political matters. In his very first letter, written in reply to Persons' report that Campion had been arrested, Acquaviva insisted that there was an obligation on Jesuits in England to be careful, which Campion had not been. At Rouen Persons began to write Campion's life, and Acquaviva urged him to make sure that what he wrote was indeed a life, not an account of his martyrdom. Either Persons found the brief too puzzling, or his patrons in France wanted something else from him, for he abandoned the 'Life' for an account of the persecution of Catholics in England, and did not return to it for thirteen years. Then he produced a torso which was a good deal more conventional than what Acquaviva seems to have had in mind, and stopped before Campion's arrest. In practice Persons surely

---

[16] Its proper title was *The Copy of a Letter written by a Master of Art of Cambridge*, and it was seemingly printed at Rouen about June 1584: see the fine edition of Dwight C. Peck, ed, *Leicester's Commonwealth: "The Copy of a Letter Written by a Master of Art of Cambridge" (1584) and Related Documents* (Athens, Ohio, 1985), pp. 5–7. Peck accepts with qualifications the attribution of the work by Hicks to Charles Arundell: Leo Hicks, S.J., 'The Growth of a Myth: Fr Robert Persons, S.J., and *Leicester's Commonwealth*', *Studies* 46 (1957), pp. 91–105. Peter Holmes, *Resistance and Compromise: The Political Thought of the Elizabethan Catholics* (Cambridge, 1982), attributes it to Persons without qualification.

[17] Clancy, *Introduction*, p. 139; Persons described one of Acquaviva's letters as '*dolcissima*,' as indeed it was: Acquaviva to Persons, 19 March 1582 (Francia I/1 f. 130ᵛ); Persons to Acquaviva, 3 May 1582 (FG 651).

made it his business to din into departing missioners the message that they were being sent to do a job not, if they could help it, to get martyred. But I wonder if he altogether grasped the inwardness of Acquaviva's thought: that their task was not to edify the Church in general but to bring help and comfort to souls in England. Martyrdom, Acquaviva told Allen in a letter about Campion, was more meritorious than a life of toil, and Campion would have his reward; we can sense his implication that the salvation of the missioner's soul was not the purpose of his mission. This strikes me as a very proper judgement, in the circumstances perhaps a brave one. I suspect that the cautious and fruitful career of Henry Garnet in England was a consequence of it, and also the missionary narratives of William Weston and John Gerard, whose freshness and durability seem to reflect Acquaviva's wishes.[18]

I come to the political issue. Acquaviva interpreted Ignatius's guidelines to the Society as including a ban on political activity, though so far as I know he never stated his interpretation publicly, or said exactly what he meant. It was particularly relevant to France, where he took the long-sighted view that the future of the Society depended upon amicable relations with the French crown; but we have seen enough to realise that it was virtually impossible to separate the English case from the French. I imagine, simply from its date, that his first intervention in the matter was to remove from the instructions of Jesuits going to England the limited permission which had been given to Persons and Campion to engage in political dealings; this was done before the beginning of his correspondence with Persons, who was still in England.[19] When Persons got to France, he must have detected a change in the wind, but he appears to have carried on regardless. When his patrons required his attendance at the invasion committee in Paris, and still more when they sent him to Portugal, Persons was nervous about explaining to Acquaviva what had happened.[20] We do not have Acquaviva's reply, but he appears to have gone along with the *fait accompli*: he had indeed little choice. But he did not like it much, and there were limits to what he was prepared to tolerate.

During Persons' year in Portugal and Spain their correspondence was sparse, and although Persons on at least one occasion told Acquaviva what he was up to,

---

18 Acquaviva to Persons, 14 October 1581, 17 February & 19 March 1582, [?]3 July 1584 (Francia I/1, ff. 109ʳ, 121ᵛ, 130ᵛ, 197ᵛ); Acquaviva to Allen, 14 October 1581 (Patrick Ryan, S.J., ed., 'Some Correspondence of Cardinal Allen 1579–85', in *Miscellanea VII* [London, 1911] CRS 9, p. 80). See above, n. 2, for the 'Life of Campian'. On the mission and martyrdom, see Michael E. Williams, 'Campion and the English Continental Seminaries' in this volume.

19 Hicks, *Letters of Persons*, p. 318, n. 19.

20 Persons to Acquaviva, 3 May 1582 (FG 651): 'molte difficultà mi se offerivano in abbracciar questo viaggio, ma bisogna pigliarlo . . .'; in his 'Notes' p. 61, Persons says that the nuncio in Paris 'imposed' the journey on him, but I doubt whether in the strict sense he had the power to do this.

Acquaviva made no comment.[21] Then Persons fell ill. Eventually, towards the end of April, he wrote from Madrid a letter which does not survive. He had just talked to Philip again, and was about to return to France, where he arrived about the end of May; Acquaviva's reply is dated 5 June, and was sent to Paris. We have it in the form of a secretary's draft which is both very difficult to read and in parts, because of Acquaviva's circumlocutions, difficult to understand.[22]

Acquaviva begins by saying that, concerning 'the business of the princes' (*principum negotium*) he will find out in Paris what William Crichton has achieved in Rome: the Pope is still very keen to promote the enterprise, but will go no farther than supplying cash. Beyond this he is not willing to offer support (I am not sure what is meant), so Acquaviva does not see what he can do but commend the cause to God in prayer. If an opportunity occurs, he will be happy to take advantage of it.[23] At the end of the letter he pours cold water on two of Persons' ideas for furthering the English cause: having a special papal representative to deal with 'those matters' who will work either in Spain or in England; and sending a Spanish Jesuit to London, to operate from or in connection with the Spanish embassy.[24]

So far, we can infer on Acquaviva's part a zealous tepidity towards Persons' Spanish dealings, but no express objection to them. He had apparently packed Crichton off from Rome with an instruction to keep out of such matters in future;[25] Persons got off more easily. But a passage in the middle of the letter shows that, on one particular matter, he put his foot down. It concerns a cardinal ('*De Cardinali*,' it begins) in connection with whom Persons has made a proposal to Rome, perhaps through the nuncio to Philip II, and has had a reply by word of mouth. This, says Acquaviva, will be confirmed by a letter from his friend, now Acquaviva's English advisor, George Gilbert. So, if Persons wants the matter to be pursued, he will have to explain why 'that matter (*ea res*) cannot obstruct the business of the princes, such that (*ut*), if there is no other obstacle than this (*hoc*), once it is removed the difficulty will cease to exist'. He goes on: 'But, whether that be the case or not, it will be proper for the Society to get mixed up in that matter (*istam causam*) with extreme caution, or rather to keep out of it altogether, as something so little in accordance with our institute that it would be better proposed to the Pope by anyone else than by ourselves.'[26]

---

21 Hicks, *Letters of Persons*, pp. lv f, 167–71; Acquaviva to Persons, 8 November 1582 (Francia I/1, ff. 142^v, 144^v). As Martin says (*Henry III*, p. 101), in the first letter Acquaviva said that he had 'learned with pleasure' what Persons had to tell him; I take this to be politeness.

22 Acquaviva to Persons, 5 June 1583 (Gallia 44, ff. 9^v–10^r). The transcription of this letter has been a joint effort of Fr McCoog, Fr László Lukács, S.J. and myself; the translation below is my responsibility entirely.

23 Martin, *Henry III*, pp. 101, 107, 113 cites this sentence of the letter, but does not quote any of it.

24 Persons had broached the last idea before: Hicks, *Letters of Persons*, pp. 52, 104f.

25 Martin, *Henry III*, p. 101.

26 'De Cardinali Reverentia Vestra a Domino Georgio [Gilbert] intelliget responsum

In the second half of the passage quoted Acquaviva is being perfectly clear; in the first half he is mincing his words so diligently that without some gloss or emendation I cannot make him mean anything at all. In a general way, the reading of the passage does not seem very doubtful: it says that, if Persons wants his proposal connected with the cardinal to get anywhere, he will have to explain why something or other is the only real obstacle to the enterprise, and if it were removed there would be no question of its successful execution. The idea, whatever it was, was clearly very embarrassing to Acquaviva, and embarrassment has interfered with his dictation or his secretary's syntax. The problem seems to be with 'cannot' (*non possit*). Leaving out the 'not' would be a possibility, though a drastic one. Otherwise we might want to read 'cannot' not as 'will not', which appears to me to make the sentence self-contradictory, but as 'cannot be allowed to', which makes good sense; but this is probably not acceptable Latin, and if that was what was meant the phrase ought surely to have been *non debet* (ought not to). I leave the question to better Latinists.

What, in any case, can Persons have been saying? The first thing we can be sure of is that it was something to do with the *principum negotium* or enterprise, at this point envisaged as the invasion of England through Scotland; it was probably something Persons had talked about at his meeting with Philip II. The second thing is that Acquaviva thought it was not in keeping with the Jesuit institute. Hence it is something dubious; it is also something political, and not simply in the sense that the enterprise in general is political: Acquaviva has already, however unwillingly, approved of the enterprise as such. The third thing is that it is something to do with a cardinal. Looking around for possible cardinals, we may think of Cardinal Bourbon, Persons's protector in Rouen, and later the Catholic League's candidate for the French throne. Was Persons suggesting a *coup d'état* in France which would make the French monarchy keener than it was on the enterprise of England? No such scheme was on foot in 1583, and there is no evidence of anything of the kind remotely proximate to Persons. But there is another cardinal in connection with whom evidence of the kind we are looking for may be found: Tolemeo Galli, Cardinal of Como, ex-*protégé* of Carlo Cardinal Borromeo and Gregory XIII's secretary of state. If Gallio was the cardinal in question, we can surmise what Persons' dubious proposal was. It has long been a cause of embarrassment to well-wishers of the Counter-Reformation papacy that Gallio, and probably under his influence his master Gregory XIII, showed a good deal of interest in the idea of promoting the Catholic cause in England by the assassination of Queen Elizabeth. Three proposals for doing this were made

quod hic habitum est; quod quidem cum eo consentit quod Reverentia Vestra scribit sibi dictum fuisse. Quare si Reverentia Vestra negotium progredi cupit, exponere debebit rationes, cur ea res impedire non possit principum negotium, ut si nihil aliud quam hoc obstet [*deleted*: (nescit [? nescitur] enim ne quid aliud quo desideratur obstet)], hoc sublato, cesset impedimentum. Quoquo tamen modo res habeat, conveniet Societati valde caute se in istam causam se immiscere, vel potius sese abstinere, ut pote parum convenientem institutis nostris, ut propterea melius sit per alios quosvis apud Pontificem urgeri.'

to them: one in 1580, through the previous nuncio in Madrid, and warmly welcomed both by him and by Cardinal Gallio; the third by William Parry, from Paris, at the end of this year, 1583. In between, precisely in April 1583 or shortly before, another offer was made to the Duke of Guise by George Gifford, a gentleman pensioner of the Queen disgruntled, it was thought, for family reasons. Guise approached the nuncio in Paris about it, and the nuncio passed it on to Cardinal Galli on 2nd May.[27] On this hypothesis Persons will already have been told of the proposal by Guise, and instructed to help it along in Rome. The nuncio in Madrid, who had changed since 1580, seems to have been discouraging. Hence Persons' letter to Acquaviva of 25 April, and Acquaviva's response of 5 June: late enough for him to have found out what the cardinal thought about the matter, and to have deputed Gilbert to write Persons a letter which was no doubt less guarded than his own. I am sorry to say I think there can be no reasonable doubt that this hypothesis is correct. What Persons was putting to Acquaviva, and Acquaviva stiffly turning down, was Gifford's offer to assassinate Elizabeth. I do not think that '*ea res*' can exactly mean 'the assassination scheme': I cannot see how it could possibly be thought to obstruct the enterprise; it would make '*hoc*' something different from '*ea res*'; and the sequence of thought between the two parts of the phrase ('*cur ea res . . .*' and '*ut si nihil*') would be baffling. So I take '*ea res*' and '*hoc*' to mean something like 'the life of the Queen', or conceivably 'scruples about taking away the life of the Queen' (though these might not seem to amount to a *res*); '*non possit*' remains a problem, as it does with any other interpretation of the passage, but with that qualification the meaning is clear enough. Persons, no doubt under instructions from Guise, has said that Elizabeth's life is the only serious obstacle to the success of the enterprise, and that Guise ought therefore to be given permission to arrange her assassination. Acquaviva is expressing doubt as to whether Persons' premise is sound, and shock at the idea that Persons, or any member of the Society, should countenance the proposal, let alone agitate on its behalf.

Acquaviva's shock is something we can all share. To say the least, he was confirmed in his view that it had been a grave mistake for Persons to go on his

---

[27] Arnold Oskar Meyer, *England and the Catholic Church under Queen Elizabeth* (London, 1916, repr. London 1967), pp. 266–74, 490–91; Thomas Francis Knox, ed., *Letters and Memorials of William Cardinal Allen* (London, 1882), pp. xlvi–xlviii; John H. Pollen, S.J., ed., *Queen Mary and the Babington Plot* (Edinburgh, 1922), Publications of the Scottish History Society, 3rd series, 3, pp. xx–xxiii, 169–75, where all the documents relevant to Gifford's case, except the one discussed here, are printed. The Jesuit Jasper Heywood, one of Persons' immediate successors on the English mission, believed that Persons had thought up the idea himself, and complained to Acquaviva about it (*ibid.*, pp. 171f, 174). This appears to be impossible, Persons being in Spain at the time; but he certainly knew about it (*ibid.*, p. 175). Persons' interview with Philip II: Hicks, *Letters of Persons*, p. lviii. George Gifford was a regular performer at tournaments at the English court around this time: Roy Strong, *The Cult of Elizabeth: Elizabethan Portraiture and Pageantry* (London, 1977), pp. 206–07. See Dennis Flynn, ' "Out of Step": Six Supplementary Notes on Jasper Heywood' in this volume for the fundamental difference between Heywood and Persons about the politics of the mission.

mission to Philip II; his conclusion was that, since Persons was evidently not going to be able to avoid such disastrous entanglements so long as he was based in France, he had better get him out of the country. Two months later, when he must have received a reply to his previous letter which has not survived, he suggested that it was time for Persons to take a holiday:

> It has occurred to me that perhaps it would be a good idea for you to make a journey to Rome; which would not only bring us and your people [meaning I presume the English in Rome] much consolation, but also perhaps be of some help to the *negotia* themselves.[28]

Martin has taken the last phrase as evidence for Acquaviva's accommodation to the English or British enterprise and an authority for Persons' participation in it. Seen by itself, that is what it is. Seen in the light of what we have just found out, it must take on a different colour. Even if we presume that assassination was no longer on the agenda, since Gifford very shortly changed his mind, I take the phrase to be a concession, offered perhaps less to Persons himself than to his political masters, intended to undercut objections to his coming. The passage is certainly very tentative in form, but I do not think it will now seem an instance, as Martin claims, of Acquaviva's feeble and disingenuous handling of the matter. He had recently given Persons an exceptionally stiff rebuke, and I take it he was now seeing what could be done by gentle pressure.

The answer, for the time being, was: not much. Acquaviva must have had another shock when his letter crossed with one from Persons saying that he was indeed coming to Rome, and *instanter*, but coming on the business of the enterprise.[29] We have seen that he was bearing a revised set of instructions from Guise about the second invasion plan, which concerned England alone and entailed, among other things, the reissue of the bull of excommunication against Elizabeth. Persons certainly saw Acquaviva on his brief and busy visit; heaven alone knows what passed between them, and perhaps we had better not try to guess. Acquaviva gave up for the present his notion of getting Persons out of France, which amounted to a permission to carry on dealing for the invasion of England.[30] At this point there may be something to be said for Martin's adverse judgement; presumably Persons had a trump card in the enthusiasm of Gregory XIII. There is not much sign that he reduced his involvement after his return to Paris; nor of any obvious *quid pro quo* Acquaviva might have managed to get out of him.

---

[28] Acquaviva to Persons, 11 August 1583 (Francia I/1, f. 170ᵛ); Hicks, *Letters of Persons*, p. lix; Martin, *Henry III*, pp. 107, 113. This is the third occasion on which Martin finds Acquaviva giving authority to Persons' political dealings; for the other two, above, nn. 19 and 21.

[29] Persons to Acquaviva, 22 August 1583 (FG 651).

[30] Persons, 'Notes', p. 111, says that he and Acquaviva 'discussed fully, though in secret, everything pertaining to the good of the mission'; Acquaviva to Claude Matthieu, 20 October 1583 (Francia I/1, f. 224ʳ).

He did indeed, as Acquaviva wanted, return for a time to a stable life in a Jesuit community. But since the community was the professed house of St Louis in Paris, the 'peace and quiet' which he claimed to be enjoying there was very relative.[31] The rector of the house was his close ally Claude Matthieu, a tireless promoter of Catholic politics in France, Scotland and England, and another Jesuit regicide;[32] it was full of people of like mind. In Paris it was the centre of the zealous party among the Jesuits in France, as the Jesuit college was of the royalists. It was here that Persons did whatever he did about *Leicester's Commonwealth*. If *Leicester's Commonwealth* had not been given to the world, the gaiety of the English nation would have been diminished; from Acquaviva's point of view, his connection with it, whatever it was, was little less deplorable than his promotion of the assassination of Queen Elizabeth. It precipitated Persons' return to his safe house at Rouen: he claimed that he had had to go into hiding again because Leicester had in retaliation sent a gang over to Paris to murder him. It also precipitated a complaint to Acquaviva from the French provincial, Odon Pigenat. Acquaviva decided that enough was enough: he had already sent Persons another polite invitation to come to Rome, which he repeated more firmly on 9 January.[33] Persons replied in a long letter, written from Rouen on 12 February 1585, which is at least the second most interesting piece in our dossier. Now that we have deciphered Acquaviva's letter of 5 June 1583, which I had not done when I first discussed this one, we cannot go far wrong in taking the later letter as a pendant to the earlier. Nobody appears to have quoted it in print before.

Persons began by saying that he had talked about the idea of leaving France to Allen, who had been very hostile on the grounds that he could not run the mission without him; but he had finally decided that he would come as soon as he had got three things out of the way. The first two involved his dealings with the Duke of Parma about a revival of the enterprise. He said that he did not believe anything would come of the idea, but that it would not do to drop it on the spur of the moment. His third and strongest reason was that he wanted three or four months to finish his *Book of Resolution*, from which he claimed that he had been 'very peremptorily summoned' by the politicians in 1582. We may think that he was saying what Acquaviva wanted to hear, or playing for time. But there was more to it than this, as the rest of the letter reveals. He now said that he

[31] Persons to Acquaviva, 29 May 1584 (FG 651).

[32] Martin, *Henry III*, p. 129: Matthieu suggests to Gregory XIII the assassination of Henri III, October 1584; and Acquaviva to Matthieu, 29 December 1583 (Francia I/1, f. 179), which appears to be about something similar.

[33] Hicks, *Letters of Persons*, pp. lxviii, 260; Pigenat to Acquaviva, 25 November 1584 (Gallia 91, f. 309); Acquaviva to Persons, 29 November 1584; to Pigenat, and to Persons, 9 January 1585 (Francia I/1, ff. 207ʳ, 209ᵛ, 210ᵛ). From Persons' 'Notes', pp. 151 ff., where he has a letter of 18 August 1584 to Acquaviva from a missionary priest, George Birkhead, asking him not to remove Persons from France, it seems that Acquaviva's pressure had begun during the summer.

would like to make a proposal which he had been turning over in his mind for the past year:

> Since for some years now I have been involved in these great distractions, I should like, according to the constitutions of the Society, to be allowed to make my third year of novitiate [tertianship] so as to recollect myself . . . For I feel myself extremely debilitated by these daily dealings with the world, and even though I were never more keen to perform them, the importunity of these affairs [*negotiorum*] does not allow me to find any satisfaction in them. The passions of my disposition [*passiones animi*] have greatly grown and strengthened, and unless I get time to attend carefully and undistracted to *this* business I do not see how I shall be able to subjugate them.

So, when he comes to Rome, he would like to go into the novice-house at Sant'Andrea

> so that I can strengthen myself [*perhaps* 'confirm my vocation'] in that place where first I received the spirit of the Society.

He hopes that Acquaviva will not want him to do a job concerned with England, at least not for the time being:

> I therefore beg that I may shut myself up inside the walls of Sant'Andrea for at least eight or ten months, and that there I may for once lay down the burden of these affairs and begin to take a look at myself. I confess to Your Paternity that when I had the advantage of the place [as a novice] I did not realise the benefits of it; but now that I have learned from the lack of them I do not doubt that I shall get more profit from it in a month than I did in the whole year I spent there.[34]

Forty years ago Philip Hughes remarked on two of Persons' letters, dating from a little earlier and published by Hicks, where he seemed to show regret on his and Allen's part for their period of political activity; the more explicit was written to Mary Queen of Scots, probably in October 1584. Here he wrote that, considering the opposition they had aroused by it and the lack of achievement, they 'had resolved . . . to leave cogitation of such matters, and to follow only our spiritual course, whereon all dependeth though in longer time'. He took the 'lets and hindrances' which had occurred as evidence that in the strategy of divine providence 'it was not yet time to relieve us temporally'. Perhaps I may make some amends for a pert remark about Fr Hughes by recording the exactitude of

---

[34] Persons to Acquaviva, 12 February 1585 (FG 651); cf. Persons to Queen Mary, 15 February 1585 (Hicks, *Letters of Persons*, p. 269), where he says that he has been 'commanded by obedience to retire my self into Lorraine for a time'. Hicks (*ibid.* p. lxxi) cites an answer to the request about the tertianship by Acquaviva, 9 April 1585 (Francia I/1, f. 221ʳ), but I have missed it in my note on this letter.

his judgement here.[35] We have now quite a dossier in its favour, which indicates some kind of cumulative crisis. In May 1584 he had gone to the professed house in Paris in search of a bit of peace and quiet. I doubt if he had got it, and wonder whether as yet he altogether wanted it. In July he had written to Acquaviva declining to be put in charge of the Scottish mission on the grounds that in that capacity he would have to deal continually, though he named no names, with the Duke of Guise and his allies, 'which would be an enormous pain (*pena*) and distraction to me'; he had enough to do with English business, and he urgently needed a rest ('*bisognosissimo di qualche riposo e ritiranza*'). Next day he told Sir Francis Englefield that he would be glad to see the back of Queen Mary and her enterprises; in October he told her herself that he and Allen would in future stick to their spiritual last.[36] In February he wrote to Acquaviva the painful letter I have quoted; and in April, to Agazzari the rector of the English College in Rome, another almost equally revealing. Agazzari had transmitted Acquaviva's anxiety about the rising feeling among English lay exiles like Thomas Morgan and Charles Paget against Allen and Persons himself, and invited him to make his peace with them. Persons' reply included an obscure passage where he said that he had no quarrel with them except in 'some matters of judgement and opinion, which is [*sic*] secret and private to myself and pertains to my status;' this seems to mean something more particular than the view that he, as a priest and a religious, should keep out of politics, but I do not understand what. Anyway, he went on, there was now on this score no reason for friction between them:

> There was a time when Allen and I had some business to conduct with them [that is, in the invasion scheme of 1583]. Now that time has passed, and so now we attend solely to our own functions, and they to theirs, without getting mixed up with one another. That will be good, I hope, for both parties.[37]

As Fr Hicks rightly said, the idea behind his going to Rome, this time, was not to get on with the enterprise of England but to get away from it.[38] It was the result of steady pressure from Acquaviva, of his own accumulated discomforts, of complaints about him from the French provincial and probably from English lay exiles, and of the collapse of the enterprise itself in the form in which he had

---

[35] Hughes, *Reformation in England*, III, p. 329, from Hicks, *Letters of Persons*, p. 246; my *English Catholic Community*, p. 3.

[36] To the two letters already cited, add Persons to Acquaviva, 23 July 1584 (Hicks, *Letters of Persons*, p. 221: not from FG 651 but from Stonyhurst); to Englefield, 24 July 1584 (*ibid.* p. 226); above, n. 31.

[37] Persons to Agazzari, 3 April 1585 (FG 651). Various points of view on this long-running dispute may be found in Hughes, *Reformation in England*, III, p. 331; Hicks, *An Elizabethan Problem*; my own 'The Character of Elizabethan Catholicism', in Trevor Aston, ed., *Crisis in Europe, 1560–1660* (London, 1965), pp. 238–39; and Mark Greengrass, 'Mary, Dowager Queen of France', *The Innes Review* 38 (1987), pp. 171–88.

[38] Hicks, *Letters of Persons*, pp. lxx ff.

promoted it. We can only guess in what proportion these determined his with-drawal from the battlefront. There were in fact still six months to go, rather than three, before he finally left for Rome. He did do some work on the *Book of Resolution*, of which he produced a new edition instead of the second part he had promised;[39] but most of the time he spent in the Duke of Parma's re-Catholicised Netherlands where, among other doings, he reconstituted the passage for priests into England and sent, on Parma's behalf, a spy to London and back to find out about the impending English military intervention in the Netherlands.[40] As he and Allen journeyed towards Rome between late September and early November 1585, the conflicts of north-west Europe were moving into a hotter phase, with which he was to have a great deal less to do than with the cold war which had preceded it. He did get some of the peace and quiet he had asked for, for in the spring he went to make the Spiritual Exercises in Sant'Andrea.[41] His correspondence with Acquaviva of course came to an end, and the story of their relationship is plunged back into relative darkness.

What, all told, does our correspondence have to say about Persons? What does it have to say about Acquaviva? I advance, in either case, with some trepidation. We are now able to peer a little farther into the 'undescried heart of Robert Persons' than A.L. Rowse, Philip Hughes, or Garrett Mattingly.[42] Our thoughts are likely to be dominated by the discovery that, during his major period of political activity, Persons advocated or, shall we say, did rather more than condone the assassination of Queen Elizabeth as a preliminary to the enterprise of England. The discovery makes the question of Persons' politics a good deal more fraught than it was before. I want to put it together with what seems to me the message of his confession to Acquaviva: that, after three years or more of *negotia*, political and other, he was in some kind of a state of incipient breakdown. What were the 'passions of his disposition', the *passiones animi*, which had been so intensified by this commerce with the world that he feared they would run away with him?

I have two suggestions. The first I shall call, following the description of a senior contemporary Jesuit, Oliver Mannaerts, the passions of magnanimity; by which I mean the tendency for Jesuits to have an excessive esteem for heroic enterprises, which might encourage individual and collective self-glorification.[43]

---

[39] See Houliston, 'Why Persons'.

[40] Hicks, *Letters of Persons*, pp. xliv, lxvii, lxx ff., 270 ff., where he cites from Acquaviva's letters to the Flemish province one to Persons of 31 May 1585, which I have not seen, about Persons' coming to Rome; Persons to Agazzari, Rheims 12 August 1585 (FG 651).

[41] Solomon Aldred to Walsingham, 27 March/6 April 1586, CSP Domestic, XII, p. 170.

[42] A.L. Rowse, *The England of Elizabeth* (London, 1950), pp. 462–63; Hughes, *Reformation in England*, III, p. 333; Garret Mattingly, *The Defeat of the Spanish Armada* (London, 1962 edn), pp. 80–81.

[43] Clancy, *Introduction*, pp. 114–15; Persons accused the French provincial, Pigenat, of 'pusillanimity' about the English mission: to Acquaviva, 20 August 1584 (FG 651). Mannaerts was quite critical of Persons, as witness his letter printed in Knox, *Letters and Memorials*, p. 392, n. 2.

I have said that I think this was of relevance to Campion: Acquaviva's comments on martyrdom were a vote against magnanimity. It is relevant to Persons too, in the temptation (which I take to have accompanied perhaps irresistible external pressure) to deal in great affairs. We can see this as a personal problem, but also as a Jesuit problem, by the light of his comments to Acquaviva about his noviceship. Persons had entered the Society at a time when the activist interpretation of the Jesuit institute was at its most influential; I think he meant that, having joined in a spirit of commitment to heroic enterprises, he had not seen the point of a year spent washing dishes and investigating his soul. During the next seven or eight years he illustrated, perhaps crudely, Jerome Nadal's famous judgement that there was no such thing as *otium* or leisure in the Society.[44] His *negotia*, more and more far-flung, always urgent, left him without leisure to consider properly what he was doing, carried away by the ambition of changing the world tomorrow which led him fatally to the condonation of political murder.

With that word I enter the second region of the passions which Persons invites us to probe: the passions of hostility. We have always known that he had difficulty in tolerating opposition; but now we seem to be approaching something more cosmic: the passions of enmity and hatred, the urge to avenge. Hatred of heresy and heretics was a cliché of sixteenth-century Catholicism: Allen taught it to the students at Rheims,[45] and it was rampant among the kind of French Catholic Persons frequented. We may feel that Persons had something more special on his mind. Perhaps it was this: Campion had been his friend, and possibly his hero in much the same way as I think he himself had been Acquaviva's; he had been executed on a spurious charge, among others, of conspiring to murder the Queen;[46] his death cried for vengeance. It would be far-fetched to see Persons as driven to take up the enterprise of England by a passion to avenge Campion; is it so far-fetched to see the passion as lowering his resistance to the idea of securing the triumph of the enterprise by doing to Elizabeth as she had done? Perhaps it entered into his project of assassinating the reputation of the Earl of Leicester; which he then transformed into an unlikely, though admittedly possible, project of Leicester to assassinate himself? He denied that the passion entered into his dispute with Thomas Morgan and other Catholics who took against him and the Society; but Acquaviva does not seem to have been convinced.[47] Are we to see this contagion spreading from Elizabeth to her ministers, and then to fellow-workers in the political enterprise imagined to be betraying it underhand? May we see it at the bottom of the

---

44 Clancy, *Introduction*, p. 110; surely remembered in Persons to Agazzari, London, 17 November 1580 (Hicks, *Letters of Persons*, p. 55): 'Nulla est admittenda in his rebus defatigatio.'

45 Knox, *Letters and Memorials*, p. 67.

46 Evelyn Waugh, *Edmund Campion: Jesuit and Martyr* (London, 1935), p. 192.

47 Above, n. 37; compare the account of Persons' feud with Christopher Bagshaw by Anthony Kenny, 'Reform and Reaction in Elizabethan Balliol', in John Prest, ed., *Balliol Studies* (Oxford, 1982), pp. 17–51.

nightmare which appears, around Christmas 1584, to have been driving him round the bend? These may be untoward suggestions; but suggestions seem to be needed.

About Acquaviva, I have three comments. I have already mentioned the first of them, in commending his insistence that Jesuits were being sent to England as missioners, not as martyrs. I wonder if either of them quite saw all the implications of this. If the first duty of the Jesuit in England was to survive, he would need to be 'worldly' in a way that Campion had not been.[48] But exactly how worldly? It was clear that he had better not, either for the sake of his own soul or for the credibility of the mission, concede as much to the world as Persons had done. On the other hand, it does not seem to me that, in falling back on a traditional separation of the temporal and the spiritual, Persons and Allen were quite meeting the difficulties of the case: in the running of what amounted to an international smuggling operation, the distinction might seem to collapse, and it was surely not, as they implied, identical with the distinction between the political and the unpolitical. It may be that Acquaviva, having excluded the explicitly political, thought that the way to solve the problem remaining was to provide a body of worked examples in the missionary narratives he asked for: which sounds a good idea.

On the political side I think we can now substantially exonerate Acquaviva from Martin's charge of saying one thing about France and something else about England.[49] It is true that he did not put his foot down about the enterprise as he did about assassination. It is also true that formal contradictions in his letters can be found. But to see his dealings with Persons as a whole is to see him making cautious progress towards the end of extracting a generally admired subordinate from a situation he disapproved of and whose disastrous consequences had been revealed. We may guess that he would have been less cautious had Gregory XIII been less keen on the enterprise of England. We nevertheless owe Martin a debt for making us see Acquaviva's concern for the English mission in connection with his long-range policy for the Society in France. During the year 1584 it began to appear as if the continuation of the Jesuit mission in England was incompatible with that long-range policy: those Jesuits in France who supported the policy, like the provincial, wanted the English mission stopped, while those who wanted the mission to go on, like Matthieu, were viciously hostile to the policy. In spite of his long commitment to England Acquaviva found the decision extremely difficult, and finally put it to the Pope, who told him to carry on.[50]

---

[48] Cf. Persons to Acquaviva, 20 August 1584 (FG 651), where Persons records an argument with Pigenat about William Weston's suitability for the mission: Persons said that he 'would need to acquire a little more experience in worldly matters (*cose mundane*)', but that the same had been true of Campion. Hicks, *An Elizabethan Problem*, pp. 117 ff. quotes part of this letter.

[49] Martin, *Henry III*, pp. 101, 113–14, 218; cf. de Guibert, *Doctrine*, p. 230 for Acquaviva's 'gentleness without weakness', which I think he showed in this case.

[50] Hicks, *Letters of Persons*, pp. lxv ff., 201 ff., 219; Persons, 'Notes', pp. 146–47, where he

There remains a point about the Jesuit life. One of Acquaviva's contributions to the inner development of the Society was to rehabilitate comparatively traditional notions of prayer against a more activist interpretation of Ignatius's doctrine about finding God in all things. He did this in his circular letter to the Society *On the Renovation of the Spirit*, written in the middle of his exchanges with Persons in 1583 and echoed by Persons himself in a judgement, probably mistaken, on the reign of Mary Tudor; later, he commended contemplative prayer.[51] He had in mind, I take it, to defend against Nadal the idea that there was room in the society for *otium*. I take it that he also had in mind the correspondence we have been reading over his shoulder, including the distasteful fact it revealed.

oddly confuses Pigenat with Matthieu; Acquaviva to Allen, 15 July 1584 (Francia I/1, f. 200; printed in Ryan, 'Correspondence', p. 96): 'Negotium . . . Anglicanae missionis, ut erat gravissimum, et non parvas nobis difficultates obiiciebat, visum erat necessario cum Summo Pontifice conferendum, ut non solum illius sancta benedictione sed etiam consilio ac lumine accedente eo certiores essemus de Dei voluntate.' I think this was a more serious crisis than Hicks indicates.

[51] de Guibert, *Doctrine*, pp. 237–42; my *English Catholic Community*, p. 17: Persons said that the Marian Church had failed in 'the renewing the spirit'. Compare David Loades' 'The Spirituality of the Restored Catholic Church (1553–1558) in the Context of the Counter Reformation' in this volume.

9

Why Robert Persons would not be Pacified: Edmund Bunny's Theft of *The Book of Resolution*

VICTOR HOULISTON

One of the latest and most apt re-publications of Robert Persons' famous *Book of Resolution* – later renamed *A Christian Directory* – was the American edition of 1845. This was dedicated to Andrew Byrne, newly consecrated Bishop of Little Rock, Arkansas, 'as a testimony to his unaffected piety – his zeal and devotion in the cause of Religion – and the amiableness and urbanity of his manners as a clergyman and a gentleman'. In 1845 the cathedral at Little Rock was projected but building had not yet commenced. The Catholic population of the diocese was about seven hundred, with five churches built and eight under construction.[1] To be reprinted with such a pioneering Catholic enterprise in mind was just the kind of afterlife that Persons would have wished for his favourite work. To be adapted for use as an aid to Protestant piety, on the other hand, was a consummation that he had to contemplate in his own lifetime and found utterly intolerable.

The Book of Resolution, first composed in the heady days of the Jesuit English Mission of 1580/1, must count as one of the most influential prose works of Elizabeth's reign, a work not only eloquent in itself but remarkably successful as an instrument of Catholic revival.[2] Pious, moving and traditionalist in its appeal to the reader to be 'resolved' in the service of God, the book, simply signed 'R.P.', seemed to Edmund Bunny, Calvinist subdean of York and rector of Bolton Percy, worth assimilating to Protestant churchmanship. Courteously, as

---

[1] *A Christian Directory* (New York, 1845; rpt. 1851); for details of the Little Rock diocese, see the *Catholic Directory* of 1845.

[2] *The first booke of the Christian exercise, appertayning to resolution* (Rouen, 1582), STC 19353, ARCR II no. 616; to be referred to as *The Book of Resolution*, enlarged and re-published as *A Christian directorie guiding men to their salvation* (Rouen, 1585), STC 19354.1, ARCR II no. 618; to be referred to as *A Christian Directory*.

he thought, he 'perused' it to cleanse it of its more blatant papist corruptions, and offered it to the public in a new, phenomenally successful edition, giving due credit to the anonymous but initialled author.[3] Persons would have none of it. He refused Bunny's appended offer of pacification with contempt; his virulent, outraged response to this act of apparently benign piracy has been taken by many observers to provide further evidence of his legendary belligerence and intolerance.

Such a reading of Persons' refusal to be pacified discounts the immediate purpose of the book and approaches it with something of Bunny's own innocence. The fact that *The Book of Resolution* had, and still has, a universal appeal does not mean that it was more or less confessionally neutral, and therefore open to appropriation without being substantially disfigured. Nor does it take away Bunny's offence to argue, as Brad Gregory has done in a recent article, that Persons and Bunny had a common aim, of challenging their respective co-religionists to a similar zeal. Gregory imagines that because Bunny implicitly endorsed so much of what Persons wrote, the two authors are virtually interchangeable. Hence such misleading phrases as 'Parsons's and Bunny's use of language' and 'Parsons's and Bunny's diatribe against "the world" '.[4] Bunny was not the co-author of the passages he reproduced, nor were these passages written by some ideological component of Persons' brain in which Bunny might be said to have participated. *The Book of Resolution* was written by a genuine prose artist, and shaped by the circumstances and vision of a nervous, relatively inexperienced Jesuit missionary agitated by extremes of hope and discouragement.

In 1580 Persons had been a Jesuit just five years. It was not for another six years, until he returned to Rome after the collapse of a series of schemes for a Catholic invasion of England, that he was able to go into retreat for his tertianship.[5] He found the intervening years of close engagement with the English

---

[3] *A booke of Christian exercise, appertaining to resolution, that is shewing how that we should resolve our selves to become Christians in deed: . . . Perused, and accompanied now with a Treatise tending to pacification*, by Edmund Bunny (London, 1584), STC 19355. This version was reprinted at least seventeen times in the following two years.

[4] Brad S. Gregory, 'The "True and Zealouse Seruice of God": Robert Parsons, Edmund Bunny, and *The First Booke of the Christian Exercise*', *Journal of Ecclesiastical History* 45 (1994), pp. 238–68; see also Elizabeth K. Hudson, 'The Catholic Challenge to Puritan Piety, 1580–1620', *Catholic Historical Review* 77 (1991), pp. 1–20, and Robert McNulty, ' "The Protestant Version" of Robert Parsons' *The First Booke of the Christian Exercise*', *Huntington Library Quarterly* 22 (1959), pp. 271–300. McNulty provides a useful apparatus of Bunny's alterations in 'Robert Parsons's *The First Booke of the Christian Exercise* (1582): An Edition and a Study' (unpublished Ph.D. thesis, Columbia University, 1955). McNulty's work is ignored by Hudson and Gregory.

[5] Leo Hicks, S.J. ed., *Letters and Memorials of Father Robert Persons, S.J.* (London, 1942), CRS 39, p. lxxii. Persons apparently made the thirty days retreat at the novitiate of Sant' Andrea as part of the third year of probation, and took his final vows on 9 May 1587. See also R. Persons to C. Acquaviva, 12 Feb 1585, ARSI, Fondo Gesuitico 651/640. Grateful acknowledgements to Fr Thomas McCoog, S.J., of the provincial archives, London, for transcripts and English translations. He is currently preparing an edition of these letters for the *AHSI*.

Mission wearing, weighed down as he was with the responsibilities of making decisions about the posting of missionaries, negotiating at a high level with potentates in France, Belgium and Spain in a fruitless attempt to create circumstances for national conversion, and writing books of controversy and piety to further the Catholic cause on the ground in England. It was during this period that he wrote and revised *The Book of Resolution* with its deceptive equanimity of voice. That he could detach himself from pressing business to write it is itself testimony to the singleness of purpose underlying all his activity, but the emotive quality and incisiveness of the writing derive at least in part from the circumstantial drama. Edmund Bunny might approve, with reservations; he could not have written *The Book of Resolution.*

Campion and Persons left Rome for England in April 1580; in April 1582 Persons became involved in discussions, in Paris, with Henri Duke of Guise and William Allen about a Scottish invasion. By that time the first edition of *The Book of Resolution* had been printed at a rather makeshift press in Rouen. It is difficult to pinpoint precisely when and where the book was composed, but it was probably begun in London and completed in Rouen. Between October 1580 and May 1581 Persons was in the London area, occupied in writing and printing English books in secret, while Campion was in Lancashire writing the *Rationes decem* in Latin, addressed to the two universities. The two books of his own that Persons had printed at this time were topical: *A brief discours contayning certayne reasons why Catholiques refuse to goe to church* addressed the urgent issue, discussed at the Southwark Synod in July, of attendance at Anglican services, and *A brief censure vppon two bookes written in answere to M. Edmonde Campions offer of disputation* responded to Protestant attacks on the prematurely publicised document known as 'Campion's Brag'.[6] Yet it is not unlikely that Persons was simultaneously engaged in writing more generally to challenge and edify the Catholic community he had found somewhat inert and unmotivated on his return to England. William Weston later reported that Persons 'had done much of his work and writing' as the guest of a gentlewoman named Bellamy, that is, at Uxenden Manor near Harrow, which at that time was a thickly-wooded retreat, ideal for the purpose. Philip Caraman goes so far as to assert as a simple fact that 'Fr. Persons wrote the greater part of his classic spiritual treatise, *The Book of Resolution*', there.[7]

Events moved rapidly during the summer of 1581, with the move to Stonor Park, the sensational distribution of the *Rationes decem* at St Mary's, Oxford,

---

[6] *A brief discours contayning certayne reasons why Catholiques refuse to goe to church* ([London], 1580), STC 19394, ARCR II no. 613 was printed by Stephen Brinkley at the 'Greenstreet House' press, East Ham, probably in December 1580; this press was dismantled early the following year but set up again in the house of Francis Browne in Southwark for *A brief censure vppon two bookes written in answere to M. Edmonde Campions offer of disputation* (Douay [vere London], 1581), STC 19393, ARCR II no. 612.

[7] William Weston, *The Autobiography of an Elizabethan*, translated and edited by Philip Caraman, S.J. (London, 1955), p. 3 and n. 10.

Campion's arrest, the seizure of the press at Stonor, and Persons' reluctant decision to fly to France. Once he was settled at Rouen, in the house of the Archdeacon, Michel de Monchy, he intended to continue with three books that he had 'either begun to write, or at least projected [in England] . . . the third, entitled *The Resolution*',[8] but leisure was at a premium. He was concerned, first, to stabilise the English mission and make plans for Scotland. Already his mind may have been turning to an alliance with the Duke of Guise through de Monchy's relative, the Bourbon Archbishop Charles of Rouen. His most pressing literary task was the Latin tract *De persecutione anglicana* which was used primarily to raise funds for the seminary at Rheims;[9] indeed, Persons at Rouen was establishing a vital link between the exiles at Rheims and the recusants in England. Throughout the winter of 1581/2 he was uncertain whether he should return immediately to England, make a venture to Scotland, or remain where he was.

It seems that in January Bernardino de Mendoza, urged by Mary Queen of Scots, applied pressure on him to hasten to Scotland, arguing (as Persons recalled) that 'it was no time to be occupied in writing books when it was a question of the salvation of kingdoms'.[10] This was, of course, a false distinction even if applied to *The Book of Resolution*, and Claudio Acquaviva, whose intervention kept Persons in Rouen by recommending the senior Scottish priest, William Crichton (Creighton) to go in his stead, would very likely have shared Persons' satisfaction with the completion of the work: 'A book has been published in English on resolution', wrote Persons to the General on 11 April, 'suited to our [present] needs.'[11]

Ostensibly *The Book of Resolution* was designed to turn readers back to devotion from a preoccupation with the blasts and counter-blasts of the propaganda war. Persons' own prefatory statement of this motive has become well known, partly because Bunny appealed to it as having ecumenical implications, and partly because it may seem to contain elements of dramatic irony in the light of Persons' subsequent career. Of books of controversy, he wrote:

> yet helpe they litle oftentymes to good lyfe, but rather do fill the heades of men with a spirite of contradiction and contention, that for the most parte hindereth deuotion, which deuotion is nothinge els, but a quiet and peaceble state of the sowle, endewed with a ioyful promptnes to the diligent execution of all thinges that appartayne to the honour of God.[12]

---

8 'Notes Concerning the English Mission', in *Miscellanea IV*, ed. John H. Pollen, S.J. (London, 1907), CRS 4, pp. 26–27.

9 Hicks, *Letters of Persons*, p. xliii.

10 Persons, 'Notes', pp. 56–57.

11 'Liber quidam editus de resolutione anglice accommodatus temporibus nostris', R. Persons to C. Acquaviva, 11 April 1582, ARSI, Fondo Gesuitico 651/640. In an earlier letter, 21 October 1581, he describes the book as 'most pertinent to our purpose' ('unum, qui ad propositum nostrum maxime pertinet').

12 *The Book of Resolution*, p. 2.

Bunny misinterpreted this. Persons was not referring to political acquiescence or confessional neutrality but to inner peace: the God-honouring deeds that were to be diligently, joyfully and promptly executed by a soul at peace were such contentious acts as absenting oneself from Anglican worship. By 'resolution', to be sure, Persons meant an unswerving commitment to the service of God, which Bunny would whole-heartedly endorse; but he also meant a readiness to suffer persecution for recusancy, which the Calvinist 'perusor' most certainly would abjure. In short, *The Book of Resolution* reinforced the uncompromising alternative for English Catholics as staked out initially in the *Reasons why Catholiques refuse to goe to church.* Church papists – those who remained loyal to the old faith while conforming outwardly – would feel uncomfortable reading such passages as this:

> [That persecution be appoynted an ordinarie meanes of mans saluation in this lyfe] is signified by the shyppe, where into Christ entered with his disciples, whiche was tossed and tumbled, as yf it wolde haue bene drouned . . . a figure of the troubles and afflictions, that all those shoulde suffer, whiche doe rowe in the same shyppe with Christ our sauiour. (p. 242)

Such insistence on the hardships a Christian 'in deed' must expect to face is consonant with the book's unmitigating assault on lukewarmness. It reflects Persons' disappointment with the spirituality of the Catholic remnant. It was his business to stir them up, make them steadfastly non-conformist, so that *The Book of Resolution,* containing motives 'to encourage Catholics to virtue and specially to patience and firm resolve to bear the present persecution',[13] was published not to correct but to complement the works of controversy.

The Book of Resolution was partisan also in that it took its place in the transmission of Counter-Reformation spirituality to England. Persons was never slow to contrast Catholic devotional literature with the poverty of the native Protestant product.[14] At first he projected nothing more than an expansion of the Spanish Jesuit Gaspar Loarte's *Essercitatio della vita cristiana* (Venice, 1561), which had been translated into English in 1579 by Stephen Brinkley, his printing associate.[15] In his epistle to 'the Christian reader' (p. 1) he implies that 'this booke' is a second English edition of Loarte. This has misled some literary historians[16] into assuming that *The Book of Resolution* is a translation of Loarte, but in fact as it stands there is virtually no overlap at all.

To understand the relation between Persons and Loarte the use of the term *exercise* is critical. Loarte's book is chiefly about the disciplining of the passions: how to combat particular temptations and make confession after a fall. *Exercise*

---

[13] Persons, 'Notes', pp. 26–27.

[14] Preface to *A Christian Directory*, ff. 21ᵛ–22ʳ.

[15] Stephen Brinkley (trans.), *The exercise of a Christian life* (London, 1579), STC 16641.5, ARCR II no. 63. The Spaniard Loarte wrote several books in Italian.

[16] E.g. Helen C. White, *English Devotional Literature [Prose] 1600–1640* (Madison, Wisconsin, 1931), p. 144.

here means the practice and strengthening of virtue by the devout Catholic. In *The Book of Resolution* Persons calls his reader to serious 'consideration' leading to a firm resolve to live a virtuous life. *Exercise* here means becoming a Christian 'in deed', converting faith into works, a necessary preliminary to the Loartean exercise. Thus the 1582 *Book of Resolution* was intended as the first of three parts of a new, expanded version of Loarte: *The first booke of the Christian exercise.* The three parts were all to be exercises appertaining to resolution: why be resolved, how to set about it, and how to maintain the resolution. This last would presumably incorporate Loarte's original.

We shall see how Edmund Bunny, in changing the title to *A booke of Christian exercise,* signalled his limited understanding of the term *exercise.* Persons himself abandoned it when he entitled his revised version *A Christian Directory.* Yet it does point us to affinities with *The Spiritual Exercises.* For in the sixteenth century Ignatius's work was used not only as part of the discipline of the Society of Jesus but also as an instrument of conversion. Persons' book, too, was directed at lay people, both Protestant and Catholic, who today might be called 'inquirers', that is, who might have an inclination, however casual or transient, to consider the claims of religion. In 1575 Persons himself had been in this position: expelled from Balliol College and planning to study medicine in Padua, he made the Spiritual Exercises with Fr William Good in Louvain. The course of his life was irrevocably altered.[17] Later, John Gerard used the exercises to great effect, but for many potential converts in England there would not normally have been a Jesuit father available to direct them. Persons, accordingly, invites his readers to ponder the four last things – death, judgement, hell and heaven – much as the exercitant is required to do in the first week of *The Spiritual Exercises.*

It would be an exaggeration to claim that Persons' vivid descriptions are quasi-Ignatian meditations, but they clearly belong to that tradition:

> Imagine then (my freende) thow I saye which art so freshe and froelicke at this daie, that the ten, twentie, or two yeres, or perhaps two monethes, which thow hast yet to lyue, were now ended, and that thow were euen at this present, stretched out vppon a bed, wearied and worne with dolour and paine, thy carnall frindes aboute the weepinge and howlinge, the phisitions departed with theire fees, as hauing geeuen thee ouer, & thow lyinge there alone mute and dumme in most pitifull agonie, expecting from moment to moment, the last stroake of death to be geeuen the. (pp. 114–15)

Effectively, this is an informal 'composition of place'. It is intended to subvert the reader's settled habits of mind by an intense exercise of the imagination. The argument of the book thus far has been to convince the reader, on logical grounds, of the necessity of amendment of life; now the fictional immediacy of

---

[17] Henry More, S.J., *The Elizabethan Jesuits: Historia Missionis Anglicanae Societatis Jesu (1660),* translated and edited by Francis Edwards, S.J. (London, 1981), pp. 49–53; Hicks, *Letters of Persons,* pp. x–xi.

death transforms a syllogism into a mental revolution. The skill lies in the handling of time and space. The intervening years are annihilated, but distance is preserved: 'euen at this present, stretched out vppon a bed . . . thow lyinge there alone mute and dumme in most pitifull agonie, expecting from moment to moment, the last stroake of death to be geeuen the'. Both present and terrified, horrified and detached, participant and observer, it would be an unusual reader that would not be ready to make up his mind.

Whatever these Jesuit antecedents, the chief source of *The Book of Resolution* is neither Loarte nor Ignatius but Luis de Granada. Persons was in fact to echo the title *Guía de Pecadores* (1556/7) in the renamed *Christian Directory*, which is not a directory in the technical Jesuit sense of the word (that is, a handbook or guide to *The Spiritual Exercises*) but rather a signpost for the beginner. Maria Hagedorn first pointed out a large number of borrowings from *The Sinners' Guide* in Persons' chapter warning against delay in making one's resolution. A.C. Southern readily accepted the attribution, but J.P. Driscoll demurred, observing that many of the borrowings could equally well have been derived from other authors.[18] As an example, he referred to a short list of arguments, in *The Book of Resolution*, why a man on his deathbed will repent with difficulty. These are found in *The Sinners' Guide*, but Driscoll points out, somewhat inaccurately, that in *A Christian Directory* Persons omits the details as given by Luis but cites an earlier source, Duns Scotus.[19]

Discovery of a common source often seems to confer finality on arguments of this kind, but Driscoll was over-hasty in concluding that Persons was at most incidentally indebted to Luis de Granada. Hagedorn's contention was vulnerable because her evidence was concentrated in one chapter of *The Book of Resolution*; even so, the sequence and number of identical ideas and references in that chapter (Part 2, chapter 5) rules sheer coincidence out of the question. Moreover, Persons adopted the broad outline of Book 1 of *The Sinners' Guide*: motives inducing men to virtue, followed by impediments or excuses men use to delay or avoid conversion. In many instances the topics follow the same sequence, as in the chapters on God's benefits and on the illusion that the way of virtue is hard.[20] Several of Persons' most striking analogies are to be found in *The Sinners' Guide*, such as how the abandonment of reason for passion may be

---

[18] Maria Hagedorn, *Reformation und Spanische Andachtsliteratur: Luis de Granada in England* (Leipzig, 1934), pp. 110–20; A.C. Southern, *Elizabethan Recusant Prose, 1559–1582* (London, [1950]), p. 186; J.P. Driscoll, S.J., 'The Supposed Source of Persons's "Christian Directory" ', *Recusant History* 5 (1959–60), pp. 236–45.

[19] Cf. *The Book of Resolution*, pp. 387–9, and Luis de Granada, *The sinners guide: a worke contayning the whole regiment of a Christian life*, trans. Francis Meres (1598), Book I, Part 3, ch. 25, p. 286. All references are to this translation, to be referred to as *The Sinners' Guide*, unless otherwise stated. Persons altered this passage in 1607, not 1585 as Driscoll claims.

[20] Persons's nine 'spirituall succours . . . for the easing of vertuous lyfe' are recognizably based on Luis's twelve 'privileges of virtue': cf. *The Book of Resolution*, Part 2, chapter 1, and *The Sinners' Guide*, Book 1, Part 2, ch. 11–24.

compared to the agony of a man who, married to a gracious noblewoman, becomes enslaved in a passionate affair with a shrewish servant girl.[21]

It is only to be expected that two sixteenth-century authors, associated with the Counter Reformation, writing for 'beginners', would have sources in common, common schemata, common illustrations. Luis de Granada was a Dominican friar, still living in Lisbon when Persons went there later in 1582, but there is no record of a meeting between them.[22] Such considerations argue caution. Still, we know that Luis was widely read and highly esteemed among the early Jesuits.[23] George Loyselet's press in Rouen was responsible for printing translations (probably on Persons' account) of two of his works: *Of prayer and meditation* (1584) and *A memoriall of a Christian life* (1586).[24] Lurid passages from both of these appear in *The Book of Resolution*, such as the dying man's anticipation of what will happen to his body after death, and 'a vision of the handling of a wicked man in hell'.[25]

In denying the influence of Luis on Persons, Driscoll no doubt wished to affirm the independent value of *The Book of Resolution*. Yet Persons' achievement is not diminished by allowing the debt. His work is neither a translation nor a mere adaptation of *The Sinners' Guide*. The crucial difference lies in the urgency of Persons' argument, the greater concentration on the immediate conversion of his reader, and the unremitting psychological pressure he brings to bear. Where Luis is often content, after setting out some evidence of God's beneficence and power, to stand back and wonder, Persons conducts a directly persuasive dialogue with his reader. From beginning to end a continuous argument for making one's resolution is built up, the momentum seldom flags, and there is no escape. Differences in the structure of the two works bear witness to this quality of *The Book of Resolution*. Luis develops the motives for virtue from God's inherent goodness and lovableness to a consideration of the four last things: Persons, echoing the 'first principle and foundation' of *The Spiritual Exercises* (Section 23), begins with the purpose of man's creation, and hence his duty and accountability to God. Only after he has explained what kind of a master God is, to whom we His servants must render account, does he move on to God's benefits. By bringing forward the treatment of the day of judgement, he early instils a sense of guilt and fear; the emotional temperature is much higher than in Luis's elegant initial tributes to God the creator and preserver. Persons' chapter on benefits, then, piles awareness of ingratitude on top of the emotions already

---

[21] *The Book of Resolution*, pp. 214–16; *The Sinners' Guide*, Book 1, Part 2, ch. 19, pp. 200–01.

[22] Hicks, *Letters of Persons*, pp. lv–lviii.

[23] Joseph de Guibert, S.J. *The Jesuits: Their Spiritual Doctrine and Practice*, trans. William J. Young, 3rd edn., (St. Louis, 1986), p. 218.

[24] ARCR II no. 444 and no. 439. Persons refers to his supervision of translations from Loarte, Granada and others ('ex Granatensi Loarte et aliis') in a letter to Acquaviva, 21 October 1581.

[25] Cf. *Of prayer and meditation*, f. 192, and *The Book of Resolution*, pp. 107–08; *A memoriall of a Christian life*, pp. 43–45, and *The Book of Resolution*, pp. 137–39.

aroused; next he turns the screw by considering 'Of what opinion and feelinge we shalbe, towchinge these matters, at the tyme of our deathe', adding another turn with a terrifying description of hell, and bringing Part 1 to a close with an acute sense of loss and yearning induced by projections of heavenly reward.

To appreciate the impact of Persons' style it is instructive to compare a parallel passage from the translation of *The Sinners' Guide* made by Francis Meres in 1598:

> What great madnes I pray thee would it be thought, if a man had many and weighty burthens to be carried to some certain place, and he had many Horses sufficient to carry them, yet he should lay all the burthens vpon one of the weakest and worst Horses, the other being sent away empty? like, or rather greater is their madnes, who doe impose the burthen of repentance to be carried of old age; sparing youth, and manly age, and letting them goe empty, which are much stronger, and farre more fit to carry then old age: seeing that old age is scarce able to support her owne infirmities.
>
> (*The Sinners' Guide*, p. 275)

Meres's elaborate parallelism, linking the two madnesses in every detail, is pedestrian and flat. Persons is able to present the same analogy with far greater vigour and realism:

> How madde a man woldest thow esteeme hym, that trauayling on the waye, & hauing great choyse of lustye strong horses, should lett them all goe emptie, and laye all his cariage vpon some one poore and leane beast, that could skarse beare yt selfe, and muche lesse stand vnder so many bagges cast vpon yt? And surelie no lesse vnreasonable is that man, who passing ouer Idlely the lustie dayes, and times of his lyfe, reserueth all the labour and trauaile vnto feble olde age. (*The Book of Resolution*, p. 377)

Persons isolates the plight of the 'one poore and leane beast', and evokes much more strongly the character of the man who passes over idly the lusty days and times of his life. His is the more uncluttered version, allowing the potent imagery to do its own work, and giving more room for the reader to infer connections.

The second part of *The Book of Resolution*, disposing of the excuses people make for not amending their lives, extends the psychological method of the first. As in a classical oration, *refutatio* follows *confirmatio*. Tightening the structure, Persons employs two bracketing devices: first, the main argument, the motives for resolution, is suspended while he deals with objections, only to return with redoubled force at the end; second, he frames excuses within excuses, making even more inexorable the process of stripping away every defence. If the reader pleads that the way of virtue is hard, Persons will not allow that to be sufficient reason to refuse God's call, in the light of subsequent reward or punishment; and then he withdraws his hypothetical concession:

> . . . in respect of all whiche, we ought to make no boones at litle paynes and labour, yf it were true that gods seruice were so trauailsome as many doe

esteeme yt. But now in verie deede the matter is nothing so, and this is but a subtile deceate of the enemie for our discouragement. (p. 187)

As each excuse falls away, Persons gradually develops a new method of winning his reader: a satirical portrayal of those who will not have this man to rule over them:

[S]o these men that wolde not heare of penance, while they were in health, will now admitt any thyng, & make straunge of nothing: Now (I saye) when they can lyue no longer, will they promyse any paynes: what prayer you will: what fasting you will: what almes deedes you can desire: what austeritie soeuer you can imagine, they will promyse it, (I saye) vpon condition they myght haue lyfe agayne: vpon condition that the daye might be prolonged vnto them: thoghe, yf God should graunt them their request, (as many tymes he doeth) they wolde performe no one point therof: but be as careles, as they were before. (p. 395)

The copiousness, the repetition, the elegant variation, are all there to mimic the desperation of the false, last-minute penitent.

Finally, with the sinner's every hiding-place laid open, Persons in his peroration is able to clinch his argument with great authority:

If all this styrre the not, what will stirre thee (gentle reader?) yf when thou hast read this, thou laye downe the booke againe, and walke on in thy careles lyfe as quietly as before: what hope (I beseeche thee) may there be conceiued of thy saluation? wilt thou goe to heauen liuing as thow doest? it is impossible: as soone thow maiest driue God owt of heauen as gett thither thy selfe, by this kind of lyfe. What then: wilt thow forgoe heauen, and yet escape hell too? this is lesse possible, what soeuer the Atheistes of this world doe persuade thee. Wilt thow perhappes deferre the matter, and think of yt heerafter? I haue tolde thee my opinion heerof before. Thou shalt neuer haue more abilitie to doe it than now, and perhappes neuer halfe so muche. If thou refuse it now: I maye greatlie feare, that thou wilt be refused hereafter thy selfe. (pp. 428–29)

Here Persons joins the tradition of great evangelists, but what makes this more than merely an emotional altar-call – however carefully modulated in tone and rhythm – is the way it imitates the movement of Part 2 of *The Book of Resolution*, each hoped-for excuse or proffered impediment firmly repudiated. The peroration also draws on the intimate relationship Persons has built up with his 'gentle reader'.

Contemporary evidence of the effectiveness of *The Book of Resolution* is manifold. The original print run of 2500 was immediately snapped up and read to pieces ('statim distracta') by a public starved of books of devotion, reported Persons to Acquaviva.[26] Thomas Clancy has drawn attention to the number of

---

[26] R. Persons to C. Acquaviva, 12 February 1585, ARSI, Fondo Gesuitico 651/640.

men whose Jesuit vocations began with reading it.[27] Yet, ironically, it is likely that more people were influenced by the Protestant adaptation than by Persons' original. It is difficult to reconstruct Edmund Bunny's original motive for 'perusing' the book. A Magdalen graduate of distinctly Calvinist leanings, he was at the time rector of Bolton Percy in Yorkshire. He claimed to be pleasantly surprised by this Roman Catholic publication which called men to be 'Christians in deede'; he welcomed an apparent suspension of controversialist hostility, and assumed a common goal of sincerity in religion. Acknowledging the peculiar force of the writing, he wanted to promote its distribution, but felt obliged to protect Protestant readers from papist infection. Given his premises, and in the confessional context of the day, his alterations were restrained and sensitive: many phrases which suggest a Catholic view of good works are allowed to remain, so long as they do not necessarily imply the building up of merit. In this account of heavenly reward, for example, he pauses only to add the italicized clause and a note in the margin that 'this must needs be warily taken':

> [What ioye will thy soule receyue in that day . . . when] al thy vertuous deeds, *al the labors that thou hast taken in thy calling;* al thy almes; al thy praiers; al thy fasting; al thy innocencie of life; al thy patience in iniuries; al thy constancie in adversities; al thy temperance in meats; al the vertues of thy whole life . . . shalbe recounted there, al commended, al rewarded: shalt thou not see now the valure and profite of vertuous life? Shalt thou not confesse, that gainful and honorable is the service of God?[28]

Here Bunny is trying to put the most charitable gloss on Persons' words. To demonstrate his good will he appended a 'Treatise of Pacification' generously conceding that papists were part of the true church but arguing that the kind of Catholic holy life Persons recommended in *The Book of Resolution* could be accommodated without recusancy.

Bunny was determinedly moderate. Richard Hopkins, Catholic translator, was even to claim that he had repudiated earlier Protestant denials that a papist might be saved.[29] He could hardly have expected the reception he got. Already in February 1585 Persons had wind of his piracy, for he reported to Acquaviva that the Puritans, exploiting the book's popularity, had reprinted it with excisions: 'a preface has been added in praise of the book, and they affirm that, after some things had been eliminated by them, the remainder was written by the spirit of God'.[30] Only a trace of satire here foreshadows his feelings when he

---

[27] Thomas H. Clancy, S.J., 'Spiritual Publications of English Jesuits, 1615–1640', *Recusant History* 19 (1989), pp. 426–46.

[28] *A book of Christian exercise*, pp. 150–51; *The Book of Resolution*, p. 173. Where Bunny has 'fasting,' Persons wrote 'fastinges.'

[29] R. Hopkins (trans.), *A memoriall of a Christian life* (Rouen, 1586), ARCR II no. 439, dedicatory epistle, p. 15; cf. John Jewel, *An apologie or aunswer in defence of the Church of England* (London, 1562), STC 14590.

[30] '[P]raemissa quadam praefatione in libri laudem, quem exceptis quibusdam iam per

actually read Bunny's version. This was not until he was seeing *A Christian Directory* through the press in August 1585. The printers had already imposed forme Dd; he stopped the press and had an annotation squeezed into the gap at the bottom of the page at the end of chapter 5: 'the print being come to this place, M. Bunneys edition of this booke was deliuered to me, out of whose infinite corruptions, maymes, and manglings, diuers things shalbe noted here-after in the margent.'

War was declared. The first acerbic marginal note appears in the next gather-ing, Ee. But the late arrival of Bunny's text at Rouen meant that there is no extended rebuttal in the main text itself; that was left to the Preface, which was printed, as usual, after the body of the work. In these pages we encounter a very different Persons from the author of *The Book of Resolution*. Now he is in contro-versialist mode, lampooning his adversary, mocking his name, ridiculing his arguments, indignantly flinging back in his face all irenic overtures:

> [Of absurd annotations] you may finde examples page 153. wher by a marginal note he discrediteth the beleefe of S. Cyprian about the knowl-edge, that we shal haue of our fathers, mothers, and other acquaintance in heaven; as though one Cyprian with Christian men of reason, weighed not more in the affaires of our soule, then ten coople of Bunis, were they neuer so vendible. (f. 12ᵛ)

Here a gamesome, irreverent, unjust Persons has entered into the *agon* of confes-sional rivalry, aiming to bolster recusant morale by seeing off a ridiculous oppo-nent.

Bunny himself was somewhat bemused by the vehemence of all this, and adopted an injured, self-justifying tone in his *Brief answer, vnto those idle and friuolous quarrels of R.P. against the late edition of the Resolution*.[31] A.L. Rowse is typical of modern commentators who portray Bunny as the honest Englishman stepping innocently into the den of a howling wolf. In this scenario we can see the influence of Ethelred Taunton, Mark Tierney and T.G. Law, who characterized Persons as bellicose and impatient, coupled with Rowse's own belief in his touchy vanity. Rowse gleefully hints that Bunny had inadvertently called Persons' bluff.[32]

Bunny was certainly 'vendible'. The bookseller John Wight registered his version with the Stationers' Company in August 1584, but the following year his printers, the so-called Eliot's Court Press, found their lucrative property threat-

ipsos resecatis, quoad caetera Dei spiritu scriptum affirmant', R. Persons to C. Acquaviva, 12 February 1585, ARSI, Fondo Gesuitico 651/640.

[31] (London, 1589), STC 4088.

[32] A.L. Rowse, *Eminent Elizabethans* (London, 1983), pp. 41–74; Ethelred L. Taunton, *The History of the Jesuits in England, 1580–1773* (London, 1901); M.A. Tierney, ed., *Dodd's Church History of England*, 5 vols (London, 1839–43); Thomas Graves Law, *A Historical Sketch of the Conflicts between Jesuits and Seculars in the Reign of Queen Elizabeth* (London, 1889).

ened by pirates on all sides. There was John Windet in London, and Joseph Barnes in Oxford, the newly-appointed printer to the university. Barnes had the book reprinted eight or nine times in 1585 alone, prompting the partners at Eliot's Court to petition the Privy Council, with the claim that they had the right 'to be the onelye woorkemen thereof; which beinge the most vendible Copye that happened in our Companie theis manie yeeres, woulde haue kept vs in worke for a longe tyme'. They even tried to counter-attack by pirating a work by Thomas Bilson, only to have their equipment confiscated by order of the selfsame Privy Council. Evidently Barnes enjoyed some privilege.[33]

The stir created by *The Book of Resolution* in the printing trade was analogous to Persons' quarrel with Bunny. Persons treated his perusal as an unwarranted infringement of his rights as an author. We can detect writerly pride, as well as Jesuit indignation, in his complaint, 'M. Buny maketh me to speake like a good minister of England' (f. 11ʳ), and his rather sardonic observation 'a man would thinke that M. Buny did take but a very strange way to pacification, in offering me the greate iniurie which before hath bene shewed, in his edition' (f. 16ᵛ). Bunny must have been naive indeed if he imagined that the author of *The Book of Resolution*, the unknown R.P., would suffer such perusal without protest, in the interest of ecumenism. In 1584, it is true, Persons' formidable power as a controversialist had not yet been fully demonstrated, nor was Bunny the last to provoke him unsuspectingly.

Persons had good reason to resent Bunny's interference, if only because of the latter's clumsy prose. This can frequently be seen in the mutilation of sentences, where he upsets the balance and rhythm for the sake of theological correctness. Trawling for evidence of heavenly consolation in times of hardship, Persons had written:

> But yet this maye I saye, that those which attend in the Catholique Churche, to deale with soules in the holie sacrament of confession, are indeede those, wherof the prophet sayeth, *that they woorke in multitudes of waters, & doe see the maruailes of God in the depthe:* In the depthe (I saye) of mens consciences vttered with infinite multitudes of teares, when God toucheth the same with his holy grace. (p. 224)

'Here', as he commented in the margin of the same passage in *A Christian Directory* (p. 615), 'Bun. is inforced to mangle extremly':

> But yet this may I say, that those which are known to be skilful, and to deal so sincerely withal, that others disburden their consciences unto them for their comfort or counsel, are some part of those, wherof the prophet saith ... (p. 204)

[33] Edward Arber, *A Transcript of the Registers of the Company of Stationers of London, 1554–1640*, 5 vols (London, 1875–94) II, pp. 793–94; CSP Domestic II, p. 296.

Much of the force of the sentence is lost when attention is wrenched from the actual experience of confessors, 'the maruailes of God in the depthe', to the laboured definition of a Protestant equivalent.

In the 'Treatise of Pacification' and the *Brief Answer* Bunny shows himself occasionally capable of eloquent, passionate discourse, especially when he abandons close argument and commends the sufficiency and glory of Christ's sacrifice. But generally his style, so lacking in Persons' lucid ease, is hamstrung by Ramist considerations of division and subdivision. He was following the vogue of the 'method' of Peter Ramus, which tended to reduce the art of rhetoric to a system of so organizing one's arguments that they could be represented in tabular form.[34] The 'Treatise of Pacification' boasts a 'table declaring the effect and method', set out with the familiar pattern of brackets resembling the draw of a knock-out tournament. This betrays him into a lot of repetition for the sake of symmetry: arguments minimising the advantages of conversion to Catholicism are virtually identical to those querying the 'inconveniences' of relinquishing recusancy. Ramism is probably also responsible for the tortuous introductions to each stage of his treatise, where he raises a veritable forest of unnecessary and bewildering signposts to advertise how methodically he has planned what is about to be delivered.

If the two authors are stylistically worlds apart, the theological divergence is also more than superficial. There were, to be sure, affinities between the Jesuits and the Puritans in their call to come out from among their co-religionists and be separate, to depend rather on the faculties of the mind as informed by the word of God or by self-reflection than on church custom. But there is abundant evidence in *The Book of Resolution* to show that Persons expected his reader, having made the all-important resolution, to look to the institutional 'helps' of the Roman Catholic church to establish and maintain that state: the panoply of sacrament, liturgy and spiritual direction that Persons' political agenda was intended to restore. Just how important these were to him can be inferred from his mockery of Bunny's ecumenism:

> [He demands] of vs in very good earnest, why we should stand so much vpon Limbus Patrum, vpon Christes descending into hel, vpon real presence, freedome of wil, and merit of workes, vpon traditions, preestood, and sacrifice, vpon worshiping of Saintes and Images, mariage of preestes, inherent iustice, and the fiue Sacramentes that we numbre more then they doe? . . . wheras notwithstanding al these things, the Protestantes faith (as he saith) and ours is al one in substance, and we al are members of one true Catholique and Apostolique Churche, albeit some of vs be somewhat better members in that Church then others.[35]

What, then, is the 'substance' of Catholic religion? Bunny's objection to Persons'

---

[34] See Walter J. Ong, S.J., *Ramus, Method and the Decay of Dialogue* (Cambridge, Mass., 1958).
[35] Preface to *A Christian Directory*, f. 19^r; see also f. 22^v.

change of title from *The first booke of the Christian exercise* to *A Christian directorie, guiding men to their saluation* indicates how deeply the two men were divided over the meaning of *exercise*. The phrase 'guiding men to their saluation' rankled, because it implied that the resolved life was a condition of salvation, and he refused to accept that practices such as fasting, almsgiving and abstinence were holy in themselves. They were only 'exercises tending to [holiness]'. For Bunny, who recommended the practice of virtue as subsequent to and arising out of justification, the title *A booke of Christian exercise* sufficed.[36] For Persons, the resolution to amend was the first step – *The first booke* – of an exercise that comprehends the whole discipline of Christian life, concurring in justification.

Persons' Catholic theology is more deeply embedded in the language of *The Book of Resolution* than Bunny will admit. The life of good works to which he calls his readers is the only thing that will save them from judgement and hell; so much more depends on resolution, and so much more is embraced by the term that his prose resonates with a controlled urgency. To remove all references to winning heaven, to specifically Catholic practices of penance and self-discipline, as Bunny does, is to tone down the book significantly. Perhaps the strongest indication of this is Persons' recurrent motif of security, never, like the elusive Protestant assurance, guaranteed by a subjective act of faith, but to be hoped for only in the bosom of mother church. This is a note that Persons often takes from Augustine, and it reflects the difference between his and Bunny's notion of the term 'Catholic'. Bunny understands it as the lowest common denominator of all true churches, Roman, Greek and reformed;[37] Persons, like John Henry Newman after him, assumes the definition offered by St Vincent of Lérins in the fifth century: *quod ubique, quod semper, ab omnibus creditum est*, where 'everyone' means the orthodox majority down the ages. Indeed, it was on this precise issue, the interpretation of Vincent's 'marks of the true church' that Campion and Persons challenged Theodore Beza at Geneva in 1580.[38]

It is clear from Persons' revision in 1584/5 that he felt constrained to protect the idea of resolution from Protestant re-interpretation by making more explicit the Roman Catholic ramifications of the original. In a new chapter, 'How a man may iudge or discerne of him self, whether he be a true Christian or not', he carefully articulated the relation between right belief and virtuous life: the former is unequivocally Roman Catholic doctrine, the latter is compared to the 'raising vp the walles, & other partes of our spiritual building, by the exercise of all virtues, and diligent obseruation of Gods commaundements. Without the which, our faith is to no more purpose or profite, then is a foundation without a building vpon it, or a stocke or tree that beareth no fruite' (p. 315). Such elaborations have the less desirable effect of reducing both the intimacy and the

---

[36] *A brief answer . . . to R.P.*, pp. 63, 135–36, and Preface, sig. *2ᵛ.
[37] See 'The Treatise of Pacification', p. 106.
[38] More, *The Elizabethan Jesuits*, p. 76. See also Thomas M. McCoog, S.J., ' "Playing the Champion": The Role of Disputation in the Jesuit Mission' in this volume.

momentum of the argument with the reader. It is as though controversy has re-entered the discourse.

Several other factors arising from the intervening history seem to have affected the coherence of *A Christian Directory*. In the preface Persons refers to criticism of *The Book of Resolution* on two counts: over-emphasis on the judgement of God, and failure to prove the philosophical and theological grounds of resolution (f. 20ᵛ). He responded to the former by writing a chapter entitled 'Mistrust and diffidence in Gods mercie', which is happily consonant with the rest of Part 2, about the impediments that hinder resolution. Less satisfactorily, the threat of atheism, allegedly arising from indifference to and distaste for controversy, was met by two excessively long chapters, 'That there is a God' and 'Particular confirmations of Christian religion'. These were convincing enough to prompt Thomas Nashe's observation that anyone who perused them and remained an atheist, would never be converted.[39] Nevertheless they were perceived to mar *A Christian Directory*. Edmund Bunny observed that Persons should thank anyone who 'would now take out the most of that which in this your second edition you haue put vnto it', and when he came to review the work for re-publication in 1607 he conceded that these chapters 'seemed to some not to be so necessary to the end heere proposed (but fitter to goe in some other worke of that argument a part)', and omitted them.[40]

By adding these bulky chapters Persons confused two related but separable kinds of atheism: philosophical scepticism and what Persons himself had called 'a secret kinde of Atheisme, or denieing of God: that is, of denieing him in life and behauiour'.[41] It was the latter that he was primarily addressing, and although the proofs he now added might strengthen resolution, they dulled the edge of persuasion. Rhetorically speaking, *The Book of Resolution* is deliberative: it exhorts the reader to decision and action. *A Christian Directory*, with two lengthy chapters inserted early in the text, veers towards the forensic: it deals with proof rather than motive. In his revision, therefore, Persons upset the rhetorical balance of his work under pressure from his friendly critics.

It was continuous pressure of business, however, that perhaps had the deepest influence on the new version. From 1582 to 1584 Persons' life was dominated by the expectations of others. It is too easy to dismiss as self-justification his frequent disclaimers of initiative: 'For reasons both necessary and urgent, as it is thought, it was judged expedient by the Archbishop of Glasgow, Mr Allen, Father Creighton, and the Spanish ambassador in England that I depart for

---

[39] *Christes Teares over Jerusalem* (1593), in *Works of Thomas Nashe*, ed. R.B. McKerrow, 5 vols (2nd edn, Oxford, 1966) 2, p. 121. See also J.M. Stone, 'Atheism under Elizabeth and James I,' *The Month* 81 (1894), pp. 174–87, and Herbert Thurston, S.J., 'Catholic Writers and Elizabethan Readers. I. Father Parsons' "Christian Directory",' *The Month* 82 (1894), pp. 457–76.

[40] E. Bunny, *A brief answer . . . vnto R.P.* (1589), p. 138; R. Persons, *The Christian directory guiding men to eternall saluation* (St Omer, 1607), STC 19354.5, ARCR II no. 620, sig. §5ᵛ.

[41] *The Book of Resolution*, p. 410.

Lisbon to see the King.'[42] He was despatched on errands to Philip II in 1582/3 and to Rome later in 1583. During the winter of 1583/4 he was in Tournai and Flanders, negotiating, it is presumed, with the Duke of Parma and attending to the pastoral needs of English soldiers. No doubt his heart was in these projects, but he was acting on behalf of others. What is certain is that throughout this period he was stretched to the limit in diplomacy, administration of the English Mission, founding the school at Eu, and tirelessly ministering to Catholic exiles, driven by his passion to create the conditions for the restoration of Catholicism in England.[43] He experienced disappointment over the invasion plans, an acute illness, which delayed his return from Portugal, and frustration even with Mendoza, who by all accounts had been the first to arouse his interest in military and diplomatic means of furthering his cause. Despite the encouragement of his happy relationships with Allen, particularly, and Philip II, these experiences were putting fully to the test his own claims, in *The Book of Resolution*, that the difficulties and hardships of the resolved life were only 'supposed'.[44]

After the death of Alençon in June 1584 Persons seems to have become extremely dispirited about the prospects of an early *coup d'état* in England; by October he was writing to Mary Queen of Scots that for the time being he and Allen were reverting to purely spiritual methods.[45] At the same time he was involved, to some degree, in the publication of the notorious *Leicester's Commonwealth*, a work better designed to promote the Duke of Guise's interests in France than to gain any advantage for Catholics in England.[46] It was, thus, with a sense of dissipated energy that he began to revise *The Book of Resolution* in the summer of 1584. In all likelihood he consulted William Weston about it when the latter spent three months with him in Paris, from June to September, *en route* to the

[42] 'Per cause necessarie et urgenti, come si pensa, s'è giudicato spediente dal archievescovo di Glasco et Signor Alano et p. Criton et l'ambassiador di Spagna in Inghilterra, che io me n'andasse in Lisbona al re', R. Persons to C. Acquaviva, 3 May 1582, ARSI, Fondo Gesuitico 651/640.

[43] Testimonials of Persons's readiness to respond to calls for help are legion, e.g. 'Persons, one of those great-souled men who are always on the look-out for the chance of doing a good work' (More, *The Elizabethan Jesuits*, p. 208); 'ther is none of our nation nowe living that hath better defended of his Countrey both at home and abroad then he hath done' (John Bavant to George Birkhead, 26 November 1608, in *Letters of Thomas Fitzherbert*, ed. Leo Hicks, S.J., [London, 1948], CRS 41, p. 80).

[44] See Hicks, *Letters of Persons*, pp. lii–lxix; A. Lynn Martin, *Henry III and the Jesuit Politicians* (Geneva, 1973), pp. 63–74; John Bossy, 'The Society of Jesus in the Wars of Religion', in *Monastic Studies: The Continuity of Tradition*, ed. Judith Loades (Bangor, 1990), pp. 229–44. See also Bossy's 'The Heart of Robert Persons' in this volume where he refines a number of the points raised in the earlier article. For criticism of Mendoza, see the letter from Tournai, probably by Persons, 8 March 1584 (Hicks, *Letters of Persons*, pp. 198–200).

[45] Hicks, *Letters of Persons*, p. 246.

[46] Dwight C. Peck, ed., *Leicester's Commonwealth: 'The Copy of a Letter Written by a Master of Art of Cambridge' (1584) and Related Documents* (Athens, Ohio, 1985).

English Mission in September.[47] In February 1585 he estimated that he would be occupied with the revision for the next three to four months.[48] Thereafter he left Rouen for St Omer and Tournai, but returned in August for the presswork before departing with William Allen for Rome in September, more or less permanently as it turned out.

By this stage Persons had a more substantial press in Rouen, operated by George Flinton and Stephen Brinkley, who had been arrested and imprisoned in the Tower in 1581 when the secret press at Stonor Park had been seized, but was now at large again. This gave Persons the opportunity to improve the physical appearance of the book, with better paper and typeface.[49] He also sought to deepen its spirituality. Despite confessing to Acquaviva that his ability and knowledge in matters spiritual were small,[50] he began to conceive of *A Christian Directory* as a reflective book, suitable for meditation, rather than a single inspirational argument. In the preface, he conceded that *The Book of Resolution* had consisted only of 'vehement matter of persuasion', and therefore 'furnished' it now with other material 'more indifferent, wherwith the reader may solace his minde, at such times as he findeth the same not willing to feele the spurre of more earnest motion to perfection' (f. 21ʳ). Accordingly, he inserted a longish chapter into Part 2, of notable examples of resolution, which add nothing to the argument but as 'speaking pictures' refresh the imagination. *A Christian Directory* thus became a book to which he could append a 'method' dividing the chapters up into a course of readings for morning and evening. The reader is given a choice of ten days or two weeks in which to cover the entire work.

A Christian Directory certainly contains food for thought. It is not, however, a book of profound spiritual insight, and it may be that Persons was misguided in trying to give it a more contemplative slant. Still, his revision suggests that he was now conscious, in the light of his own recent experience, of the limitation of mere resolution and action. However ready he was to throw his everything into varied and to some extent conflicting schemes in what he earnestly believed to be God's service, he could write: 'I feel myself very weakened as a result of these dealings with the world; and although I have had keener desires, nevertheless, the importunity of affairs in no way allows me to satisfy myself.'[51] The 'keener desires' he mentions refer to 'personal consolation', the retreat and its time of recollection. If this is what he was longing for, it is no wonder that he turned the

---

[47] 'Personio lo trattenea . . . per servirsi dell' opera sua e spedire per la stampa quelle opere che andava scrivendo', Persons, 'Notes', pp. 156–57; cf. Weston, *Autobiography*, p. 1.

[48] R. Persons to C. Acquaviva, 12 February 1585, ARSI, Fondo Gesuitico 651/640.

[49] Preface to *A Christian Directory*, f. 4ᵛ.

[50] '[E]xigua mea facultate et scientia in rebus spiritualibus', R. Persons to C. Acquaviva, 12 February 1585, ARSI, Fondo Gesuitico 651/640.

[51] 'Sentio enim me diuturnis his cum saeculo commerciis debilitatum valde, et licet nunquam acriora habuerim desideria; tamen negotiorum importunitas nullo modo mihi ipsi satisfacere me permittit', R. Persons to C. Acquaviva, 12 February 1585, ARSI, Fondo Gesuitico 651/640.

'vehement' *Book of Resolution* into the more spacious, leisurely *Christian Directory*, which gives room for the reader to expand and relax.

The subsequent history of *A Christian Directory* is one of extraordinary textual instability. As published in 1585, it was virtually twice the length of *The Book of Resolution*. When he revised the work for a new edition in 1607, the omission of the chapters proving the existence of God and the truth of the Christian religion reduced it to a manageable length with a view to adding the second and third Books before long. The next edition, of 1622, was published twelve years after Persons' death, but may represent his final intentions, for the two transitory chapters are back, in an intelligently abbreviated form, and there are other minor changes.[52] The 1633 edition drops them again, but they re-appear in 1650 and, to the best of my knowledge, are included in all the many reprintings that followed, down to 1861.

Evelyn Waugh noted that *A Christian Directory* 'has proved a text book of sturdy piety to thousands of Catholics up to the present day', an observation somewhat compromised by his rechristening the book the *Spiritual Directory*.[53] J.P. Driscoll, doughty apologist, confused the 1585 and 1607 editions. Helen C. White thought it was a translation from Loarte. Brad Gregory re-invented the wheel thirty years after Robert McNulty had provided a thorough analysis of parallel passages from Persons and Bunny. These are not, perhaps, egregious errors. But they do suggest that *The Book of Resolution* is a book more talked about than read, and read, when it is, in ignorance of its complicated textual history and circumstances of composition. Yet it may be the final irony of the book's fortunes that now, in today's ecumenical climate, it will be read again with sympathy and patient interest.

---

[52] *A Christian directory, guiding men to eternall saluation* (St Omer, 1622), STC 19354.7, ARCR II no. 622.

[53] Evelyn Waugh, *Edmund Campion: Jesuit and Martyr* (London, 1935; rpt. New York, 1956), p. 82.

10

'Out of Step': Six Supplementary Notes on Jasper Heywood[1]

DENNIS FLYNN

I

Among the earliest discussions of a Jesuit mission to England one seems to have originated in Belgium. Dr Thomas Wilson, William Lord Burghley's agent at Brussels in 1574, wrote to the Lord Treasurer about a mooted petition to be addressed to Queen Elizabeth through King Philip II of Spain. The point of the proposed petition was that William Allen, Nicholas Sander, Jasper Heywood, and his brother Ellis be allowed to re-enter England for the purpose of peaceably preaching Catholicism.[2] Considering the background of Wilson's report, it seems highly probable that the source of this rumour was Ellis Heywood himself: Wilson had been probing him for information about the Catholic exiles and their plans.

The Jesuit General in 1574 was hard-headed Everard Mercurian, who had come to Rome after having served as Jesuit Provincial in Belgium. There is no evidence that any petition involving a mission for the Heywood brothers had ever been discussed within the Society, nor would it be surprising if Ellis Heywood had not mentioned the proposal to superiors. Ellis must at least have suspected that Mercurian would be cool to any such notion. In any case, Heywood also knew that his own physical condition could not recommend him to Mercurian for this kind of work. In successive annual and triennial

---

[1] Material presented here supplements my 'The English Mission of Jasper Heywood, S.J.', *AHSI* 54 (1985), pp. 45–76.

[2] Dr Thomas Wilson to William Cecil, Baron of Burghley, 14 February 1574, printed in *Queen Elizabeth and Her Times*, ed. Thomas Wright, 2 vols (London, 1838), II, pp. 3–6. Four and a half years after his brother Jasper, Ellis Heywood had entered the Society at the end of 1566, in the Jesuit college at Dillingen, Bavaria, where Jasper had been stationed since 1564. See Thomas M. McCoog, S.J., *Monumenta Angliae*, 2 vols (Rome, 1992) MHSI 142, 143, II, pp. 351–52.

evaluations his superiors in Germany had described him as 'infirmarius'; partly for this reason he had been transferred to Belgium, perhaps also in part to help care for his aging, exiled father.[3] Although Ellis was in no condition for the rigorous trials awaiting the first Jesuit missionaries, his fond idea was that the mission could be quietly negotiated with the Queen and her Council. It was a way of thinking about the problem that naturally tended to characterize his and his brother's approach, whereas Mercurian's quite different way of thinking brought him to the conclusion that no English mission was practicable in the 1570s.

Ellis Heywood, however, may have talked with William Allen about the idea. During the winter of 1575–76, writing to Mercurian about the need to do something for English Catholicism, Allen recommended that Ellis and Jasper Heywood, John and Edward Rastell, and Edmund Campion were ideal missionary prospects because of their reputations in England as men of learning. At this date Robert Persons still did not figure in Allen's thoughts.[4] Mercurian was not swayed by Allen's advice, perhaps because as Jesuit General he would know some things about these men that Allen probably did not know. Apart from Ellis Heywood's long-standing physical problems, Mercurian learned that Jasper Heywood too had for years been suffering from afflictions both physical and mental. Beginning early in 1572, reports had begun to come to Mercurian's predecessor Francis Borgia, that at the Jesuit college in Dillingen Heywood was experiencing acute terror every night, troubled by what he called a 'demon'.[5] This psychological debilitation continued for over six months, when Heywood was transferred from Dillingen for a vacation at Augsburg.[6] But the terror still did not wane until the end of 1572.

Moreover, Jasper Heywood and John Rastell had both by 1577 been called to the General's attention as disciplinary problems. Both men were increasingly restive with their assignments to the Bavarian province of the Jesuits. Their provincial, Paul Hoffaeus, had written to Rome suggesting that in view of growing tension Rastell should be transferred out of Bavaria inasmuch as he was not working well and was becoming a centre of discontent that could spread.[7] Perhaps to head this off and as part of a general policy to acknowledge the

[3] Heywood is termed 'infirmarius' in catalogues of Munich in 1567 (ARSI, Sup. Germ. 44, f. 56); Innsbruck in 1568 (ARSI, Sup Germ. 44, f. 49); and Halle in 1572 (ARSI, Germ. 131, f. 186ᵛ). At Halle in 1571 his limited work was described as primarily nursing the sick (ARSI, Germ. Sup. 44, f. 73). These catalogues were published in McCoog, *Monumenta Angliae*.

[4] William Allen to Everard Mercurian, n.d., in Patrick Ryan, S.J., 'Some Correspondence of Cardinal Allen', in *Miscellanea VII* (London, 1911), CRS 9, pp. 67–69.

[5] Heywood's agitation is suggested in his letter to Jerónimo Nadal, 6 January 1572 (ARSI, Germ. 134/I, f. 25). Explicit reports are in Theodore Canisius to Nadal, 28 March 1572 (ARSI, Germ. 134/I, f. 141); Paul Hoffaeus to Borja, 29 March 1572 (ARSI, Germ. 179, ff. 300–01); Hoffaeus to Borja, 3 May 1572 (ARSI, Germ. 134/I, f. 213); and Heywood's own detailed letter to Borja, 6 June 1572 (ARSI, Germ. 134/I, ff. 245–46ᵛ).

[6] Hoffaeus to Nadal, 23 June 1572 (ARSI, Germ. 134/I, ff. 271–72).

[7] Hoffaeus to Borja, 20 September 1572 (ARSI, Germ. 134/II, f. 458).

painful problems of English Jesuits in exile, Rastell instead was given a more responsible position as vice-rector at Ingolstadt University. But by 1577 Mercurian had received further bad reports about Rastell, ultimately learning that Rastell had actually disappeared from his post and had to be replaced.[8]

Heywood too had been complaining about his assignment since the early 1570s, when he wrote to Borja that for nine years he had been a useless appendage at Dillingen College. Listing his fluency in Italian, French, Latin, and English as qualifications for a different assignment, Heywood pointedly omitted German.[9] But though Dillingen had perhaps not been the best assignment from Heywood's point of view, his troubles as a Jesuit went deeper than the local conditions in Bavaria. Heywood had been admitted into the Jesuits at Rome in 1562. This date seems significant in two respects: first, it had been just six years since the death of St Ignatius, during a period when the Society's character was still fluid, relatively open to Erasmian currents, and not yet irrevocably identified with enforcing the Council of Trent; and, second, it had been just three years since the death of Giampietro Carafa, Pope Paul IV, at whose election in 1555 Loyola is said to have shaken in every bone of his body.[10]

Joining the Jesuits in 1562, under the less rigorist pontificate of Pius IV, Heywood seems likely to have thought the Society a more congenial organization than it turned out later to be. The Erasmian cast of mind with which Heywood joined the Jesuits is reflected in his bookish admission statement, a required list of possessions inscribed by each novice at the 'professed house' of the Jesuits in Rome:

> I, Jasper Heywood, Englishman of the City of London, have . . . brought with me a black coat with a belt; Macrobius's *On the Dream of Scipio*; Marsilio Ficino's *On the Immortality of the Soul*; Gerson's *On the Imitation of Christ*; the *Book of Psalms*; and the *Office of the Blessed Virgin*.[11]

Pages of adjacent entries by other novices in the spring of 1562 do not mention any books, let alone such books as the first two of these. It may be that Heywood

---

8 Antonio Baldvini to Mercurian, 1 May 1577 (ARSI, Germ. 138/I, f. 25); Hoffaeus to Mercurian, 15 July 1577 (ARSI, Germ. 138/II, f. 227); Jacob Rabenstein to Mercurian, 12 August 1577 (ARSI, Germ. 138/II, f. 290); and Hoffaeus to Mercurian, 13 August 1577 (ARSI, Germ. 138/II, f. 291). The policy issue had been addressed by Jacob Brunellus in a letter to Mercurian from Louvain (co-signed by William Allen and Nicholas Sander) on 6 April 1572 (ARSI, Germ. 134/I, f. 154).

9 Heywood to Borja, 6 June 1572 (ARSI, Germ. 134/I, f. 245): 'hoc collegio (cuius iam per novem tantum annos inutile membrum fui)'. To Nadal, Heywood wrote more bluntly on the same day that he would prefer to work in Rome because of the relatively greater intellectual stimulation available there (ARSI, Germ. 134/I, f. 140).

10 Peter A. Quinn, 'Ignatius Loyola and Gian Pietro Carafa: Catholic Reformers at Odds', *Catholic Historical Review* 67 (1981), p. 391; and John W. O'Malley, S.J., *The First Jesuits* (Cambridge, Mass., 1993), pp. 33, 161.

11 ARSI, Rom. 170, ff. 55–55[v].

had heard about similar baggage carried by the first Jesuits on their travels and was trying to imitate Ignatius and his original companions.[12]

Unfortunately for Heywood's irenic, Erasmian expectations as a Jesuit, after only four years Pope Pius IV was succeeded in 1566 by Pius V, who not only excommunicated Queen Elizabeth but established as a policy, for his and succeeding papacies, casting the Jesuits more and more in the role of Catholic reformers according to the dictates of the Council of Trent. Increasingly disenchanted with this role, during these years Heywood demonstrated, and acquired some reputation for, a maverick tendency in the Erasmian vein.

Moreover, by the time Mercurian was getting advice from Allen to send Heywood to England, the General had also become aware of Heywood's central role in another turbulence affecting the Bavarian Province. In a notorious controversy with local merchants Heywood, rather than remain a useless appendage at Dillingen, had taken to preaching at the Court of the Duke of Bavaria that business contracts charging 5% interest were usurious and illicit. This rash act brought Heywood and the Jesuits into dangerous conflict with the Bishop of Augsburg, who began to consider expelling the Society from his diocese.[13]

As for the fourth member of William Allen's brace of brothers, Edward Rastell too cannot have been judged well-qualified for an English mission in Mercurian's eyes, again for reasons of health. Before the decade was over, in fact, Edward Rastell had died.[14] Only Edmund Campion among those recommended by Allen could not be disqualified for various reasons; but Campion was also comparatively new in the Society, younger than the other four men, and (however promising) not yet entirely a known quantity from Mercurian's point of view. In an evaluation of March 1577, Campion was described as grappling with and overcoming his difficulties,[15] a report that to Mercurian's point of view would only suggest the pattern of difficulties characterizing the progress of Allen's other four candidates. These had all been promising men whose promise had generally been clouded by the difficulties of transplantation into exile.

II

Campion, himself possibly having met Heywood while travelling in the spring of 1580 from Prague to Rome, early favoured calling Heywood to the English mission.[16] Prior to the spring of 1581 Robert Persons also thought highly of

---

[12] O'Malley, *The First Jesuits*, pp. 32–33.

[13] Hoffaeus to Mercurian, 1 February 1576 (ARSI, Germ 137/I, ff. 55–55ᵛ); and Dietrich Canisius to Mercurian, 12 February 1576 (ARSI, Germ. 137/I, ff. 72–72ᵛ).

[14] Henry Foley, S.J., *Records of the English Province of the Society of Jesus*, 7 vols in 8 (Roehampton/London, 1875–83), VII/2, p. 675. Cf. Thomas H. Clancy, S.J., 'The First Generation of English Jesuits', *AHSI* 57 (1988), p. 140.

[15] J. Campanus to E. Mercurian, 4 March 1577 (ARSI, Germ. 138/I, f. 128ᵛ).

[16] Campion's letter to Pope Gregory XIII, no longer extant, recommending Heywood for

Heywood as a prestigious former Oxford don, poet, and translator, and a Latin preacher as a Jesuit, who would represent precisely those qualities for which Campion himself was thought invaluable.[17] Heywood's reputation with both Persons and Campion must have been based more on what they knew or heard of his career at Oxford than on any detailed knowledge of his problematic activities as a Jesuit.

However, Persons' opinion of Heywood changed abruptly after their first meeting in the summer of 1581. Heywood had landed in England, not like Persons and Campion on the southern coast but at Newcastle in the north, coming to London out of Percy country, evidently under the auspices of Henry Percy, eighth Earl of Northumberland, Captain of Tynemouth Castle.[18] In this contrast we may find some indication of how the two priests' disagreements derived from differences in age, background, and style as missionaries. Heywood evidently saw himself as a loner, coming to the mission directly from the Court of Bavaria at the special request of the Pope.[19] Persons on the other hand saw himself as more the administrative officer in a chain of command. He tended to

the mission, was cited by Ignaz Agricola, *Historiae Provinciae Societatis Jesu Germaniae Superioris*, 4 vols (Augsburg, 1727–46), I, p. 244.

[17] Persons' repeated requests for Heywood are mentioned by Acquaviva in a letter to Allen, 28 May 1581, Ryan, 'Correspondence', p. 78. Cf. Allen to Alfonso Agazzari, 20 April 1581: '[Persons] asks for subjects for England who are eloquent in the Latin tongue and suitable for disputations'; Penelope Renold, ed., *Letters of William Allen and Richard Barret, 1572–1598* (London, 1967), CRS 58, p. 30.

[18] Heywood had disembarked with a fellow Jesuit, William Holt; Examination of William Holt, 1 and 2 March 1583 (Bodleian Library, Tanner MS 79, f. 187). Northumberland's man at the castle, Captain William Pullen, had probably helped arrange for the Jesuits' passage to Newcastle on an earlier trip to France; see Henry Carey, Baron of Hunsdon, to Sir Francis Walsingham, 13 March 1581 (Joseph Bain *et al.*, *Calendar of State Papers relating to Scotland and Mary Queen of Scots*, 13 vols in 14 parts [London, 1898–1969] V, 653). The furtive participation of Percy followers in such landings is illustrated in a report to Walsingham by one of his spies, conveying information from a servant of William Allen, that 'preists most commonly do come over in French boates that come to Newcastle for Coales, whoe do land the sayd Preists either at Newcastell, or in some Creeke nere to the same. They make choyce of that place the Rather for that Robert Higheclyf her Majesty's officer at Newcastell is a papiste in harte & made acquaynted with there comynge, & that his wyef is and hathe bynne a papiste this iii or iiii yeres, and that by her Directions the sayd preists with there bookes do passe in Securitie, And that the sayd Higheclif hathe certen servants dwellinge aboute the Creeks nere to Newcastell which willingly do R[eceive] the Preists and helpe to convey them farder into the lande, Unto the houses of one Gooderiche, hareclif, Grymshawe, and Nevell, all gents of great livinge, where the sayd Preists are R[eceived] and change there apparrell, and are provided of horses for there Jorney to London or ells where' (Thomas Rogers to Walsingham, 13 April 1585, PRO, SP 12/177, f. 19). Likely through Pullen, Northumberland had similarly arranged not only for Heywood's and Holt's sailing from France but also for their hiding in one of the safe houses after their arrival at Tynemouth.

[19] Pope Gregory XIII had written specially to Wilhelm Wittelsbach, Duke of Bavaria, on 9 May 1581, requesting Heywood's participation in the English mission; Augustin Theiner, *Annales Ecclesiastici*, 3 vols (Rome, 1856), III, p. 300.

expect from fellow Jesuits a kind of discipline foreign to Heywood's manner. Where Heywood understood their work as requiring dramatic personal initiatives, Persons (especially after a year on the job) saw a need for security, secrecy, and carefully planned procedures. Something of the same difference in style, though less pronounced and not a cause of friction, had marked a contrast between Persons and Campion.[20]

Again, Heywood was twelve years older than Persons, having grown up at court during the reigns of Henry VIII and Edward VI. His personal acquaintance not only with Queen Elizabeth but with other aristocrats in England and abroad led him to think of the mission largely in terms of influencing the great noble houses. In contrast Persons, a yeoman's son and a scholarship student at Oxford, tended to consider the English nobility a lost cause from the Catholic point of view. Their supine acquiescence and even complicity in Tudor looting of Church property and revenues ultimately suggested to Persons that England might best deprive the House of Lords of all effective power and govern itself instead by a combination of Catholic Crown with an enlarged House of Commons, fortified by the transfer of some newly appointed Catholic bishops to the Commons from the House of Lords.[21] No doubt because of such differences the two men irritated each other.

III

After a short stay in London, Heywood travelled to the north, where Catholic feeling ran strong and where in three months he was able treasonously to reconcile hundreds to Catholicism. With a remarkable boldness, evidently exceeding that of Persons and Campion, Heywood defied detection by travelling with much display, 'in coach accompanied with many and in costly apparel'.[22] In October 1581 he returned triumphantly to London bringing with him alms for imprisoned Catholics from the northern nobility and gentry. Heywood's methods of operation are seen in the way he soon collected first payments of pledges for the work of the mission totalling about £1300 annually, 'by even porsions to be payde', from a long list of wealthy Catholics and Catholic sympathizers

---

[20] Elsewhere in this volume, John Bossy's essay, 'The Heart of Robert Persons', makes a perceptive estimate of Persons' political style.

[21] So Persons argued in 'A Memoriall for the Reformation of Englande', which he never published but circulated widely in manuscript after 1596; see Thomas H. Clancy, S.J., *Papist Pamphleteers* (Chicago, 1964), pp. 40–42; and John Bossy, *The English Catholic Community, 1570–1850* (London, 1975), pp. 15–34.

[22] John H. Pollen, S.J., ed., 'The Notebook of John Southcote, D.D. 1628–36' in *Miscellanea I* (London, 1905), CRS 1, p. 112; and P.H. to Walsingham, n.d. (PRO, SP 12/155, f. 96), where Heywood and Holt, along with one 'Dr Henshawe', are reported to have made 228 conversions. The letter is mistakenly calendared as if written on 17 November 1582; but it seems rather to have been written in the winter of 1581 or spring of 1582.

headed by Henry Stanley, Earl of Derby (£300 a year). Other Catholic nobility on the list of Heywood's contributors were Anthony Browne, Viscount Montague; and Lords William Vaux, Thomas Paget, John Lumley, Henry Morley, and Philip Wharton.[23] All these noblemen or their deceased fathers had grown up with Heywood at court (as had a group of noble women contributors on the same list); and all were key figures, able in more ways than financially to facilitate missionary operations throughout the country.

Heywood also continued his relations with the Earl of Northumberland, through whose bailiwick he had entered England. Though Northumberland had been required (on account of earlier involvement in plotting to liberate Mary Stuart) to reside in Sussex, through his retainers and relations he continued to open and close many doors not only in Sussex,[24] but in London and even in the north, where (it was still said) people knew no prince but a Percy; and he had long since felt sufficiently harassed and limited by the Privy Council to have developed a sympathy for the cause of the missionaries. Thus Heywood was assisted in moving from safe house to safe house, using and ramifying a network for underground activity provided by the Catholic nobility and gentry for the seminary priests, and before them for the old Marian priests.

By this time, of course, Campion had been tried for treason and executed. Heywood nevertheless continued with his missionary work, following his success in the north with a campaign at Oxford and Cambridge designed to make the two universities 'perpetual aqueducts' through which would pass young English scholars bound to finish their studies at continental seminaries. As a result of Heywood's work, twenty English students came to Rheims from the universities in November 1582; and fifty more arrived in August 1583, a group including several 'sons of noblemen'.[25] When the resources of the Rheims seminary were strained by this dramatic influx of defectors, various solutions to the problem were proposed and implemented, including transfer of some of the students to the English College at Rome and also creation of new Jesuit colleges such as

---

[23] P.H. to Walsingham, n.d. (PRO SP 12/168, f. 31). The letter is conjecturally calendared as if written in 1584 (CSP Domestic, II, 160); but its references to the imprisonment of the priests Christopher Small and Ralph Collyer show that it must have been written after mid-spring 1582 and before mid-winter 1582–83. On Small, see Godfrey Anstruther, *The Seminary Priests* 4 vols (Ware/Durham/Great Wakering, 1968–77), I, 319; on Collyer, see Clink certificates printed in John H. Pollen, S.J., ed., 'Official Lists of Prisoners for Religion from 1562–80', in *Miscellanea II* (London, 1906), CRS 2, pp. 225–26, 231. Heywood's return with funds from the North is noted by Persons to Acquaviva, 26 September–21 October 1581 (Leo Hicks, S.J., ed., *Letters and Memorials of Father Robert Persons, S.J.*, [London, 1942], CRS 39, p. 108); and by the Spanish Ambassador Bernardino Mendoza to King Philip II, 20 October 1581 (CSP Simancas, III, p. 195).

[24] For example, Heywood used the house of Northumberland's adherent and Sussex neighbour William Shelley; Examination of Edward Jones, 23 June 1586 (PRO, SP 12/190, f. 50).

[25] Allen to Agazzari, 5 November 1582 and 8 August 1583 in John H. Pollen, S.J., ed., 'Notes Concerning the English Mission' in *Miscellanea IV* (London, 1907), CRS 4, pp. 73, 115.

those at St Omer and Eu, endowed for several purposes by the Duke of Guise.[26] But not all these young fugitives can have been interested in becoming priests, and seminary education leading to ordination was not the only activity Heywood's aqueducts were likely to be feeding.

While Guise sponsored the new college at Eu, he was also cultivating a related plan, for an 'Enterprise' or invasion of England. Beginning as early as 1578, Guise had tried through the Spanish ambassador at Paris to negotiate King Philip's support for such an invasion. By 1582 these plans had crystallized: Spanish forces would be landed in Scotland where, with the cooperation of the Duke of Lennox, an effort could be launched southwards into England to free Mary Stuart and restore Catholicism. One element of the plan was to organize fugitive gentry and nobility as officers for companies of English soldiers, to be attached temporarily to the Spanish and allied forces fighting Dutch Protestant rebels.[27]

Raw materials for such an English unit were on hand at least as early as the summer of 1582, when four hundred unpaid English soldiers, sent covertly by the Privy Council to fight for the Dutch rebels, deserted to the Spaniards and were received and paid by Alessandro Farnese, Prince, later Duke of Parma, the leader of the Spanish forces. From England, the Spanish ambassador Bernardino de Mendoza pointed out that these former enemy troops would remain useless (except as decoys to attract further English deserters) without well-trained and reliable English Catholic officers.[28] But here the increasing flow of young nobility and gentry could become a factor. Such emigration for military training would have to be carefully organized on both sides of the

---

[26] 'The young gentlemen go over by heaps from hence out of all places, and most by the creeks, and in fisher-boats, carrying with them great provisions of all necessaries. There is a new-erected seminary at Eu, a town of the Guises' inheritance, by the sea-side in Picardy. You shall hear there how it is filled in a short time, so as the revolt and falling away increaseth daily, notwithstanding all the prisons be full of them here'; Nicholas Faunt to Anthony Bacon, 20 November 1583 (Thomas Birch, *Memoirs of the Reign of Queen Elizabeth*, 2 vols [London, 1754], I, p. 41).

[27] This was originally an idea of the 1569 rebel emigres, many of whom already were doing scattered service with the Spanish army. The Earl of Westmorland and Lord Thomas Copley were among those who had urged this course on King Philip; and Lord Copley (given his title by the Spanish king) had been observed suspiciously conversing with Lord Percy, eldest son of the Earl of Northumberland, during a tournament at the French Court. But King Philip of Spain remained scrupulous about diplomatic problems connected to the scheme, irresolute so long as he and England were officially at peace. See Robert Lechat, *Les Réfugiés Anglais dans les Pays-Bas Espagnols Durant le Règne d'Élisabeth* (Louvain, 1914), pp. 64–65; and Cobham to Walsingham, 10 October 1581 (CSP Foreign, XV, p. 336). On Guise's support of Eu and his early negotiations with Spain, see A. Lynn Martin, *Henry III and the Jesuit Politicians* (Geneva, 1973), pp. 65 and 70–73; and elsewhere in this volume John Bossy's 'Heart of Robert Persons'.

[28] Mendoza to King Philip, 30 August 1582 (CSP Foreign, III, p. 398). On the 1582 plans for the 'Enterprise' see Leo Hicks, S.J., *An Elizabethan Problem* (London, 1964), pp. 6–7; and Hicks, *Letters of Persons*, pp. lii–lv.

channel with the help of some powerful Catholic sympathizer in England. In view of what we know about Northumberland's various activities, he seems likeliest to have been coordinating Heywood's perhaps unwitting activities with those of Guise and the exiles in their effort to develop an English force that could eventually be used in an invasion.

After a few months, Heywood's recruiting at the universities was curtailed (so he surmised) by the severe reaction of the Privy Council to one of Persons' several pamphlets printed at Rouen, smuggled into England, and distributed at Oxford and Cambridge. Persons arranged all this from France, and it must have involved a considerable apparatus of underground workers, all of them evidently unknown to Heywood, who was simply bypassed by Persons. The result, Heywood later complained, was devastating to his efforts: heads of colleges were suddenly directed by the Privy Council to require the Oath of Supremacy from selected students twelve to fourteen years of age, many of whom did swear, thus undercutting Heywood in his attempts to lead them toward the seminaries.[29]

IV

Heywood took another important initiative in developing his contacts with some 'big fish'.[30] By early 1583, implementing a policy to further the reconciliation to Catholicism of the most prestigious members of the old nobility, Heywood had been in touch with all three of the most ancient earldoms of the realm in the persons of the Earls of Arundel, Derby, and Northumberland. Philip Howard, Earl of Arundel, was a godson of Spain's King and son of Thomas Howard, the Duke of Norfolk who, despite having deserted the northern Earls in 1569, was himself later beheaded for treason. Arundel had been tutored as a child by the Catholic scholar Gregory Martin, and then had led a worldly life at Elizabeth's Court, troubled in conscience about Catholicism. In 1581 he acceded to his Earldom and became reconciled with his estranged wife. Lady Arundel within a year became a Catholic, as did Arundel's sister. Later in the same year Arundel attended a disputation in the Tower of London between the imprisoned Edmund Campion and some Anglican ministers, an experience that strongly influenced him to become a Catholic.[31] Heywood contacted Arundel early in 1583.

---

[29] Heywood to Acquaviva, n.d. (ARSI, Anglia 30/I, f. 118ᵛ). The increasing apprehension of the Oxford authorities through the early 1580s is detailed elsewhere in this volume by James McConica, 'The Catholic Experience in Tudor Oxford.'

[30] Allen to Agazzari, 14 March 1583; Thomas Francis Knox, ed., *The Letters and Memorials of William Cardinal Allen* (London, 1882), p. 182. Allen's phrase 'magnos pisces' he must have had from his brother Gabriel, who in turn carried it from Heywood himself. Persons glosses the apparent reference to the Earls of Arundel and Northumberland in Pollen, 'Notes', p. 92.

[31] John H. Pollen, S.J. and William MacMahon, S.J., ed., *The Venerable Philip Howard, Earl of Arundel, 1557–1595* (London, 1919), CRS 21, pp. 20–23, 32.

Politically the most important of the Earls was Northumberland, who like Arundel since the early years of the reign had changed in his religious sympathies. His helping Heywood infiltrate England committed him ever more strongly toward an overt, sacramental reconciliation to the religion he now favoured and his father and brother had died for. His continuing contacts with exiles and French ultramontanists probably accentuated his spiritual development toward Catholicism. Perhaps the most pointed indication of the Earl's state of mind shortly after the beginning of 1583 is the last mission of his most trusted aide, Captain William Pullen, who left Tynemouth Castle for Rheims to become a priest and then, through the offices of Robert Persons, a chaplain to the company of English fugitives stationed in the camp of the Prince of Parma.[32] Moreover, late 1582 or early 1583 must have been the time when Northumberland himself, in contact with Heywood, was formally reconciled to Catholicism.

V

By the summer of 1584, both Heywood and Northumberland had for several months been imprisoned in the Tower of London, Northumberland awaiting trial and Heywood's trial having been suspended *sine die*. In September Persons dispatched a replacement for Heywood from Paris. William Weston immediately sought out Heywood's sister Elizabeth Syminges after successfully evading the port watchers and arriving in London. With her help he was able to exchange letters with Heywood in the Tower. Weston learned how, prior to the trial, Heywood had been tortured on the rack. Gradually, with repeated persuasions to cooperate better and thus spare himself, Heywood had been put to torture 'in as charitable a manner as such a thing might be'.[33] Since his trial, during the summer months of heightened persecution, he had been held in solitary confinement in a little, dark cell without any furniture. Weston gained through his correspondence a conviction of Heywood's staunch resistance but no clear sense of any continuing enthusiasm for martyrdom.

Weston learned in any case that, despite the general expectation among Catholics that Heywood would be executed, the government was probably going

---

[32] Arriving at Rheims on 7 January (Thomas Francis Knox, ed., *The First and Second Diaries of the English College, Douay* [London, 1878], p. 192), Pullen was ordained subdeacon on 3 March (*ibid.*, p. 194), deacon on 7 April (*ibid.*), and priest on the Vigil of Pentecost in May (*ibid.*, p. 195). On his subsequent commission as a chaplain see John H. Pollen, S.J., ed., 'Memoirs of Father Robert Persons, S.J.', in *Miscellanea II*, CRS 2, p. 33 and Pollen, 'Notes', p. 125).

[33] The phrase is Burghley's in his 'Declaration of the Favourable Dealing of Her Majesty's Commissioners'; see *'The Execution of Justice in England' By William Cecil and 'A True, sincere, and Modest Defence of English Catholics' By William Allen*, ed. Robert W. Kingdon (Ithaca, N.Y., 1965), p. 47.

to deport him along with numerous other priests held in various prisons. The policy of Lord Burghley with regard to the priests had begun to prevail over the policy of the Earl of Leicester and Sir Francis Walsingham, who had strongly urged show trials and public executions during the preceding three years. As Burghley now argued, these brutal executions had largely backfired: 'Death doth no Ways lessen them, since we find by Experience that it worketh no such Effect, but, like *Hydra's* Heads, upon Cutting off one, seven grow up.'[34] Therefore, it would be better to clear out all the priests: summarily deport those in custody and then put new legislation through Parliament banishing the rest and making it simply illegal for them ever to set foot in England again. Heywood, in custody since December 1583, was thus to be deported with twenty others in January 1585.

These plans, along with preparations for the Parliament of 1584–1585, had become a main concern of Catholics. To counter the new legislation a group of Catholic nobility and gentry, headed by Heywood's friend Lord William Vaux and including a representative of Northumberland,[35] had worked with Heywood to prepare a petition boldly appealing to the Queen herself for toleration of Catholicism. The Catholics were planning to present the petition to the Queen before Parliament convened. Weston learned of these plans through correspondence with Heywood and relayed word to Persons in France. Probably on instructions from Persons, Weston now sought more searching conversation with Heywood than could be had by letters. The petition contemplated had the potential to compromise the whole political design of the mission. Thus at Christmas 1584, evidently under the guise of a family visit, Mrs Syminges daringly brought Weston to Heywood's cell in the Tower. To make the family visit more plausible, they brought with them into the Tower Heywood's nephew, the twelve-year-old John Donne.

Weston's memoirs, tersely describing the meeting, were written twenty-seven years afterwards. But even at such great distance of time, his traitorous penetration into the Tower of London had left a deep impression on him:

> I accompanied her to the Tower, but with a feeling of great trepidation as I saw the vast battlements, and was led by the warder past the gates with their iron fastenings, which were closed behind me. So I came to the cell where

---

[34] William Cecil, Baron of Burghley, 'Lord Treasurer Burleigh's advice to Queen Elizabeth, in Matters of Religion and State' in *A Fourth Collection of Scarce and Valuable Tracts*, 4 vols (London, 1752), I, p. 104.

[35] Representing Northumberland as this petition was drawn up, and perhaps even participating in the conference with Weston, was James Price, a gentleman servant of the Earl. See Roger B. Manning, 'Richard Shelley of Warminghurst and the English Catholic Petition for Toleration of 1585', *Recusant History* 6 (1962), p. 270.

the Father was confined. We greeted one another and then, as was natural, exchanged the information we had about the affairs that concerned us.[36]

The specifics of these affairs Weston does not mention; undoubtedly various sensitive political matters were involved. One thing Weston does mention is that Heywood had been in touch with the Earl of Northumberland, imprisoned elsewhere in the Tower, and that the Earl had been informed by his sources that the Privy Council was already aware of Weston's presence in England.

Donne has left us his own account of the visit, the earliest experience of his life of which we have any personal testimony: 'at a consultation of *Iesuits* in the *Tower* in the late Queenes time, I saw it resolved, that in a Petition to bee exhibited to her, shee might not be stiled *Sacred*'.[37] Although even more laconic than Weston's account, Donne's remark also tells characteristically more than Weston does about the heart of the matter, the meeting's political focus on the petition for toleration. We may be sure, however, that this quibble over wording the petition was not the only thing about his visit to the Tower that had made an impression on the boy. Weston concludes:

> At last, when I had finished talking to Father Heywood – we spent almost the whole day together – I embraced him and said goodbye. Then I returned the same way that I had come; and the moment I reached safety outside the walls I felt as if I had been restored to the light of day.[38]

VI

At length following Heywood's deportation in January 1585, he arrived at the English College in Rheims. Heywood spent most of March there conferring with Persons and Allen, being debriefed on affairs in England, and discussing his own future in relation to the English mission. Heywood wanted to return to England, to contest his illegal deportation and to continue the work he had been forced to abandon. But Heywood's ideas about the continuing conduct of the mission diverged considerably from those of Allen and Persons. After a few days of conferences at Rheims, it became clear to Heywood that his views and opinions, so highly regarded by Mendoza (expelled from England and by now serving as Spanish ambassador in Paris), had little standing with the leaders of the English mission.

Emerging again into exile after three and a half years underground and behind prison walls, Heywood found dramatic changes in the attitudes of the

---

[36] William Weston, *An Autobiography from the Jesuit Underground*, translated and edited by Philip Caraman, S.J. (London, 1955), p. 10.

[37] John Donne, *Pseudo-Martyr* (London, 1610), STC 7048, p. 46.

[38] Weston, *An Autobiography*, p. 11. Unlike Donne, Weston carefully omits all mention of the visit's political context; but see Manning, 'Richard Shelley', p. 270.

exiles. In 1581 he had left the continent triumphally, a descendant of Sir Thomas More returning to England with the personal blessing of the Pope and the endorsement of his fellow Jesuits. But in the time that had elapsed, his own stature in the exiles' eyes had diminished, especially in relation to that of Robert Persons. By 1585 Persons had become the acknowledged co-leader of the English mission along with William Allen. Heywood's initial differences with Persons had now hardened and multiplied, so that a definite friction appears to have grown between them. These differences ran so deep that they could no longer work together.

Heywood complained about the way Persons had slighted him on his arrival in England and about his treatment by Persons in ensuing correspondence across the Channel. Heywood also criticized a whole list of Persons' real or supposed decisions as Superior in England, the most lurid criticism being Heywood's charge that Persons had conspired with one George Gifford to assassinate Queen Elizabeth.[39] How many of these complaints and suspicions Heywood divulged immediately in the spring of 1585 is not known. The most immediate and pressing source of disagreement however was probably the petition for toleration, which Heywood had been working on with the Catholic gentry and nobility, including Northumberland. William Allen soon sided with Persons in concluding that Heywood was 'out of step' and unsuited to work connected with the English mission. Despite this rejection, Heywood seems to have thought he still had influence enough to overcome their opposition and return to England. He took the position that he would need word from Rome before he would accept orders from Allen and Persons to stand down.[40]

Ultimately Heywood was disappointed and perhaps stunned by the refusal of his superiors to permit his return to England. William Allen, writing to Claudio Acquaviva about Heywood's appeal of this decision, remarked with some asperity that Heywood 'has made it his convenience' to await the General's decision at Rheims. Robert Persons too wrote at length to Acquaviva about Heywood and the future of the mission. The General was in agreement that 'they who handle those matters should all have the same sentiments and views, and with consentient minds advance by the same paths'. Siding with Allen and Persons, Acquaviva recalled Heywood to Rome early in April.[41] But by this time, his stubborn presence unwelcome, Heywood had already left Rheims. Retiring to Paris, he visited an old friend from his days at Dillingen, the English Jesuit

---

[39] Heywood to Acquaviva, n.d. (ARSI, Anglia 30/I, f. 119). Elsewhere in this volume, John Bossy's 'Heart of Robert Persons' argues that Persons knew of and probably sympathized with Gifford's project.

[40] Allen to Acquaviva, 8 March 1585 (Renold, *Letters of Allen and Barret*, p. 142); Allen to Acquaviva, 18 March 1585 (*ibid.*, p. 143); and Allen to Acquaviva, 3 April 1585 (*ibid.*, pp. 147–48).

[41] Allen to Acquaviva, 18 March 1585 (Hicks, *Letters of Persons*, p. 143); and Acquaviva to Allen, 9 April 1585 (Ryan, 'Correspondence', pp. 97–99). Persons's letter is not extant, but is mentioned in another letter to Acquaviva on 10 May 1585 (Hicks, *Letters of Persons*, p. 148).

Thomas Darbyshire, with whom he could more congenially recover from the shock of emerging into exile.

Never again would Heywood play a role with the Jesuits in England, but he found it difficult to withdraw immediately from affairs of the mission, troubling himself along with Darbyshire to advise one of Allen's seminary priests about a consignment of books, probably some pamphlets by Persons being smuggled into England.[42] Considering his past behaviour whenever conflict arose with superiors, it is probable that Heywood did not intend easily to accept assignment elsewhere. He may, as at earlier points in his career, have thought to appeal directly to the Pope; but such a tactic was prevented by the death of Gregory XIII in mid-April. Heywood did not leave Paris until the beginning of June 1585, travelling in the company of James Hill, a recent fugitive with whom he had worked during his time in England. Hill arrived at the English Hospice in Rome on 16 June.[43]

According to Henry More, the seventeenth-century Jesuit historian of the English mission, Heywood did not go to Rome in 1585. Instead, by More's account, Heywood was reassigned directly to the Jesuit college at Dôle in France and stayed there until he went to Rome four years later, eventually to be stationed for the remainder of his life at Naples.[44] However, this account appears to be wrong. In fact, Heywood must already have come to Rome when on 10 April 1586 he was granted permission to travel from Rome to Naples.[45] Moreover, the generally precise and comprehensive annual and triennial personnel reports from Dôle make no mention of Heywood during this period.[46] On the other hand, Heywood's name appears in the personnel reports from Naples as early as October 1587.[47] Evidently More was mistaken about Heywood's whereabouts from 1585 to 1589.

---

[42] Examination of Thomas Simpson, 14 May 1585 (PRO, SP 12/178, f. 57.viii). Darbyshire had taught at Dillingen with Heywood in the 1560s (Foley, *Records*, III, 710).

[43] Allen to Acquaviva, 3 July 1585 (Renold, *Letters of Allen and Barret*, pp. 164–66 and note on p. 166).

[44] Henry More, S.J., *The Elizabethan Jesuits: Historia Missionis Anglicanae Societatis Jesu (1660)*, translated and edited by Francis Edwards, S.J. (London, 1981), p. 172.

[45] ARSI, Hist. Soc. 61, f. 44[v] (cited as ARSI, Hist. Soc. 62, f. 44[v] in McCoog, *Monumenta Angliae*, II, p. 352).

[46] Eg., ARSI, Lugd. 12, ff. 59, 103, 126, and 146; ARSI, Lugd. 13, ff. 1–4; ARSI, Lugd. 18/I, ff. 14–15; and ARSI, Francia 10, ff. 103–106[v]. Alfred Hamy, S.J. found no mention of Heywood in his survey of the Lyons province's annual and triennial reports: *Province de Lyon, 1582–1762. Noms, Prenoms, Lieu d'Origine, Dates de Naissance, d'Entree, de Degre, Lieu et Date de Mort de Tous les Jesuites Demeures Fideles a Leurs Voeux jusqu'a la Fin* (Paris, 1900). Nor have I been able to find any mention of Heywood in reading ARSI, Lyons provincial correspondence from 1585 through 1590.

[47] ARSI, Neap. 80, f. 3.

11

Robert Southwell:
The Mission of the Written Word

NANCY POLLARD BROWN

As Philip II of Spain prepared for his great Enterprise to reclaim the throne of England, an even greater enterprise was being undertaken by the ground troops being trained in the seminaries and colleges on the continent to reclaim the country for Catholicism. The plans for the conversion of England gradually evolved, an act of faith on the part of those who suffered the hardships of exile, sustained by the conviction that numbers of English people, in some areas whole communities, would return to the old ways as soon as the possibility was presented to them through the work of the Mission priests. The seminary priests sent into England from the new college at Douai were a widening stream: four led the way in 1574; then seven; then eighteen; fifteen in the fourth year. A similar college was developed from the English Hospice in Rome in 1578. By 1580, when the Jesuit fathers Edmund Campion and Robert Persons set out from Rome, there were a hundred seminary priests at work.[1]

But however zealous these pioneers, however well-intentioned those who sent them, it was impossible for them to reach all areas. Nor could they respond promptly to the charges made against them by a government and an ecclesiastical authority that regarded their priestly ministry as traitorous and subversive. Books were seized at the ports or confiscated in the homes of Catholics. Proclamations condemning the importation and the possession of books of religious controversy were frequently issued during the reign, beginning with the Proclamation of 1 March 1569 and followed by similar edicts on 1 July 1570, 14

---

[1] Arnold Oskar Meyer, *England and the Catholic Church under Queen Elizabeth* (London, 1916), p. 132, citing Thomas Francis Knox, *The First and Second Diaries of the English College, Douay* (London, 1878), pp. 24–27. The number of 100 priests by 1580 is taken from Humphrey Ely, *Certaine briefe notes upon a briefe apologie* (Paris, 1602), preface, p. 29 (STC 7628; ARCR II, no. 187).

November 1570, and 28 September 1573,[2] all directed against books published on the continent. From the opening of the Jesuit Mission the need was recognised to extend the work of the priests by their own writing and by the printing and distribution of their books. In particular, they would be able to counter the defamation of their activity by immediate response to the polemical challenges issued by their adversaries.

The faculties granted to Campion and Persons on 14 April 1580 included permission to print and issue books anonymously, overriding the decree of the Council of Trent which expressly forbade such freedom.[3] Both priests were gifted writers, richly endowed to enable them to take advantage of the new policy. Their writing in England was addressed directly to the government authorities. Campion's 'Brag', apparently written in great haste as he set out on his first extended missionary tour, was specifically concerned to clear his good name in the event of his capture. Through it he asked that he should be allowed to defend Catholicism before representatives of the State, the two universities, and the civil and ecclesiastical law, and he begged to be allowed to put his case to the Queen herself. The succinct and moving statement of faith addressed to the Privy Council was put into the hands of Thomas Pounde, a prisoner in the Marshalsea. Pounde, finding it unsealed, allowed a copy to be made, and other copies followed. It was soon circulating widely in manuscript. On the other hand, Persons' longer defence in Latin, addressed to the London magistrates, apparently never gained such extensive currency.[4] To respond to the attacks printed in reply to Campion's manifesto they established a printing press with the help of a layman, Stephen Brinkley, first at Greenstreet House, East Ham, Essex, then at the house of Francis Browne, and then, when discovery seemed imminent, at Stonor Park, near Henley-on-Thames. The works the two Jesuits wrote for the press were all of a controversial or apologetical nature, each volume forged by the urgency of the time. Although some were addressed to the authorities, they were of concern to Catholics and served to strengthen their resolve and to clarify their position in some ambiguous areas, as on the subject of attending the English church services. Persons settled the issue in his *A briefe discours contayning certayne reasons why Catholiques refuse to goe to Church*, addressed to

[2]   Paul L. Hughes and James F. Larkin, C.S.V., eds, *Tudor Royal Proclamations*, 3 vols (New Haven, 1964–69), II, nos. 561, 577, 580, and 598.

[3]   Copies of the Jesuits' faculties are in the PRO, SP 137/26, 27, and 28. The decree forbidding the printing of books anonymously was issued at Session IV (8 April 1546), which forbade Catholics 'imprimere vel imprimi facere quosvis libros de rebus sacris sine nomine auctoris' (Norman Tanner, S.J., ed., *Decrees of the Ecumenical Councils*, 2 vols [London and Washington D.C., 1990], II, p. 665) The licence to print books reads: 'Ut liceat libros catholicos imprimere et edere tacito nomine auctoris, loci, et typographi, non obstante concilio Tridentino' (Meyer, *England and the Catholic Church*, Appendix xvii, p. 487).

[4]   On the 'Brag' and the consequent controversy, see Thomas M. McCoog, S.J., ' "Playing the Champion": The Role of Disputation in the Jesuit Mission' in this volume.

the Queen, and attributed to 'John Howlet', one of his many pseudonyms.[5] To disguise the existence of the press the volumes were given false imprints. Campion's challenge to debate matters of belief, issued to members of the two universities, *Rationes decem* (STC 4536.5; ARCR I, no. 135.1), was printed at Stonor and distributed in St Mary's University Church, Oxford, on 27 June 1581. Three weeks later he was taken at Lyford Grange. With prescience Campion had written to Claudio Acquaviva, Father-General of the Society, on 9 July: 'Nothing else was lacking to this cause than that to our books written with ink should succeed those others which are daily being published, written in blood.'[6]

The establishment of the press was a daring undertaking, highly dangerous to those involved. It was also an extremely costly venture, for the books could not be sold but were distributed widely to both Catholics and others in order to confuse the pursuivants. Funds were supplied in part by George Gilbert, who was responsible for the organisation of the band of young noblemen and gentlemen who supported the priests, and in part from alms.[7] As it was, the equipment was hardly adequate for the tasks that were planned. The press was so small that only half-sheets could be printed; there was no Greek fount, and some types were in such short supply that substitutes from mis-matched founts had to be used; completed formes had to be printed off before the next pages could be set. In view of this limited operation it is difficult to understand why as many as seven printers seem to have been needed at one time.

At every stage there were alarms. When the press was first set up at Greenstreet House, Persons was afraid that suspicion had been aroused by the purchase of paper in sufficient quantity for printing; Persons' servant, Robert Alfield, was mistrusted after he stayed away overnight; the owner of the house was nervous and apprehensive concerning the use made of it and the number of strangers who frequented it; one of the printers was arrested and questioned under torture. Later it was reported that an employee of the Oxford bookbinder Roland Jenkins – a workman who had been employed by Persons to bind books for him in London – had made charges against his master, with the result that Persons' store of books and papers in London was raided and the priest Alexander Briant was taken. Finally, after the arrest of Campion, the press was discovered, and Stephen Brinkley and four printers seized.[8]

---

[5] STC 19394; ARCR II, no. 613. Persons also issued from the press *A brief censure vppon two bookes written in answere to M. Edmonde Campions offer of disputation* (STC 19393; ARCR II, no. 612) and *A discoverie of J. Nicols minister* (STC 19402; ARCR II, no. 625). Apologetical works published included Richard Bristow's *A reply to Fulke* (STC 3802; ARCR II, no. 72), two editions of Thomas Hide's *Consolatorie Epistle* (STC 13376, 13377; ARCR II, nos. 430, 431), and two editions of *A Manual or Meditation* [sic] (STC 17278.4, 17278.5; ARCR II, nos. 664.3, 664.5).

[6] Cited in Richard Simpson, *Edmund Campion: A Biography* (London, 1867), p. 217.

[7] Ethelred L. Taunton, *The History of the Jesuits in England, 1580–1773* (London, 1901), p. 74.

[8] The history of the press is gathered from various sources originating in the accounts

These difficulties were not sufficient to persuade Persons to abandon the policy he had instigated. For the next few years, however, the dispersal of Catholic writing in manuscript or printed book depended on laymen. Persons, busy on the continent, with a press established at Rouen, was occupied with successive editions of *The first Booke of the Christian Exercise, appertayning to resolution* (1582; STC 19353; ARCR II, no. 616), enlarged in 1585 as *A Christian Directorie* (STC 19354.1; ARCR II, no. 618), in which his skills in pastoral instruction, expressed in a pellucid and vivid style, are splendidly demonstrated, in contrast with the controversial works that occupied so much of his life.[9] He was never to return to England.

II

On 8 May 1586, when Persons rode out to the Milvian Gate with Henry Garnet and Robert Southwell, newly appointed to the Jesuit Mission in England, he committed them to a ministry that was to continue the work that he and Campion had inaugurated.

As a young man Henry Garnet had been employed in the workshop of the printer Richard Tottel and during his three years' experience he learned the intricacies of the craft. This training was to stand him in good stead during his twenty years on the mission. No doubt he was responsible for the press set up in Southwell's house in London, and after Southwell's arrest in 1592 he was able to operate two presses in succession. Unlike the books printed by Campion and Persons he generally avoided works of controversy and issued mainly popular works of piety, many of which he translated and edited. His concern for those to whom he ministered is revealed in the number of works on meditation he chose, and directives to enable Catholics to live a devout life, including the first edition of Southwell's *Short Rule of Good Life* (STC 22968.5; ARCR II, no. 721).[10] He was aware of the danger inherent in the printing of works likely to enrage the authorities. He refused permission for the printing of Southwell's *Humble Supplication to Her Majestie* in 1591, and was so chary about the dissemination of a work

written by Persons and summarized in Leo Hicks, S.J., ed., *Letters and Memorials of Father Robert Persons* (London, 1942), pp. xxxi–xxxix, CRS 39. Details are given in John H. Pollen, S.J., ed., 'Memoirs of Father Robert Persons, S.J.,' in *Miscellanea II* (London, 1906), pp. 29, 182, CRS 2; and 'Notes Concerning the English Mission' in *Miscellanea IV* (London, 1907), p. 17, CRS 4; see also Simpson, *Campion*, pp. 184–86, 200–17, and E.E. Reynolds, *Campion and Parsons* (London, 1980), p. 128, citing the account given by Edward Rishton, a priest who was condemned with Campion.

9   On these works, see Victor Houliston, 'Why Robert Persons Would not be Pacified: Edmund Bunny's Theft of *The Book of Resolution*' in this volume.

10   The books issued from Garnet's two presses are listed in ARCR II, p. 225 (Presses nos. 8 and 10). See also A.F. Allison's critical bibliography, 'The Writings of Fr Henry Garnet, S.J. (1555–1606)', *Biographical Studies* (now *Recusant History*) 1 (1951), pp. 7–21.

on equivocation by Southwell that he could not find a copy in 1598 and was forced to write a defence himself, a treatise that was circulated in manuscript.[11]

The selection of Robert Southwell for the mission confirms the policy that the work of the priests was to be extended by means of the written word. He had proved his ability from the time of his entrance into the Society in Rome on 17 October 1578 when with an impassioned plea in English he persuaded the Jesuit authorities to allow him to enter the novitiate after their initial refusal.[12] When he moved to the English College in 1580 he appears to have acted as secretary to Alphonsus Agazzari, Rector of the College. He prepared the Annual Letters, compiled news reports, and on the death of Edward Throckmorton, a student who had been admitted to the Society on his deathbed, and whom Southwell had known since they were both children in England, he wrote the obituary required by the Father-General. He had time also for testing his literary skills in English. The private papers that have survived from this time include a translation of a medieval meditation on Mary Magdalen, attributed at that time to Origen, and a draft of part of Luigi Tansillo's 'Le Lagrime di San Pietro' translated from the original Italian.[13] He was clearly trying to recapture his native facility in English, longing for the opportunity to return to minister to his parents and friends, as he wrote later, believing that they would be damned in hell if they did not embrace once again the Catholic Church:

> I was the childe of a Christian woman and not the whelpe of a tygar; I could not feare, and foresee, and not forewarne; I had not a crueller heart then a damned caytiffe, to despise their bodies and soules, by whome I received myne. But this was an inveigled zeale, a blinde, and now abolished faithe; a zeale notwithstanding, and a faithe yt was. And god allmightie is my wittnes I came with no other intention into the realme.[14]

Once in England, Southwell applied his gifts both in verse and prose to the furtherance of his work on the mission, and in so doing he reached beyond the policy established by Campion and Persons. The body of literature that he left in manuscript and in printed form served not only to encourage and instruct, but through the precepts he advocated, through the devotional life he proposed for

---

[11] Two contemporary MS copies have been preserved, one with marginal notes in Garnet's hand in the Bodleian Library, Laud Misc 655, and one dated 1607, sent out of England to Persons, in the English College, Rome. See also Philip Caraman, S.J., *Henry Garnet (1555–1606) and the Gunpowder Plot* (London, 1964), pp. 253–54.

[12] Southwell's 'Querimonia' exists only in a fragment quoted in a Jesuit Catalogue of 1640 (ARSI, Anglia 14, f. 80, under date 1578). A Latin translation is in Henry More, S.J., *Historia Provinciæ Anglicanæ Societatis Jesu* (St Omer, 1660), Book V, pp. 173–75.

[13] Stonyhurst College MS A. v. 4.

[14] Letter to Sir Robert Cecil, Folger Shakespeare Library MS V. a. 421, f. 57ᵛ. A modern spelling version is included in *Robert Southwell, S.J.: Two Letters and 'Short Rules of a Good Life'*, ed. Nancy Pollard Brown (Charlottesville, Virginia, 1973), p. 81.

lay men and women, he helped to formulate the kind of life possible for Catholics living in the midst of an alien society.

Except for his one polemical work, *An Humble Supplication to her Majestie*, written in white-hot response to the proclamation published in November 1591 – a defence that would be taken up by Persons on the continent – all the writing that has survived from the six years Southwell laboured on the mission reflects his care for those whose lives he touched. For the young men with whom he rode on missionary journeys he wrote lyrics in the popular rhythms of the day, speaking not of the love-longings of this world, but of divine love. In 'Loves servile lot' he describes the troubles of the worldly lover:

> Love mistris is of many mindes,
> Yet few know whome they serve:
> They recken least how little love
> Their service doth deserve. . . .
>
> A honnie shower raines from her lippes,
> Sweete lights shine in her face:
> She hath the blush of virgine mild,
> The mind of viper race. . . .
>
> May never was the Month of love,
> For May is full of flowers,
> But rather Aprill wet by kind,
> For love is full of showers.   (lines 1–4; 13–16; 37–40)[15]

The theme is directly expressed in 'Lewd Love is Losse':

> Gods love alone doth end with endlesse ease:
> Whose joyes in hope, whose hope concludes in peace.
>
> (lines 17–18)[16]

Imagery in these poems is frequently drawn from the experience shared by these men who risked so much to assist the priests. John Gerard reported that Southwell found difficulty in remembering the technical terms for the gentleman's sports of hunting and falconry,[17] but in the poems he refers familiarly to country activities such as trapping birds, fishing, coursing, and the way of life in country houses, farming and gardening. At times it is possible that such images disguise a political statement:

> The Marlyne cannot ever sore on high,
> Nor greedie greyhound still pursue the chase:

---

15 *The Poems of Robert Southwell, S.J.*, ed. James H. McDonald and Nancy Pollard Brown (Oxford, 1967), pp. 60–61.

16 *Ibid.*, p. 63.

17 John Gerard, *The Autobiography of an Elizabethan*, ed. Philip Caraman, S.J. (London, 1951), p. 15.

> The tender Larke will find a time to flie,
> And fearefull Hare to runne a quiet race.
> He that high growth on Ceders did bestow
> Gave also lowly mushrumpes leave to grow.
> ('Scorne not the least', lines 13–18)[18]

In the sequence of poems based on incidents in the life of Christ and his Mother the imagery springs from the liturgy and the ancient teachings of the Church. In 'Christs returne out of Egypt' Southwell plays on the traditional meaning of Nazareth as the city of a flower (possibly originating in St Jerome), the title of Mary, *rosa mystica*, and the pun *virgo/virga*, together with the description of Christ as flower of the house of Jesse – a display of ingenuity of baroque complexity:

> For flower he is and in a flower he bred,
> And from a thorne now to a flowre he fled.
>
> And well deservd this flower his fruit to view
> Where he invested was in mortall weede,
> Where first unto a tender bud he grew
> In virgin branch unstaind with mortall seede.
> Young flower, with flowers, in flower well may he be:
> Ripe fruit he must with thornes hang on a tree.   (lines 11–18)[19]

The lyrics were not printed in Southwell's lifetime, but were circulated in manuscript. A prose dedication accompanied a group of the poems sent to a cousin, and indicates Southwell's intention that they should be disseminated, 'to invite some skillfuller wits to goe forward in the same, or to begin some finer peece, wherein it may be seene, how well verse and vertue sute together'.[20]

At some time shortly after the end of Southwell's active ministry the poems were gathered up and set in order, headed by the prose dedication and another introductory poem he had written for the selection he had dispatched as a gift. The work was very possibly Garnet's, although he does not speak of this great charge. Copies were made by scribes who faithfully reproduced the order that was now established. Some added short prose pieces and letters that by implication were also attributed to Southwell. Five of these early manuscripts have survived, testimony to the value set upon these writings by his contemporaries. Two are bound in with printed copies of Southwell's single long poem, 'Saint Peters Complaint'. This poem, amongst his last work and perhaps left in draft, has been preserved in two early manuscripts, neither of them reliable as textual witnesses.

The London printers, however, recognised the importance of a substantial

---

[18] Southwell, *Poems*, p. 69.
[19] *Ibid.*, p. 10.
[20] *Ibid.*, p. 1. The dedication is found in three of the early manuscripts and in the first edition of the lyrics printed by John Wolfe in 1595.

long poem to precede a collection of shorter work, and John Wolfe's edition, *Saint Peters Complaint, With other Poemes* (STC 22955.7) was published shortly after Southwell's execution in February 1595. Twelve lyrics were selected from the manuscript compilation, omitting poems of specifically Catholic doctrine. In an edition that followed rapidly on the first (STC 22957) Wolfe added another eight poems and corrected the text of 'Loves servile lot' by the addition of twenty-eight lines. But it would appear that he did not have a complete manuscript of the lyrics, otherwise he would not have yielded the advantages of publication to John Busby, who produced another selection in the same year, entitled rather mysteriously *Mœoniæ* (STC 29955). Drawing on materials that had presumably not been available to Wolfe, Busby published ten of the fourteen poems in the sequence on the Virgin Mary and Christ, nine lyrics from the manuscript collection, and three further poems found elsewhere only in one manuscript.[21] Busby also obtained a copy of the prose piece to which he gave the title *The Triumphs over Death* and published it in the same year (STC 22971).

Wolfe handed on his rights in the printing of the poems to Gabriel Cawood, another publisher with Catholic sympathies, who registered the volume with the Stationers' Company as *Saincte PETERs Complainte with MARY MAGDALENs blusshe and her Complaint at CHRISTes deathe with other poemes* on 5 April 1595.[22] He issued an edition in the same year, followed by two further editions (STC 22956, 22958 and 22959), and then in 1602 he renewed public interest by the addition of a further seven poems, an indication that by this time he had been able to obtain a manuscript of the complete compilation (STC 22960a).

Southwell's poems, gathered up after his arrest, had now become the property of dedicated Catholic scribes and of London printing houses. What had been first written to strengthen the resolution of his co-religionists, to be treasured after his death as the work of a martyr, had become more widely diffused amongst Anglican readers. The series of eighteen editions, later combined with some of his prose works, continued until 1636, when the pressures of Puritan influence put an end to printing until the nineteenth century. For many years the reputation of Southwell as a poet depended very largely upon entries in anthologies, a small number of poems giving some sense of the delicate tracery of sound, and of the deep conviction of faith on which they were built.

III

The history of Southwell's prose pieces is similarly a history that extends from their first inception to fulfil specific needs to their presentation to a wider range of readers. His output in the brief six years of his work on the mission

---

[21] Details of the early editions are to be found in Southwell, *Poems*, pp. lv–lxxvii.

[22] Edward Arber, *A Transcript of the Registers of the Company of Stationers of London, 1554–1640*, 5 vols (London, 1875–94), II, p. 295.

demonstrates the intensity with which he committed himself to a written record of his pastoral activity. One of the first works is his longest: *An Epistle of Comfort, to the Reverend Priestes, and to the Honorable, Worshipful, and other of the Laye sort restrayned in Durance for the Catholicke Fayth* (STC 22946, ARCR II, no. 714), printed from the press in his own house in 1587 or 1588. The address 'To the Reader' explains its evolution in terms echoed in his other works. It was based on letters written in the first instance to 'an especiall frende of myne', and later adapted for use by others who found themselves in similar need 'though it cost me no smale labour in altering the style'. The volume incorporates a number of letters written to Philip, Earl of Arundel, then in prison in the Tower. Southwell never met the man whom he speaks of as his 'espeaciall frende', but references to their correspondence recur in the life of the Earl written by a Jesuit priest who in later years served as chaplain to the Countess. She was always a devoted supporter of the Society. In the early months of his ministry Southwell had succeeded Martin Aray as her spiritual adviser, and she had enabled him to set up a press in the house she allowed him to use in Spitalfields.[23] *The Epistle of Comfort* is well printed, and it is probable that the work was carried out by a London printer with Catholic sympathies, and corrected by Southwell himself.

The first of Southwell's works to appear from a commercial press, *Marie Magdalens Funeral Teares*, was printed by John Wolfe for Gabriel Cawood in 1591 (STC 29950), and again the accuracy of the text suggests that Southwell corrected the work of the press. As he writes in 'The Epistle Dedicatorie', he had chosen a theme 'fittest for this time'. As in the introductory letter prefacing the poems, Southwell rebukes those whose life is regulated by passion, and particularly the pursuit of profane love, 'the Idol to which both tongues and pennes doe sacrifice their ill bestowed labours', and he urges them to redirect this outflow of emotion: 'Passions I allow, and loves I approve, onely I would wishe that men would alter their object and better their intent' (1591, sig. A 3ᵛ). In his address 'To the Reader' his criticism of contemporary writing on frivolous topics is expressed even more strongly:

> . . . the finest wittes loose themselves in the vainest follies, spilling muche Arte in some idle phansie, and leaving their workes as witnesses, howe long they have beene in travaile to be in fine delivered of a fable. And sure it is a thing greatly to bee lamented, that men of so high conceite should so much abase their habilities, that when they have racked them to the uttermost endevour, all the prayse that they reape of their employment, consisteth in this, that they have wisely tolde a foolish tale, and carried a long lie verie smoothlie to the ende. (sig. A 7–7ᵛ)

---

[23] The press in Southwell's house was reported by John Gerard in his *Autobiography*, p. 26. For the house in Spitalfields, see Nancy Pollard Brown, 'Paperchase: The Dissemination of Catholic Texts in Elizabethan England', in *English Manuscript Studies, 1100–1700*, ed. Peter Beal and Jeremy Griffiths (Oxford, 1989), I, pp. 123–25.

Southwell recognises that his work will be no more than an 'eye-sore' to readers who favour these fashionable productions, and he admits that he would not have undertaken the printing except for his fear of the work of over-zealous editors:

> Yet sith the copies therof flew so fast, and so false abroad, that it was in danger to come corrupted to the print: it seemed a lesse evill to let it flie to common viewe in the native plume, and with the owne wings, then disguised in a coate of a bastard feather, or cast off from the fist of such a corrector, as might happily have perished the sound, and imped in some sicke and sory fethers of his owne phansies. (sig. A 8)

The comment is important in showing the enthusiasm with which Southwell's work was being received, and how quickly copies were being circulated. None of these manuscripts have survived.

The *Funeral Teares* may well have been written in the first instance to encourage a young woman entering religion. A tradition originating from the dedication to 'Mistres D.A.' associates it with Dorothy Arundell, daughter of Sir John Arundell of Lanherne, Cornwall. Through her aunt, Mary Arundell, who married Henry FitzAlan, Earl of Arundel, as his second wife, Dorothy was connected with Philip Howard, whose mother was a daughter of the Earl, married to the fourth Duke of Norfolk. Dorothy's parents sheltered Father John Cornelius, a seminary priest and a friend of Southwell, who had known him in Rome. The family had a London house in Clerkenwell, where many eminent Catholics had their town houses, and later in Isleworth. After Sir John's death in 1590 his wife, Lady Stourton, moved to Chideock, Dorset, where Cornelius was taken in 1594.[24] Dorothy and her sister Cecily both fled to the continent to enter religion. Dorothy was one of the first group of nuns to be professed at the convent of the English Benedictine nuns in Brussels on 4 November 1599.[25] At this earlier period in London she was part of the society among whom Southwell moved and worked and found his friends, and the traditional identification may indeed have a firm foundation.

In his study of Mary Magdalen at the Tomb of Jesus Southwell returned to a subject that had engaged his interest in Rome. He incorporates into his meditation the full text of the medieval sermon known as 'Audivimus Mariam', augmenting it at length with his own exposition. His additions intensify the

---

[24] Cornelius had applied for membership in the Society of Jesus while he was in Rome, and continued to plead for admission during the ten years of his missionary work. Garnet promised to try to get permission for him to be admitted in England, but before arrangements could be made Cornelius and three lay companions were hanged in Dorchester on 3 July 1594. On the scaffold Cornelius declared that he died a Jesuit. Garnet's account, sent to Acquaviva on 9 August 1594, can be found in ARSI, Fondo Gesuitico 651/624, and is printed in Caraman, *Garnet and the Gunpowder Plot*, p. 189). See also Thomas M. McCoog, S.J., ed. *Monumenta Angliae*, 2 vols (Rome, 1992) MHSI 142, 143, II, pp. 274–75.

[25] Report of John Petit to Privy Council, CSP Venetian V, p. 343, printed in Peter Guilday, *The English Catholic Refugees on the Continent, 1558–1795* (London, 1914), p. 258, n. 1.

emotional impact of the account as it is given in the Gospel of St John, developing in turn all the reactions of the senses as Mary realises the extent of her loss, so that she will not be comforted, even by the appearance of the angels:

> Thy eies seeme to tel thee that every thing inviteth thee to weepe, carrying such outward shew, as though all that thou seest were attired in sorrow to solemnize with generall consent the funerall of thy Maister. Thy ears perswade thee, that all sounds and voices are tuned to mourning notes, and that the Eccho of thy own wailings, is the cry of the very stons and trees, as though (the cause of thy teares being so unusuall) God to the rocks and woods, had inspired a feeling of thine and their common losse. And therefore it soundeth to thee as a straunge question, to aske thee why thou weepest, sith al that thou seest and hearest, seemeth to enduce thee, yea to enforce thee to weepe. (sig. E 3ᵛ–4)

Mary explains the source of her misery in terms of a love that cannot be consoled with worldly possessions:

> Without him I were poore, though Empresse of the worlde. With him I were riche, though I had nothing else. They that have moste are accounted richest, and they thought to have moste, that have all they desire: and therfore as in him alone is the uttermost of my desires, so hee alone is the summe of all my substance. It were too happie an exchaunge, to have God for goodes, and too rich a poverty, to injoy the only treasure of the world.
> (sig. F 7)

Her grief leads her to almost hysterical plans of action to try to recover the body of Jesus by force, and in this state she does not recognise Jesus when he first speaks to her. The narrator suggests that she cannot see him because her eyes are blinded with tears, but at the same time he justifies her mistake in thinking that he was a gardener:

> For as our first father, in the state of grace and innocency, was placed in the garden of pleasure, and the first office allotted him, was to be a Gardener: so the first man that ever was in glorie, appeareth first in a Garden, and presenteth himselfe in a gardeners likenes, that the beginnings of glory, might resemble the entrance of innocencie and grace. And as a Gardener was the foyle of mankind, the parent of sinne, and author of death: so is this Gardiner, the raysor of our ruines, the ransome of our offences, and the restorer of life. (sig. G 6)

The figure of Mary Magdalen in the garden during these hours when the world was a desolate place, when the body of Christ was no longer to be found, was indeed fitting for the time when Southwell attempted to minister to Catholics who felt themselves deserted and abandoned, threatened by powerful authorities who had forbidden them access to the Sacrament. It spoke with particular force to a young woman contemplating a religious life which would entail giving up a place in English society for the uncertainties of a life of poverty in exile. Southwell's moving and eloquent account of this night of weeping is essentially a study of Christian hope, driven to the very edge of despair, but finally redeemed at the moment of revelation.

Printer and publisher could be assured that nothing in the work could trace its origins to a Catholic priest, and their confidence in their property is proved by its popularity. Successive editions were issued: Cawood published it three more times, in 1592, 1594, and again a year or so later (STC 22950.5, 22951, and 22951.5); after his death other editions appeared in 1602 and 1609 (STC 22952, 22953). Very few copies of these editions are now to be found, and although some no doubt were destroyed in Catholic libraries by raiding parties, their scarcity suggests that copies were worn out with use. The work was certainly read by readers other than Catholics, and it was chosen for William Barrett's 'collected works' issued first in 1620, and reprinted in 1630 and 1634/36, a selection of Southwell's writing that had been carefully edited to please Protestant taste (STC 22965, 22966, and 22968). In the *Funeral Teares* Southwell's ministry had extended far beyond what was first envisaged, beyond the instruction and consolation of a young woman to the world opened up by commercial printing and open distribution.

IV

The other prose work issued by a commercial press shortly after Southwell's execution was given the title *The Triumphs over Death*, printed by Valentine Simmes for James Busby in 1595 (STC 22971). Like the earlier *Epistle of Comfort* it was written for the Earl of Arundel at a time of great distress, after the death of his half-sister Lady Margaret Sackville in August 1591. The Earl had been condemned for treason in 1589, and access to him was even more sternly forbidden. Under these circumstances Southwell clearly doubted whether his words of consolation would ever reach the Earl or his friends who shared his sorrow:

> But I thincke the philosophers rule wilbe here verified, that it shalbe last in execucion, that was first designed, and he last enjoy the effect, that was first mover of the cause. This let chaunce overrule, sith choyse may not, and into whichsoever of their handes it shall fortune, much honor and happynes may it cary with it, and leave in their hartes as much joy, as it found sorowe.
> (Stonyhurst College MS A.v.27, f. 20)

There is no indication that Southwell envisaged the printing of this very personal document. Unlike his adaptation of the *Epistle of Comfort* the precise nature of this situation, that of a brother mourning a sister's death, is unchanged, and general interest further limited by a lengthy account of the special qualities of Lady Margaret. The last section plays on her name:

The base shell of a mortall body, was an unfitt roome for so pretious a margarite. And the Jeweller that came into this world to seeke good perles, and gave not onely all he had, but himself also to buy them, thought it nowe tyme to take her into his bargaine, finding her growen to a Margarites full perfection. (f. 35–35ᵛ)

Southwell committed the work to manuscript dissemination, and it is included in three copies of the collection of the poems, providing a much more accurate text than in the printed version. Nevertheless the printing was clearly a commercial success. Two later editions followed from the same press, both dated 1596, but actually printed at wider intervals, the second edition (STC 22973) a year or so after the first, and the third (STC 22972) shortly after 1600. It also found a place in Barrett's 'collected works' of 1620, and its later editions.

For the first time Southwell's authorship was used as a selling point. On the title-page he is described as '*R. S.* the Author of *S. Peters Complaint*, and *Mæoniæ* his other Hymnes'. In introductory poems, including a dedication to the Sackville children, the editor John Trussel spells out Southwell's full name, leaving no doubt in the mind of the purchasers whose work they were buying.

During Southwell's lifetime there was no attempt to print a similarly personal letter addressed to his father Richard Southwell. It was written in fulfilment of an undertaking that had seemed utterly frustrated when he was refused admission to the Society of Jesus, when he wrote in agony that he lived 'prived of my purpose defeated of my desire, restrained from the perfetting my designement',[26] and of which he wrote again in his last letter:

> . . . on the one side being indebted to my parents for my very being, to freinds for many benefitts, on the other, having a faithe to discerne, and not so brutishe a minde to neglecte their miseries, bothe the Lawe of God and man inforced mee to indevour their redresse. (Letter to Cecil, f. 57ᵛ)

Richard Southwell was the eldest son, though illegitimate, of Sir Richard Southwell, one of the commissioners for the dissolution of the monasteries in Norfolk. From the monastic properties that he acquired for himself he built a substantial house out of the refectory building of a monastery dedicated to St Faith for Mary Darcy, the mother of all his children except his one legitimate daughter. His son Richard succeeded to great wealth, although harassed throughout his life by the charge of illegitimacy. No doubt it was to defend his riches that during the time of Robert Southwell's training overseas he made his peace with the Established Church. His son's letter makes a passionate plea for his return to the Old Faith:

> Yowe have longe sowed in a feilde of flynte, which could bringe yowe nothinge forthe, but a cropp of cares, and affliction of spiritt, rewarding your labours with remorse and affording for your gaine eternall damages. It

---

[26] 'Querimonia', in ARSI, Anglia 14, f. 80.

is nowe more then a seasonable tyme, to alter the course of so unthrivinge a housbandrye, and to enter into the feilde of Gods churche, in which sowing the seedes of repentant sorrowe, and wateringe them with the teares of humble contricion, yowe may reape a more beneficiall harvest, and gather the fruites of everlastinge comforte. Remember I pray yowe, that your springe is spente, and your sommer overpaste, yow are nowe arrived to the fall of the leafe, yea and winter collours have alreadye stayned your hoary heade. (Stonyhurst College MS A.v.27, f. 7ᵛ)

The letter is dated 'This 22 of october 1589', but by this time Richard Southwell had followed his son's urgent counsel. He is named in a Norfolk recusant list of March 1588, and in the same year the family house at Horsham St Faith's was sold to Sir Henry Hobart, although the sale may well have been one to avoid seizure if recusancy fines remained unpaid.[27] By July 1589 he was in prison for debt, and his attempts to raise the immense sum of £9,000 by mortgaging lands in order to help his two oldest sons, Richard and Thomas, had failed.[28] It is most likely, therefore, that the date repeated on copies of the letter is the error of an early scribe, and that the letter was in fact written soon after Southwell's return to England, possibly in October 1586.

The force of the argument made the *Epistle to his Father* a valuable tool in the work of the mission. Nine manuscript copies are known, three of them with copies of the lyric poems. The letter was printed with *A Short Rule of Good Life*, issued from Garnet's second press about 1596–97 (STC 22968.5; ARCR II, no. 721), and included in the four later editions (STC 22969, 22969.3, 22969.5, 22970; ARCR II, nos. 722–725). A translation into Welsh is dated 1612 (ARCR II, no. 725.5).

By the time of the printed editions there was little question of the identity of the author, although Garnet reduced references to initials only. Except for the Stonyhurst MS early copies are equally cautious, even at the point in the letter when Southwell recalls how his father was 'wonte in merimente to call me father R. which is the customary stile nowe allotted to my present estate' (f. 6ᵛ). The printing history of the letter is all the more unexpected: something more than half of the *Epistle* is reproduced as the second part of Sir Walter Raleigh's *Instructions to his Sonne, and to Posterity* with the title *A Religious and Dutifull Advice of a loving Sonne to his Aged Father*. The two items were first published by Benjamin Fisher in 1632 (STC 20642 and 156), with frequent reprintings during the seventeenth century.[29] With the omission of the lengthy introductory section and

---

[27] John H. Pollen, S.J., ed., 'Recusants and Priests, March 1588', in *Miscellanea XII* (London, 1921) p. 120, CRS 22; Francis Blomefield, *A Topographical History of the County of Norfolk*, 11 vols (London, 1805–1810), X, p. 441.

[28] APC, XVII, p. 351 (6 July 1589).

[29] The first edition was followed by five more, after which the two items were included first in editions of Raleigh's *Maxims of State* (1650, 1651, and 1656) and later in the collection entitled *Remains* (1657, etc.).

of the final pages (containing the only direct reference to the Catholic Church) Southwell's appeal to his father, which reads as a fierce polemic against the dangers of remaining outside the shelter of Catholicism, is equally powerful as an appeal to an unbeliever to rejoin the Christian community. In the part of the *Epistle* issued by Fisher, although frequent unauthorised textual revisions have been made, the only significant phrase that might have indicated a Catholic work is the reference to 'the folde and familye of Gods Church' (f. 10ᵛ), which was changed to read 'that fold and family of Gods faithfull servants' (1632, p. 40).[30] Southwell's very private purpose was transformed by a publisher's ingenuity that linked the work to an even more famous name, ignoring the incongruity with which the letter is placed beside Raleigh's devout *Instructions to his Sonne*. As in the case of those works issued from commercial presses the *Epistle* became public property, and its robust challenge in the face of his father's schism was transferred implicitly to the atheism of which Raleigh was accused by his enemies.

V

Like the other prose works *A Short Rule of Good Life* was a compilation prepared to supply a particular need. From the account given by her biographer Anne, Countess of Arundel, had no intention of offering Southwell a permanent place in her household when he was first brought to her. He assumed that he was to take the place of the banished priest Martin Aray, and having asked the servant who fetched him 'whether he should reside with her or no', he began to make arrangements for a hiding-place in case the house was raided. The misunderstanding proved of the greatest advantage, for otherwise 'both she, her Lord, and many of their friends had wanted that great help and Comfort, which they found by him in all occasions'.[31]

Since her conversion to Catholicism several years previously the Countess had tried to live a life of great devotion in the midst of a succession of almost unsupportable difficulties. After her husband's arrest at sea in 1585 he was imprisoned in the Tower and Anne was subject to long years of deprivation at the whim of the Queen. At one time her only living quarters were a few rooms in Arundel House, empty except for beds. She sold jewels for food and to pay her few servants. But gradually she was able to regain sufficient control of her jointure to rent houses, one in Spitalfields – a Catholic enclave – and one in Acton. She made no secret of her Catholicism; rank still had privileges and powers that were perhaps greater than she herself was aware of. While he remained with her Southwell seems to have been protected.

[30] Copy in the Bodleian Library, 8 P 75(3) Art.
[31] *The Life of the Right Honourable and Virtuouse Lady, the Lady Anne Late Countesse of Arundell and Surrey*, Arundel Castle Archives MS, pp. 21–22.

As her biographer records, Southwell wrote for her *A Short Rule of Good Life*.[32] It is not a rule made up of prescriptive regulations, but as in the earliest religious rules, it offers a number of guiding principles, showing how inflexible standards of life should control flexible patterns of action, with the end always in view of the restoration of the individual soul. It offers a directive for a life spent in a worldly context with mind and heart fixed upon a life beyond, so that the earnest Christian might learn, in Southwell's own use of the Pauline phrase, 'howe our conversation maye be in heaven', that is, to live on earth a heavenly life. It is the theme of many of his lyrics, and of one of the poems preceding the *Rule*, when Southwell puns on the rule he is offering and a carpenter's rule, seeing an equivalency in his labour and in that of the craftsman. It is, he writes,

> A rule to leavill lyfe and death so true
> As leaveth hell, and leades to heavenly crue. (p. 116)

For many years the work was known only in the rare copies of early editions. The earliest was issued from Garnet's second press soon after Southwell's execution, and the writer of the 'Preface to the Reader' – probably Garnet himself – commemorates the martyrdom of his friend and records that

> he himselfe hath left behind him for thy benefitte, and even amongst the last of his fruitefull labours for the good of soules, had designed to publish unto the world the description of this most gainfull voiage to heaven, bedecked with the most pretious ornamentes of all christian vertues, and with the most pleasant and comfortable brightnes of notable rules of spirituall life: every one of which may be as it were a lantern unto thy feete, and a continuall light unto thy steppes (sig. a 5–5ᵛ).

This is the only independent evidence of the precise date of any of Southwell's writing, although other pieces may be linked to external events, such as the death of Lady Margaret Sackville and the publication of the Proclamation in November 1591. Southwell's work on the *Rule* in his last year of freedom was not its original composition, however, but its revision for its dissemination for a general readership. The identification of six substantive manuscripts during recent years has revealed that in its earliest form, as preserved in manuscripts in the Jesuit House of Studies, Dublin, and in York Minster Library, the *Rule* was clearly written for a woman. Southwell's revision, apparently undertaken in the spring of 1592 before his arrest in June, attempted to remove all such limiting references. His work was not finished, but the textual changes are preserved in

---

[32] *Ibid.*, p. 23. The spelling of the title and of quotations is from the most authoritative text, Gonville and Caius College MS 218/233, collated with the other substantive manuscripts and the printed edition. References are given to chapters and page numbers. The only modern edition, *Two Letters and 'Short Rules of a Good Life'*, is a modern-spelling version of the Folger Shakespeare Library MS V. a. 421, a non-substantive text copied from an early printed edition.

four manuscripts, those in the Library of Gonville and Caius College, Cambridge, in the Hunter collection in the Library of the Dean and Chapter, Durham Cathedral, in the possession of the late Lord Kenyon, and in the Throckmorton Papers, now in the Warwickshire Record Office.[33] The editor of the printed text continued the process of revision by removing the introductory sonnets, the final section – 'A breefe forme of confession for such as use to confesse often' – which is intended for the use of women, and a diagrammatic meditation on the four last things that, although included in three manuscripts, may not be Southwell's. The editor also worked over the text in detail, making some substantial deletions, and softening phrases that seemed to him too spirited or too violent, or that suggested theological ambiguity. These changes are certainly unauthoritative and undermine the value of the printed edition as a substantive text.

In the Countess, Southwell had a most pliant subject, a woman whose natural inclination welcomed the spiritual discipline of the *Rule*. In the main body of the text he wrote in the first person, following the form used by St Ignatius in the *Spiritual Exercises*, putting himself in the place of the exercitant. It is an all-encompassing directive, affecting every aspect of life. From the beginning it is clear that Southwell is writing for a person of rank, someone accustomed to the hierarchy of service. In the world of the faithful Christian the normal assumption of the highest place is reversed, and 'Gods creature' must learn instead the place of the steward. The responsibility for body, soul, and goods is held

> as bayliffe, tennaunt, or officer to demayne, and governe thease thinges to his best service. And therefore when the tyme of mye stewardshipp is expired, I shalbe sommoned bye death to appeare before mye landlorde, whoe with moste rigorous justice will demaunde accoumpte of everye thinge and creature of his that hath beene to mye use . . .
>
> (Chap. 1, pp. 125–26).

Like her co-religionists the Countess lived in the midst of non-Catholics, surrounded by people from all walks of life. Only when the difficulties of this existence are fully imagined are some of Southwell's injunctions made clear, as when he starts his chapter on the care of servants with the admonition: 'I must see that they lie not out in the night but that I knowe what is become of them' (Chap. 8, p. 169). This abruptness is less surprising when it is remembered that the servant who slips out at night is likely to be the servant who is the hidden informer.

For the Countess, a recent convert, the way of salvation must have often seemed a harsh and dangerous road walked in silence and solitude. Born in 1557, she could have had no memory of the Catholic Church as the

---

[33] For my knowledge of these manuscripts I am indebted to the late Christopher Devlin, S.J., Dr Peter Beal, and the late Dr David Rogers.

acknowledged religion of the country; she could not now share the ancient inspiration to devotion, when every church and cathedral offered evocative images and pictures to rouse lagging spirits and stimulate imitation of the lives of favourite saints with sung liturgy and festival procession. The *Rule* gave her a substitute order of Catholic devotion. It organised an exemplary Christian life from the hour of getting up in the morning to the hour of going to bed, assigning particular times for prayer and meditation. It made some practical concessions, as a thought for what business had to be transacted that day before turning to morning prayers, and advising a pause for the rosary before dinner only 'yf companye and other more waightie occasions will permitt'. At dinner grace is to be said by the children, leftovers given to the poor, then later in the afternoon there is evensong, followed by the reading of 'parte of some good booke', with special instruction, twice stated, that one book should be finished before another begun – a note possibly arising from Southwell's observation of the Countess' habits. The day ends with self-examination, first with thought of business completed and promises kept – or forgotten – and secondly 'touching the thoughts, wordes, and deedes of that daye'. Sundays and feast days are days to get up earlier, with preparation for communion, and meditation after it, and these days are to be spent with more attention to 'godlye exercises', although it is understood that 'I ame likelye to be troubled with companye more those dayes then others . . .'. Even visiting friends might be a source of danger (Chap. 6, pp. 152–67). As far as is possible under these circumstances the devout life is aligned with the traditional cycle of the worship of the Church, marked by the feasts, and in a series of appendices Southwell suggests ways in which these days of commemoration may be recalled at home, by associating the specific occasions – incidents in Christ's life and the examples of the saints – with the days of the week, the rooms of the house, or walks in the garden. In such ways the incentives given by attendance at church are replaced by an interior life of imaginative richness of devotion.

The two final chapters, on temptation and on perseverance, are the most substantial in their analysis of difficulties that are to be met on a spiritual course of life. The study of temptation is largely based on the 'Rules for the Discernment of Spirits' for the First Week of the *Spiritual Exercises* and its parallel section for the Second Week, 'Rules to the same effect, containing a fuller Discernment of Spirits'. Southwell makes a significant change in a passage when he is translating directly from the Ignatian text by substituting the image of a cowardly soldier for the original one of a woman to describe the devil, a change that points to consideration for the Countess (Chap. 10, pp. 188–89). In this section the dangers of temptation are most vividly portrayed, as in this passage omitted from the printed version:

> Allsoe the devill is like a wicked, and unchaste lover, whoe goeinge about to entice some godlye mans daughter, or honest wife, at his first entraunce with them barganeth that his counsell maye be kept, and his drifte concealed

from the parent or husband. For he knoweth that yf they were privye of his lewd intent, they would cutt him of from all hope of his purpose.

(Chap. 10, p. 189)

In the discussion of scruples, a subject where the prescribed examination of conscience might lead to unwarranted self-condemnation in a woman of over-zealous sensitivity, Southwell makes an important addition to the Ignatian rules, and one that was to be a cause of much dispute at a later time, when he asserts that sinful thoughts should not disturb a Christian aspiring to live a virtuous life:

> For not to have them, is not in mye power, but onelye not to consent unto them. And soe longe as with deliberacion I have not consented, nor will-inglye, nor with delight stayed in them, I have not synned anye more, then yf I hadd onelye hadd them in a dreame. (Chap. 10, p. 184)

Southwell then qualifies his statement with a tortuous sentence:

> It is never lawfull for me to take delight in thinkinge of anye acte or pleasure, which at that tyme, wherin I thinke it, it is not lawfull for me to use. (p. 185)

He is awkwardly trying to avoid direct reference to lustful thoughts or sexual fantasies, and he has some diffidence in introducing the subject to the Countess. The reference to a woman's day-dreams that follows indicates the particular sin:

> And therfore for an unmaried woman to delight advisedlye in thinkinge what pleasure shee would take yf shee were married to such a man, weare a mortall synne. (p. 186)

This is the reading of Southwell's revised text; the earlier version has 'virgin' for 'unmaried woman'. It is puzzling to guess why Southwell thought a change necessary, for neither phrase would relate to the Countess.

Southwell armed the Countess well against such womanly weakness. She seems to have been terrified of any charge of impropriety. Her biographer reports that after the Earl's death she took a vow of chastity, regularly renewed. At a time when some ladies were showing their willingness to be wooed by the Scotsmen who followed King James south, the story is told that when one Scot appeared at the door of her country house uninvited, she could not avoid entertaining him and his large retinue, but early next morning she drove off in her carriage before he was up and refused to return until he had left.[34]

Her biographer confirms her acceptance of the life Southwell outlined for her:

> In the observance whereof she was alwayes as carefull and diligent, as others are remisse, carelesse, and negligent; for that settl'd course of vertue

---

[34] *Life*, p. 31.

and devotion to which he then advis'd her, she continu'd with great exactness and perseverance even to her death, which was more than five and thirty years after his imprisonment and glorious Martyrdom.[35]

He chronicles her life of good deeds, of charity, of her service to the sick, of her ability to respond to the questioning of her Protestant acquaintances. She frequently referred to Southwell's precepts. She had a relic, one of the small bones from his feet, and wore it constantly, exerting herself in every possible way to follow his edicts.

Southwell's *Rule* was proved to be more than a personal guide to spiritual growth. In the Countess he created an exemplar of the English Catholic woman. He chose a woman of the highest rank, and therefore most noticeable – a *grattacielo* among women – resilient in the face of direct hardships, making a private life for herself in which the practice of a forbidden religion was quietly carried out. In her strength of resolution even so strong an adversary as the Queen was outwitted, and as she gradually regained her fortune she was able to support the Jesuit mission with the foundation of the tertianship at Ghent. In all her acts, a known Catholic, she stood as a demonstration of Christian virtue.

In her life Southwell's apostolic mission was carried on. With the dissemination of the manuscripts and the publication of the printed recension of the *Rule* others also would direct their lives in the way he urged in the prefatory poem:

> Then read, remember, put it well in ure,
> And have it ofte in hand, more ofte in harte,
> For profitt smalle or none it will procure
> Till will do take the understandinge parte,
>   No more then drugg or foode will stand in steed
>   Err they be usd to cure or ells to feede.
>   Take then a taste, and trye howe sweet it is
>   To lyve in love, which leades to endles blisse. (p. 116)

In his care to revise texts, and to control, as far as he could, their distribution among the faithful, Southwell foresaw the way in which his work was to extend beyond his death. His immediate aims to serve his family and his friends became immersed in the need to have written texts to guide and strengthen Catholic life – needs felt by Anglicans also, as shown by the demand for the commercially printed books and for manuscripts suitably modified not to offend their points of faith. Behind the concern shown by Campion and Persons that they should be permitted to debate their position with the civil and ecclesiastical lawmakers was the dream of an England restored to Catholicism. The reality five years later was no longer a conversion of England by an army of priests sweeping away the changes, awaiting the accession of a Catholic monarch to the English throne, but those who laboured on the English Mission faced a sterner future. Catholic life

[35] *Ibid.*, pp. 23–24.

had to be led apart and in secret. In the poems and in the prose pieces, the written evidence of six years of freedom, Southwell achieved what he had long felt to be his task as a priest. The work of the written word was acknowledged in a note he made when he was still a student in Rome, quoting Psalm 45 [in the Authorised Version]: 'My tongue is the pen of a scrivener that writeth swiftly'.[36]

36 *Spiritual Exercises and Devotions of Blessed Robert Southwell, S.J.*, ed. J.M. de Buck, S.J., trans. P.E. Hallett (London, 1931), p. 37.

12

Intrigues of a Scottish Jesuit at the Spanish Court: Unpublished Letters of William Crichton to Claudio Acquaviva (Madrid 1590–1592)[1]

FRANCISCO DE BORJA MEDINA, S.J.

The fourth centenary of the Spanish Armada (1588–1988) saw a revival of interest among Spanish and British Historians not only in the causes, preparations and execution of the plan, but also in its disastrous termination and consequences. There has also been increased study of the post-Armada period, special attention being given to the British Isles and neighbouring regions: Ireland, Brittany and the Low Countries. However almost no attention has been given to the repercussions felt in Scotland after the defeat of the Armada.[2] The present article will attempt to deal with one small aspect of this question, and I shall concentrate my attention on the person of the Scottish Jesuit, William Crichton (or Creighton, though he signs himself 'Creytton')[3] and on the years

---

[1] My thanks to Fr Wiktor Gramatowski, S.J., Director of the Archivum Romanum Societatis Iesu in Rome, and also to Frs Geoffrey Holt, S.J., and Thomas M. McCoog, S.J., former and current archivists of the British Province of the Society of Jesus, for their kindness, competence and fraternal support.

[2] In recent studies, *After the Armada: Elizabethan England and the Struggle for Western Europe 1588–1595* (Oxford, 1984); and *The Return of the Armadas. The Last Years of the Elizabethan War against Spain 1595–1603* (Oxford, 1994), R.B. Wernham devotes part of one chapter to this theme (*After the Armada*, pp. 455–460), and there are other scattered references throughout the book. Many years earlier Albert J. Loomie, S.J. had studied the post-Armada years in connection with the English Catholics: 'The Armadas and the Catholics of England', *The Catholic Historical Review* 59 (1973), pp. 385–403.

[3] William Creighton (1530–1615): he entered St Salvator College and matriculated in the University of St Andrews in 1552, taking his B.A. in 1554 and his M.A. in 1555. He became a Jesuit in Rome, 5 December 1561, and was ordained priest in 1562. He made his solemn profession in Lyons, 28 August, 1568. See D. Fernández Zapico, S.J., 'La Province d'Aquitaine de la Compagnie de Jésus d'après son plus ancien catalogue (1566)', *AHSI* 5 (1936), pp. 268–292, and Thomas M. McCoog, S.J., ed., *Monumenta Angliae*, 2 vols (Rome, 1992), MHSI 142, 143, II, p. 280.

1590–1592 while he was engaged on a mission at the court of the Spanish King. Given the purpose of this volume and the limitations of space, I shall restrict myself to presenting and publishing some unedited letters, written from Madrid to the Father General of the Society of Jesus, Claudio Acquaviva, during the period from 1 February to 18 July, 1592.

It was at the end of that same year, December 1592, that an incident occurred that seriously threatened the Scottish Catholic party, then fighting for its ideals and for its survival: the affair of the 'Spanish blanks'. George Kerr was arrested on the Scottish island of Cumbrae as he prepared to set sail for Spain. He was found to be carrying a number of blank letters, signed and sealed by the Earls of Angus, Huntly and Errol; they were thought to be directed to the King of Spain or some other important personality. Under torture Kerr confessed that a plot was under way, set in motion by the Jesuit William Crichton. Its aim was to gather support from the Catholic nobility for a planned invasion of England. There were indications that James VI was informed of the conspiracy, but he firmly denied all knowledge of this to the English ambassador. The affair of the 'blanks' was discussed by the Privy Council, 25 December 1592, and a little later, 17 January 1593, information was presented at Holyrood Palace concerning Crichton's plan.[4]

What credence should be given to Kerr's accusations against Crichton and to the implication of the Catholic earls who had signed these blank letters? An answer becomes possible in the light of the correspondence published below. This consists of six holographs written by the Scottish Jesuit: five letters addressed to Acquaviva from Madrid and the copy of a document presented to Philip II in March, outlining the pros and cons of carrying out the 'English enterprise' in 1592, which is included with one of the letters. All these texts, handwritten by Crichton himself, are in Italian; they are preserved in the Archivum Romanum Societatis Iesu (ARSI), originally the 'Archives of the Superior General of the Society of Jesus in Rome', section Tolet. (= Provincia Toletana). Their placement in this section, and a lack of familiarity with the organisation of these archives in function of the general government of the Society,[5] probably explain why this correspondence has so far escaped the attention of scholars. Among these is to be included Hubert Chadwick, who published with commentary one unedited Latin letter of Crichton to the General, written from Brussels, 29 October 1589.[6]

---

4   Thomas Graves Law, 'The Spanish Blanks and the Catholic Earls', ed. P. Hume Brown, *Collected Essays and Reviews of Thomas Graves Law*, (Edinburgh, 1904), pp. 244–76. There is a report on the affair, dated 1 July 1593, presented to Idiaquez (Archivo General de Simancas [henceforth AGS], Estado 839, f. 61.

5   For further comments on the ARSI, see Francisco de Borja Medina, S.J., 'La Compañía de Jesús y la Evangelización de América y Filipinas', *Memoria Ecclesiae* V (Oviedo, 1994), pp. 31–61, esp. pp. 32–33.

6   Hubert Chadwick, S.J., 'Father William Creichton S.I. and a recently discovered letter (1589)', *AHSI* 6 (1937), pp. 259–86.

Crichton's mission to Scotland (1587–1589)

In the letter discovered by Chadwick, Crichton reveals the role he played during his mission to Scotland, and gives his account of the affairs of that kingdom in relation to the Armada and its defeat. According to him, two-thirds of the population were waiting hopefully for the Armada, and he himself had been sent to welcome the invaders. Thus it was a cause of great disappointment, and even anger, when the Armada sailed past the coast and was eventually wrecked. This disaster could have been avoided with a disembarkation in Scotland,[7] as was subsequently demonstrated when more than a thousand ship-wrecked soldiers and sailors who landed on the coasts of Scotland were hospitably received and cared for by the Catholics (with the King's consent). The Jesuits assisted them and stayed on in the capital, Edinburgh, partly for their sake and partly for other reasons, even if they could not communicate with the Spaniards publicly. The Jesuits would join them at night and some of the Spanish officers even went to call on Crichton at his lodgings in the house of the young Earl of Angus, on the outskirts of the city near the Canongate. Once their presence was discovered by heretics, Crichton at once left his lodgings, on advice from his friends, and that same night the house underwent an official search which was unsuccessful. At about this time or a little later some letters were intercepted by English spies and sent to Scotland; they alerted those who were looking for the Jesuits. According to Crichton, they were searching for him because he had reconciled to the Catholic Church the Earl of Crawford, and for his colleague Edmund Hay because he had done the same with the Earl of Errol.[8]

Actually Crichton had undertaken missions in Scotland on two previous occasions. The first, in February of 1582, was to the Duke of Lennox on behalf of Pope Gregory XIII, in order to discuss the liberation of Queen Mary and the return of Scotland to the Catholic faith. On that occasion Crichton had been accompanied by Brother Ralph Emerson, who earlier had come to England with Edmund Campion. Crichton returned to Paris with the Duke's reply, which he delivered to Juan Bautista de Tassis, the ambassador of the Spanish King, on 7 March 1582, before going on to Rome to report to the Pope on his mission.[9] The

---

[7] 'Diu classem expectavimus Regis Catholici, non minore devotione quam illi Christi adventum qui dixerunt: utinam disrumperes coelos et descenderes. In hac expectatione et desiderio scio fuisse duas tertias partes regni. Missus sum ego ut illis essem obviam et significarem quo animo essent affecti, et quo in statu essent nostrates. At illi nunquam nostra littora attigerunt, fugientes nemine persequente, et circumeuntes omnes insulas nostras, Horcadas ac Hebrides per medias Syrtes et scopulos, sine nautis qui ullo pacto nossent illa maria; unde secuta est mira illa iactura hominum et navium. Si vero in nostra venissent littora, ne navem quidem unam aut hominem ullum amississent; sed rem per Dei gratiam sine ullo alio auxilio confecissent, ob quam mare sunt ingressi. Sed Deo omnia in melius disponente, meliora erant expectanda tempora' (Chadwick, 'Creichton,' p. 282).

[8] Chadwick, 'Creichton', pp. 274, 278, 281–84.

[9] Ludwig Freiherr von Pastor, *History of the Popes*, 40 vols (London, 1891–1953), XIX,

second mission, in 1584, had taken place together with the Jesuit James Gordon, uncle of the Earl of Huntly. They were betrayed and captured by the Zealanders of Flushing. Gordon was allowed to go free, but Crichton was taken to London, interrogated before the Privy Council (3–16 September 1584), and then imprisoned in the Tower of London (16 September 1584 – May 1587).[10] He recovered his freedom in May 1587 after giving a promise to the members of the Privy Council that he would not attempt to return to Scotland. He reached Rome about 1 July and had an interview with Persons.[11] In the summer of 1587 Claudio Acquaviva appointed him to accompany the Bishop of Dunblane, the Carthusian William Chisholm, sent by Sixtus V on apostolic mission to Scotland.[12] The letters patent, signed by Acquaviva on 17 August, stress as justification for his return an order given under holy obedience. This was intended to circumvent the promise made by Crichton to the Privy Council not to do anything for his part to procure his return to Scotland; the General affirms in the patent that Crichton had kept his word.[13]

In the autumn of 1589 Crichton left Scotland along with the Jesuit Edmund Hay. He had been there two years. The next stage of his mission to help the Catholics of Scotland would be in Madrid. Already present in Spain were the English Jesuit, Robert Persons, busy with the foundation of English Seminaries there, and the Irish Jesuit James Archer, the first Rector of the Irish College in Salamanca. Both had been appointed chaplains to the Catholic military forces assembled at the time of the Armada. The first had been given the post of superior to all the English Jesuits serving as chaplains in the army of the Spanish King in Flanders, and also put in charge of the Jesuits living in England (5

pp. 429–31. A deciphered copy of the letter to Tassis is preserved in AGS, Estado K 1560 (B53); it talks of Crichton's mission and expresses acceptance of the proposals made by the Pope and the King of Spain.

10 On Crichton's stay in the Tower, see John H. Pollen, S.J., 'Memoirs of Father William Crichton, S.J. 1584–1589', *The Month* 139 (1922), pp. 317–24. On the interrogations and the replies or confessions, see Thomas Francis Knox, ed., *The Letters and Memorials of William Cardinal Allen* (London, 1882), pp. 425–34.

11 Enrique de Guzmán, Count of Olivares, to the King, Rome 3 July 1587, CSP Simancas, IV, p. 119.

12 Chadwick, 'Creichton', pp. 262, 264–66.

13 This is the tenor of the letters patent, one of the few that has been preserved in its entirety: 'Missio P. Creyttonis in Scotiam. Claudius, etc. Carissimo fratri in X° Gul° Creyttoni eiusdem Societatis sacerdoti salutem, etc. Quamuis cum in Anglia in vinculis detinereris Consiliariis eiusdem Regni Reginae, illorum coactus imperio, promisisse te asseras, nunquam te curaturum, quod reuera praestitisti, ut in Scotiam mittereris, nec eo iterum nisi nostra et superiorum qui pro sua in te potestate tibi id iniungere possent, obedientia compellante: Nos tamen qui divinam tantum gloriam et animarum salutem spectare debemus, tibi per praesentes iniungimus atque in virtute Sanctae obedientiae mandamus, ut in Scotiam te conferas, ubi fidei propagationi atque animarum tantum lucro iuxta instituti nostri rationem diligenter incumbas, divinam interim Maiestatem obnixe rogantes ut tibi in omnibus luce atque auxilio suae gratiae adesse dignetur. Amen. Romae 17 Augusti 1587' (ARSI, Hist. Soc. 61, f. 27ᵛ., summary, f. 45).

November 1588).[14] The second was at this period (1588) chaplain to the Irish Regiment of the Army under Alessandro Farnese, Duke of Parma.[15]

In August 1590 Crichton was held up in Genoa, recovering from attacks of tertian fever that had forced him to take to his bed for long periods.[16] Towards the end of October or beginning of November he arrived in Madrid, from where he wrote to Acquaviva.[17] His mission at the Spanish court would last a little under two years, as he departed from Madrid in August 1592.

Crichton's mission in Madrid (1590–1592)

Nearly all the correspondence sent to Crichton from Rome during his residence in the Spanish capital has survived. However of the letters sent by him to Rome only the documents mentioned above have been preserved covering the period from 1 February to 18 July 1592. Eleven letters from Acquaviva addressed to Crichton were transcribed and kept in the Register of Letters of the Superior General directed to the Jesuit provinces of Milan and Toledo for the period from December 1590 to July 1592. Thanks to these it is possible to reconstruct at second hand the various steps taken by Crichton in his negotiations at the Spanish court from November 1590 to February 1592, the date of the first of Crichton's letters from Madrid that has been preserved giving first-hand evidence about his efforts. From March 1591 the General uses in his letters to Crichton a code, for which no detailed key has been found; however from the context and a comparison with other documents on the subject, it is not difficult to decipher the meaning in its main lines. Thus 'Georgio Cottomo' (G.C.), a merchant, must be William (Gulielmus) Creytton. The 'business' is the 'enterprise of England' and the 'merchandise' is everything connected with it.

From Acquaviva'a reply to Crichton's report, 9 November 1590, it is clear that his proposals had been favourably received at the Spanish court. The King, on hearing of the offers made by the Scottish noblemen in support of the 'enterprise', had suggested that either Crichton or another member of the Society should go to Scotland to inform the nobles of possible plans. The General was absolutely convinced that it would not be suitable for Crichton or any other member of the Society to return to Scotland unless he were to go openly with the Armada. The reason was that it would be quite impossible to hide the purpose of such a visit; the opposing forces in England were well provided with intelligence, as Crichton well knew, and they might easily discover

---

[14] 'Institutio Superioris nostrorum Anglorum qui Castra Regis Catholici sequuntur . . . Romae, 5 Novembris 1588', ARSI, Hist. Soc. 61, f. 28.

[15] Francisco de Borja Medina, S.J., 'Jesuitas en la Armada contra Inglaterra (1588). Notas para un Centenario', *AHSI* 58 (1989), p. 29n.

[16] Acquaviva to Crichton, Rome 25 August 1590, ARSI Med. 21/II, f. 308[v].

[17] Acquaviva to Crichton, Roma 24 December 1590, ARSI Tolet. 4, f. 79[v].

the move, through informers or by guesswork; the outcome would be disastrous for the common good. Acquaviva gave instructions that Crichton might show his letter to the authorities, if no other means was available, in order to block the journey. Should the King decide that somebody of Scottish nationality should go to Scotland, a person that had been recommended to Acquaviva as the most appropriate was Robert Bruce, 'an excellent agent for such an undertaking'. The reports on him could not be better: he was 'a man of great zeal and readiness for the task, gifted with great prudence and intelligence', as Crichton already knew. People had informed the General that he was a person 'of rare parts', and that no one similar was to be found in that nation. He was then in Flanders where he was well known to the lords of the *Cámara Real,* and therefore it was quite appropriate that Crichton should put forward his name, if necessary, to the King so that he could be summoned to the court. If this might involve a risk of too much delay, the King could send the appropriate instructions to Flanders.[18] Crichton had known Bruce for some time and had recommended him to the King as a faithful and intelligent gentleman, who had already rendered valuable services to his Catholic Majesty. He was trustworthy and capable of undertaking any sort of service.[19]

Acquaviva's warnings against returning to Scotland seem to have led Crichton to propose an alternative plan: he urged (1 February) that he might be allowed to visit Flanders in order to comply with the request of a certain 'Ruberto Hiberno' (Robert Bruce?). His departure from Madrid appeared to be imminent because the General sent a reply, in code, addressed to Genoa, advising him not to go to Flanders for the same reasons that he had advised against a journey to Scotland. His presence in Flanders would arouse even further those who already suspected something, it would lead to fresh jealousies and cause more harm than good. The line of action recommended by the General to Crichton ('Georgio Cottomo') was to send instructions, written or verbal, to the representative of the said 'Robert' concerning the place and the person best suited for negotiating about his wares, and also the measures to be taken, and inform him of the names of his three brothers, who were in Flanders, then leave him to settle the affair as he thought best. When the appropriate time came, he would entrust the transport of those commercial goods to one of the two that Cottom himself had mentioned.[20]

Despite the General's opinion, it seems that a decision had already been reached by June 1591 in favour of the journey to Flanders. In reply to Crichton's dispatch of 30 March Acquaviva sent a letter patent in duplicate (one to Genoa

[18] Acquaviva to Crichton, Rome 24 December 1590, ARSI Tolet. 4, f. 79ᵛ.

[19] 'La Nobiltà principale di Scotia di titulo di Conte e di Lord', AGS Estado 839, f. 34. They had worked together on the latest mission to Scotland, and Bruce had been the link with Parma and Philip II. See Chadwick, 'Creichton', pp. 276, 284. On his possible role as a double-agent, see p. 266, note 16.

[20] Acquaviva to Crichton, Rome 16 March 1591, ARSI Med. 22, f. 024ᵛ.

and another to Turin) authorising him, as he had requested, to reside in Lower Germany, i.e. present-day Belgium, *ad fructificandum in vinea Domini* ('to produce fruit in the vineyard of the Lord').[21] Acquaviva also sent a letter in triplicate (to Madrid and the two cities mentioned), 11 June, in which he informs Crichton, using his cryptic terminology, that he has sent the letters patent that had been requested, authorising the transfer to Flanders, should the other pilgrimage, about which mention had been made in previous letters, not prove possible in a convenient way. However he needed to inform 'Georgio Cottomo' that he should come to Rome because 'Edoardo Hoffeo' (Edmund Hay) wanted to speak to him. Therefore, on arriving in Italy he should wait for an invitation from Hay, unless some urgent business forced him to depart for his own country. Unless he happened to land in Italy before the end of June, he should wait in Lombardy, at either Florence or Siena, until the weather had cooled a little. However, if he had business to deal with which he considered extremely urgent, such that it would not be convenient to make such a detour and spend such a long time just for a second opinion, then he should not put obstacles in the way of the main business but rather set off at once for Flanders, *cum modis et mercibus* ('with the means and the merchandise'); it would be possible to deal with the other matter by letter. As for the successful outcome of the negotiations to found a Scots College in Flanders, a letter would be sent to the Provincial of that province.[22] In fact in a letter to Oliver Mannaerts, Provincial of Flanders, the General explains that Crichton would be going there in connection with the seminaries of the Society in Belgium.[23]

It is possible that this journey was linked with the activities in Madrid of Sir William Stanley, who was getting ready to return to Flanders at about this time. To judge from a report sent by the spy William Sterrell, Sir William arrived in Flanders in August.[24] He would find himself in Rome on 5 October along with two servants, guests at the Hospice of the English College.[25]

Given Crichton's insistence on the journey (in his report of 17 August), Acquaviva in his reply referred to his previous letters in June and confirmed that provided the 'merchandise' was in order, 'Cottomo' could travel with it wherever he was required.[26] On 13 October Crichton informed Acquaviva that the 'merchandise' (= 'the enterprise') and the journey had been delayed indefinitely and asked him to speak with 'Signor Pompeo' (= the Pope); however the General did

---

[21] Patent for Lower Germany, Rome 7 June 1591, ARSI Hist. Soc. 61, f. 47ᵛ.

[22] Acquaviva to Crichton, Rome 11 June 1591, ARSI Tolet. 4, f. 85ᵛ. The copy of the letter sent to Madrid is in such a bad state that several sentences are illegible. However the main points can be confirmed from the copy of the other letter sent in duplicate on the same day to Genoa and Turin.

[23] Acquaviva to Mannaerts, Rome 10 June 1591, ARSI Fl. Belg. 1, f. 474.

[24] Wernham, *After the Armada*, pp. 449–50.

[25] Henry Foley, S.J., *Records of the English Province of the Society of Jesus*, 7 vols in 8 (Roehampton/London, 1875–83), VI, p. 564.

[26] Acquaviva to Crichton, Rome 1 October 1591, ARSI Tolet. 4, f. 90ʳ⁻ᵛ.

not see how the latter could be of any help, as he was very busy with matters all over the place, as Crichton might have already heard from information received from the Low Countries.

On 4 November Edmund Hay died of dysentery, with acute colic pains, an illness from which he had suffered habitually. His death would deprive Crichton of a valued support. Hay had held office with great humility, prudence and fidelity.[27] It was only in 1591 that Edmund Hay had been appointed assistant for Germany (which included all provinces north of the Alps and the missions to England, Ireland and Scotland), taking the place of Paul Hoffeus, who had been both the oldest of the assistants and admonitor to the General.[28]

There was a new letter from Crichton to the General on 7 December, but the latter restricted himself in his reply to a promise of prayers, both his own and those of the Society, for the success of the negotiations undertaken by Crichton, as indeed for that of other matters. Among these was the election of a new pope, and Acquaviva expressed the wish that he might be similar to the deceased Innocent IX (who had died 30 December 1591).[29] On 30 January 1592 Hipolito Cardinal Aldobrandini was elected and took the name of Clement VIII.

In the meanwhile Crichton had not been idle, and a new opportunity had arisen. In November 1591 the King decided to send a Scottish gentleman to invite Baron Fyntrey (or Fintry), a statesman and a very faithful Catholic, to come from Scotland to the Spanish court on behalf of the Scottish nobility so that he might discuss the offers made to His Majesty and inform him of the situation.

David Graham, the Laird of Fintry,[30] was held in high regard by Crichton. In a report on the Scottish nobility that he drew up for the King he mentions him among the lower grade earls, who nevertheless were to be greatly esteemed as they possessed no less power than the others. It is highly probable that this report, in addition to others given earlier, decided the King to choose Graham as the person most suitable to establish contact with the highest Scottish nobility.[31]

---

[27] Acquaviva to Crichton, Rome 25 November 1591, ARSI Tolet. 4, ff. 95ᵛ–96.

[28] The removal of Hoffeus was a decisive coup by Acquaviva. He had ousted him because he represented an obstacle to Acquaviva's form of government. Hoffeus, as both assistant and admonitor had criticised Acquaviva's style of government, which he considered too removed from the paternal simplicty shown by Ignatius Loyola and the first generals, all of whom Hoffaeus had known personally as friends and colleagues. See Burkhart Schneider, S.J., 'Der Konflikt zwischen Claudius Aquaviva and Paul Hoffaeus. Ergänzungen und Berichtigungen', *AHSI* 27 (1958), pp. 279–306.

[29] Acquaviva to Crichton, Rome 20 January 1592, ARSI Tolet. 4, f. 99.

[30] Chadwick, 'Creichton', p. 276.

[31] In his report, Crichton writes: 'buonissimo catholico e zeloso per il quale ha fatto seruitii per tirar molti al fauore et parte de sua Maestà Catholica più que nessun altro per il che è excomunicato per gli Ministri heretici et persecutato dal Re et priuato delle sue baronie et beni, è signor fedele, intelligente nelle lingue et costumi di forastiere, et degno d'esser impieghato in qualsi uoglia cosa', 'La Nobilità Principale di Scotia di titolo di Conte o di Lord', AGS Estado 839, f. 34.

In fact he had already undergone several arrests and imprisonment, and some months later, when the 'Spanish blanks' were discovered, he was beheaded as he refused to accept the condition proposed for his liberation – conformity with the Kirk.[32]

Crichton was to complain to the General that even in March 1592 not the slightest news had reached Madrid about the mission sent to Fintry. The long wait had prevented his departure to Rome to give a verbal report to the General on his progress. He had presented two or three requests for royal permission to leave, subject to the King's better judgement. He had received no reply, but he was aware that the King was not inclined to let him go. However Crichton was prepared to do whatever the General ordered him.[33]

On 1 February 1592 Crichton was writing to Acquaviva, though in veiled terms, to inform him that he had become aware of growing inactivity in relation to the 'enterprise'. Like others he criticised the slowness in settling matters of business and he expressed fears that nothing or too little would be done, or too late. To convey the strength of the Queen of England he used the simile of the spider in her web. Unless one were to sweep away the spider along with the web, which would be the simplest move, she would continue to spin her threads in other parts of the house. Once the spider were removed, no more webs would appear and those already there would have no strength against the sweeper. The conclusion was clear for anyone capable of hearing: Philip was wasting his time fighting on various fronts – Flanders, France, the Indies with their fleets – all of which were inspired or supported by Elizabeth; the best move would be to attack her in her own house.

As Crichton was uncertain if the King intended to undertake the 'enterprise', his stay at the court had no meaning; he suggested to Acquaviva that Fr Gil González, then holding the position of Visitor to the province of Toledo and present in the court, should decide about the advisability of his staying or leaving. The fleet from the Indies had arrived recently in Spain with coffers to the value of ten to twelve million ducats, counting together all that corresponded to the King and to private individuals. The Flemish Jesuit Jacob de Zeelander had been sent to the court to deal with the business of Flanders, but this was still in the hands of the King.[34]

All this news gave the impression of considerable confusion and impotence. However by 6–7 April 1592 Crichton could explain clearly to Acquaviva, by means of the bearer of his letters, Baron Dacre, the steps he had taken on behalf of the 'enterprise' and its present state. This nobleman was Francis Dacre, the younger brother and heir to Leonard, Lord Dacre. Towards the end of September 1589 (near Michaelmas) he had escaped into Scotland and sought refuge with his

---

[32] William Forbes-Leith, S.J., ed., *Narratives of Scottish Catholics under Mary Stuart and James VI* (Edinburgh, 1885), pp. 220–21.

[33] Crichton to Acquaviva, Madrid 7 April 1592, ARSI Tolet. 37a, f. 218.

[34] Crichton to Acquaviva, Madrid 1 February 1592, ARSI Tolet. 37a, f. 212.

wife and children in the house of the Earl of Bothwell. He was ready to serve the King of Spain at the time of the 'enterprise'. He spent about two and a half years in Scotland. Early in 1592 he came to Madrid, where he stayed for three months, receiving a pension from the King of 100 ducats a month.[35] He was lodged at the house of Jane Duchess of Feria.[36] Crichton made use of his services when he left for Rome in April of the same year, sending with him several letters (this time not in code) to Acquaviva. By 28 May Dacre was already in Rome, lodged at the English College.[37]

Crichton explained that he had communicated considerable information to the Spanish court, but received no reply. Officials there were not displeased, but they came to no decision, only informing him that the King was well disposed and that all would be done in due time. Crichton sent Acquaviva a copy of the various reasons for and against carrying out the 'enterprise of England' in that same year, that he had communicated to the King in March.[38] However the situation in France prevented, for the time being, the undertaking of anything new. On the other hand, they had promised him help for the Society's mission to Scotland, without being more precise except for a grant of 700 ducats, delivered some five or six months earlier, for his own upkeep and that of his secretary, a layman. The latter was an excellent person, and Crichton had sent him to Lisbon to be admitted into the Society, as the college in Madrid lacked the necessary conditions to receive novices.

The General, in agreement with Crichton's proposal, replied on 13 April, that he should discuss with the Visitor, Gil González, or anyone else that he considered suitable, on the advisability of his departure. Acquaviva would send his letters to Genoa, and informed him that he should pay a visit to Rome before setting off for Flanders, if his business allowed this detour.[39] On 23 May 1592 Crichton wrote to tell the General that in agreement with the fathers consulted he would be leaving for Rome to inform him personally about the goings-on at court. He intended to go to the Escorial on that very day to request the royal permit. He would leave with the first ship he could find, and expected to arrive in Rome at the height of the summer.[40] In June Acquaviva expressed to Crichton his own view about the expediency of meeting with Persons in order to decide what was most convenient.[41]

---

[35] '1593, June 30. Examination of John Whitfield in Northumberland, servant to Francis Dacre', Historical Manuscript Commission, *Calendar of the Manuscripts of the Most Hon. the Marquis of Salisbury preserved at Hatfield House*, 24 vols (London, 1883–1976), IV, pp. 333–34.

[36] Albert J. Loomie, S.J., *The Spanish Elizabethans* (New York, 1963), pp. 105–06, 247.

[37] Foley, *Records*, VI, p. 565.

[38] 'Pro e Contra', March 1592, ARSI Tolet. 37a, ff. 214–15.

[39] Acquaviva to Crichton, Rome 13 April 1592, ARSI Tolet. 4, f. 103ᵛ.

[40] Crichton to Acquaviva, Madrid 23 May 1592, ARSI Tolet. 37a, f. 220.

[41] Acquaviva to Crichton, Rome 6 June 1592, ARSI, Epp. NN. 2, f. 20. This letter, registered among the *Litterae Extraordinariae ad NN*, is addressed to 'Gioan' Creytton in Madrid,

On 18 July Crichton was informing Acquaviva about his visit to Valladolid to speak with Persons in order to reach an agreement with him; on reaching Rome, which he hoped to do, following the General's instructions, at the end of August or beginning of September, he would tell him what had been agreed. For the time being there was nothing further to be done over the principal matter of business, despite much goodwill and a desire to bring the affair to a conclusion when possible. The King had granted him permission to leave, on condition that he would return when called. Crichton had referred this point to the General, assuring the King that the latter would always do his best to please him. As for the projected foundation in Douai of a seminary college for Scottish noblemen, it had been put off until word was received from the Duke of Parma and negotiations for the granting of funds for the Society's mission to Scotland had been settled.[42]

Crichton's departure from Madrid must have occurred early in August. On the third of that month the Nuncio, Pietro Millino, handed him a letter of presentation to Pope Clement VIII. The Nuncio had known and had dealings with Crichton during his two years in Madrid, and considered him to be very zealous in God's honour and a confirmed enemy of all heresies and their partisans. He informed the Pope that this Father had been in contact with the King and his ministers about the return of Scotland to the Catholic religion and the expulsion of heretics; although they had listened to him willingly, he had not been able to obtain what he desired, perhaps because the King was too preoccupied with the wars in France and Flanders, and wanted first to see the outcome of his negotiations with France. The father would personally inform the Pope in detail about the affairs of Scotland and England dealt with by him at the Spanish court. The Pope could also question him about the affairs of France, as he was well informed about those as well.[43]

On 17 August Crichton was in Valencia, where he intended to wait for a month.[44] By 22 October he had reached Barcelona.[45] He probably arrived in Rome in November 1592. Towards the end of January 1593, he set out for Flanders, accompanied by Fr William Baldwin.[46] By 21 April 1593 he had reached Douai, passing via Pont-à-Mousson.[47]

---

but it is certainly meant for William Crichton, the only Jesuit at the time with this name. Evidently the secretary interpreted the G° in Crichton's signature as Gioan (=Giovanni).

[42] Crichton to Acquaviva, Madrid 18 July 1592, ARSI Tolet. 37a, ff. 225–26ᵛ.

[43] Pietro Millino to Aldobrandini, Madrid 3 August 1592, ASV Spagna 40, f. 18. Pastor (*History of the Popes*, XXIII, p. 200 n. 2) is mistaken when he allots these reports of Millino to 3 August of the following year, 1593.

[44] Crichton to Sebastián Hernández, Valencia 17 August 1592, ARSI Angl. 30/I, f. 102.

[45] Crichton to Sebastián Hernández, Barcelona 22 October 1592, ARSI Angl. 30/I f. 104.

[46] Letters patent, 13 January 1593, ARSI Hist. Soc. 61, f. 48ᵛ.

[47] Crichton to Acquaviva, Douai 21 April 1593, ARSI Germ. 171, f. 510; Acquaviva to Crichton, Rome 5 June 1593, ARSI Fl.Belg. 1, f. 518.

1590–1592: The worst possible moment

Crichton could not have chosen a worse moment to open negotiations with the Catholic King about the 'enterprise of England'. Philip II was fully occupied with the war in France in defence of the Catholic League against the pretender, Henry of Navarre, head of the Huguenot party, which was supported by Queen Elizabeth of England, the Dutch United Provinces and the German Protestant princes.

On two occasions Parma had been ordered by the King to enter French territory with his *tercios* to help the League, thus leaving Flanders defenceless and at the mercy of attacks by Maurice of Nassau, supported by English troops. Between August and November 1590, Parma entered to bring help to the Duke of Mayenne, at the head of the League, and raise the siege of Paris. Between December 1591 and the middle of June 1592 he liberated Rouen, besieged by Henry of Navarre with his English auxiliaries. When on the point of invading France for a third time at the King's orders, he died at Arras on 3 December 1592, succumbing after a long illness.[48] In 1590 the Catholic King had sent other troops to support the League: in July they entered Languedoc, and in September, Brittany, when Juan del Águila went to the assistance of the Governor, the Duke of Mercoeur, who had placed at the King's disposal the port of Blavet. Control of this base assured communications with Flanders and facilitated the invasion of England.[49]

Meanwhile in Spain, the ex-Secretary of State, Antonio Pérez, fled from prison on 20 April 1590 to seek refuge in Aragon where disturbances followed in May 1591. In September 20,000 Castilian troops were sent into Aragon under the command of Alonso de Vargas. In February 1592 there came an invasion, instigated by Pérez and his followers and supported by Henry of Navarre, of troops from the Béarn into northern Aragon, but nothing came of it.[50]

During this period, August 1590 to 30 January 1592, Rome had seen the passing of three popes between the death of Sixtus V and the election of Clement VIII: Urban VII (15–27 September 1590), Gregory XIV (5 December 1590 – 16 October 1591), and Innocent IX (29 October – 30 December 1591). This series of interruptions at the head of the Catholic Church prevented the

[48] For a good summary, see M.J. Rodríguez Salgado, *Felipe II y la crisis Post-Armada: política exterior y rebelión, 1588–1594 / Philip II and the Post-Armada crisis: foreign policy and rebellion, 1588–1594* (Madrid, 1993), Cuadernos monográficos del Instituto de Historia y Cultura Naval, Supplement to No. 20, pp. 78–86.

[49] Manuel Gracia Rivas, 'La Campaña de Bretaña (1590–1598) una amenaza para Inglaterra', in *Después de la Gran Armada: la historia desconocida (1588–16..)* (Madrid, 1993), pp. 41–56, Cuadernos monográficos del Instituto de Historia y Cultura Naval, No. 20.

[50] John Lynch, *Spain under the Habsburgs*, 2 vols (Oxford, 1964, 1969), I, pp. 337, 345.

establishment of any stable policy vis-à-vis the problems of the Spanish King: in particular, the succession of a Catholic as King of France and the 'enterprise of England'.

Crichton's negotiations at the Spanish court

The two letters sent by Crichton, 6 and 7 April, along with his memorandum to the King on the pros and cons of undertaking the 'enterprise of England' in 1592, are fundamental documents for understanding the subjects discussed by Crichton while in Madrid, and his personal opinions on these matters.[51]

Despite the general lack of interest arising from the political situation just described, Crichton worked night and day to persuade the King that he should launch the 'enterprise of England' as soon as possible: he stressed the favourable feelings of the Scottish nobility, and the ease of the undertaking. The nobles offered to take ('pigliar': literally 'grab') their King (James VI) and place at the disposal of Philip some of their castles and their own sons. To house the latter Crichton proposed to found a seminary in Douai for the education of the young Scots under the patronage of His Catholic Majesty.

Philip II seemed satisfied with the support of the Scottish nobility, but he was unable at that stage, owing to the wars in Flanders and France, to undertake 'the enterprise'. However, he had other motives, that he did not disclose, such as his fear that he would not be able to keep England for himself or as a friendly power. The disastrous loss of the Grand Armada had deprived him of forces and left him hesitant, fearful, and reluctant to engage himself in massive expenses when other ventures had a prior claim. It was really up to the Pope to legitimise Philip's rights and to come to the appropriate decisions about the 'enterprise', then communicate them to the Spanish ambassador. Unless he did this and added his own encouragement and financial support, another ten years would go by with nothing achieved. Ten had already passed since Crichton's mission to the Duke of Lennox on behalf of Gregory XIII, and everything was still in the preliminary stages.

As for the question of the succession to the English throne,[52] it would be most helpful if William Cardinal Allen could be persuaded of the advisability of the Catholic King taking over the kingdoms of England and Scotland, and that these should be united under one head.

Crichton kept Persons informed about all his plans, but the latter remained firmly opposed to starting the 'enterprise' in Scotland. As a result, he was making the 'enterprise' much more difficult. His hostility to Scotland made people

---

[51] ARSI Tolet. 37a, ff. 214–15, 216–18ᵛ.

[52] On this point, cf. M.J. Rodríguez Salgado, 'The Anglo-Spanish War: the final episode in the "War of the Roses" ', in M.J. Rodríguez Salgado and Simon Adams, eds, *England, Spain and the Gran Armada, 1588–1604* (Edinburgh, 1991), pp. 1–44.

suspect that he, Cardinal Allen and others intended to make use of the Catholic King simply to get rid of the heretics and then set up their own King. Crichton regretted that the contradictory nature of the reports reaching the King, and of the opinions among the English themselves, quite apart from those dividing the English and the Scots, concerning the place where the 'enterprise' should begin, would delay any project. He implored the General to moderate, by means of Allen, the opinions of Persons, whose judgement carried great weight in both Spain and England, far greater than that of anyone else. Persons was liable to error.[53]

The Catholic King as guarantor of the faith and of justice

Crichton was convinced, as were others, that England was the root cause of all the difficulties and hardships faced by the King in different quarters: Flanders, France, the Indies, etc. He calculated that there would be a saving of five to six million ducats a year if the 'enterprise' were to be launched at once.[54] He insisted, rather optimistically, on the ease of the operation: in relation to its importance, not much money would be needed to complete it, and only one commander with some troops. Many thought that the Duke of Feria would be an excellent person for the task as he knew the language and was the son of an English lady.[55]

The General was advised to discuss the matter with the ambassador, the Duke of Sessa, so that the new nuncio, Camillo Caetani, could be well informed on his arrival. Crichton himself would give him further information in Madrid.[56]

Crichton maintained that every effort should be directed to carrying out the 'enterprise'. If the disembarkation did not take place in Scotland, so much the better. Provided the English were able to gain control of one of the northern English ports, it could be organised there. His own hope, as was that of all

---

[53] This difference of opinion with Persons did not mean that they were enemies. Crichton had always defended and supported Persons, even if he did not always approve of his policies: Crichton to George Duras, German assistant in Rome, Chambéry, 4 May 1602, ARSI Angl. 42, f. 158ᵛ.

[54] On the back of Crichton's letter of 7 April, there is a summary from the pen of the secretary which characterizes the 'enterprise' as 'la guerra contro quella Jezabel', which is hardly Crichton's style (ARSI Tolet. 37a, f. 217ᵛ).

[55] Lady Jane Dormer was the wife of the Count of Feria who later became the first Duke (Loomie, *Spanish Elizabethans*, p. 94).

[56] Camillo Caetani, Patriarch of Alexandria, reached Madrid in February, 1593. The Pope had announced his appointment to the King on 1 October 1592, and Caetani received his instructions on the 27th (Pastor, *History of the Popes*, XXIII, p. 197).

Scotsmen, was that the Spaniards would not enter Scotland, as they would only bring ruin and hardship.[57]

The whole purpose of the 'enterprise' was to restore the faith, to allow the practice of the Catholic religion, and to save souls. He strongly opposed those in Rome who supported James VI, the Scottish heretical King, with a faint hope of his conversion. Their aim might be good, but the means chosen was harmful. He did not mind who should be King, but he could see no better candidate than His Catholic Majesty if the aim was the expulsion of heretics and their long-term exclusion. The best legal justification for Philip's right to the throne would have to be supplied by the Pope, and would require the excommunication and deposition of both the Queen of England and the King of Scotland, as cruel and obstinate heretics, and the granting of the right of succession to the first Catholic to take the throne who showed himself capable and willing to return the kingdom to obedience to the Catholic Church.[58]

Crichton had hoped at least until 1587[59] for the conversion of James VI. New hopes appeared in 1593, perhaps as a result of his disappointment with the attitude he had found in Madrid and his new confidence in closer contact with Scotland, which was now less distant.[60] But at least at this juncture, 1592, there was only one possible candidate capable of guaranteeing the spiritual and temporal ideals of the Catholics who found themselves caught in the fire of persecution in England and Scotland, and who wanted to free themselves: the Catholic King. He would give them a good viceroy, and this move would have the added advantage that if found not to be good, he could be replaced, whereas if a king took over who was evil, a tyrant or a heretic, there would be no remedy but to suffer him in patience.

On the other hand,

> if the Catholic King were to be the king, not only would he be able to maintain faith and justice and defend the inhabitants against enemies, but he would also, by making use of the resources of both kingdoms on behalf of the inhabitants, not draining them out of the country, enable our countrymen to share in his great ventures, honours, wide-spread Empire and wealth.[61]

---

[57] Crichton to Acquaviva, Madrid 7 April 1592, ARSI Tolet. 37a, f. 219.

[58] 'Pro e Contra', March 1592, ARSI Tolet. 37a, f. 215. This was in substance the plan drawn up by Sixtus V and agreed to by Philip II on 29 July 158 (Pastor, *History of the Popes*, XXII, pp. 50–51).

[59] Persons noted this in his reply to Crichton's negative reaction to the book on the succession: in Rome, 1587 [he writes 1586 by mistake], Crichton was still showing hopes about the conversion of his King, but the situation had changed when they met in Spain (Persons to Crichton, Seville 10 May 1596, Knox, *Letters and Memorials*, p. 382).

[60] This is discussed in greater detail later.

[61] Crichton to Aquaviva, Madrid 6 April 1592, ARSI Tolet. 37a, f. 216ᵛ.

This utopian vision, which was shared more or less by quite a few who were suffering because of fidelity to their consciences, was to prove an illusion. Crichton left the court completely disillusioned. The King had a good heart, and his way of life and noble intentions were quite saintly. But in the opinion of many his great weakness was that all too often he showed no will to do what lay in his power, and great will to do what lay outside it; as a result many of his undertakings remained simple velleities. Crichton drew attention to the King's lack of confidence in possible collaborators: he could have taken over any of the kingdoms of England, Scotland and Ireland, with one competent leader and the assistance of the English, Scottish and Irish Catholics, but it was impossible to say if he was willing to trust them and use their collaboration. On the other hand, without their support and friendship, it was impossible to take over those kingdoms and hold them for very long. Crichton followed Pedro Ribadeneira, who noted at the time of the defeat of the Armada[62] that the King was advanced in years, overwhelmed by the weight of governing his kingdoms and other preoccupations, and beset by uncertain health. Unless he shifted the burden to prudent and faithful commanders, allowing them to discuss in his presence and carry out the decisions, everything would continue as before, or even worse. Crichton had clearly described to the General the indecisive character of the King, inspired in part by his fears and uncertainties about taking the throne: the Pope should set the King's conscience at rest with regard to his rights to that kingdom, and Allen should work out the best way to preserve the affection and support of the nation when the take-over was complete. For 'those who are lacking in resolve, and are slow, fearful and distrustful, need to be given efficacious help, as otherwise they cannot produce a generous response, even though they are most holy people, of excellent goodwill'.[63] This was exactly the position of Sixtus V in his reply, often misinterpreted, to Philip II in 1589 after the disastrous outcome of the Armada. He was ready to give the help promised in 1587, but not to make an advance payment, 'because Your Majesty takes so much time to consult about your undertakings that both the occasion and the money are gone before you come round to carrying them out'.[64]

Crichton was not far from the truth in his assessment of Philip II, and the course of history was to prove him right. The Catholic King was incapable of carrying out any of his plans for the map of Europe. The 'English enterprise' failed once more in 1596 and 1597; the French venture ended with the Peace of Vervins (2 May 1598) four months before his death in his retreat in the Escorial (13 September 1598); he left to his son the unresolved (and insoluble) problem of

62 Medina, 'Jesuitas en la Armada', p. 24.

63 Crichton to Acquaviva, Madrid 6 April 1592, ARSI Tolet. 37a, f. 216ᵛ.

64 'Copy of a letter written by Pope Sixtus V to the Lord King, Philip II, on the occasion of his taking up arms against England', [25 July 1589], ASV Ottoboni Mss 2.640, f. 578. See Knox, *Letters and Memorials*, p. 435. The Pope was ready to provide more money once there had been a disembarcation in England; he had the money and it had been gathered to bring the 'enterprise' to a successful conclusion.

the rebellion in the Low Countries. But prior to all this there had been the state bankruptcy of 1596, the result of the excessive expenditure required by so many different projects, all going on simultaneously with very poor administration.

Crichton was not lacking in Scottish humour. His own description of his failed mission refers to the myth of the Egyptian elephants, who were supposed to have given birth, after prolonged labours, to abortions. He said that he had come pregnant with an elephant, and wished that there might be produced at least a kid![65]

Perhaps the 'kid' was the Scots College that was so close to his heart. Crichton was sent to Douai to look after the mission to Scotland and at the same time to take care of the students at the college with whatever means he could find. Acquaviva strongly urged the Provincial, Mannaerts, with insistence to help Crichton with his help, advice and authority.[66]

Winds of change:
Crichton in favour of James Stuart

Upon his arrival in Flanders in 1593, Crichton's confidence in the person of his King and natural lord, James Stuart, started to surface again. This change could have been due, in part at least, to the ineffective if not indifferent attitude respecting the Scottish plan, experienced by Crichton at the Spanish court, which was controlled by the English faction led by Persons. But what most decisively justified his change of attitude was the arrival of encouraging news from Scotland, where he had managed to establish trustworthy informers.[67] The situation had become considerably better than it had ever been before. The King found himself betrayed by those he trusted the most, both by heretical ministers and by those of his own family, the Stuarts, and his closest relatives, the Hamiltons, who handed him over into the power of an outlaw, the Earl of Bothwell. James had been able to escape and had placed himself in the hands of the Catholics, who proved to be most faithful and most powerful. For her part the young Queen of Scotland had separated herself from the heretics and showed favour to the Catholic ladies, who in their turn had a great opinion of her and the greatest hopes in her.[68] The King had appointed Baron Hume, a confessed Catholic, captain of his guard of two hundred horse and three hundred

---

[65] 'De mea expeditione in mentem venit quod scribitur de eliphantibus Aegypti qui diu parturiunt, et tandem pariunt abortum. Ego veni ex eliphanto gravidus, vtinam pariat haedulum', Crichton to Sebastián Hernández, n.d. [August 1592], ARSI Angl. 30/I, f. 101.

[66] Acquaviva to Mannaerts, Rome 26 January 1593, ARSI Fl. Belg. 1, f. 510.

[67] Crichton to Acquaviva, Douai 21 April 1593, ARSI Germ. 171, f. 136. Crichton had sent to Scotland a young man who wanted to join the Society of Jesus so that, while he put his own affairs in order, he would set up reliable informers.

[68] Crichton to Acquaviva, Antwerp 23 October 1593, ARSI Germ. 171, f. 290.

infantrymen. Crichton acknowledged his former opposition to the candidacy of James, about whom he had a very poor opinion, but now, even though the King had not yet embraced the Catholic faith, there were genuine hopes for his conversion, whether willingly or by force. Perhaps at that moment, the example of the abjuration of Henry of Navarre on 15 July 1593 was working in favour of Crichton's change of opinion concerning the possibility of a similar gesture by James Stuart. At least he already had an immediate precedent to rely on in the change of religion of an ally of Elizabeth of England.

In January 1594 Crichton, writing from Brussels to Acquaviva, informed the General about the failed attempt to draw the Earl of Derby to the Catholic cause, which had been aborted by the execution in the environs of London of the gentleman sent to England for that purpose. And he criticised those who had tried to entrust the 'enterprise' to the Earl by offering him the crown. Derby would have been unable to carry out the 'enterprise' for lack of means and of people who would follow him, since many would have vied with him with equal right for the crown. On the contrary, James possessed a better right, one as incontestable as the right of his mother. He counted on the support of the entire kingdom of Scotland, and of all the English Catholics, and, indeed, of many Protestants – all those who had backed the cause of his mother. Crichton proposed that, when the Pope and the King of Spain came to an agreement about the 'enterprise's' leader, James should be considered; if the forces and assistance allegedly promised to the Earl of Derby were given to James, the King of Scotland would side with the Catholics. It was also convenient that the apostolic nuncio, currently resident in Cologne, move to Brussels where he would be able to discuss any developments with Archduke Ernest, Governor General of the Low Countries. From there it only took three or four days to sail to Scotland; indeed, if the weather was favorable, the crossing could even be made in two.[69]

In this hopeful climate Crichton's reaction against the *Book of Succession*,[70] in which the rights to the English crown of Philip II and his daughter the Infanta Isabel Clara Eugenia were supported and those of James Stuart rejected on the basis of heresy, causes no surprise.[71]

---

[69] Crichton to Acquaviva, Brussels 13 January 1594, ARSI, Germ. 172, f. 11[r–v]. Crichton referred to the abortive attempt to persuade Ferdinand Stanley, the new Earl of Derby, in the autumn of 1593. Sir William Stanley had sent his agent Hesketh to England with this purpose. See Wernham, *Return of the Armadas*, p. 16.

[70] The proper author and title are R. Doleman, *A Conference about the Next Succession to the Crowne of Ingland* (n.p. [Antwerp], 1594 [1595]), STC 19398, ARCR II, no. 167.

[71] Persons to Crichton, Seville 10 May 1596 and Madrid 2 November 1596, Stonyhurst College, Coll P 316, 318 (in response to Crichton's letters of 20 January and 20 August 1596). On Crichton's reaction, see also Persons to Acquaviva, Seville 10 May 1596, ARSI, Hisp. 136, ff. 316–17. Regarding authorship, see Leo Hicks, S.J., 'Father Robert Persons S.J. and *The Book of Succession*', *Recusant History* 4 (1957–58), pp. 104–37. Hicks' interpretation has been challenged by Peter Holmes. See his 'The Authorship and early Reception of *A Conference about the Next Succession to the Crown of England*', *Historical Journal* 23 (1980), pp. 415–29.

Crichton's change in attitude with regard to James had been perceived by Elizabeth's spies. In August 1594 they informed her of it, as well as of the fact that the Jesuits had taken into their hands the management of Scottish affairs, to the great displeasure of Robert Bruce.[72]

Although it may seem paradoxical, it was Persons notwithstanding opposition to Crichton's for Scotland, who in future would look after the negotiations connected with the Armada and the contacts between the Scottish lords and the Catholic King, the contacts being made through his protégé, John Cecil, a double agent, who had been a pupil at the English College in Valladolid. On 1 July 1593 Cecil delivered a Report on the affair of the Spanish blanks and its consequences: the previous Easter, now that the persecution whipped up against the Catholics by the Protestant ministers had calmed down, the Scottish lords had decided to send John Cecil, who had crossed into England from Scotland, with their requests for help and their own offers to the Catholic King. Not daring to send their signatures, they entrusted Cecil with trustworthy tokens, and sent him to Persons.[73] Cecil had an interview with Idiaquez and later drew up for him a memorandum with the requests of the nobles. These were the same as those that Crichton had been explaining to the court during his two-year mission.[74] On 31 August 1593 Persons corroborated Cecil's trustworthiness and the validity of the petitions presented on behalf of the Scottish noblemen.[75]

It would be interesting to compare Persons' views in this document with those of Crichton, and to investigate how far the conversations that had taken place between the two men in Valladolid (July 1592), when Crichton thought they had arrived at an agreement, had been influential. Again one would like to know what were the negotiations and plans of Persons concerning England and Scotland prior to the sailing of the second Armada in 1596/97. However these themes would take us far beyond the limits set for the present essay, and deserve a study to themselves.

---

[72] M. Moody to Thomas More [Sir Robert Cecil?], 3/13 August 1594, *Cecil Manuscripts*, IV, p. 577: the informant mentions that 'Crichton [Craton], the Jesuit, and his confederates do feed themselves with more than hope that the King of Scots will turn to the Pope', and notes that Bruce [Bruise] 'is much displeased for that the Jesuits have taken the management of the Scots affair in their own hands'.

[73] 'Relación de Escocia a p(rimer)o de Julio 1593. Lo que ha pasado en Escocia el mes de Diciembre del Año passado de 1592 por causa de vna embaxada que los Señores Catholicos de aquel Reyno quisieron embiar a su Magestad', AGS Estado 839, f. 61.

[74] *Ibid.*, f. 78.

[75] *Ibid.*, f. 76.

DOCUMENTS[1]

I

Madrid, 1st February 1592

ARSI Tolet. 37a, f. 212.
Molto R^do in Xpo. Padre nostro
Pax Xpi.

Ho ricevuto quella de V.P.R. delli 25 9bre; per la quale ho inteso della morte del Padre Edmondo Hayo la quale ho resentito più ch'io non doua perché credo che ci adgiutarà nel celo più che non puoteua in terra.

La ragione, la occasione, la facilità, la necessità de nostri negotij douerrebbono persuader ogni uno che facessero il progresso debito; dicono de si, et stanno nella volontà o velleità, non mancha altro che gratia et virtus pariendi ma veggo la natura tanto fiacca, et le preparationi tanto pocche, che dubito che pocco o tarde, o niente si farà.

Due cose li danno la vita: il secreto, et il modo. Perché sapendo il mondo che si deue et si può fare, pensa che si farà et poi non si fa niente et resta il mondo ingannato; et si mal auiene, il modo che si tiene basta per risuscitar et tener la vita nel negotio. L'aragna sta nella sua tela, et de più fa tele per tutta la casa, et stanno a trauagliar per leuar via queste tele, et con pocco progresso, et in tutta la casa non c'è tela tanto facile a leuar via che quella stessa nella quale stà l'aragna et insieme con essa lei: et pur stanno perdendo il tempo, quando leuata via l'aragna non faria più tele, et quelle che stanno fatte pocco forze haueriano per resistere al spacciatore.

Io non posso saper per certo si faranno o non faranno, così V.P.R. puotria pensar del mio star o partir da qui, et come la cosa è dubia con quanta facilità o difficoltà puotria esser, pare a me ch'il meglio saria de rimettere il negotio al R. P. Egidio González visitator che, segondo l'exigentia della cosa, disponesse di me nel star o partir.

Le saffare colli thesori sono gionte dall'Indie chi dice diece chi 12 millioni tra quello ch'è del Re et delli particolari. Delli negotii de Fiandra per gli quagli venne il Padre Giacomo Zelandra non è espedito niente per anchora ma stanno tra le mani del Re.

Altro non ho da scriuere se no le mie hummilissime raccomendationi alli santi sacrificii et orationi de V.P.R. a cui Iddio signore nostro dia l'abondantia de suoi santi doni et gratia. De Madrid, Adì primo de febraro 1592.

De V. P. Rda. humilissimo figliolo et seruo,

G° Creytton

---

[1] I would like to thank Fr Mario Colpo, a member of the Jesuit Historical Institute in Rome for his great assistance in revising my transcription of these documents.

II

Madrid, 6 April 1592

ARSI Tolet. 37a, ff. 216–217.
Molto R^{do} in Xpo. padre Nostro,
Pax Xpi.

Fin adesso non ho potuto scriuere così chiaro et distesamente a V.P.R. come adesso per mancamento de portitore securo, così darò informatione più ampla delle cose.

Ho trauagliato con sua Maestà Catholica per far l'Impresa d'Ingliterra dandoli l'Informatione come in Scotia nella nostra missione haueuamo guadagnato tutta quasi la nobiltà de quel regno non solamente alla fede catholica ma anche al seruitio de sua Maestà, per spendere le vite loro per la restitutione della fede catholica et vendetta della crudele et ingiusta morte de lor Regina de Scotia, et che il Re de Scotia non tiene altre forze che della sua nobiltà, perché non tiene grand intrata ne denari, ma solamente l'obedienza de suoi subditi gli quali sono obligati in tempo de guerra de seruirli a spese loro, et essendo più oblighati de seruire a Dio et alla sua chiesa, s'offeriuano de pigliar lor Re, et far de sorte che ne lui ne nessun heretico puotesse impedirli de concorrere con sua Maestà per l'Invasione d'Ingliterra, et per secortà de questo dariano tra le mani de sua Maestà tutte le terre grosse, et forti, et tutti gli porti del mare, et insieme mettariano tra le mani de sua Maestà gli lor figlioli primogeniti, o più prossimij parenti e heredi, per dispor di lor a suo beneplacito se mancassero de lor promesse.

Sono parimente nelle parti settentrionali d'Ingliterra che confinano colla Scotia alcuni conti e Grandi signori catholici molto puotenti et altri catholici in grandissimo numero che si giontariano colle forze de sua Maestà, et come afferma il Baron de Dacre Inglese, il quale arriuarà a Roma con questa, che saranno bastanti d'occupar tutto il paese, da Scotia insino a Eboraco, vulgo York detta, che sono circa cento miglia, poi tutta la Vallia è catholica et subito se leuaria, oltra de ciò che tutte le prouincie d'Ingliterra sono piene de catholici gli quali si leuariano de sorte che se si comminciasse vna volta quella impresa andaria da se innanzi con grandissima facilità.

Mostra sua Maestà d'esser molto contenta de questa buona dispositione delle cose, et d'auer buon animo et desiderio che questa impresa si faccia, ma che per adesso le guerre de Fiandra et Francia et altre occupationi li danno tanto a fare che non può così presto mettere la mano. Sopra de questo, questi dì passati io diedi a sua Maestà le ragioni pro et contra, le quali mando a V.P.R. ma so bene ch'ha altre ragioni chi lo ritardano, come puotriano esser la difficoltà de mantener quel regno o suo, o amico, e la grand perdita che fece de huomini et de spese nell'ultima armata [216ᵛ] che fece per questo, tiene anchora sua Maestà suspesa et spauentata. Poi tiene scrupolo de spendere tanto in quell'impresa, et altri de tener meglior dritto de posseder il Regno. 3° credo che sia molto persuaso che gli catholici d'Ingliterra vorrebbono seruirsi delle sue forze per scacciar li hereteci et poi far vn Re catholico tra loro, et scacciarlo, et tutti forastieri delli cui imperio sono molto impatienti.

Tocca a sua Santità de securar sua Maestà in conscienza de puoter possedere quel regno, et all'Illmo Cardinal d'Ingliterra, adesso capo delli catholici de quello, de pensar delli mezzi per securar sua Maestà per puoter possederlo coll'amore et fauore della natione. Quelli che sono irresoluti, lenti, timidi et suspetosi, hanno bisogno de adgiuti forti altrimente non possono vscire in effetti generosi benché siano santissimi et de buonissima volontà.

Se Sua santità non fa le resolutioni coll'Illmo Cardinal de Ingliterra costì et conferite coll'ambassador de sua Maestà et non li dia ogni sorte d'adgiuto dato et gagliardo, tanto de comminatione che de denari credo che staremo altri dieci anni senza far niente come dieci anni sono che V.P.R. m'impieghò in questa missione et rapportai allo hora come il Duca de Lenox [sic] alhora era contento de rendere il Re de Scotia et farlo catholico per forza. Io portai la nuoua a Roma et il P. Personio in Spagna. Il buon Papa Gregorio 13°, de buona memoria, rimesse la cosa a sua Maestà Catholica con offerta de far la quarta parte delle spese dell'Impresa, et adesso siamo per recomminciare.

La Ingliterra è la radice de tutti gli mali che patisce sua Maestà in Fiandra, nelle Indie et in Francia et altroue per mare et per terra, et tiene sua Maestà più che la metà dell'Impresa fatta senza che li costa niente tenendo tutta la Scotia et le parti settentrionali de Ingliterra, che è la parte più forte et bellicosa, sparagnaria ogni anno per il mancho cinque o sei millioni che spende, oltra alcuni millioni che gli Inglesi robbano ogni anno de sua Maestà et suoi vassalli. Et per manco de duoi millioni se puotria far et finire l'Impresa d'Ingliterra; mezzi bastanti non mancano, ma pare che mancha la naturalezza generosa et gagliarda o la gratia per far questa Impresa et che Iddio uuol anchora castighar gli nostri peccati, et espiarli per il sangue de più martyri de quei regni.

Mi pare che saria buono che Monsegnor Cardinal Allano fosse persuaso che saria per la più grand gloria de Dio et bene de quei populi che l'Ingliterra et Scotia fossero uniti et dati a questo buon Re percioche non c'è altro che possia espellere gli heretici, et quando fossero espulsi tenerli fuori et poi ci daria sempre buon ViceRe, et se non fosse buono presto si puotria mutarlo, et darci vn altro, doue se fossemo suggetti a Re nostro particolare, se fosse catiuo, tyranno o heretico, non saria altro rimedio che patientia et sopportarlo. Ma auendo vn Re de Spagna per nostro, non solamente si puotria mantener la fede, et la giustitia et defenderci dalli nemici, ma etiandio (senza tirar il succo delli Regni fuora ma spenderlo tutto tra li incolini, farli partecipi de sue grandezze, honori, amplissimi imperij et ricchezze.

Tra gli mezzi suaui per contentar gli [217] incolini, et securar sua Maestà Catholica de lor fideltà et obedientia tre m'occorono che paiono molto a proposito. p° Che sua Maestà prometta de lasciarli le sue antiche leggi et custumi de gouerno et administratione de giustitia senza mutarli. 2° de non dar beni hereditarii de quei regni a nessun fuorastero per nessuna caggione se non alli naturali stessi delli regni. 3° de rendere tutti gli signori principali obligati a sua Maestà per beneficij et commodità signalata, quel che si puotria far delli beni delli stessi delli regni come de dar a quelli che parerà a sua Maestà et a chi li faranno più notabili seruitij gli beni di quelli che saranno trouati obstinati nelle sue heresie, o chi verranno con arma hostili contra de lui in questa impresa.

Credo che la diuersità delli informationi per doue s'habbia de comminciare l'Inuasione ritarda la cosa non pocco. Perche gli più principali segnori Inglesi eccetti gli settentrionali Inglesi sono de parer che si debba cominciar per la Vallia o porti meridionali d'Ingliterra benche non habbino in quei parti alcun porto in mano ne alcuni grandi segnori o seguita de gente che nel principio puotesse giongersi colle forze de sua Maestà. Gli scozesi et Inglesi settentrionali dicono che si debba comminciar dalla parte settentrionale d'Ingliterra doue haueranno buonissimi porti in Scotia a 10 o 15 miglia discosti d'Ingliterra et poi tutti gli scozesi et inglesi settentrionali puotriano giongersi et far molti millia de caualli et piedoni per seruire altrimenti non puotrianno seruir de niente o de pocco, se da lì non si comminciase.

Io non curarei de altro se non che si facesse l'impresa, et se si poutesse farla senza che l'armata descendesse in Scotia, tanto più felice saria quel regno, se gli Inglesi puotessero guadagnar qualche porto nelle parti settentrionali de Ingliterra saria buono de descendere lì.

Per effectuar questa impresa non se manca altro che denari et in pocca quantità in rispetto dell'importanza dell'impresa per il riposo della chiesa d'Iddio, et un capo con qualche gente. Al parer de molti sua Maestà non puotria fare elettione de Capo più a proposito che del Duca de Feria, perché saria estimato naturale tra loro, per essere la sua madre Inglesa [Lady Jane Dormer], et per saper la lingua Inglesa ch'è cosa che daria grand contento et sodisfattione a tutti; con ogni altro che non intendessero sariano mille scontenti et murmurationij.

Piaccia a V.P.R. conferir de queste cose con sua santità et coll'Illmo. Cardinal d'Ingliterra et coll'Illmo duca de Sessa Ambasciadore, come parera a V.P.R. accioche Monsegnor R^{mo} Patriarcha Caietano Nuncio vengha qui ben instrutto de queste cose, a cui venuta saro per dar a sua segnoria Illma più intiera informatione.

Et qui fo fine colle mie humilissime raccommendationi alli santi sacrificij et orationi de V.P.R. preghandoli dal Signore ogni gratia, sanità et consolatione. Da Madrid Adì 6 d'Aprile 1592.

De V.P. R.,

Humilissimo figlioglo et seruo in X°.
Guglielmo Creytton

III

Madrid, 7 April 1592

ARSI Tolet. 37a, f. 218^{r-v}.
Molto Rdo. in Xpo Padre Nostro,
Pax Xpi etc.

Ho riceuuto quelle de V.P.R. del mese de febraro, In nouembre il Re uuolse ch'io mandasse vn gentilhuomo scozese in Scotia per chiamar il Barone de Fyntrey ch'è huomo de stato et molto constante catholico, il quale doueua venir con commissione da quella nobiltà per trattar le particolarità delle lor offerte a sua Maestà et per saper la dispositione delle cose, il quale non è venuto, ne risposta verruna de quella missione. Se non hauesse stato per aspettar quella risposta o venuta de quel segnor, haurei fatto grand instantia d'hauer dato queste informationi a bocca a V.P.R. et ho ben domandato due o tre uolte licentia de partir con remettermi pur al parer de sua Maestà. De questo non m'han dato risposta et pare che non è inclinata sua Maestà ch'io parti, pur farò quel che piaciara a V.P.R. commandarmi. Non mi fanno replica nessuna alle informationi che do, et intendo che non li dispiaciono pur non risoluono niente. Al manco io non posso intendere niente ne affirmatiue ne negatiue se non un freddo dire che sua Maestà tiene buona volontà et che tutto si farà, et che le cose de Francia l'impediscono molto. Et così stanno. M'hanno promesso adgiuto per la nostra missione in Scotia, ma non posso tirar niente. Cinque o sei mesi fa mi diedero 700 ducati per le mie spese le quali pagho qui et vn compagno scozese secolare ch'io teneua ch'haueua desiderio d'intrar nella Compagnia, il quale ho mandato a Lisbona per esser riceuuto et formato nella Compagnia, et mi scriuono che fa molto bene et che sarà molto buon suggetto: questo collegio non è per formar nouitij.

Io conto tutte le cose che fo qui col P. Personio, et sta sempre saldo che non si habbi de far principio dell'Impresa della banda de Scotia. Quel che mi pare che fa duoi mali effetti: l'uno è che rende l'Impresa più difficile, et d'hauer bisogno de più grande gente, et sopra tutto che non possono transportar cauallaria in numero bastante et in Ingliterra non puotranno hauer cauallaria se non nelle parti settentrionali uerso Scotia. Il 2º male è che questa auersione sua da Scotia augmenta molto la suspitione grande che tengono che tanto il Cardinal d'Ingliterra ch'il P. Personio et altri inglesi non vorrebbono seruirsi di loro se non per scacciar gli heretici et poi far qualche Inglese catholico Re d'Ingliterra, et le pretensioni de sua Maestà sono altre, et questo io ho dalla bocca de collui che gouerna il tutto sotto il Re [Juan de Idiaquez]. Già ho scritto nell'altra mia come si habbia d'occorrere a questa paura et ho detto che hauendo sua Maestà tutta la Scotia per se et le fortezze et porti de [218^v] l'un et dell'altro regno molti amici de dentro come tutti gli Inglesi settentrionali et la Vallia, et porti che può fortificar et lasciar guarnizone [sic] de dentro, et commodità de mettere quanta gente vorria de dentro il regno quando vuolesse, non hauerà occasione de dubitar de rebellione, o seditione. Poi si tratta de fondar vn seminario delli nobili a Duai [sic] doue sariano notriti gli primogeniti delli nobili sotto la mano de sua Maestà che saria retinacolo molto gagliardo. V.P.R. puotrà trattar coll'Illmo Cardinal d'Ingliterra per mitighar questa opinione del padre Personio il cui uoto pesa più qui et in quella natione che de tutti gli altri, et pur si può ingannarsi.

Io sarei molto contento come sariano anche tutti gli scozesi, che spagnogli non intrassero in Scotia, perché non apporteranno che ruina et disgusto, et non curarei niente chi fosse Re, se hauessimo la restitutione della fede et esercitio della religione catholica, et salute dell'anime ma non vedo altro mezzo tanto a proposito per scacciar et tener fuori gli heretici et heresie, che quel de sua Maestà catholica. Et quando hauessimo naturali per Re in quei regni non saressimo securi per molto tempo ne de l'un ne dell'altro. Et a me pare che doueressimo cerchar la più grand gloria de Dio et ben de sua chiesa et non disegni particolari. So ben che nostro Re heretico, colla magra speranza che tengono alcuni de sua conuersionone [sic] hauerà gli suoi protettori in quella corte, lor fine puotria esser buono, ma il mezzo è molto cattiuo. Non ho altro a scriuere, et fo fine per le mie humilissime raccommendationi alli santi sacrificij et orationi de V.R.P. preghandoli dal signore ogni gratia sanità et contento. Madrid 7 d'Aprile 1592.

De V.P.R.

humilissimo figliolo et seruo in Xpo.
Gulielmo Creytton

IV

Madrid, 23 May 1592

ARSI Tolet. 37a, f. 220.
Molto Rdo. in Xpo. Padre Nostro
Pax Xpi.

Ho riceuuto quella de V.P.R. delli 13 d'Aprile nelle quali quanto al mio star o partir da qui mi rimette al auiso de questi padri de qui, et a quel che mi parerà. Loro sono de parer ch'io vadi a referir a V.P.R. et costì quel che passa qui; et io sono del medesimo parer et così hoggi andarò al Escurial per domandar licentia, et colle prime galere passarò, per la gratia de X°, et credo che sarà colli più grandi caldi ch'entrarò a Roma.

Molta buona volontà trouiamo et buone parole, ma altri effetti non c'è de sperar così presto. Altro mezzo si puotria trouar bastante a nostro proposito, come più a pieno dirò a V.P.R. a bocca, et a quel tempo rimetto il restante che sarà il più presto che puotrò.

Alli S^{ti} sacrificij et orationi de V.P.R. molto humilmente mi raccommando, et pregholi dal Signore ogni gratia et consolatione. De Madrid Adì 23 de Maggio 1592.

Humilissimo figliolo et seruo in x°

G° Creytton

V

Madrid, 18 July 1592.

ARSI Tolet. 37a, ff. 225–226ᵛ.

Molto Rᵈᵒ in Xpo Pʳᵉ Nro. etc.

Alli 12 de questo mese riceuetti quella de V.R.P. delli 6 de Guigno [sic]. Questi dì passati fui a Valliadolid per conferir col Padre Personio, et siamo stati molto conformi nel medesimo parer come dirò a V.R.P. a bocca per la gratia de Xpo, et penso per questo effetto d'esser a Roma ò circa il fine d'agosto ò principio de settembre. Nel negotio principale per altre occupationi non si può far altro per adesso, ma pur c'è molta buona intentione et volontà per far il tutto col tempo. Me lasciano partir con conditione de retornar quando sarò chiamato, et in questo mi sono rimesso a V.R.P. la quale ho detto che sarà sempre per compiacerli. Il seminario è differito insino che venghi l'auiso del duca de Parma e concesso alcun adgiuto per la missione delli nostri, nel paese mio. Et questa è la somma de quel che posso scriuere a V.R.P. per adesso. . . .

Et alli santi sacrifici et orationi de V.R. Paternità molto humilmente, etc. et pregholi dal Signor ogni gratia sanità et contento. De Madrid, Adì 18 de Luglio 1592.

De V.R.Paternità indegno figliolo et seruo

G° Creytton

VI

[Pro e contra]
March 1592

ARSI Tolet. 37a, ff. 214–15.

Se si ha de fare l'inuasione d'Ingliterra
questo anno o no. Le ragioni pro et contra

Le Ragioni contra

Pᵃ   Le Guerre et occupazioni in Fiandra, Francia, Aragonia, et la conseruatione delle flotte delle Indie et coste et stretti marini richiedono tutti quanti gli denari ch'ha sua Maestà de spendere questo anno / et da queste cose comminciate non può retirarsi ne differirle. Et però questo anno non può vacar all'Inuasione d'Ingliterra.

2. L'Impresa d'Ingliterra saria delle spese de somma non mediocre, et per via extraordinaria non puotria sua Maestà fornir tanta somma questo anno.

3. Non si puotria trouar questo anno naui et vittuaglia per vna armata bastante per questa Impresa.

4. Il Re non è computato il prossimo de sangue (escludendo gli heretici) per godere giustamente de quei regni quando haueria guadagnatoli. Et de far tanta spese per ben d'altri non saria espediente per la Spagna percioché, benché fossero adesso amici et propinqui alli quagli acquistaria quei regni, fra pocco puotriano deuentar nemici, et contrarij a i suoi stati et successori.

Le Ragioni pro

1. Tutte quasi le ragioni sopradette contra, probabilmente saranno delle medesime forze l'anno che viene come questo anno, Percioché probabilmente non mancharanno a sua Maestà Catholica le medesime occasioni de spendere in Fiandra, Francia, per il mare et per tutto. et forse che gli denari non l'abondaranno più che questo anno, et l'occasioni de spendere puotriano crescere et durar per più anni, perche le cose della Fiandra, Francia et del mare paiono de disporsi a luonghi trauaglij.

2. Il primo modo che trouara sua Maestà de sparagnar le spese che fa in Fiandra et per mare, et vna grande parte de quella che fa in Francia, saria de far l'Impresa d'Ingliterra, percioché che fatta che saria, tutti gli Inglesi che tengono gli luoghi et le chiaui de suoi stati in Fiandra li rendariano per hauer lor perdono et beni in Ingliterra, et gli ribelli de sua Maestà verriano a tal compositione de pace che vorria, et così cessariano le spese et per terra et per mare. Et il Re de Nauarra saria presto abandonato da molti suoi hauendo perso il fondamento de suo credito per hauer gente forastiera, ch'è la Regina d'Ingliterra. Et quanto prima si puotria far questo tanto meglio, et se fosse possibile questo anno pare che non si doueria differirlo all'altro.

[214ᵛ]

3. Certo che sua Maestà non puotria far l'Impresa d'Ingliterra et star sotto le spese ordinarie ch'è sforzato de fare senza qualche sforzo et prouisione extraordinaria de denari, et se questo è vero meglio saria de farlo questo anno che d'aspettar l'altro con tanta perdita de denari, della reputatione et de bellissime occasioni che si perdano atteso che probabilmente l'anno che viene hauerà le medesime difficoltà ch'ha questo anno.

4. Gli catholici Inglesi et scozesi chi stanno nel fuogho della persecutione con pericolo de perdere la vita et gli beni, et chi questo anno possono et vorebbono spendere la vita in questa causa et seruitio de sua Maestà catholica cerchano il più corto camino de uscire fuora de lor tribulationi.

Se questo anno non si serui sua Maestà de loro forsa che presto si puotriano offerirsi ad altri come degià si parla ch'alchuni sariano contenti de darsi al duca de Lorena il quale col adgiuto de suo genero puotria abbracciar et finir quell'impresa, perché escludendo gli heretici il principe de Lorena è nel medesimo grado de sangue colla signora Infanta figliola de sua Maestà, a quelle corone d'Ingliterra et Scotia come sono anche il duca de Sauoya, et il duca de Guysa et de Mayena.

5. Questo anno il Paese Basso sta occupato per le forze de sua Maestà ma se si perdesse la Frisia che sta in pericolo et più anche de quei stati, si puotria giongersi talmente colla Regina d'Ingliterra, che poi saria molto difficile de guadagnarla et però saria buono de non perder tempo.

6. Se questo anno facesse sua Maestà l'Impresa d'Ingliterra la Francia non puotria impedirla. Ma se fosse fatto vn Re de Francia, benché fosse il più stretto de sangue che tenesse sua Maestà catholica non permetteria che'occupasse l'Ingliterra et questa consideratione è importantissima come sono parimente le due immediatamente sopradette.

7. Molto è da considerare che le spese dell'Impresa d'Ingliterra duraranno poco, per non esser in fortezze et terre forti per assediar et prolunghar la guerra, et quelle che sono si puotria ricuperar per intelligentia ch'è de già pratticata.

8. Se le naui et galere de Spagna non fossero bastanti per questa Impresa, si trouaria per supplir abondantamente [sic] nelli soli porti de St Malo et Haure de Gracia in Francia, luoghi affettionatissimi al seruitio de sua Maestà.

9. Il più securo dritto che si puotria hauer de quei regni saria per l'escommunicatione et depositione della Regina d'Ingliterra et Re de Scotia obstinati et crudeli heretici per il papa, il quale puotria dar il dritto primo occupanti catholico ch'hauesse le forze et la volontà de ricuperarli all'obedienza della chiesa catholica. Questo non puotria far la signora Infanta sua figliola ne nessun'altro si commodamente come sua Maestà Catholica et questo dritto de posseder quei regni per via del papa per excommunicatione et depositione de heretici saria più securo che per via et dritto de sangue il quale è suggetto a molte competentie et pretensioni de molti, et così possiede sua Maestà il Regno de Nauarra.

[215]

10. Le forze che tiene don Alonso de Vargas in Aragonia, et le spese che fa sua Maestà per mare per far la guerra defensiua, sariano bastanti poco più o meno per far la guerra offensiua et finire l'Impresa d'Ingliterra col concorso che si trouaria delli catholici in Ingliterra et Scotia.

[215v] A tergo: [Crichton's hand] + Pro et contra. Dato a sua Maestà in Marzo 1592.

VII

Creytton to Aquaviva
Antwerp, 23 October 1593

ARSI Germ 171, f. 290.

Admodum Rᵉ in Xpo. Pʳᵉ

Pax Xpi. etc.

Accepi litteras R.P.V. datas 17 7bris quibus quod respondeam parum est nam fusius omnia scripsi ad P. Tyrium (ne istis tempporibus litteris prolixioribus R.P.V. distineam), qui singula referet. Nostri in Scotia per Dei gratiam bene valent, et bene occupantur. Videntur res illius regni esse modo in longe meliori statu quam vnquam prius. Nam legatus quem misit rex Scotiae in Angliam redijt, negotijs pro quibus missus fuit incomplectis, et tanto melius, ita enim auertetur animus regis ab illa impiisima regina. Rex proditus ab illis qui erant sui nominis ex familia Stuarta, et auersus ab illis qui sunt ex familia Hamyltonia sanguine ei proximis, cogitur catholicis adherere, quos nouit fidelissimos, et potentissimos. Propterea Regina Scotiae est omnino auersa ab hæreticis et fouet apud se dominas catholicas quæ optimam hauent de ea spem et opinionem. Nunc, si offererentur suppetiæ, optima esset spes rei bene gerendæ, sed de his fusius ex P. Tyrio, et bonum esset, istud secretum tenere.

R.P.V. dixit mihi discedenti, vt si qui Scoti idonei ad Societatem sese offerrent, eos Romam mitterem. Misi igitur Magistrum Thomam Abercromby qui iam cursum philosophiae audiuit, juuenis pius et præstans viribus corporis, qui istud cælum bene ferre posset, puto gratum futurum R.P.V. Sunt nonnulli alii qui cupiunt admitti in Societatem, sed qui dubito an cælum Romanum ferre possint eos non mitto.

Postquam R.P.V. concessit Anglis vt aliqui hic reciperentur, rogamus R.P.V. vt concedat idem priuilegium nonnullis Scotis. Ex Hispania datur ncbis spes alicuius auxilij pro nostro seminario duacensi; Illmus. Cardinalis Caietanus protector noster isthinc quoque nobis pollicetur multa nomine pontificis, si dignaretur R.P.V. rem suæ Dominationi Illmæ commendare maturiorem et abundantiorem, sperarem effectum. Dominus Jesvs custodiat semper et multa gratia consoletur R.P.V. cuius santissimis sacrificijs et orationibus humiliter me commendo. Antuerpiæ, 23 octob. 1593.

R.P.V.

Humillimus filius et seruus
Gˢ Creytton

VIII

Creytton to Aquaviva
Brussels, 13 January 1594

ARSI Germ 172, f. 11^{r-v}.
Molto Rdo. in Xpo. P^{re} Nro.
Pax Xpi.

Questa sarà per auisar V.P.R. del infelice successo del gentilhuomo mandato in Ingliterra per indurre il conte de Darby [sic] d'a[do]porarsi per la restitutione della fede catholica il quale è stato messo a morte apresso di Londra nel mese di xbre. Et dopo che sua Santità e Maestà Catholica siano d'accordo de terza persona per far quell'Impresa d'Ingliterra forsa che non saria fuora di proposito de pensar della persona del Re de Scotia del quale benché io ho auuto sempre malissima opinione, pur adesso trouandosi tradito da tutti gli suoi più confidati, tanto Ministri heretici che quelli del suo sangue, et messo a tradimento tra le mani del conte de Boduel [sic] suo sbandito, al quale fu sforzato precibus armatis de perdonare, adesso scampato da le lor mani s'è messo tra le mani delli catholici hauendo fatto il Baron de Hume capitano della sua guardia ch'è de 200 caualli et 300 pedoni ch'è signore chi fa professione pubblica della fede catholica. Pare che si può sperare meglio de lui che non s'ha potuto da qui inanzi, perche benche non habbi abbracciato la fede catholica pur s'hauesse le forze e adgiuto che si dice fu promesso al conte de Darby, si tiene per certo che si scopreria per gli catholici et tenendolo gli catholici tra le mani, lo putriano [sic] far giongere per forza o per amore a quel che saria di bisogno, et si tiene per certo che saria contento d'esser sforzato a questo. L'Impresa per il conte de Darby haueria stato molto difficile, de molto luongha guerra et de grossissime spese, per la multitudine de quelli chi lo precedono in dritto, gli quagli mai haueriano ceduto a lui, et per la moltitudine de signori suoi uguali et compagni nel regno gli quali molto mal uolontieri se fossero sottoposto a lui come lor Re. Ma il dritto del Re de Scotia è chiaro come quello de sua madre, et oltra tutto il regno di Scotia, tutti quelli in Ingliterra ch'erano per sua madre, chi sono moltissimi, si dariano al figliolo, de sorte che saria senza competentia, et non haueria altro contra che la sola Regina d'Ingliterra, et d'Inglesi haueria il Re di Scotia seco grandissimo numero come tutti gli catholioci et moltissimi hereteci. Piaccia a V.P.R^{da}. informar sua Santità de queste cose, perche tengo per certo che si può guadagnar questo Re. Ma bisogneria che sua Santità hauesse persona qui col quale si puotesse trattare, perche quando va de guadagnar o perdere regni o re, non bisogna trattar come de cose beneficiali currrendo a Roma perche perdendo l'occasione si perde il tutto, et però se sua Santità non manda persona espressa saria bisogno che il Nuntio de sua Santità in queste bande chi reside [sic] in Colonia, facesse la sua residentia qui con potestà et modo de prouedere a quelle che saria de bisogno col Archiduca Ernesto, et preuenire alli pericoli et mali, perché con vasello a proposito si può sempre andar da qui in Scotia in tre o 4 dì et alcune volte in duoi.

De Spagna mi scriuano che saria buono ch'io andasse in Scotia, et alcuni qui sono del medesimo parer, ma non mi pare che sia espediente, et de questo et molte altre cosette particulari scriuo al P. Tyrio assistente per non dar fastidio a V.P.R. il quale raguagliarà del tutto. Et non essendo questa per altro, prego Iddio signor nro dia a V.P.R. buon principio et felicissimo progresso de questo nuouo anno in ogni gratia et sanità, a cui S^mi sacrificij et orationi humilmente mi raccomando. Da Brussella, Adí 13 de Genaro 1594.

De V.P.R^da   Humilissimo figliolo et seruo

G° Creytton

PART III

CAMPION'S LEGACY

13

Popery and Pounds:
The Effect of the Jesuit Mission
on Penal Legislation

JOHN J. LAROCCA, S.J.

Time and death joined together to stop the restoration of Catholicism in England when they ended the lives of Mary Tudor and Reginald Cardinal Pole before the former had produced her longed for heir and before the latter's efforts for the reform of the Church had taken root. Pole's reforms included the foundation of schools and seminaries, the production of a prayer book and a set of homilies.[1] His attempts to restore traditional Catholic doctrine and practice built on a large base of popular piety which wished to go back to the Church of 1547, if not all the way back to medieval Catholicism.[2]

[1] The nature of theology under Pole's leadership of the Church in England is interesting. In 1555 Edmund Bonner, bishop of London, published a set of homilies (*Certaine homelyes* [London, 1555], STC 3285.1–3285.10) and a catechism and a book entitled *A profitable and necessary doctrine* ([London, 1555] STC 3281.5–3283.7) to instruct the faithful in his diocese. I am currently investigating the theological content of these works and have discovered that they do not fit neatly into either medieval or counter-reformation theology. In some instances, e.g. the nature of humanity after original sin they borrow from the reformers and in explaining what the Counter-Reformation would call sacramentals they rely on the interpretations to be found both in the Henrician *Bishop's Book* and *King's Book*. Professor Loades has touched on some of these points in his contribution to this volume 'The Spirituality of the Restored Catholic Church (1553–1558) in the Context of the Counter Reformation'.

It is necessary to remember that before the end of the Council of Trent (1562) what was heresy and what was orthodoxy had not been clearly defined. Pole had been aligned with a group within the Council who had been sympathetic to the reformers and one of his friends, Gasparo Cardinal Contarini, had developed a definition of salvation by faith and good works with Philip Melancthon at the Colloquy at Regensburg (1541) which had been condemned as had Pole's own theology of redemption at the Council. On Pole, see also Dr Thomas Mayer's 'A Test of Wills: Cardinal Pole, Ignatius Loyola, and the Jesuits in England' in this collection.

[2] Eamon Duffy, *The Stripping of the Altars* (New Haven, 1992), Chapter 16; Susan Brigden, *London and the Reformation* (Oxford, 1989), Chapter 13; Christopher Haigh, *English Reformations* (Oxford, 1993), Chapter 12.

The nature of that piety, the number of those sympathetic to it, the number of those who thought the Pope essential to the Church, the nature of the Reformation (i.e. was it a popular movement led by the monarch or a movement imposed on the masses by the monarch) have been the subject of debate between historians from 1533 until the present. The result of recent scholarship indicates that there was widespread support for the restoration of traditional forms of piety and for some traditional doctrines of the medieval Church.[3]

Elizabeth would have liked to move slowly in imposing a religious reform and would have liked, like a good number of her subjects, to return to the Church of her father; personalities and events outran her. Both the Treaty of Cateau-Cambrésis (April 1559), which ended Mary's war with France, and the refusal of the Marian bishops to accept her supremacy forced her to turn to more radical men to govern her Church in her name. Parliament accomplished that Reformation in April 1559 by passing the Acts of Supremacy and Uniformity (1 Eliz. c. 1 & 2).[4] That Reformation was defined in both political and religious terms.

The Elizabethan Act of Supremacy revoked all of Mary's religious legislation. In doing that, it abolished all foreign jurisdiction, both spiritual and temporal, and united all jurisdiction in the person of the Queen.[5] It had, therefore, defined the establishment of the Anglican Church in the authority and

---

[3] The best summary of the debate is contained in Rosemary O'Day, *The Debate on the English Reformation* (London, 1986). There is need for a new edition of this book to include the revisionist material which has been published since 1986. Dr O'Day's work includes the beginning of the revision in the early work of Christopher Haigh and J.J. Scarisbrick's *The Reformation and the English People* (Oxford, 1984); it omits the works of Susan Brigden and Eamon Duffy. The nature of the old religion and its transformation in early Elizabethan England as it came in contact with the Counter-Reformation is not really germane to the argument of this article and can be traced in the following works: J.C.H. Aveling, *The Handle and the Axe: The Catholic Recusant in England from the Reformation to Emancipation* (London, 1976), pp. 9–74; John Bossy, 'The Character of Elizabethan Catholicism', in Trevor Aston, ed. *Crisis in Europe* (London, 1973), pp. 235–60, and 'The Counter Reformation and the People of Catholic Europe', *Past and Present* 47 (1970), pp. 51–70, and *The English Catholic Community, 1570–1850* (London, 1975); Duffy, *Stripping of the Altars*, pp. 565–93; Christopher Haigh, 'The Continuity of Catholicism in the English Reformation', in *The English Reformation Revised* (Cambridge, 1987), pp. 176–215, and 'From Monopoly to Minority: Catholicism in Early Modern Europe', *Transactions of the Royal Historical Society*, 5th series, 31 (1981), pp. 129–47, 'The Church of England, the Catholics and the People', in Christopher Haigh ed., *The Reign of Elizabeth* (London, 1984), pp. 195–220, *English Reformations*, pp. 187–284; Arnold Pritchard, *Catholic Loyalism in Elizabethan England* (London, 1979); Alexandra Walsham, *Church Papists* (London, 1993), pp. 1–50; Elliot E. Rose, *Cases of Conscience* (Cambridge, 1975); Peter Holmes, *Resistance and Compromise: The Political Thought of Elizabethan Catholics* (Cambridge, 1982); and Adrian Morey, *The Catholic Subjects of Elizabeth I* (London, 1978).

[4] The best discussion of the politics involved in passing the Acts is to be found in Norman L. Jones, *Faith by Statute: Parliament and the Settlement of Religion, 1559* (London, 1982). This study replaces the previous works by Sir John Neale, *Elizabeth I and Her Parliaments, 1559–1581* (London, 1953), pp. 51–84 and 'The Elizabethan Act of Supremacy and Uniformity', *The English Historical Review* (1950), pp. 304–32.

[5] 1 Eliz. c. 1 § 7 and 8.

jurisdiction of the Queen and rejected the power of the Bishop of Rome as usurped authority. The implications of this were clear: to be a loyal subject of the Queen meant accepting her authority and attending her Church. Realizing the danger which had faced her father, her brother, and her sister in changing the religion of the realm, Elizabeth determined to move slowly. She would depend on time, death, and the next generation to impose her religious settlement on her people.[6] The Queen and Parliament wanted all those who held office under the Queen and all who were potential office holders to accept the settlement. The Supremacy Act, therefore, insisted that all civil and ecclesiastical office holders, magistrates, those suing for livery and maintenance, university graduates, and all who took possession of a new office had to swear to accept the new settlement.[7] This desire to impose conformity on office holders was not completely successful. The Justices of the Peace could, and did, avoid taking the oath.

Elizabeth and her Council realized that their gradual religious policy depended on time and the death of the old clergy. They were willing to wait, but they were aware that devotion to Catholic practice was widespread. The survival of that practice and devotion to the old is surprising given the lack of leadership from the Roman Church. Some Catholics had approached the Spanish ambassador and through him the Pope to ask whether it was possible for them to attend the Queen's Church. They received no answer.[8] Until the arrival of the first seminary priests in 1574 and the Jesuits in 1580 the old faith was kept alive through a combination of religious observance in the household and the work of the Marian priests;[9] even without active leadership from Rome, Catholicism survived.

Elizabeth, while attempting to wean the next generation from Catholicism, was faced with the attempts of various popes to weaken her régime. The revolt of the northern Earls covered itself in religious rhetoric.[10] In response to the revolt Pope Pius V issued the bull *Regnans in Excelsis* on 25 February 1570; his intended help for the northern rebels of 1569 was too late. The bull declared '. . . that Elizabeth was an excommunicated heretic and supporter of heretics . . .

---

[6] For a fuller description of this policy, see John J. LaRocca, S.J., 'Time, Death, and the Next Generation: The Early Elizabethan Recusancy Policy 1558–1574', *Albion* 14 (1982), pp. 103–17 and 'English Catholics and the Recusancy Laws 1558–1625: A Study in Religion and Politics' (unpublished Ph.D. thesis, Rutgers University, 1977), Chapter 1.

[7] 1 Eliz. c. 1 § 10, 11, 12, 13.

[8] William R. Trimble, *The Catholic Laity in Elizabethan England 1558–1603* (Cambridge, Mass., 1964), p. 22.

[9] The lives of those devoted to the old religious practice and to Catholicism and the work of Marian priests in serving that community are best described in the works of Christopher Haigh listed above in n. 3 and in the works of John Bossy also in n. 3. See especially Bossy's 'Nature of Elizabethan Catholicism' and *English Catholic Community*.

[10] The revolt had more to do with old noble families, local politics, and the tension between the northern nobility and the Queen and her Privy Council than it did with religion.

Freeing all people from their obedience to her, it cursed all who supported her.'[11] The excommunication of Elizabeth, therefore, not only attacked the legitimacy of the regime, but it also gave the impression that everyone who favoured the old religion was a potential traitor. *Regnans in Excelsis* also 'pushed the Queen into a direct confrontation with the papal church . . . henceforth there was an avowed hostility and an expectation of warfare'.[12] Pius V's successor Gregory XIII (1572–1585) had already negotiated, and would continue to negotiate with both Spanish and French leaders to remove Elizabeth from the throne.[13] In 1574, while Gregory was still negotiating for a crusade, Richard Bristowe, Gregory Martin, Thomas Ford, and Thomas Robinson returned to England from the seminary at Douai. Neither Elizabeth nor her Council had expected the realm to be invaded by young, enthusiastic priests who promised to spend their lives keeping the old faith alive and winning converts from Elizabeth's Anglican Church;[14] because of that, they underestimated the importance of their arrival.[15] In bringing people back to the old religion the missionaries and their followers continued to deny the Queen the authority she had claimed in the Act of Uniformity; the presence of those priests in England defeated the policy which Elizabeth had used for fifteen years: to wait for death to remove the Marian clergy and those attached to the old religion. The new priests vowed obedience to the Pope and the time they spent in lands ruled by the King of Spain allowed the Council to question their loyalty and made them appear to be minions of the Pope and the King of Spain. The actions of French and Spanish ambassadors in interceding for recusants also increased the impression that the priests were 'foreign agents'. Spain continually demanded that the English improve the lot of the recusants. The Queen and the Council did not know what effect the new priests would have in organizing the recusant community as a Spanish tool. The French even tried to use the recusants in their negotiations for the proposed marriage between the Duke of Anjou and Elizabeth.[16]

This was the England which Edmund Campion and Robert Persons entered in 1580. A country with a significant number of people devoted to the old religion, a Queen and her Council which saw the war which had been waged in foreign policy negotiations and in Ireland brought into the realm by the secular priests. Their arrival, therefore, was not, as it has once been gratuitously described, '. . . an olive branch from the universal church; an appeal for talks if

---

[11] Norman L. Jones, *The Birth of the Elizabethan Age* (Oxford, 1993), p. 260.

[12] Wallace McCaffrey, *Elizabeth I* (London, 1993), p. 329.

[13] Conyers Read, *Lord Burghley and Queen Elizabeth* (London, 1960), p. 236; R.B. Wernham, *Before the Armada: The Emergence of the English Nation, 1485–1588* (New York, 1966), p. 339.

[14] For the early Elizabethan recusancy policy, see LaRocca, 'English Catholics and the Recusancy Laws', pp. 1–56 and 'Time, Death, and the Next Generation'.

[15] McCaffrey, *Elizabeth I*, p. 329.

[16] John Bossy, 'English Catholics and the French Marriage 1577–1581', *Recusant History* 5 (1959), p. 506.

only about talks'.[17] The Queen and her Council interpreted their arrival differently. The Jesuits arrived in an England where attraction to the old religion was not dying with deaths of the Marian clergy, but was, according to the reports sent to the Privy Council, growing. Catholics and recusants were in the universities as professors and students, in the Inns of Court and in the Commission of the Peace. For six years William Allen's seminary had been sending priests into England; an army supported by papal funds had just invaded Ireland. The Queen and her Council, therefore, saw Campion's and Persons' arrival as connected with treason and the safety of the Queen.

The bull *Regnans in Excelsis* would dog the steps of Campion and Persons and allow the Council to present them as traitors; they brought with them an interpretation of the bull from Gregory XIII which stated 'that the Bull should always bind the Queen and the heretics; on the other hand that it should in no way bind the Catholics, as things then stood, but only in the future when the public execution of the Bull should be made'.[18] This, then, did not appear to be an 'olive branch' but a rationalization to make adherents of the old religion appear to be loyal until such time as the Pope invaded the realm. Rather, in the words of Professor Elton, '. . . the new vigour infused into English catholicism by the opening of the Jesuit campaign made these issues one of the chief reasons for the recall of Parliament in 1581'.[19] That Parliament passed the statute 'to retain the Queen's majesty's subjects in their due obedience' which, with some alterations in 1587, would control the Catholic community until the seventeenth-century Interregnum.[20]

Campion's arrival and the beginning of the Jesuit mission hastened the transformation of Marian Catholicism into recusancy and church papistry and was seen by Elizabeth, her Council, and Parliament as a part of the war policy of the papacy and Spain; their arrival brought that war onto English soil at the same time that the papacy was supporting rebellion and invasion in Ireland (1579–1580). These new priests were not subject to the authority of the Englishman William Allen, but belonged to a religious order founded by a Spanish soldier, directly subject to the Pope through their vow of obedience, and associated with Spain.[21] This paper will examine the machinery which was in place

---

[17] Francis Edwards, S.J., *The Jesuits in England* (London, 1985), p. 258.

[18] Evelyn Waugh, *Edmund Campion: Jesuit and Martyr* (London, 1935; rpt. New York, 1956) p. 95; the implications of the instructions and how they proved to divide Catholic from Protestant are explored in Michael L. Carrafiello, '*Rebus Sic Stantibus* and English Catholicism, 1606–1610', *Recusant History* 22 (1994), pp. 29–40.

[19] G.R. Elton, *The Parliament of England 1559–1581* (Cambridge, 1986), p. 185.

[20] 23 Eliz. c. 1 and 29 Eliz. c. 6.

[21] The Jesuits seem to have developed a reputation during the mission and afterward which far outdistanced the number of Jesuits in England at any one time. They were always a small part of the priests on the mission. That reputation continues to the present. A recent work (Jones, *Birth of the Elizabethan Age*, p. 77) cites Jennifer Loach's claim ['Reformation Controversies' in James McConica, ed., *The Collegiate University. The History of the University of*

during the period before the Jesuits arrived and how that machinery was changed in 1581 because of their arrival.[22]

The best description of the recusant community at this time is contained in a letter from William Allen to Everard Mercurian, Superior General of the Society of Jesus. Allen was attempting to obtain Jesuit cooperation in the English mission and described for Mercurian the conditions in which the Jesuits would work if he sent them to England. Allen's account is outstanding for its accuracy in numbering, locating, and estimating the strength of the English recusants. He divided England into Catholic districts: York, Winchester, Newcastle, Durham, Chester, Derby, Lancaster, Richmond, Lincoln, and almost all of northern England. He noted that there were also 'certain noble women whose names are sufficiently well known for their adherence to Catholicism' on whom the priests could depend.[23] In noting the importance of women,[24] Allen pointed to one of the problems which the Council never adequately attacked – the recusant wife. He continued his letter by noting that Oxford was more responsive to the Ancient Faith than Cambridge,[25] but nonetheless students came to his seminary even from the latter school. Many of those students who arrived at Douai answering the biographical questions put to them could answer 'tota vita inter catholicos educatus'.[26]

Until 1581 William Cecil Lord Burghley depended, as he had in the past, on the Church to impose uniformity and to report and prosecute recusants.[27] The bishops depended either on the High Commission or the local Ecclesiastical Commission as their best weapon in fighting recusancy.[28] The records of the Bishop's Visitation and the High Commission in York indicate that in 1575 the total number of non-communicants was less frequent than ten years earlier. A.G. Dickens attributes the decline in non-conformity to the work of Archbishop Edmund Grindal. After Grindal left York in 1575 there was a resurgence of

Oxford vol. III (Oxford, 1986) pp. 378–87] that Campion and Persons were the first missionary priests martyred by the Elizabethan régime. The first missionary martyred was Cuthbert Mayne. Robert Persons was not martyred, but died in Rome on 15/25 April 1610.

[22] This paper will examine the reporting of recusancy to the Privy Council and the nature of the reports made. It will not deal with the reason for the non-conformity; those reasons are contained in the material contained in note 3.

[23] Patrick Ryan, S.J., 'Some Correspondence of Cardinal Allen 1579–85', in *Miscellanea VII* (London, 1911) CRS 9, pp. 63–65.

[24] On the importance of women in the recusant community, see Bossy, 'Character of Elizabethan Catholicism', p. 237; Diane Willen, 'Women and Religion in Early Modern Europe', in Sherrin Marshall, ed., *Women in Reformation and Counter-Reformation Europe* (Bloomington, 1989), pp. 140–65; and Mary B. Rowlands, 'Recusant Women 1560–1640', in Mary Prior, ed., *Women in English Society 1500–1800* (New York/London, 1985), pp. 149–66.

[25] On this, see James McConica, 'The Catholic Experience in Tudor Oxford' in this volume.

[26] A.C.F. Beales, *Education Under Penalty* (London, 1963), p. 81.

[27] Reed, *Lord Burghley*, pp. 288–93.

[28] John Strype, *Annals of the Reformation and Establishment of Religion*, 4 vols (Oxford, 1820–1840), III/1, p. 138, n. 97; p. 346, n. 239; p. 260, n. 100.

Catholicism. Without Grindal the High Commission could not deal effectively with recusants.[29] The effectiveness of the York Commission was more severely damaged when its two chief members, Lord President Henry Hastings, Earl of Huntingdon and Archbishop Edwin Sandys, began to feud.[30] The number of recorded cases grew from 21 in 1578 to 329 in 1582.[31] The growth in recusancy did not confine itself to the north. John Aylmer, Bishop of London, after conferring with the Archbishop of Canterbury and the rest of the bench of bishops,[32] wrote to Mr Secretary, Sir Francis Walsingham, with a plan to reduce Catholic social standing by fines rather than imprisonment. The reason given for the suggested policy was the growth in number of recusants.[33] This growth in recusancy occurred after the arrival of Mary Stuart in England, after the 1569 Northern Rebellion and subsequent excommunication of Elizabeth 'that forced a distinction between the merely conservative and those willing to become recusants and remove themselves from their parish churches',[34] and after the Ridolfi Plot of 1571 that involved the proposed marriage of Mary Queen of Scots and Thomas Howard, Duke of Norfolk. Catholicism was growing when the first Jesuits arrived in England.

The religious-political problem facing the Council grew. Ten years after the first census of the religious convictions of the Justices of the Peace the Council still felt that it was necessary to deal with the justices who absented themselves from the church service. The bishops had informed the Council that the men listed in the memorandum were non-conformist.[35] The Council ordered the J.P.s to take the Oath of Supremacy before the Justices of the Assize. The oath was administered in a few counties; some of the justices absented themselves with the excuses they had used a decade before for avoiding the oath.[36] In short, the attempt to administer the oath to the J.P.s was not successful.

---

[29] A.G. Dickens, 'The First Stages of Romanist Recusancy in Yorkshire', *Yorkshire Archeological Journal* 35 (1943), pp. 160, 165, 167.

[30] Philip Tyler, 'The Significance of the Ecclesiastical Commission of York', *Northern History* 2 (1967), p. 41. The evidence for the poor functioning of the Commission for Ecclesiastical Causes in York is supported by the evidence from Cheshire. Records are available for fines levied by the High Commission in Cheshire between 28 June 1580 and 1 July 1583. Most of the fines levied on recusants during his period were for contempt of court 'for recusants and others treated citation before the high commission with no more deference than they did the secular courts' (K.R. Wark, *Elizabethan Recusancy in Cheshire* [Manchester, 1973], p. 48, Chetham Society, English Remains Historical and Literary, Series 3, No. 19).

[31] Dickens, 'First Stages of Romanist Recusancy', pp. 169–79. This is all the more impressive since the methods of discovery had not improved.

[32] Trimble, *Catholic Laity*, p. 72. This policy is similar to the one suggested to Mary I by Stephen Gardiner rather than the burning of heretics. It also foreshadows the legislation of 1581 and 1587.

[33] CSP Domestic, I, p. 549.

[34] Jones, *Birth of the Elizabethan Age*, p. 78.

[35] APC, IX, 49.

[36] Trimble, *Catholic Laity*, p. 90. APC, XI, p. 178 (28 June 1579); XI, p. 292 (25 October 1579).

The Council itself was not consistent in its dealings with recusant J.P.s. The Council minutes for 1578 contain the case of one Richard Shelly, Esq., of Lewes, Sussex who had been evicted from the Commission of the Peace in accordance with the Council order that all who were backward in religion should be removed from the commission. The Council nonetheless ordered that he be reinstated, not because he had conformed, but because he was a gentleman who was faithful and who had been of good service to Her Majesty.[37] On 12 September 1581 a letter was sent to a Mr Keynes, a Justice of the Peace in Somerset, asking him to support his two sons who were imprisoned because they had been arrested with Campion the Jesuit.[38] Hugh Aveling concludes that throughout this period the Commission in the North Riding of Yorkshire had its quota of Catholic justices or justices with Catholic relations.[39] The problem of the recusant justices faced Elizabeth in 1580 and became more complex when a member of the Commission of the Peace had sons arrested with Campion.

Education and schoolmasters were also a problem when the Jesuits arrived. Catholic schoolmasters existed and educated their charges. As we have noted above, some of the seminarians at Douai had been educated only by Catholics. The universities had never successfully been cleared of Catholics. Beales' examination of the records of Oxford and Cambridge reveals that the universities had their share of church papists, lax Anglicans, and many Catholic dons.[40] He has also found evidence of many Catholic students living in the university towns who could make use of the university, attend lectures, and be tutored even though they could not receive a degree.[41] There were, however, ways around the taking of the oath before proceeding to the degree. Despite the vigilance of the Council and the university officials Catholics still came up to the universities.[42]

The Council was vexed that in 1580 Balliol College was still unsound in religion and a home for papists.[43] In 1581 the Council again wrote to the Vice-Chancellor and doctors of the university informing them that most of the seminary priests who were then disturbing the peace of the Church had been scholars at Oxford. Since the letter was written after the arrival of Persons and Campion, it may have referred to them. The survey also gave indications that there might be close connections between the Oxford recusants and the English Catholic exiles.[44] The letter further accused officials of tolerating absence from Common Prayer and the Lord's Supper. The Council ordered them to search and inquire after all those who were associated with the university and suspect in matters of religion. The names of the disaffected were to be sent directly to the

---

37 APC, X, p. 168 (19 February 1578).
38 APC, XIII, p. 204 (12 September 1584).
39 Hugh Aveling, *Northern Catholics* (London, 1966), p. 21.
40 Again, see McConica, 'Catholic Experience'.
41 Beales, *Education Under Penalty*, p. 57.
42 Beales, *Education Under Penalty*, p. 52.
43 CSP Domestic, I, p. 693.
44 LaRocca, 'English Catholics', p. 65.

Council. They instructed university officials to use all means within their powers to reduce the disaffected to conformity until the Council had time to deal with them.[45]

The census of the Inns of Court did not encourage the Council either. The Middle Temple submitted a list of fifteen Catholic recusants, including three exiles at Louvain, and Edmund Plowden and Edward Vavasour. The Inner Temple had the largest number, reporting that sixty-two of its members habitually absented themselves from the Anglican services. Thirty-two of the recusants were either absent or had withdrawn from membership in the Inner Temple. The thirty-two members bear names which connect them with prominent recusant families; in fact, most of the thirty-two could be classed as prominent recusants. Lincoln's Inn reported sixteen Catholics, including Thomas More's son-in-law and grandson, William and Thomas Roper. Grey's Inn had fourteen.[46]

The survey of the Inns of Court and the universities revealed that William Allen's assessment of the religious situation was accurate. Many members of the Inns still clung to the old religion; some were recognizable as recusants, others were probably church papists, or at least in sympathy with the members of the Inns who were recusants. Otherwise it would have been difficult for a large number of recusants to stay unnoticed at the Inns. Oxfordshire reported large numbers of recusants who were generally located in the city or university. Allen's observation on the adherence of Oxford to the old religion seems accurate. The Queen and the Council were also aware of the facts which Allen had conveyed in his letter to Mercurian. They realized that the policy they had been using had failed. The Marian clergy who had kept the old religion were dying, but they had been replaced by new priests from Douai who had been joined by a small, but notorious, group of English Jesuits. The Council had failed to keep young recusants out of the universities and the Inns of Court. The next generation had been educated in popery and would return to take their proper place in the counties and to assume local office. The Council could not stop them because in the Catholic areas of the realm there were either not enough Protestants to fill local offices or they had to appoint Catholics to office if they were to gain the cooperation and good will of those governed. They realized that neither the Ecclesiastical Commission nor the J.P.s had succeeded in enforcing the recusancy statutes. The actions of the local officials told the Queen and Council that local and familial ties were still stronger than any notion of loyalty to the Queen which included prosecuting friends and neighbours for religious beliefs. Because of that lack of obedience, because of the strength of local ties, because of the work of the Marian and non-conforming clergy, and because of the presence of the seminaries and the Jesuits, recusancy was a permanent feature of English life. The Queen and Council would have to analyse the social structure of recusancy and attack it, if they wished to successfully eliminate or control the growth of

---

[45] APC, XIII, p. 170 (14 August 1581).
[46] Trimble, *Catholic Laity*, pp. 86–87 nn. 96, 97, 98, 99, 100.

recusancy; or, if they chose a more moderate tack, they would have to accept recusancy as a permanent feature of English life and decide how they would control and contain it, and in some way force the recusants to visibly accept the Queen's authority in matters of religion.

The Council began to take steps against upper class recusants in 1574 after the arrival of the seminary priests. After 1574 the government adopted a much stricter policy in its attempt to destroy Catholicism. Its haphazard methods were replaced with consistent efforts to enforce conformity.[47] The Council's goal was lay conformity; but, as in previous years, occasional conformity would satisfy since it was at least a token acknowledgement of the Queen's authority to regulate religion in the realm. The new policy became obvious when on 12 August 1575 the Council issued warrants for the appearance before their bishops of six recusants living in Stafford; two of them were Justices of the Peace. All except one appeared before their bishop on the 17th; they were questioned separately and declared that they were following the dictates of their conscience and the example of their forefathers. They were ordered to appear before the bishops and the divines again on the next day. Upon hearing that the bishops could not bring the recusants to conformity, the Council called the recusants before them and told them that they could not be suffered to return home because of their non-conformity and because a breach of Her Majesty's laws in men of their stature could not be tolerated. They were all assigned to the custody of different bishops until Michaelmas although they were given temporary liberty to return home to finish business or to obtain their papers.[48] In December 1576 Alexander Nowell, Dean of Westminster Abbey, petitioned for the release of his half brother, John Townley who had been willing to attend the established Church but not to receive Communion. Nowell's petition was denied.

The Council's actions in dealing with the recusants indicated that they were interested in weakening the position of the recusant gentry by keeping them in confinement and then by releasing them and subsequently forbidding them to meet with friends and neighbours. The recusants were harassed by continual conferences with divines and bishops over their non-conformity. Apparently the Council was willing to accept the promise of conformity and weak excuses for absence from church, if those promises resulted in occasional conformity. Then, at least, the tenants and friends of the recusant gentry would see them obediently attending the Queen's Church. In that case the Council would not touch the recusant household, the centre and chief support of recusancy. They also displayed their own strength against the gentry and revealed that a recusant could not protect his dependants and tenants from the Council. The place in country society of recusant gentry would be destroyed if they refused to compromise with the Council and conform occasionally.

---

[47] Trimble, *Catholic Laity*, p. 68.
[48] APC, XII, p. 157 (15 August 1580); APC, IX, pp. 13, 15, 17–21, 26; Trimble, *Catholic Laity*, pp. 77–78.

A new drive to induce recusants to conform began in 1580. That drive cannot be understood without reference to papal actions. In 1578 Gregory XIII commissioned an Irishman, Thomas Stuckley, to raise an army and invade Ireland; Stuckley stopped in Lisbon and joined a Portuguese crusade to Africa where he and his army were massacred. In 1579, however, a crusade under the leadership of James Fitzmaurice Fitzgerald, cousin of the Earl of Desmond, landed in Ireland; papal reinforcements arrived in 1580 as Campion and Persons disembarked in England. The 1580 anti-recusant campaign attempted to keep the recusants under surveillance and to have them support the Queen's army in Ireland; they were to be made to pay for the expense of fighting the papal invasion by being rated for the support of light horse and lances for the Queen's service in Ireland.[49]

In 1580 the Privy Council wrote to the Archbishop of York, the Earl of Derby, and the rest of the Ecclesiastical Commission informing them that after consultation with men learned in the law, it had been decided to punish recusants by some mulct.[50] The Queen, herself, took more direct economic action in Lancaster by granting the fines imposed by law on those who violated the Acts of Supremacy and Uniformity to Nicholas Anesley. The Council wrote to the Sheriff to insure that the recusants made a composition with Anesley. The Queen needed money to pay for the war in Ireland and would get it from her recusant subjects; they, however, preferred imprisonment. Anesley only managed to compel the poorer recusants to appear before the commissioners; the prominent recusants from whom the Queen and Council expected money refused to appear and answer according to law. Anesley had to obtain writs of *distringas* (the remedy for collecting the 12d fine proscribed in 1 Eliz. c. 1 §v).[51]

During the year 1580–1581 the Council used the 1577 census to rate the wealthy recusants throughout the realm for the supply of Light Horse and Lances for the Queen's service in Ireland.[52] The rate seems to have been one lance and one light horse for each 100 marks or fraction thereof of the rented value of a recusant's land. Occasionally goods were also included in the valuation at the rate of one lance or light horse for each £200–300.[53] The result of the levy on the 22 dioceses of England and Wales was 274 persons were assessed[54] for lances and 200 for light horse.[55] This is more evidence which indicates that the Queen and Council were looking for a way not only to follow Aylmer's previously cited advice to attack the social structure of recusancy but also to make the recusants pay for the army which would face the Pope's army in Ireland.

[49] PRO, SP 12/142/33 (?Sept. 1580).
[50] APC, XII, p. 76 (3 July).
[51] APC, XI, p. 446 (14 April).
[52] The two plans described above, i.e., the mulct and the composition with Anesley were confined to the north.
[53] Trimble, *Catholic Laity*, p. 181.
[54] *Ibid.*, Trimble gives the number as 283.
[55] *Ibid.*, Trimble gives the number as 213.

Later in 1581 the Privy Council attempted to bring into court recusants who had been called into the ecclesiastical courts and who had failed to appear. Most of those who had failed to appear were excommunicated. Because they had been called into ecclesiastical court, they must appear to be tried there according to the Act of Uniformity. The Council, therefore, sent letters to the sheriffs of Wiltshire, Berkshire, Worcester, and Herefordshire chiding them for their leniency to excommunicated recusants.[56] The Council included writs *de excommunicato capiendo* from the chancery and instructed the sheriffs to imprison the men named in the writs in the common jail until their cases were called. In Hereford the Council directed that the two previous sheriffs be sent to London to answer before them why they had ignored the writs *de excommunicato capiendo* which had been sent to them during their terms of office.[57]

Between 1574 and 1581 the Queen and Council found that they could not keep the missionaries out of the realm; in response to that invasion, therefore, they had attempted to limit the effectiveness of the missionaries by making occasional conformity necessary on the part of the gentry if they wished to retain control over their households. In doing that the Council ensured that wives and women became the centre of the recusant household.[58] The second part of the government's programme to contain recusancy was to have the recusants pay in the form of mulcts and levies for the expense caused by the papal invasion of Ireland. Both of the above tactics imply that the government realized that recusancy was now a permanent feature of English life and that the function of the Council was not to eradicate recusancy from the realm but to contain it by making it profitable to the Crown. The attempt to levy an occasional mulct on the recusant was first tried in the north at the direction of the Privy Council in order to hasten conformity. In Winchester it was done at the instruction of Sir Francis Walsingham. His name seems to be associated with plans to make recusancy profitable to the Crown.

Parliament met in January 1581; part of the agenda was to solve the problem of the missionary and the recusant. That resulted in the passage of An Act to Retain the Queen's Majesty's Subjects in Their Due Obedience (23 Eliz. c. 1).[59] That statute, if it had been successfully enforced, would have obliged the heads of recusant households to conform at least once a month or face financial ruin. It would have achieved the two goals of the Council's policy during this period: first, they would have forced the recusant to acknowledge the Queen's authority in religious matters by forcing them to conform once a month; secondly, if the recusant failed to conform, he would suffer financial and social ruin.

On 25 January a Commons committee was formed to draw up articles for a

---

[56] APC, XII, p. 90 (8 July); APC, XIII, p. 146 (30 July 1581); XIII, p. 191 (5 September 1581). They were excommunicated either for not coming to church or for not appearing when cited before a church court and, therefore, being declared contumacious.

[57] APC, XIII, p. 191 (5 September 1581).

[58] Bossy, *English Catholic Community*, pp. 152–60.

bill to deal with recusants. Burghley apparently wanted them 'to sharpen the measures against Catholics', to write whatever new provisions were necessary, while allowing 'mercy to the repentant'. On 7 February the committee was prepared to present its work to the Commons. At that time Sir Christopher Hatton announced that the Lords also had a recusancy bill and suggested a conference of both houses; 'the Council was not united'.[60] The bill which the Lords produced was a bill which had been introduced and vetoed in 1571, now made more stringent. It would have given statutory authority to the provincial and diocesan commissions to imprison and impose heavy fines on both recusants and those who overlooked recusancy. Failure to attend church once a quarter would result in a fine of £12; failure to receive Communion twice a year involved an increasing scale of fines starting with £20 for the first offence and reaching a peak of £100 for the fourth offence.[61] The power given to the ecclesiastical judicial system and the provision for compulsory Communion imply that the bill was written and backed by the bishops in an attempt to make the normal ecclesiastical judicial work. That attempt was killed because the Puritans in both houses realized that the bishops would use their authority against them.

The joint committee met eighteen times. They produced a second bill which resembled the first Commons bill. This would have made it treason to reconcile or be reconciled to Rome by reason of the missionaries, priesthood alone. The Commons bill made saying a Mass a felony punishable by death and hearing Mass punishable by imprisonment for six months for the first offence and penalties of *praemunire* for the second. Both bills made a distinction between Catholic non-attendance and Protestant non-attendance of the Established Church. Catholics would suffer fines of £20 for the first month, £40 for the second, and £100 for the third month as well as the penalties of *praemunire*. Non-Catholic recusants were to pay fines of £10, £20, and £40 for the same offence. Other provisions of both bills attempted to keep recusants out of positions of influence. Lawyers were to be barred from office and the right to practice law if they refused the Oath of Supremacy; all schoolmasters were to take the oath and to subscribe to the articles of 1571. The oath was also obligatory for all law students and for all who were connected with either ecclesiastical or civil courts.[62] All offices and positions of influence in the realm would have been closed to recusants. On 27 February after the committee bill was awaiting a second reading before the Commons, the Lords asked for a new meeting of the

---

[59] Sir John Neale saw the act as the result of the Queen's intervention thus stopping a bill which originated with the Puritans in the Commons and which was too vindictive for her (*Elizabeth and Her Parliaments*, pp. 195–96, 385–90). Sir Geoffrey Elton sees the bill as one which originated in the Council, which was not united on the approach to take in framing the bill, and the differences became evident in the bill offered in the Commons and in the Lords; the bill which became law was, for Elton, written by Burghley (Elton, *Parliament*, pp. 185–87).

[60] Elton, *Parliament*, pp. 185–86.

[61] Neale, *Elizabeth and Her Parliaments*, pp. 195–96, 385–86.

[62] Neale, *Elizabeth and Her Parliaments*, pp. 386–90.

joint committee. From that meeting a new bill emerged, which with some perfunctory debate would become 23 Eliz. c. 1.

The bill opened with the statement that 13 Eliz. c. 2 – Against Bulls From
Rome – had not been enforced and that great numbers of recusants had withdrawn their obedience from Her Majesty's laws for the establishment of religion.
The bill concluded, therefore, that any who absolve, persuade, or withdraw any
of the Queen's subjects from their natural obedience 'or for that intent' withdraw them from the religion of the land, would, if convicted, be guilty of high
treason. Anyone who was reconciled to Rome suffered the same penalty. That
distinction followed in the spirit of the earlier distinction which set up a difference between silent non-conformity and active opposition to the religious
settlement. That distinction also allowed recusants to seek reconciliation with the
Queen on the ground that their recusancy was based only in religion and not in
questions of treason.

The next section of the act dealt with those who had knowledge of treason-
able act of reconciliation. Anyone who knew of any person, who either
reconciled someone to the old religion or who knew of someone who was
reconciled and failed to report that to a J.P. or higher official within twenty days
after the reconciliation, was to be found guilty of misprision of treason for so
concealing that knowledge.[63] If a priest were convicted of saying Mass, he was to
be imprisoned for the space of one year and fined 200 marks. Anyone convicted
of hearing Mass was to pay a fine of 100 marks and be imprisoned for the space
of one year.[64]

Everyone above the age of sixteen years was to attend the church or chapel as
specified in the Act of Uniformity. Every month's absence from church after the
closing of that session of Parliament incurred a £20 fine. If non-attendance
lasted twelve months, then it was to be certified into the King's Bench either by
the Ordinary of the place or by a J.P. The offender was to post a bond of £200
for his good behaviour.[65] The statute gave the recusants a choice: they could
attend the established church once a month or they could be fined heavily –
£260 *per annum* plus a bond of £200 for a total of £460 *per annum*.

Anyone guilty of an offence against this Act could escape all penalties, if,
before indictment, he appeared before the bishop of his diocese, made his
submission, and conformed. After being indicted a recusant could make a recognition of his submission in open court and be discharged for all offence against
the Act except treason and misprision of treason, if that were his first indictment
for recusancy.[66] The fines from this Act were to be divided into three parts. One
went to the Queen, one to the poor of the parish in which the recusant lived, and
the last part, to whomever would sue in court for the third part of the recusant's

---

[63] 23 Eliz. c. 1 §2.
[64] 23 Eliz. c. 1 §3.
[65] 23 Eliz. c. 1 §4.
[66] 23 Eliz. c. 1 §7.

fines. Anyone who failed to pay the fine within three months of conviction was to be imprisoned until he had paid the fine.[67] It should be noted that the £20 fine did not remove the necessity of paying the 12d fine for weekly absence form the church.

This Act produced the answer to one of the principal reasons for recalling Parliament back in 1581: recusancy. The problem had become too difficult for the Queen and her Council. They had initially hoped that recusancy would die out with the last of the Marian priests, but to their shock, the universities, the Inns of Court, and the Justices of the Peace were riddled with adherents of the old religion. The nature of recusancy was also changed by the papal excommunication of Elizabeth. Pope Gregory XIII had taken the offensive. By 1580 the papacy was waging both a spiritual war and a material war against Elizabeth: Campion and Persons in England and an army in Ireland. In response to this threat the Council, through Parliament, enacted 23 Eliz. c. 1 which would govern recusancy through the Tudor-Stuart period. The Act would be clarified in 1587 when Parliament decided that after the initial conviction for non-attendance the fines were to be collected automatically month after month without the necessity of further conviction. James I again further changed the Act by making it easier for recusants and conforming heirs of recusants to receive back their lands. 23 Eliz. c. 1 also led to the establishment of the recusant rolls which carried from term to term, and from year to year, the debts of all convicted recusants in the realm. The purpose of the Act was to attack the standing of those whose support was necessary to the continuation of recusancy: the nobility and the gentry. Elizabeth and her Council realized that their policy to contain recusancy had failed; further legislation might be necessary in the future. Any satisfaction with the *ad hoc* policy that was being developed throughout the late 1570s dissipated because of papal policy. A simple glance at the entries in the *Calendar of State Papers Domestic* from 1580 until the end of Elizabeth's reign indicates how obsessed the Council was both with Campion's name and those associated with him.

In 1580 the secular clergy realized that the presence of Campion and Persons would change the relationship between Catholics and the Queen's government. At a meeting in Southwark between Jesuits, Marian priests, and seminary priests, a seminary priest explained to the Jesuits that many believed that they had been sent to England on a political mission. He suggested therefore that, for the sake of the mission, the Jesuits should leave England lest their presence intensify the persecution.[68] Their presence in England did affect governmental policy but despite repeated pleas to abandon their mission, the Jesuits refused. Their hand had been placed on the plough and any turning back would signal a victory for Elizabeth's efforts to control recusancy.

[67]   23 Eliz. c. 1 §8.
[68]   E.E. Reynolds, *Campion and Parsons* (London, 1980), p. 73.

14

'Like Locusts over all the World': Conversion, Indoctrination and the Society of Jesus in late Elizabethan and Jacobean England*

MICHAEL QUESTIER

If the polemical literature is to be believed, the Society of Jesus was feared by English Protestants after 1580 more than any other Catholic body. And the quality which made the Society so terrifying, more even than its subscription to dangerous political doctrines, was its capacity for self-ingratiation, deception, and proselytisation. It seems that however small the number of Jesuits in England, the Society's brand of subversion was exercised on a massive scale, and at all social levels. Robert Tynley warned of their capacity to transform 'themselves into as many shapes as they meete with obiects', 'now a Courtiour, then a Cittizen; heere a countrie Gentleman; there a countrie Swaine: sometimes a Servingman; a swaggerer, Pot-companion; another while [even] a Priest'. It is by these means that 'they may come within men of all sorts; insinuate themselves into their companies . . . that so they may more easily beguile them unawares'.[1] William Crashaw (who followed a well-established Protestant tradition in comparing them with locusts) said that they worked 'themselves into the favours, at least into the Courts, Coaches, & counsels of Princes; & diving into mens consciences & counsels, by the stratagems of their confession, and after into their purses & estates, by benefit of their absolution, & lastly into the conceits of the Vulgar . . . they have hereby gained more to the Pope . . . then all the Romish Clergie in the world besides'.[2]

To their Protestant opponents they certainly seemed to have all the qualities

* I would like to acknowledge the advice and assistance for the writing of this essay given by the Revd Geoffrey Holt, S.J., the Revd Thomas McCoog, S.J., and the Revd Norman Tanner, S.J.

[1] Robert Tynley, *Two Learned Sermons* (London, 1609), STC 24472, p. 6.
[2] William Crashaw, *The Iesuites Gospell* (London, 1621), STC 6017, sig. Aᵛ.

of locusts.[3] They were ubiquitous; they swarmed; they were entirely parasitical and brought nothing but destruction. They did not distinguish between those whom they approached; they were content to devour all. In this respect, as in the type of Christianity which they peddled, it was easy for Protestants to see them as representatives not just of a debased Church, but of a false one; a total inversion of all true religion.[4] Their proselytising zeal was purely for the purposes of political domination, the accumulation of wealth, and self-aggrandisement. They were cast as the principal exponents of the extreme corruption in the Roman Church which had set in after the Council of Trent as the papacy exerted total dominance over it: Henry Yaxley called them the 'now divines of Rome'. They seemed more enthusiastic for the novel doctrines of infallibility than other clergy were. Their success had accelerated Rome's plunge into superstition and error. In Thomas Bell's words, 'since the Jesuites began, (which was about the yeare 1537.) popish religion is ten times more absurd, then it was afore'.[5]

There seems, then, to have been relative unanimity among English Protestants about the Society's operations. The Jesuits were the instruments of the mystery of iniquity and the apocalyptic Babylon. For the tendency in the English Church which is frequently described by historians as 'Arminian' the threat they posed seemed as great, even if it was not given an apocalyptic twist. Laud equated their qualities with those of the Protestants whom he perceived as his enemies in the Church of England.[6]

The English Catholics' perception of the Society was more complex. Some of them saw the Society as the jewel in the crown of English Catholicism, sometimes even the whole crown. William Allen wrote to Campion in December 1579 that 'our harvest is already great in England: ordinary labourers are not enough; more practised men are wanted, but chiefly you and others of your

---

[3] For the Protestant tradition which equated the Jesuit with the locust, see Theodore Beza, *Ad Tractationem de Ministrorum Evangelii Gradibus* (Geneva, 1592), p. 113; the image was exploited in popular polemic, e.g. George Webbe, *Catalogus Protestantium* (London, 1624), STC 25160.7, sigs. g^{r-v}; Beza's tract, chapter 19 of which argued against indiscriminate conversions in foreign missions, and said that such work should be left to the Jesuits, 'locustis illis', drew a counter-reply from Hadrian Saravia, *Defensio Tractationis de Diversis Ministrorum Evangelii gradibus* (London, 1594), STC 21748, p. 309; for the background to the dispute, Tadataka Maruyama, *The Ecclesiology of Theodore Beza* (Geneva, 1978), pp. 174–92. Saravia's dissenting voice was picked up by e.g. John Sweet, *Monsig' fate voi* (St Omer, 1617), STC 23529, ARCR II, no. 739, p. 195, and Nicholas French, *The dolefull Fall* (n.p. [Louvain?], 1674), Wing F 2178, pp. 34–35.

[4] Cf. Peter Lake, 'Anti-popery: the Structure of a Prejudice', in Richard Cust and Ann Hughes, eds, *Conflict in Early Stuart England* (London, 1989), pp. 72–106.

[5] Henry Yaxley, *Morbus et Antidotus* (London, 1630), STC 26090, pp. 13–14; Thomas Bell, *A Christian Dialogue* (London, 1609), STC 1816, p. 7.

[6] William Laud, *Works*, 7 vols in 9 (Oxford, 1847–60), Library of Anglo-Catholic Theology, II, p. xv.

order'.[7] In July 1618 an English friend of the Spanish ambassador in London told him that in England 'the penitents of the Society were as Catholic as those in Spain and those of other orders and priests were like those in the kingdoms infected with heresy'.[8]

Other English Catholics were unsure which they hated more: Protestants or Jesuits; it was hard to decide whose persecution was worse.[9] This group of Catholics, particularly during the Appellant controversy, produced an anti-Jesuit polemic which was soon exploited by Protestant writers.[10] Though they wrote from a different political and theological perspective, these Catholics also insisted that, for base motives, the Society, through its proselytising activities, established an inexorable domination to the exclusion of all other clerics. The religious ideals of the entire mission were perverted by their desire to accumulate power and wealth. For Christopher Bagshaw, the Jesuits made 'merchandise of the conversion of England'. William Watson, the most violent of the Appellants, said that the Jesuits 'labour to stirre up all men, under colour of religion and zealous desire in them, of our countries conversion: against our Soveraigne, the present State, and above all against the seculars, accusing them to be fautors of heretikes'.[11]

Even if contemporary opponents of the Society differed about the source of the evil which the Jesuits propagated, and, of course, the Society and all its opponents were poles apart about its qualities generally, there does seem to have been a consensus that its proselytising was as all described it – exceptionally effective and widespread. No such consensus exists among modern historians. Some virtually endorse the Society's own claims. Helen White thought that the 'visible peak of that great iceberg of human effort [the English mission]' was the Persons-Campion enterprise. John Bossy and Caroline Hibbard have argued that the Society was bound to operate more effectively in England than its clerical opponents, the secular clergy.[12] But John Aveling in a biting modern polemic against the Society questioned whether it had any special ethos at all – nothing

[7] Richard Simpson, *Edmund Campion*, revised edition (London, 1896), p. 134; until this time Mercurian had been blocking Allen's requests for a Jesuit presence in England, Thomas M. McCoog, S.J., ed., *English and Welsh Jesuits: Catalogues (1555–1640)*, 2 vols (Rome, 1992), MHSI 142, 143, II, p. lxi.

[8] Albert J. Loomie, S.J., ed., *Spain and the Jacobean Catholics*, 2 vols (London, 1973, 1978), CRS 64, 68, II, p. 109.

[9] Christopher Bagshaw, *A True relation* (London, 1601), STC 1188, ARCR II, no. 39, pp. 73, 77–78.

[10] For the Appellant agitation against the Society, see Arnold Pritchard, *Catholic Loyalism in Elizabethan England* (London, 1979), chap. 10.

[11] Bagshaw, *True relation*, p. 72; William Watson, *A Decacordon* (London, 1602), STC 25123, ARCR II, no. 794, p. 149; cf. pp. 184–87, 213, contrasting the secular clergy's manner of proselytising with the Jesuits' political methods; cf. Thomas Bluet, *Important Considerations* (London, 1601), STC 25125, ARCR II, no. 62.

[12] John Bossy, 'The English Catholic Community 1603–1625', in Alan G.R. Smith, ed., *The Reign of James VI and I* (London, 1973), pp. 97–9; Caroline Hibbard, 'Early Stuart

beyond rebelliousness and rejection of liberal values; its operation was crippled by the pursuit of misguided policy and by inadequate leaders, an unworkable constitution, a pointless mission, undermined by disputes with other orders and internecine strife between its leading members.[13]

Although Aveling is in no sense a supporter of the 'revisionist' strain in Elizabethan Catholic history, the revisionists express similar opinions about the influence of the Society in England. Historians like C.A. Haigh have argued that the entire continental Catholic clerical influx did as much as the government to wipe out indigenous Catholicism by failing to capitalise on the Marian reaction of the 1550s. By this token, the Jesuits as much as the secular clergy, if they had any grand design to proselytise extensively or nationally, failed dismally as the missioners fled to their seigneurial retreats, eschewing the prospects of associating with social and intellectual inferiors.[14] Such historians argue additionally that the 'mission' in England had never been a proselytising venture because the aim of the priests dispatched from the seminaries was to make contact with those whom they called 'schismatics' (the floating body of church papists in England), not to tackle Protestantism (though, even in this limited aim, it must be deduced that they failed).[15] In that the missioners not only included increasing numbers of Jesuits but were partly trained and led by Jesuits, this failure in proselytising can be laid at the insufficiently demotic Society's door.

From all this it might be thought that a seventeenth-century consensus about the effectiveness (if not the virtues) of the Jesuits' propaganda and proselytism has now broken down. Twentieth-century spectators have divided over whether the Society was effective at all. Of course, it is not disputed that following the initial furore caused by the Persons-Campion venture, natural enthusiasm for persuading the masses to accept Roman doctrines and obedience was scaled down. Retrenchment was inevitable in the face of the obstacles which the regime imposed and, as the Jesuits themselves readily admitted, cramped their style.[16] But mere numerical and geographical assessments of how the Jesuits spread and proselytised are not in themselves sufficient to assess their approach to

Catholicism: Revisions and Re-Revisions', *Journal of Modern History* 52 (1980), pp. 1–34 at p. 23.

[13] J.C.H. Aveling, *The Jesuits* (London, 1981), p. 22, and *passim*.

[14] Christopher Haigh, 'From Monopoly to Minority: Catholicism in Early Modern England', *Transactions of the Royal Historical Society*, 5th series, 31 (1981), pp. 129–47, at p. 136; and 'The Continuity of Catholicism in the English Reformation', *Past and Present* 93 (1981), pp. 37–69, at p. 59 and *passim*.

[15] Christopher Haigh, 'The Fall of a Church or the Rise of a Sect? Post Reformation Catholicism in England', *Historical Journal* 21 (1978), pp. 182–86, at p. 184.

[16] Henry Foley, S.J., *Records of the English Province of the Society of Jesus*, 7 vols in 8 (Roehampton/London, 1875–83), II, pp. 3–6. Only in the brief period of the Persons-Campion mission were claims made for numerical gains by it which matched the numbers the Society claimed to have converted in France, e.g., London, PRO, SP 12/149/51, f. 122^r; cf., for claims of numbers proselytised in France, Henry FitzSimon, *The Justification* (Douai, 1611), STC 11026, ARCR II, no. 290, p. 140.

proselytisation. The argument that the Society abandoned large sections of the population draws too much on the Appellants' polemical claim that the Jesuits 'looke not after the cottages of the poore'.[17] This essay will argue that such views are simplistic because conversion is itself a complex matter. Only in the crudest sense were the Jesuits an army of propagandists who might either succeed or fail in 'signing up' large numbers of otherwise passive laymen. It will assert that the Society was effective because its programme and ethos tapped into different sorts of conversion – and that this was the case because their understanding of change of religion was more wide-ranging than that of the seculars. By reviewing what it meant to convert people this essay will question whether the Catholic retreat into a minority sect was as much of a surrender as some historians have thought; and it will argue that the Society's rift with the secular clergy and ensuing administrative problems were a natural corollary of the thing which it did best – namely to proselytise.

The first question then must be – what did the Society do when it tried to convert Englishmen? The most visible evidence of its proselytising activity is of course its polemical books. The Society was extremely enthusiastic about sustaining the flow of printed works persuading Englishmen to embrace Catholicism for political as well as religious reasons.[18] Certainly, its superior educational programme for its postulants gave it an advantage in this area, something of which the secular clergy were painfully aware.[19] Whether or not the seculars were less polemically able, it does seem that the Jesuit writers had a different attitude towards controversial theology. The tendency of the secular writers was to pursue polemic as an exercise separately from the English mission. For the Jesuits the two activities, merging with semi-public disputations, seem to have been more closely connected. It is notable that the stream of propaganda in the 1610s and early 1620s which revolved around the issue of the visible characteristics of the true Church was undertaken principally by Jesuits in England like John Percy and William Wright (occasionally backed up by seculars like Thomas Worthington who were mistrusted by their own secular colleagues for being too well affected towards the Society).[20] John Percy's printed works on this subject started off as manuscript treatises which were distributed specifically in order to

[17] Bagshaw, *True Relation*, p. 72, which accusations the Society flatly denied, Penelope Renold, ed., *The Wisbech Stirs (1595–1598)* (London, 1958), CRS 51, p. 293.

[18] On this aspect of the Society's mission, see Nancy Pollard Brown, 'Robert Southwell: The Mission of the Written Word' in this collection.

[19] Archives of the Archdiocese of Westminster [henceforth AAW], A X, 409; cf. AAW, A X, 181–82; J.C.H. Aveling, 'The English Clergy in the 16th and 17th Centuries', in J.C.H. Aveling, D.M. Loades, H.R. McAdoo and W. Haase, *Rome and the Anglicans* (Berlin, 1982), pp. 100–02, 128–31; cf. AAW, A XVI, 39–42.

[20] Peter Milward, S.J. *Religious Controversies of the Jacobean Age* (London, 1978), pp. 143–47, 216–26; Michael Questier, 'The Phenomenon of Conversion: Change of Religion to and from Catholicism in England, 1580–1625' (unpublished D. Phil. thesis, University of Sussex, 1991), pp. 65–68.

proselytise among non-Catholics.[21] The surviving conversion manuals which were based on this polemical approach were produced by the Society.[22] And the proselytising disputations in which Catholics engaged with Protestants, either in the prisons, or semi-publicly at times of relative toleration, were generally fronted by Jesuits.[23] In fact, the Jesuits and those secular priests who were on good terms with them were much more enthusiastic than other clergy in such exercises.[24] Admittedly, it would not be true to say that the seculars never engaged in such disputes; Richard Smith confronted Daniel Featley in September 1612, and William Bishop emphasised that he had actively propagated Catholicism in this way, 'preaching, disputing . . . in prison and out of prison'.[25] But it is an observable fact that, in the few places where priests could be assured of an audience, the secular clergy did not confront the authorities so readily as the Jesuits.

Among the types of conversion which Jesuit polemic recommended was the separation of the 'Catholic' element of the population from the established Church (and, after 1606, an attempt to make them avoid the Jacobean oath of

---

[21] John White, *The Way to the True Church* (London, 1616), STC 25397, sig. d7[v]: the copy of Percy's 'Treatise of Faith' which White answered was a manuscript one, and the basis of White's printed reply was the arguments which he had used in refuting it verbally; Timothy H. Wadkins, 'The Percy-"Fisher" Controversies and the Ecclesiastical Politics of Jacobean Anti-Catholicism, 1622–1625', *Church History* 57 (1988), pp. 153–69, at p. 156.

[22] Oxford, Bodleian Library, Jones MS. 53, no. 3; Bodl., Rawlinson MS D 853, f. 22[r–v].

[23] For example, the confrontation between John Percy and John Sweet and Archbishop Abbot's chaplain Daniel Featley (assisted by Francis White) in June 1623, technically in order to resolve the religious doubts of a cousin of Sir Humphrey Linde, Milward, *Religious Controversies of the Jacobean Age*, pp. 220–22; Daniel Featley, *The Fisher Catched in his owne Net* (London, 1623), STC 10732; British Library, Additional MS 28,640, f. 22[r]. Sweet had already challenged Featley from prison in 1622, George Roberts, ed., *Diary of Walter Yonge* (London, 1848), Camden Society, first series, 41, p. 63. In 1622 Percy had disputed with Francis White, John Williams and William Laud before the king in connection with determining the Countess of Buckingham's religious orientation, Wadkins, 'Percy-"Fisher" Controversies'; also the disputation between Sylvester Norris and George Walker in May 1623, in virtually identical circumstances to those already cited – the resolution in religion of a wavering individual, a relation of Sir William Harrington, *The Summe of a Disputation* (London, 1624), STC 24960. Paul Spence, the Marian cleric and seminarist who disputed with Robert Abbot in Worcester Castle in the early 1590s, was said to be a stooge for the Jesuits, Robert Abbot, *A Mirrour of Popish Subtilties* (London, 1594), STC 52, sigs. A4[v]–*[v]; PRO, SP 14/14/40, f. 95[r–v].

[24] Among those of Campion's generation, Thomas Pounde S.J. attached great importance to public disputation, and while in prison took on Robert Crowley and Henry Tripp, Robert Crowley, *An Aunswer to six Reasons* (London, 1581), STC 6075, sig. Aii[r]. For instances of two active proselytising seculars who had connections with the Society: John Ainsworth, Godfrey Anstruther, *The Seminary Priests*, 4 vols (Ware/Durham/Great Wakering, 1968–77), II, p. 3; AAW, A XIV, 209–11; PRO, SP 14/80/84, f. 125[r]; PRO, SP 14/80/93, f. 140[v]; and George Fisher, Anstruther, *Seminary Priests*, II, pp. 102–09; and for the rumours that he had become a Jesuit, AAW, A XII, 523, XIII, 382; John Gee, *The Foot out of the Snare* (fourth edition, London, 1624), STC 11704, sig. Q[r].

[25] George Wickes, 'Henry Constable, Poet and Courtier, 1562–1613', *Biographical Studies* [later *Recusant History*] 2 (1953–54), pp. 272–300, at p. 293, 299 n. 101; AAW, A XI, 348.

allegiance). A primary object of the Persons-Campion mission was to persuade large numbers to withdraw from the churches. Very few of the Catholic clergy dissented from the official Roman policy on recusancy, but, on the surface, the Jesuits would sometimes appear to have been more active in getting people to declare their Catholicism in this way, and more hostile to those who seemed to disagree with their line. Although Jesuit confessors were as capable of casuistic laxity over the question as any secular, in public they took the lead against those who wished for some sort of compromise. Thus Robert Persons wrote his *A brief discours* to counter the effects of the manuscript tract supposedly by Alban Langdale, circulated by William Clitherow.[26] Henry Garnet was largely responsible for the pressure put on Thomas Bell, the northern secular priest, who was ostracised for his views about occasional conformity. A similar situation arose over the problem of the oath of allegiance of 1606. Secular priests like John Mush who proposed a modified form of the oath in order to placate the government came under attack from the Society, even though the secular newsletter-writers fulminated that Jesuit confessors were extremely sympathetic towards their penitents in this respect.[27]

Finally, the Jesuits were notoriously associated with a more aggressive kind of proselytising – namely by force of arms. Despite their occasional professions of loyalty, the English Jesuits were almost always thought to favour the use of military power. Richard Simpson wrote that Campion thought 'all was done when he had reconciled his convert to the Catholic Church', but Persons 'desired and laboured for the conversion of England, and he thought that nothing could effect this but the overthrow of Elizabeth' and so worked tirelessly to create a belligerent party for this purpose.[28] The Society could not sympathise with a view which said that national reconversion should be carried out, if at all, by a process of gradual assimilation. This is reflected in Persons' infamous 'Memorial'; its implication of violent political change as a necessary condition for the national conversion it envisaged was viewed unfavourably by the seculars.[29]

If all of this were taken to mean that the Society thought in terms merely of trying to recruit a purely 'institutional' sort of convert, then the revisionists would be able to make some sort of case. In other words, if the Jesuits tried in their books just to make people (and people above a certain social level at that) accept some manner of allegiance to Rome, or to make as many people as

[26] John H. Pollen, S.J., ed., 'Memoirs of Father Robert Persons, S.J.,' in *Miscellanea II* (London, 1906), CRS 2, pp. 179–80.

[27] AAW, A X, 513; the Jesuits undermined the seculars' position in England by making accusations that they compromised in the matter of the oath, AAW, A X, 411, though the seculars retaliated in kind, 413–15; cf. Richard Sheldon, *The Motives* (London, 1612), STC 22397, sigs. X4^{r-v}, B3^{r}.

[28] Simpson, *Campion*, p. 276; Aveling, *Jesuits*, p. 60.

[29] Robert Persons, *The Jesuits Memorial, for the Intended Reformation of England*, ed. Edward Gee (London, 1690), Wing P 569; cf. Andrew Willet, *An Antilogie* (London, 1603), STC 25672, p. 34; Watson, *Decacordon*, p. 213.

possible (but mainly those who were sufficiently influential and wealthy to support them) become classifiable as recusants, non-jurors, or political malcontents, then they, and the English clergy who followed their lead, might well be thought to have 'failed'. On such grounds it would be possible to see them directing their persuasions only at those on the borderline between mere schism and Roman Catholicism (so they ignored English Protestants); and it might be deduced also that they ignored the residual body of indigenous English Catholicism while concentrating their efforts on a minority of gentry, and on a political revolution which never came. However, such a thesis flies in the face of the evidence. I propose to demonstrate this by looking again at their proselytising in England. The Society's conversion strategy will be examined in the first instance from two sources – the instruction manuals which told them what to do, and the evidence about converts who became Catholics under Jesuit auspices.

The basic source for English Jesuit proselytising is the manuscript instruction, partly tactical, partly doctrinal, written by George Gilbert in 1583 and based on the system employed by Campion and Persons.[30] There are four sorts of people the missioners must deal with. The first is the reliable Catholic. His house is to be used to preach in to his relations, friends and dependants whether Catholic or heretic. There remain three other broad classes to be approached – 'heretics', 'schismatics' and 'lukewarm Catholics'; the 'heretics' and 'schismatics' are divided again into sub-groups. Although there are no directions to concentrate the missioners' energies on one type rather than another, Gilbert does not say that any of them are not to be contacted; his only caveat against dealing with those termed 'malicious' heretics is that they should not be approached 'without an introduction from a friend'. Other Jesuit proselytising manuals are also specifically labelled for use with 'heretics'.[31]

What Gilbert says about dealing with 'heretics' is not that they should be avoided but that there may be little return obtained by disputing with them about doctrine alone: 'the heretical spirit is so much given to pride that few of them are converted by argument'; success is likely with them only if the priest can find some means 'whereby to make them more inclined to humility and submission, such as the consideration of their own worth, contempt of the world and such-like thoughts', and that, in their case, 'more fruit is gained from sermons giving advice for the direction of one's life, for the saving of one's soul and from other such-like meditations, than from those on subjects of dispute and controversy, which are more likely to stir up contention than bring about amendment of life and conversion'.[32]

---

[30] Leo Hicks, S.J., ed., *Letters and Memorials of Father Robert Persons, S.J.* (London, 1942), CRS 39, pp. 331–40.

[31] Questier, 'Phenomenon', pp. 298–300; Stonyhurst, MS Collectanea P I, f. 203ᵛ.

[32] Hicks, *Letters of Persons*, pp. 334, 336; Persons said that when dealing with a heretic, it is best 'never to dispute with him in publick as neer as may be, for that heresy is pride and wil not yield before others', and that 'when there is difficulty and much obstinacy in the partie the

This passage is the key to what conversion meant for the Jesuits working in England. They did not see themselves as limited in their proselytising to particular grades of non-Catholic, certainly not in the sense that revisionist historians have argued. This was at least in part because they did not think primarily of turning people who appeared to be 'Protestants' (because they approved of the established Church) into people who appeared to be Roman Catholics (because they did not). There is hardly a source concerned with the Society which does not manifestly illustrate that 'conversion' in England had at least as much to do with their own evangelical ethos as with the mechanical process of catechising the ignorant into the paths of the extremely artificial contemporary polemical formulations of the Roman faith.

In this period, of course, the word 'conversion' has generally been used to refer to exchange of loyalty between one institutional Church and another. But most theology of conversion tends to stress that change of religion in the sense of coming to belong to the true Church has a moral element because of participation in its sacraments, so that every true conversion 'must of necessity be a conversion of life', not merely the adoption of a denominational label.[33] Change of ecclesiastical institution is only one aspect of change of religion understood as the central practical expression of the theology of grace – repentance and regeneration, assurance and perseverance. This is an uncontroverted element of Christian faith. Disagreements occur over the urgency with which conversion is stirred up within the individual, and assurance sought that he is indeed subject to the regenerative workings of grace. Those in both Churches who stressed the pursuit of grace more enthusiastically than others are frequently referred to as evangelicals. Evangelical conversion in the Roman Church has a tendency to be associated with vows in religion, escape from the world, and entry into the house of a religious order. At least, this is how Catholic theology visualises the search for assurance of grace at its most intense. The Jesuits, of course, were not monks. They strongly dissociated themselves from many aspects of monastic observance as being contrary to their order's basic purposes. But the Society, though out in the world, was an order of clerks regular. Their vows in religion were at the centre of their clerical activities. It was inevitable that Jesuit proselytising should be influenced by this central characteristic of the Society, the pursuit of evangelical perfection.[34] Though change of religion in the sense of abandoning the Church of England might be an important part of conversion, the essence of that conversion was not contained in a movement between one ecclesiastical institution and another. It was principally a matter of progress in grace.

---

best way is to desist from urging of controversy and rather talke of matters of devotion'; a heretic should be argued with about doctrine only to the extent of getting him to accept the Catholic theology of penance, Stonyhurst, MS Collectanea P I, f. 204ʳ.

[33] 'Conversion', IV (Obligation of), Cornelius William Williams, O.P., *New Catholic Encyclopaedia*, 17 vols (Washington, 1967–74), IV, p. 289.

[34] Cf. John W. O'Malley, S.J., *The First Jesuits* (Cambridge, Mass., 1993), p. 16.

Jesuit proselytisers, therefore, were interested in sin as much as in heresy. Their converts not only recanted Protestantism but made general confessions, which Jesuits envisaged as part of a process of evangelical change.[35] In this respect the 'schismatic' and the 'lukewarm Catholic' confronted the Jesuit missioner with as many problems as the 'heretic'. They sometimes required more converting than a convinced Protestant who might at least be zealous already even though ensnared in error. Robert Persons contrasted formal reconciliation with the 'sound Reconciliation' which produces 'a sure and constant Christian afterwards'. Though Persons is referring in this instance to 'Schismaticks', their conversion, 'whether they have been Hereticks or no, ought to be made with great attention and deliberation'.[36] John Gerard distinguished between Sir Francis Fortescue who was a schismatic ('but there was no hope of converting him' because he lacked zeal and was content with 'wanting to be a Catholic') and the openly heretical/Protestant Grace Fortescue who was 'already interested in the Catholic faith and there was a chance she might come over in time'. Gerard believes that he can stir up her will into an appreciation of the Catholic model of evangelical activity, and persuade her that it could not be found 'in a false religion where no account' is taken of it.[37]

A crucial piece of evidence then is the use of the *Spiritual Exercises* by English Jesuits. There is no evidence that the Exercises ever induced anyone to abandon doctrinal Protestantism. As John O'Malley says, they are clearly meant to be given to 'believing Catholics', though Jesuits like Nadal thought they could be applied to Protestants and even to non-Christians. They are not intended to 'convey any special theological viewpoint'.[38] Their whole purpose is the re-orientation of self and turning in religion which is at the centre of evangelical change. In practice, the Exercises frequently provided a vehicle for an evangelical stage of conversion of an individual who was travelling between the Churches of England and Rome. The Protestant cleric, Francis Walsingham, as he drew towards the end of his fruitless polemical odyssey, said to his Catholic contact (evidently a Jesuit) that 'having now setled now my mind [i.e. intellectually] . . . I felt a good desire also in myself to accommodate my life for the time to come to a more diligent observation of Gods commandements', and the man points him in the direction of the first week of the Spiritual Exercises. Walsingham's reading of polemical tracts has already convinced him (if he needed it) of the truth of Roman Catholic doctrine. But it leaves him unresolved. His active

---

[35] O'Malley, *First Jesuits*, pp. 137–8; cf. A. Lynn Martin, *The Jesuit Mind* (London, 1988), pp. 88–89.

[36] Persons, *Jesuits Memorial*, p. 31.

[37] John Gerard, *The Autobiography of an Elizabethan*, edited by Philip Caraman, S.J. (London, 1951), pp. 161–62; the English Jesuit annual letter for 1614 says that it 'is more difficult to uproot evil habits, especially when strengthened by lapse of time, than to get people to unlearn heresy', Foley, *Records*, VII/2, pp. 1056–57. Cf. Kenelm Digby, *A Discourse* (Amsterdam, 1652), Wing D 1430, Clancy 319, p. 6.

[38] O'Malley, *First Jesuits*, pp. 37–39, 42.

rousing of his will towards resolution is the principal element of Catholic evangelical conversion. This aspect of his change of religion is channelled into the first week of the Exercises 'with its . . . purifying meditations on the malice of sin and the sufferings of hell', and its emphasis on permanently turning from sinful life.[39] John Gerard excelled in employing the Exercises to assist conversion in this sense.[40] The Jesuit proselytising text entitled 'How to proceede with heretickes in their conversion' says that Protestants might be proceeded with first by general motives to turn to Rome, supplemented by particular points of doctrine, but 'secondlie theie muste have some cheife motives gyven them to move them to hartie sorrow for their synns' and 'to such as cann reade maie be given the cheife points of the exercise of the first weeke drawen into einglishe for that purpose'.[41]

Of course, the Society did not see its role limited to any one kind of proselytising. Robert Persons wrote that by the zeal and industry of the Jesuits 'many a separation is made between good and bad, many a heat enkindled in Christian hartes, where deadly cold occupied the place before . . . many an heathen and heretique made Christian, many a frostie catholique made a hoat recusant, many a vitious lyver made observant, many a careles and earthly mynd stirred up to apprehend and think of eternitie'.[42] The point is that proselytising arguments would be based first upon assertions of the need for evangelical change, and then the convert would gradually be made aware that the Church of Rome was the best, in fact the only, Church in which this was possible. Conversion in the first sense ultimately necessitated conversion in the second sense. John Sweet, in his polemic against Marc'Antonio de Dominis, said that the virtues of 'Humility, Obedience, Pennance . . . Chastity, Poverty, Patience, [and] Austerity' as well as 'Charity and Zeale in the conversion of others' were the way in which 'Augustine the Monke' had spread Christianity in Britain, and 'so now the Jesuits and other Religious men of this tyme, do overcome' equally 'the ignorance of the barbarous, the fallacies of Hereticks, the pollicyes, pryde and ostentation of worldly wisedome, in the conversion of sundry Nations to the Faith of Christ'.[43] Jesuits did not merely capitalise on a few instances of a common fund of doctrinal alterations of belief. Jesuit spirituality was not confined to the later

---

[39] Francis Walsingham, *A Search* (St Omer, 1609), STC 25002, ARCR II, no. 785, pp. 505–07; Questier, 'Phenomenon', pp. 105–06; cf. Joseph de Guibert, *The Jesuits: Their Spiritual Doctrine and Practice*, trans. William J. Young (St Louis, 1972), pp. 129–30, 532, describing the place of the counsels of perfection in the making of the Exercises; O'Malley, *First Jesuits*, p. 39.

[40] Gerard, *Autobiography*, p. 184.

[41] Bodl., Jones MS 53, ff. 236ᵛ–37ʳ.

[42] Robert Persons, *A Temperate Ward-Word* (Antwerp, 1599), STC 19415, ARCR II, no. 637, p. 66.

[43] Sweet, *Monsig'*, p. 159.

stages of a shift of allegiance to Rome. It could be exploited heavily before the doctrinal stage was over, sometimes even before it had begun.[44]

A subtle proselytiser like Gerard could produce a doctrinal change of religion by placing his arguments in an evangelical passage from the flesh to the spirit. He ensnared Sir Oliver Manners into meeting him through an invitation to play cards, but the worldly pursuit of the card game rapidly turned into a discussion of religion. It is evident from the way that Gerard describes the persuasions exercised on Manners that his subsequent resolution for Catholicism was more than a denominational change of religion, and Gerard signals its evangelical rather than doctrinal character by saying that 'from that time on he wanted to do more than just keep the commandments'.[45]

The significance of the Jesuit understanding of conversion now becomes obvious. The Jesuit-minded proselytiser drew his evangelical concept of conversion from an area of theology and spirituality which was of common concern to Protestants and Catholics; he did this rather than base his rhetorical persuasions exclusively in the stark and off-putting monotony of Catholic polemical doctrinal arguments. The way to Rome was then opened up through a central stream of evangelical consciousness which was equally alluring to zealots of both sides, Protestants and Catholics. Contrary to every indication of the 'poles apart' polemic produced about the Society by Protestants, the Jesuits' theology of conversion took them into Protestant doctrinal and devotional enclaves. To demonstrate the spiritual havoc which Jesuits could wreak among Protestants, one needs to look no further than the '*Responsa Scholarum*', the replies of the students who entered the English College in Rome. It is evident from such records that there is a direct path from the condition which contemporary Catholics described as 'heretical' to Rome through the evangelical state of conversion which Jesuit proselytisers aimed to induce. It is frequently thought that only those at the 'high church' end of the Protestant spectrum were likely to convert to Rome; principally on the ground that they would be more sympathetic to Catholic theology and liturgy. As Anthony Milton suggests, summarising the opinion of Laudian writers, 'the problem was that those who were most in danger of converting to Rome . . . [because of perceived irreverence in the Church of England] were precisely those people who placed most importance in the "beauty of holiness" ', that is, 'those who were most likely to form the bedrock of support for the Laudian programme'.[46] There was, though, a point of exchange between elements of Protestantism which were strongly Reformed (rather than moderate), and evangelical Catholicism, frequently in the shape of the Society. This might seem odd when the target of so much Protestant vitriol was the Catholic evangelical spectrum of monasteries and vows in religion, the

---

[44] E.g., Foley, *Records*, I, pp. 145, 167, 176; III, p. 547; IV, pp. 407–08.

[45] Gerard, *Autobiography*, pp. 185–86.

[46] Anthony Milton, 'The Laudians and the Church of Rome, c.1625–1640' (unpublished Ph.D. thesis, University of Cambridge, 1989), p. 145, cf. pp. 143–44.

absolute negation of the entire Reformed understanding of the doctrines of grace. But, while James I remarked to general applause that he noted certain political similarities between Jesuits and Puritans, far more substantial ones existed on an ecclesiastical and theological level.[47] Of course, all this depends somewhat on the definition being offered of the word 'Puritan'. Still, it is possible to argue that, although their expressions of practical piety might differ, theologically there were more points of contact than difference between Jesuits and Puritan Protestants over the issue of evangelical conversion.

This can be seen first from a biographical survey of English Jesuits themselves. Though the evidence of their religious opinions before they entered the order often remains imprecise, it seems clear enough that converts who progressed subsequently to the Society frequently said that there had been strongly Protestant elements in their past, Calvinist tenets which they or members of their families had held. Robert Persons' own family was divided; his brothers Richard and George were Catholics, but Thomas and John were Protestants, and John was ardently so.[48] George Gilbert, formerly Protestant, had an 'earnest nature' which 'inclined him rather to Puritanism', confirmed in him by daily resort to the sermons of Edward Dering; Gilbert was converted in Paris by Thomas Darbyshire, S.J.[49] Henry FitzSimon, though there were Catholics in his family, was very Protestant in his youth, as was his education at Manchester. He was related to James and Henry Ussher.[50] Edward Walpole was converted by Henry Walpole, S.J., a near relative; but until then, according to Henry More, he had been a 'diligent puritan'.[51] Francis Walsingham said that his Protestant ideas had been drawn from, *inter alia*, the works of John Foxe and John Napier.[52] One wonders too about the jesuited Tobias Mathew jnr and his religious inheritance in the house of his father, the Archbishop.[53] Between 1598 and 1640, of the seminarists who left an account of their religious background at the English College in Rome, 124 were ordained and professed as Jesuits. Of these forty-nine said that they had been formerly heretical and gave the names of those who converted them. Two-thirds said that where a priest was involved it was a Jesuit as opposed to a secular.[54]

Secondly one may observe a closeness in evangelical Catholic and Protestant

---

[47] James I, *An Apologie for the Oath of Allegiance . . . Together with a Premonition* (London, 1609), STC 14401, sig. f. 4ᵛ.

[48] Pollen, 'Memoirs of Persons', pp. 38, 40.

[49] Simpson, *Campion*, p. 173.

[50] Edmund Hogan, S.J., ed., *Words of Comfort* (Dublin, 1881), pp. 201–02.

[51] Henry More, S.J., *The Elizabethan Jesuits: Historia Missionis Anglicanae Societatis Jesu (1660)*, translated and edited by Francis Edwards, S.J. (London, 1981), p. 255.

[52] Walsingham, *Search*, sig. **2ᵛ.

[53] CSP Domestic, IV, p. 168.

[54] Of those twelve seminarists who entered the Society but died before ordination, four were formerly heretical and six schismatic, Anthony Kenny, ed., *The Responsa Scholarum of the English College, Rome*, 2 vols (London, 1962, 1963), CRS 54, 55, *passim*; cf. Questier, 'Phenomenon', p. 102.

concepts of change in religion, both ecclesiastically and in the wider sense of turning under the influence of grace. The problem which confronted all Catholic priests who came to England from the Continent was how to persuade people to belong to 'the Church'. But 'belonging to the Church' for some Catholic clergy might be loaded with emphases which other clerics would not want to acknowledge so readily. There were tensions among them about the way in which the true Church should be described as visible, infallible and so on, just as there were disagreements among Protestant clergy on these issues; and this was expressed in differing attitudes to conversion. The Jesuits (with their alienation from aspects of the Tridentine emphasis on the primacy of the ecclesiastical structures of the institutional Church) entertained an idea of conversion which resembled the one held by English Protestants who adhered to more uncompromising doctrines of grace, and who played down the extent to which the institutional Church was necessary for grace to be efficacious.[55] Of course, it will always be misleading to regard Jesuits simply as 'Catholic Puritans'; it risks importing too many qualities associated with the word 'Puritan' which have no connection with Rome. But just as Jesuit proselytisers were instructed to instigate conversions at the most propitious time of the day, as the light was fading, so the Jesuit concept of conversion occupied the penumbra between the two institutional Churches where competing theologies were not clearly distinguishable, and where evangelical impulses could be capitalised upon by like-minded proselytisers from either side. It was inevitable that opposition would come from those in both Churches who saw elements of that type of activity as being in conflict with the structure, purpose and potential of the institutional Church, its hierarchies and authority. Francis Bacon, in his 'Advertisement' against Puritan demands in the Church of England, wrote that he had heard 'some [Puritan] sermons of mortification, which I think (with very good meaning) they have preached out of their own experience and exercise, and things [which] in private counsels [are] not unmeet; but surely no sound conceits, much like to Persons' *Resolution* [the *Christian Directory*] . . . apt to breed in men . . . weak opinions and perplexed despairs'.[56] It is easy to see why Puritans like Edmund Bunny should have been so quick to bring out Protestant editions of Robert Persons' *Christian Directory*. This tract was popularly known as the *Book of Resolution*. It is closely related to the first week of the *Spiritual Exercises*, and it was a proselytising work in every sense. Despite its outwardly non-controversial character it was recognised as a solver of doubt which extended to doctrine, or rather, obviated doctrinal doubt altogether. It was aimed at Protestants as much as Catholics. A spy reported in February 1584 that Catholics were distributing it to Protestants, and that it and the Rheims New Testament 'are as much sought for, of the pro-

---

[55] Cf. J. Sears McGee, 'Conversion and the Imitation of Christ in Anglican and Puritan Writing', *Journal of British Studies* 15 (1976), pp. 21–39.

[56] James Spedding, R.L. Ellis, D.D. Heath, eds, *The Works of Francis Bacon*, 14 vols (London, 1858–74), VIII, pp. 92–93.

testanttes as papistes'.[57] George Birkhead, the future Archpriest who, later, could never wind himself up to the pitch of hatred for the Society of which some of his secular colleagues were capable, wrote in August 1584 that because of 'its special object, viz., the reformation of a sinful life', the *Book of Resolution* 'has borne immense fruit; the number of conversions of heretics to faith by reading it can scarcely be believed'.[58] More of the converts in the English College in Rome said that their conversions were the result of reading this book than any other.[59] Protestants like Bunny recognised the book's potential almost immediately. The Puritan expurgated editions, shorn of their Roman terminology, are an attempt to prevent readers thinking that Rome was the natural focus for latent evangelicals.

It is easy to see also why the secular Catholic clergy should have begun to voice opposition to the Jesuits' attitude to conversion (and the mission in general) when the Society, rather like some Protestants, seemed to have little respect for hierarchies and the institution of episcopacy. It was no accident that Christopher Bagshaw in Wisbech, in his more angry moments, should refer to the fathers of the Society as 'Genevans' and 'precisians'.[60] In the area of conversion, there really was more conflict between Puritan and 'Anglican' than between Puritan and Jesuit. England's peculiar circumstances meant there was likely to be as much disagreement among Catholics, notably seculars and Jesuits, as among Protestants over conversion and the balance between emphasis on the institutional Church and 'community of the godly'.

With this Jesuit model of conversion in mind, let us ask whether it enables us to resolve some of the historiographical paradoxes concerning the Society in England. To remind ourselves, the revisionist argument is a two-fold one – that the Catholic proselytising spearhead, in which the Society was so prominent, had no intention of converting Protestants, and secondly, in that it was intended to reclaim the Catholic-minded at all, it ignored residual English Catholics who were consequently abandoned to the Church of England. (It is frequently alleged as well that Jesuit efforts to induce recusancy and to persuade people away from the Jacobean oath of allegiance were merely an attempt to discomfort their Catholic clerical opponents.) Jesuit proselytising, however, suggests that a different model may be substituted for the revisionist one. I wish to look again at the categories of proselytising activity which we examined first: the production of

---

[57] PRO, SP 12/168/31, f. 75ʳ. For crucial new research on the source material and construction of Robert Persons's *Christian Directory*, and for its relationship to the *Spiritual Exercises*, see Victor Houliston, 'Why Robert Persons Would Not Be Pacified', in this collection.

[58] John H. Pollen, S.J., ed., 'Notes Concerning the English Mission' in *Miscellanea IV* (London, 1907), CRS 4, pp. 153, 155.

[59] Kenny, *Responsa Scholarum*, I, pp. 11, 140, 150, 198, 207, 236; cf. Thomas Worthington, *A Relation* (Douai, 1601), STC 26000.9, ARCR II, no. 847, p. 73; BL, Lansd. MS 72, f. 122ʳ (for the effect of chapter seven in part two); cf. Foley, *Records*, I, pp. 215–16.

[60] Renold, *Wisbech Stirs*, p. 330.

books and engagement in disputes; the polemical campaign for separation from the established Church, and the virulent criticism of secular priests who went against the official Roman line, when the Society itself was notorious for its casuistic (some said lax) attitude to its penitents in this respect; a similar situation over the oath of allegiance; and finally, the whole question of politics and the 'reconversion of England' (in which the historians have seen English Catholicism going into decline by following a path dictated by the Society).

I think that in all these cases the essence of Jesuit concerns has to be seen below the polemical surface of the books or the institutional structure of the mission. For example, as has already been suggested, evangelicals had doubts about the value of controversial theology on its own. Robert Persons, incontestably the greatest English Catholic polemicist of the period, himself stated it as a general principle that intellectual persuasion, in the form of disputation 'as it is a fit meanes to styrre up mans understandinge to attend the truth, by layinge forth the difficultyes on both sides; so is yt not always sufficient to resolve his judgement, for that yt moveth more doubts than he can aunswere or dissolve'.[61] In the preface to the first edition of his *Christian Directory* of 1582 Persons states that the 'principall cause and reason' for publication was

> to the ende our countrye men might have some one sufficient direction for matters of life and spirit, among so manye bookes of controversies as have ben writen, and are in writinge dailye. The whiche bookes, albeit in thes our troublesome and quarrelous times be necessarie for defence of our faithe, against so manye seditious innovations . . . yet helpe they litle oftentymes to good lyfe, but rather do fill the heades of men with a spirite of contradiction and contention.[62]

Francis Walsingham, who wrote his conversion tract, *A Search Made into Matters of Religion*, partly at Persons' direction, said that after extensive reading of Catholic and Protestant polemical tracts, he was still 'fearfull to make any change in Religion for many respects'. He 'felt such a warre betweene . . . [his] understanding, will, and affection, as . . . [he] could not tell . . . what to do'.[63] Jesuit proselytisers knew this, and they proceeded upon psychological rather than polemical lines when making their final assault. This is clearly reflected in the Gilbert manuscript. In part, his advice is mere common sense; the proselytiser is told to make use of prevailing conditions, for example the state of the weather, to provide topics and similes for religious discourse. But there are also more specific instructions deliberately to induce a particular mood, and render the intended

[61] Robert Persons, *A Review of Ten Publike Disputations* (St Omer, 1604), STC 19414, ARCR II, no. 636, pp. 19–20.

[62] Robert Persons, *The first booke of the Christian exercise, appertayning to resolution* (Rouen, 1582), STC 19353, ARCR II, no. 616, p. 2.

[63] Walsingham, *Search*, pp. 473, 481–82; cf. similar assertions made by Tobias Mathew, Jnr and Sir Kenelm Digby, A.H. Mathew, *A True Historical Relation* (London, 1904), pp. 39–40.

proselyte liable to evangelical suggestion without a single mention of Rome's doctrinal claims to authority. The proselytiser should 'make use of certain methods and of times that are propitious – as for instance, if he should see him in a fit of melancholy or desolation of soul, he will then be able, under the pretext of consoling him, to speak about human misery . . . telling him that we shall have no rest until we are united with God in heaven; that the soul of man is often in desolation because, sharing as it does in the divine nature, it cannot be contented and find rest in these things below . . . ' telling him also 'of the causes which have led souls to damnation'. Thus might the Jesuit trigger the sudden moment of illumination and onset of grace; 'The evening, after the Ave Maria, is the time most apt to make a man receptive and adopt a reflective mood, because then there is quietness everywhere and repose; the world appears to be deserted and lonely; . . . the adornments and pleasures of the daytime are in abeyance, and the sun has fled to other regions, and the earth has been clothed in darkness, the image of death and the end of the world'.[64]

The apparent anomalies in the Society's attitude to the thorny problem of recusancy can also be resolved by reference to the Society's concept of change of religion. A reading of the tracts by which Jesuits like Persons refuted the 'conformist' arguments of their Catholic opponents shows that they had a different perception of occasional conformity and the nature of recusancy. Of course, there was a political angle to it. William Clitherow, Persons' opponent in 1580, came to belong to the anti-Jesuit Gifford faction.[65] But the church attendance issue could be seen on more than the political level, or even the need to avoid scandal and to protect people from the infection of Protestant services and preaching. In Persons' tract against Langdale, recusancy is written about in terms of the positive value of separation. Persons employs the sort of language and citations, notably Revelation 18:4, which those of a Puritan evangelical cast of mind used when they described separation from Babylon, a combination of abandoning a false particular Church *and* the company of the reprobate.[66] It is perhaps significant that Persons refers to those, represented by the figure of Naaman, whose resolve is as yet insufficiently great for their Father confessor to insist on their strict recusancy, as 'novices'.[67] The confessor's insistence on his penitent gradually accepting the need for absolute separation from an heretical Church coincided rather well with the Catholic concept of evangelical conversion as a gradual progress towards perfection.

The quarrels over the oath of allegiance of 1606 can be seen in the same light. What the Jesuits really attacked was the loyalist argument, adopted by some

---

[64] Hicks, *Letters of Persons*, pp. 334–35. O'Malley notes the Society's particular focus on the connection between death and conversion, and the importance of the Society's ministry to the dying, a reflection of the Jesuits' own evangelical experience, *First Jesuits*, pp. 174–75.

[65] Pollen, 'Memoirs of Persons', p. 36.

[66] BL, Add. MS 39,380, f. 18ʳ; Henry Garnet, *A Treatise* (n.p., 1593), STC 11617.8, ARCR II, no. 322, pp. 102–03.

[67] William Fulke, *A briefe Confutation* (London, 1581), STC 11421, f. 54ʳ.

among the secular clergy who approved of the oath, that papal political power might be abrogated when it was exercised '*ad destructionem ecclesiae*'. This was the Archpriest Blackwell's consistent argument in favour of the oath from the moment that the English clergy first discussed whether Catholics could take it. Loyalists like Blackwell argued that large numbers of English Catholic families would be driven into penury if they held out and thus reduce their capacity to support priests. So the papal *caveat* against it could be said to be damaging to the Church, i.e. the physical, financial structure of the Church, and thus ought to be ignored. It is possible to discern in the Jesuit rejection of this, a different attitude towards what the Church in a mission territory like England actually was. The Jesuit model of the way in which people became and remained Catholics, constantly underpinned by Jesuit ideas about conversion, meant automatically less stress would be put on the visible material superstructure of the Church, and more on the Church as the body of the Elect, regenerate in grace. If the true Church was regarded in terms of persons, rather than materially or territorially, then Blackwell's arguments were more easily dismissed. Such reasoning hints at emphases in a definition of the Church with which a Reformed Protestant might sympathise.[68]

A similar explanation is possible also for the ambiguities in the divisions between the Jesuits and their opponents over politics and 'national reconversion'. Traditionally the contrast has been drawn between the seculars who wanted Catholicism to spread in England by a slow progression as the structure of the disestablished Roman Church in England gradually expanded, and the Jesuits who wanted to see a sudden reconversion, preferably through a favourable successor to Elizabeth, but if necessary by foreign military assistance. In fact, Jesuits themselves were divided over the way in which policy towards national reconversion should be formulated as well as over which candidate to the Crown should be supported.[69] But Jesuit unity was maintained because they subscribed to the same evangelical ideal about the way that people ought to become and remain Catholics. Their essential unanimity demonstrates John Bossy's dictum that the Society's concept of mission concentrated on persons rather than territories, and that, in England, where special circumstances prevailed, conversion should be focused primarily upon individuals, rather than the essentially secondary aim of turning England back into a Catholic state.[70]

It has been suggested by this review of the Society's attitude to conversion in England that when the Jesuits there thought about proselytisation, it was principally in terms of the evangelical identity of their own order, and not the more straightforward political and ecclesiastical aims generally associated by historians

---

[68] Stonyhurst, MS Collectanea P I, ff. 165ᵛ–67ʳ.

[69] Peter Holmes, *Resistance and Compromise: The Political Thought of the Elizabethan Catholics* (Cambridge, 1982), pp. 215–18.

[70] H. Outram Evennett, *The Spirit of the Counter Reformation* (Cambridge, 1968), pp. 135–38; cf. John Bossy, *The English Catholic Community 1570–1850* (London, 1975), p. 24.

with the mission to re-Catholicise England beginning in the 1570s. This explains much of the polemic against the Society by both Catholics and Protestants. They were not really saying just that the Jesuits were greedy and dangerous; they were saying that their vows were hypocritical and worthless. This is the basis for the notorious picture of the Jesuit drawn by the Protestant John Gee (partly from Catholic sources), the 'good smug Fellow in a gold-laced suit, a cloke lined thorow with velvet, one that hath good store of coin in his purse, Rings on his fingers, a Watch in his pocket, which hee will valew at above twentie pounds'. Gee's caricature is a direct denial of the Jesuit evangelical character. As Gee says, 'This man hath vowed *poverty*. Feare not to trust him with thy wife: hee hath vowed also *chastity*.'[71]

In what way does all this illuminate our understanding of post-Reformation Catholicism in England? In one sense it takes us no further than what John Bossy has already said about the counter-reforming agenda of the Society in England. His sophisticated model comprises both an analysis of the sectarian position of English Catholics and the way in which the Jesuits' programme fitted into this sectarian Church. But the 'revisionist' argument about English Catholicism has largely ignored it and confused many of the issues by introducing anachronistic ideas into contemporary disputes. The problem lies with the meaning of the words 'English Catholicism'. The 'revisionist' definition of post-Reformation English 'Catholicism' as a mass movement (or not at all), described by reference to a concept of continuity which is social rather than religious or ecclesiastical, obscures rather than clarifies the question of how Catholicism was propagated in England after 1580. It is argued from the material presented in this essay that we can more easily begin to understand what post-Reformation English Catholicism was if we look at the different ways in which Catholic clerics in England thought about proselytisation, rather than the numbers in which they were sent over, how they were distributed geographically, and whether they gravitated towards the gentry or not. The Society's understanding of conversion was broader than that of the secular priests in England. This is not to imply crudely that the seculars were incapable of proselytising.[72] But their approach was much less flexible than the Society's because they thought in terms of re-Catholicisation through the medium of the structure of an established institutional Church which they did not have. The conflict which the Society engendered among the Catholic clergy illustrates that Catholicism in England during this period is misunderstood if it is seen merely as a rump Church or a species of political dissent. The Jesuits' proselytising activity, even as they

---

[71] Gee, *Foot out of the Snare*, p. 51; cf. Bell, *The Anatomie* (London, 1603), STC 1814, p. 130, 'Of the Iesuiticall exercise and their profitable effects thereof'.

[72] In December 1599 Christopher Bagshaw was named by the prisoners in York Castle as one of their choices for a clerical disputant in a prospective debate with the roll-call of puritan ministers assigned to preach to them, BL, Add. MS 34,250, f. 11ᵛ; cf. PRO, SP 12/199/91, f. 172ʳ; AAW, A V, no. 2. William Bishop, a leading secular, stressed in his reports to Rome the ardour with which he went about the gathering of souls, AAW, A XI, 348.

persuaded individuals towards Rome within an evangelical framework of grace, demonstrates that, after 1580, English Catholicism was not just a slide into seigneurial torpor and a hermetically sealed religious separatism, and that some Catholics had more in common with their Protestant opponents than they did with each other. It is interesting to speculate whether, in the event of a political reversal of fortunes suddenly in the 1590s, a Catholic 'John Foxe' might not have written an ecclesiastical history in which the Jesuits were the representatives of the 'true church' and of a 'little flock' persecuted previously by a godless regime, and who continued to contemplate the mystery of how difficult it was to engender in the institutional Church the godly community represented by their own proselytes.

15

Campion and the English Continental Seminaries

MICHAEL E. WILLIAMS

The establishment of colleges abroad for English Catholics began at the start of the reign of Elizabeth Tudor. At first the houses at Louvain and Douai were regarded as temporary abodes until such time as England might be restored to the Catholic faith and communion with Rome. As the years passed, it became more and more likely that the Elizabethan settlement would continue for the foreseeable future. Political developments, the absence of a strong, Catholic leadership within the country, and legislation unfavourable to the profession and practice of the Catholic religion were accompanied by an effective system of spying and policing. Among the scholars at Douai, men were being prepared to serve as priests and some showed themselves eager to cross over to England immediately rather than wait upon events. Cuthbert Mayne was captured and executed in 1577 and is regarded as the pro-martyr of the seminary priests. Although Douai College is often looked upon as a seminary, it differed from the Tridentine ideal since its alumni were not exclusively candidates for the priesthood and those who were ordained had little prospect of working within a stable diocesan structure; they had to minister to a flock that was persecuted and they themselves were hunted men. From the point of view of the English government, 1579–81 were crucial years. There was opposition from Puritans as well as Papists.[1] Not only was there an attempt by papally assisted forces to invade Ireland but William Allen succeeded in enlisting Jesuit support for a mission to England.[2] The coincidence of these two projects was unfortunate in so far as the

[1]   Patrick McGrath, *Puritans and Papists under Elizabeth I* (London, 1967), deals at length with this dilemma for the Elizabethan government.

[2]   Although Allen was not directly involved in the Irish expedition, he must have been aware that an invasion was being organised since he was in Rome when the preparations were taking place. One of the reasons of the reluctance of the Jesuits to participate in a mission to England was that it would entail adopting a different style of life with less opportunities for regular spiritual exercises and retreats in a country where the church was persecuted. See

spiritual mission of Edmund Campion, Robert Persons and their companions could easily be confused with the political and military campaign of James Fitzmaurice especially as such a distinguished apologist as Nicholas Sanders formed part of the expeditionary force.

This is the context in which we must view Campion's missionary activity and death. It is also the background to the increasingly severe legislation against Catholics and particularly against the seminary priests on the grounds that they were guilty of treason.[3] To William Allen fell the difficult task of distinguishing between a political uprising against the Queen in Ireland and a religious mission to England. As he records in his account of Campion's martyrdom,[4] on the scaffold the Jesuit priest denied he was a traitor and professed his loyalty to the Queen.[5] However, our concern here is not so much with Campion's loyalty as with his links with the seminaries. The subject of this chapter divides itself into two sections. Firstly there is a consideration of the extent to which Campion's own life and missionary activity was related to the seminaries and secondly some of the ways in which the martyrdom of Campion and his companions influenced the preparation and training of missionary priests.

I

Although the seminary priests Ralph Sherwin and Alexander Briant accompanied Campion on his mission and suffered with him at Tyburn, Campion himself had very little to do with the seminary. His residence at Douai was extremely brief.[6] He had already completed a distinguished academic career and

Richard Simpson, *Edmund Campion: A Biography*, revised edition (London, 1896), pp. 139–40, 144–46.

[3] The acts of 1559 and 1563 had asserted the crown's supremacy in religious matters. Further acts in 1571, 1581 and 1585 placed penalties on those who reconciled people to the Catholic faith and also banned Jesuits and seminary priests from the country. See John J. LaRocca, S.J., 'Popery and Pounds: The Effect of the Jesuit Mission on Penal Legislation' in this volume.

[4] *A Briefe Historie of the Glorious Martyrdom of XII Reverend Priests* (np [Rheims], 1582), ARCR II, no. 7; STC 369.5.

[5] Allen himself takes a similar view in his *An Apologie and True Declaration of the Institution and Endevours of the Two English Colleges* (Mons, 1581), ARCR II, no. 6, STC 369. It is interesting to speculate whether it was Allen who was influenced by Campion or whether it was Allen who highlighted Campion's loyalty to the Queen when writing up the account of his martyrdom in order to defend the seminary priests from the charge of treason. Concerning Campion's loyalty see Thomas M. McCoog, S.J., ' "The Flower of Oxford": The Role of Edmund Campion in Early Recusant Polemics', *Sixteenth Century Journal* 24 (1993), pp. 899–913.

[6] In his account of the trial Simpson has a rather puzzling passage which seems to assert that Campion disclaimed that he and his companions were seminary men. 'What oath seminary men do take at their first entrance, or whether Bristow's motives be repugnant to our cause or no, is not anything material to our indictment, for that we are neither seminary men nor sworn at our entrance to any such motives. But were it so that any seminary men stood

had received deacon's orders in the established Church when he arrived at Douai in 1571. Moreover his doubts about the new religion and his conversion from a secular career and the national Church to the service of God in the Catholic faith had taken place some time previously during his residence in Ireland. So in a sense there remained little for him to do except complete his theology course and engage in a little teaching as was the custom.[7] But he was not alone in this. Many of his contemporaries who came to Douai in the 1570s had already begun an academic course in England. Neither was Campion's departure from Douai before ordination, unprecedented. He went to Rome to join the Society of Jesus in the spring of 1573. In those days, Douai, not being a diocesan seminary felt no proprietorial right over the students. It was a place – the only place – where an Englishman could study in accord with the Catholic tradition and where one could prepare oneself for the Catholic priesthood. But service of the Church in the priesthood at this early period of Douai College did not necessarily include pastoral activity or immediate work in England, although many expected and hoped that their labours would be in their native land. But as yet there was no missionary oath binding them to return to their own country. As to the Society of Jesus, this too was attracting vocations, but at this stage there was no English Province and this meant that from Rome Campion was directed to Prague in Bohemia for his formation and further studies and it seemed as if he would be unable to spend his life on the English mission. This was until Allen was able to persuade the Jesuits to take part in the mission to England.[8]

But Campion's connection with the continental seminaries was not restricted to the few months he spent resident at Douai. The college at Douai was at the hub of a growing Catholic intelligence service which kept English exiles in touch with each other and with events in their native country. So it was through correspondence with Gregory Martin at Douai that Campion in Bohemia was able to be kept informed about the progress of the college and such matters as

---

here for trial, this matter could prove no great evidence against them, for that none are sworn to such articles as Bristow's but young striplings that be under tuition; whereas unto men of riper years and better grounded in points of religion (as most of England are before they pass the seas) that oath is never administered; and then many a study else flourisheth in Rome, wherein both seminary men and others are for better employed than they otherwise could be in reading English pamphlets'. (Simpson, *Campion*, p. 407). In 'Blessed Edmund Campion at Douay' (*The Month* 61 [1887], pp. 30–46), John Morris, S.J. discusses Campion's annotations to St Thomas' *Summa Theologiae*.

[7] According to Simpson (*Campion*, p. 69), Cuthbert Mayne was Campion's pupil at Douai. Joseph Gillow, *Biographical Dictionary of the English Catholics*, 5 vols (London, nd [1885]), I, p. 386 lists *De Iuvene Academico*, an oration pronounced at Douai while he was professor there. See Henry More, S.J., *The Elizabethan Jesuits: Historia Missionis Anglicanae Societatis Jesu (1660)*, translated and edited by Francis Edwards, S.J. (London, 1981), pp. 364–65.

[8] For the early recruitment of English and Welshmen to the Society, see Thomas H. Clancy, S.J., 'The First Generation of English Jesuits 1555–1585', *AHSI* 57 (1988), pp. 137–55; Thomas M. McCoog, S.J., 'The Establishment of the English Province of the Society of Jesus', *Recusant History* 17 (1984), pp. 121–39.

the political development in Flanders that necessitated the removal of the college from Douai into French territory at Rheims.[9] He also learnt about the opening of another seminary in Rome at the former English Pilgrim Hospice and Allen wrote to him from Rome about matters concerning English affairs.[10] He was also in receipt of the latest news concerning the publication of controversial works by Thomas Stapleton, Allen, Richard Bristow and Martin. He knew about the current disputes between Protestants and Catholics in England. His sojourn at Douai might have been brief but it had lasting effects. He had made many friends who wanted to hear news of him and who urged him to write to them more often.

It was the Mission of 1580 that brought Campion back to England and into closer personal contact with the seminaries. The idea of sending men who had been ordained on the continent back to England to preach and minister to the people there had formed in William Allen's mind only a few years after the founding of Douai and he had approached the Father General Everard Mercurian with a request for assistance.[11] In Rome the links between the seminary and the Society were close and it was the students themselves who had requested Jesuit superiors. The daily timetable and course of studies at Douai resembled those at Jesuit houses.[12] Recently, Robert Persons had written expressing the wish to serve on any mission to England.[13] The original composition of the party that set out for England was very broadly based. It included the Marian Bishop of St Asaph Thomas Goldwell, Dr Nicholas Morton from Douai, priests from the hospice in Rome, Sherwin and other seminary priests as well as the three Jesuits, the priests Campion and Persons, and the lay brother Ralph Emerson. In the course of the journey there were some alterations in the composition of the group, notably the withdrawal of Bishop Goldwell because of the state of his health and fear that his age might prove a handicap to the progress of the company.[14]

---

9   Martin's letters to Campion, the originals of which are in the ARSI, Fondo Gesuitico 651/636, can be found in Thomas Francis Knox, ed., *First and Second Diaries of the English College, Douay* (London, 1878), pp. 308–320. Persons kept Campion in touch with the political situation in Flanders (Simpson, *Campion*, pp. 129–31). On Campion's interest in England, see Thomas M. McCoog, S.J., ' "Playing the Champion": The Role of Disputation in the Jesuit Mission' in this volume.

10   Thomas Francis Knox, ed., *The Letters and Memorials of William Cardinal Allen* (London, 1882), p. 84. For other correspondence with Campion, see Simpson, *Campion*, pp. 117 ff.

11   Allen to Mercurian, 16 October 1578, in Knox, *Letters and Memorials*, pp. 68–69. His memorandum to the general on the subject of the conversion of England is to be found in Patrick Ryan, S.J., 'Some Correspondence of Cardinal Allen, 1579–85', in *Miscellanea VII* (London, 1911), CRS 9, pp. 62–68.

12   'Memoirs of Robert Persons, S.J.', edited by J.H. Pollen, S.J. (London, 1906) CRS 2, p. 190.

13   This was on 30 March 1579 (Philip Hughes, *The Reformation in England*, 3 vols (London, 1952–54), III, p. 305n).

14   For details see Simpson, *Campion*, pp. 152, 168–69.

Before leaving, Campion spent fifteen days in Rome preparing for the journey and as Persons records in his 'Memoirs',[15] he 'put great desire in some many priests of the College'. From Rome they set out for Rheims and we learn something of the impact made by Campion on the college from a letter of Allen to the Rector of the college in Rome, Alfonso Agazzari:

> Fr Edmund gave us an address in our own language to try whether, after eight years disuse, he still remembered his native tongue. But so rapid was the torrent of his words that with impetuous violence it seemed to overflow its boundaries.[16]

At Rheims the group split up to find England by different routes.

The progress of the mission was followed with great interest in Rheims and Rome and news of Campion's successful preaching in London was conveyed from Allen to Agazzari, the Jesuit Rector of the college in Rome,[17] as was the news of his arrest.[18] Acquaviva, who was elected to succeed Mercurian in 1581, wrote to Allen expressing the high hopes that had been placed on Campion and scarcely concealing his disappointment at his early capture:

> His exertions . . . gave us great consolation and we were daily looking for greater results; yet since it has so seemed good to the Lord, to whose honour those achievements were devoted, we have with joy resigned ourselves to divine providence. Nay, we even more hope that, in as much as there is more in merit in enduring torture rather than toil, so for the conversion of that people Fr Campion will have greater influence in prison or being racked than on the platform or by preaching or any of his former occupations.[19]

Two months later Acquaviva again wrote to Allen:

> As to Fr Campion, very consoling is what your reverence recounts, of how great service will prove even this calamity that has befallen him, if it is not rather to be called felicity, seeing that it has come about through his love for Christ and true religion. May our Lord give him courage and fortitude to

---

[15] Persons, 'Memoirs', pp. 160, 195.

[16] Ryan, 'Correspondence', p. 27. Simpson (*Campion*, p. 167) refers to Campion taking as the text of his sermon 'Ignem veni mittere in terram.' Is this the origin of the text on the Martyrs' Picture that is today venerated in the college church? This painting by Durante Alberti based on the frontispiece of the old English Hospice account book has no text appended, neither does the engraving of the picture which is reproduced in the Cavalleri book of engravings. It is said that the painting was carried out in 1580. Did Campion see it before he left Rome for the mission? Did it already bear the inscription and so give him his text for the Rheims sermon? Or was the text added after his sermon and subsequent martyrdom?

[17] Ryan, 'Correspondence', pp. 29, 31.

[18] Ryan, 'Correspondence', p. 39.

[19] Ryan, 'Correspondence', p. 81.

render a good testimony and bear the brunt of battle for his glory. We wait what should be done in his regard.[20]

One should not underestimate the shock that Campion's trial and subsequent execution created. The mission had raised great expectations. On leaving Rome the party had been accompanied by a procession of dignitaries to the Milvian Bridge, they had been received with great joy at Rheims and news of success in England was eagerly awaited. The martyrdom of Campion, Sherwin and Briant was seen as a serious check to the idea of winning back the English people to Catholicism by a campaign of preaching the Gospel and ministering the sacraments to the Catholic community. Capture might be felicity to Campion and his fellow martyrs but it was a calamity for the mission. It was with some hesitancy that the Jesuits had agreed to participate in the mission to England as it would involve a somewhat different lifestyle from their ideal. There was need of some clarification as to the relationship between mission and martyrdom. John Bossy has noted Acquaviva's anxiety lest Persons in his projected life of Campion should give undue prominence to the martyrdom and neglect to relate the life of a missioner.[21] The loss of Campion to the mission set in motion a consideration about the value of martyrdom and to what extent it should be deliberately sought. We shall have occasion to return to this theme later.

But whatever the inner misgivings, outwardly the deaths of the missioners were treated as triumphs. Prayers were offered at the English College in Rome.[22] From Rheims Allen wrote to Agazzari in Rome telling him of how verses in Latin, Greek and English in praise of the martyrs were circulated in the streets and fixed on doors. At Oxford young men who were suspected of having published poems in praise of Campion were forced to flee the country and were considering joining the college at Rheims.[23] Simpson tells us that Henry Walpole in the fervour of his own conversion estimated that the martyrdom converted ten thousand persons on the spot.[24] The Regius Professor of Divinity complained that the ghost of the dead Campion had given him more trouble than the *Rationes* of the living: 'It used to be said "dead men bite not"; and yet Campion

---

[20] Ryan, 'Correspondence', p. 87. For other letters of Allen to Acquaviva about Campion, see Penelope Renold, *Letters of William Allen and Richard Barret (1572–1598)* (London, 1967), CRS 58, pp 35–38.

[21] John Bossy, 'The Society of Jesus in the Wars of Religion', in *Monastic Studies: The Continuity of Tradition*, ed. Judith Loades (Bangor, 1990), pp. 229–44, especially pp. 233–34. This matter is further developed in Bossy's 'The Heart of Robert Persons' in this volume.

[22] 'Agazzari, the Rector of the English College caused the organ to be sounded and all the students to come to the chapel, and then and there he himself, pulling on his back a white surplice, and stole about his neck, sang a collect of martyrs, so after his manner canonising Campion the rebel as a saint'. (Simpson, *Campion*, pp. 467–68 [quoting Bell's *Anatomy of Popery*, p. 97]).

[23] Knox, *Letters and Memorials*, p. 122.

[24] Simpson, *Campion*, p. 462.

dead bites with his friends' teeth.'[25] Allen himself seems to catch some of the fire of Campion's Brag in the exhortation to martyrdom that is to be found towards the end of his *Apology*:

> No martyrdom of what length or torment soever, can be more grevious than a long sickness and languishing death: and he that departeth upon the pillow hath as little ease as he that dieth upon the gallows, block or butcher's knife. And our Master's death, both for pain and ignominy passes both sorts and all other kinds either of martyrs or malefactors.[26]

That intransigence that was characteristic of Allen and was evidenced in his attitude towards attendance at Protestant services is stirred into life by Campion's fate and his behaviour on the scaffold.

A true reporte of the death & martyrdom of M Campion, published anonymously in 1582, would seem to be the main source of the Catholic accounts of his death.[27] It was the work of Thomas Alfield, a seminary priest, and the work created a stir when it was printed in London. Richard Verstegan, the printer, was forced to flee abroad.[28] Translations were soon circulating on the continent of Europe.[29] But an even more significant account, influential because of the author's reputation, was William Allen's *A Briefe Historie of the Glorious Martyrdom of Twelve Reverend Priests Father Edmund Campion and His Companions*.[30] This relies heavily on Alfield and it too was translated, into Italian by a member of the English College in Rome in 1583, and into Spanish so that it forms a whole chapter of Diego de Yepes' *Historia particular de la Persecucion de Inglaterra*.[31] Allen's work shows the stamp of one who is concerned with his responsibilities as rector of a seminary

---

[25] Simpson, *Campion*, p. 462. Simpson does not identify this professor but both Regius Professors of Divinity, William Whitaker at Cambridge and Laurence Humphrey at Oxford, wrote against Campion. Whitaker was one of Campion's opponents in the disputations in the Tower of London. Henry Foley, S.J., *Records of the English Province of the Society of Jesus* 7 vols in 8 (Roehampton/London, 1875–83) gives other examples of converts from Campion's martyrdom (VII/2, pp. 702, 787). Michael Questier in the present volume deals with the question of conversion as it affected the Jesuits after the death of Campion (' "Like Locusts over all the World": Conversion, Indoctrination and the Society of Jesus in late Elizabethan and Jacobean England').

[26] Allen, *Apologie*.

[27] (npd [London, 1582]), ARCR II, no. 4; STC 4537.

[28] Simpson, *Campion*, p. 471.

[29] Simpson, *Campion*, pp. 468–70, gives a general account of writings about Campion's death. A more specific list of works is given in ARCR II, nos. 196–204. Even more numerous than accounts of Campion's death were the continental editions of his *Rationes decem* (npd [Stonor Park, 1581]), ARCR II, nos. 135.1–193.

[30] This work first published in Rheims in 1582 (ARCR II, no. 7; STC 369.5) was edited by John H. Pollen, S.J. (Roehampton, 1908). His introduction gives an account of the history of the work.

[31] (Macerata, 1583) ARCR I, no. 8; (Madrid, 1599) ARCR I, no. 284. The Gregg reprint 1971 has an introduction by D.M. Rogers.

and is somewhat perturbed by Campion's quick arrest and death. We must not forget that in the indictment of Campion and the seminary priests there were in all twenty people accused of acts of treason committed in Rome, Rheims and other places overseas. The list included not only Robert Persons but also Allen and his assistant at Rheims, Dr Nicholas Morton.[32] Thus the trial of Campion can be said to have imperilled the whole English seminary system. In his *A Briefe Historie* Allen does not only include those who died with Campion but other seminary priests, including Cuthbert Mayne, who died some years before Campion and Sherwin. It was as if Campion's fate had called attention to previous deaths and made Allen realise their full significance for the first time.

It was at the same time as this that Allen also composed his *Apology* for the two seminaries at Rome and Rheims so that this work of his can be said to be a consequence of Campion's death. The writing was inspired by a new urgency to defend the overseas colleges. After giving an account of their origins and the studies pursued in them, Allen takes up most of the treatise with defending the seminaries against the charge of treason and he expresses their loyalty to the person of the Queen. This theme issues from Campion's own lips on the scaffold as Allen records them in the *A Briefe Historie*.[33] In the *Apology* Allen goes so far as to say that if it had not been for the clemency of the Queen even more priests would have been put to death, thus seeking to lay the blame on her counsellors rather than on her personally. This loyalty theme is to be found in some of the verses that were composed on the occasion of Campion's martyrdom.[34] Allen could not have been unaware of the accusations of men like Anthony Munday, Charles Sledd and Laurence Caddy who claimed to be in possession of incriminating evidence obtained from their own contacts with the seminaries.[35]

It was the question of loyalty that came to the fore in the Catholic defence. It seems to take precedence over martyrdom itself. John Foxe's *Book of Martyrs* had a wide circulation and his examples of the sufferings of Protestants under Mary Tudor weakened some of the apologetic arguments that might be adduced in favour of the Catholic martyrs under Elizabeth. Allen did attempt to show that the reign of Mary was superior to that of her sister, but this was on the grounds

---

[32] A fully documented account of Campion's trial is to be found in the *Official Presentation of Documents on the Martyrdom and Cult of 40 Blessed Martyrs. Sacred Congregation of Rites, Historical Section 148* (Vatican City, 1968), pp. 231–351.

[33] Another book that appeared about this time was the compilation *Concertatio ecclesiae Catholicae in Anglia* (Trier, 1583), ARCR I, nos. 524–530 by the Jesuit John Gibbons. In the first section there are a series of writings directly relating to Campion, his *Rationes decem* and various letters. The second section includes Allen's *Apology*.

[34] See e.g. 'The complaynt of a Catholike for the death of M Edmund Campion', in Pollen's edition pp. 44–46.

[35] Peter Milward, S.J., *Religious Controversies of the Elizabethan Age. A Survey of Printed Sources* (London, 1977), p. 173.

of justice. She was not less severe in her punishments, but whereas Mary put people to death for offences against God and His Church, Elizabeth refused to do this, for her the highest crime was treason against her own person.[36]

II

But the value of martyrdom and its relationship to mission was not completely forgotten and it was especially evident in the seminaries themselves. Bursts of fervour such as had arisen at the time of Campion's trial and after his death might not be sufficient to inspire perseverance during a prolonged persecution. Nor might they be adequate to sustain enthusiasm if the persecution were to be mitigated in favour of a measure of toleration, and even indifference. At the same time news of arrests, torture and execution of former students were constant reminders of the dangerous occupation for which the inhabitants of the colleges were preparing.[37] In order that there would be no mistakes about the possible future that awaited them, a series of thirty-four frescoes were painted on the walls of the church of the English College in Rome in 1583. They were the work of the artist Niccolo Circignani (Pomerancio) and they depicted a history of Christianity in England and Wales, laying particular stress on martyrdom.[38] The first scene shows the link with apostolic times as it presents St Peter ordaining priests and bishops and Joseph of Arimathea and Simon the Apostle preaching in England. Because they were considered to have English connections, the Emperor Constantine and his mother St Helena, St George of Cappadocia as well as St Augustine of Canterbury figure in the paintings. However the majority of the pictures are gruesome portrayals of martyrdom. They include Saints Alban, Lucius, Oswald, Ethelbert, Edmund, Winefrid, Aaron of Caerleon, Thomas Becket, the boy martyr Hugh of Lincoln and many others including Thomas More, John Fisher, the Carthusian martyrs and Campion, Sherwin and Briant. The latter trio figure together in three distinct scenes: on the rack, on the hurdle and their disembowelling and dismemberment. The final scene of all is of the reigning pontiff, Gregory XIII who founded the college together with

---

[36] Michael E. Williams, 'William Allen: The Sixteenth Century Spanish Connection', *Recusant History* 22 (1994), pp. 123–40.

[37] Lionello Puppi, *Torment in Art: Pain, Violence and Martyrdom* (New York, 1991) traces the route of the processions of criminals to public execution in 16th and 17th century Rome. They passed by the Monte Savello prison on their way to the Castel San' Angelo. This would mean that they were within sight of the English College and so students at the College would be well aware of what a public execution entailed.

[38] Circignani painted frescoes of a similar nature in the church of San Stefano Rotundo in Rome. The original ones at the English College perished during the neglect the college suffered in the French occupation in the nineteenth century. Copies were made from the engravings of G.B. Cavalleri by the Italian artist Capparoni in 1893 for the tribune of the new church.

students and the Cardinal Protector at prayer.[39] The horrors of martyrdom are vividly portrayed, but they are put in a particular context, that of the history of the local church and its loyalty to Rome. One is reminded of Campion's own words:

> In condemning us you condemn all your own ancestors. All the ancient priests, bishops and kings, all that was once the glory of England, the island of saints and the most devout child of the see of Peter.[40]

Although intended for a seminary chapel these pictures were soon given a wider public. Two years after they were painted copies were made in engravings by G.B. Cavalleri to form the book *Ecclesiae Anglicanae Trophaea*[41] and so these Roman pictures took their place in the many representations of martyrdom that were circulating throughout Europe at this time.[42] As with the engravings that are found in Foxe's *Book of Martyrs* the intention behind this fashion for vivid portrayals of martyrdom was to illustrate the cruelty and evil intentions of those who were inflicting the torture and so arouse feelings of admiration and wonder at the courage and sanctity of those who suffered. The sufferings of Christ were frequently visualised in a similar way by contemporary artists.

As with the Circignani frescoes so sixteenth-century writers used martyrdom for apologetical purposes. Thomas Bozio[43] however drew attention away from individuals and their sufferings to the Church of which they were members. In

---

[39] The historical sources for these representations are varied. It would seem that Baronius was the chief medium through which foreigners gained access to English chroniclers.

[40] According to Simpson, *Campion*, p. 435, these words were spoken by Campion at his trial in reply to Lord Chief Justice Wray's question, 'What can you say why you should not die?' Simpson's source would appear to be British Library, Lansdowne MS 33, no. 65.

[41] (Rome, 1584) ARCR II, nos. 944–946.

[42] As an example we can note Richard Verstegan, *Theatrum Crudelitatum Haereticorum Nostri Temporis* (Antwerp, 1587), ARCR II, no. 1297. This is an illustrated account of the persecution in England under Henry VIII, the cruelties of the Huguenots in France, the brutalities in the Dutch Calvinists and the sufferings of Elizabethan Catholics. It went into several Latin and French editions, ARCR II, nos. 1298–1304.

[43] Tommaso Bozio (1548–1610) as a young man met St Philip Neri at the Oratory at S. Girolomo della Carità and abandoned a career in law to enter the community at the church of S. Giovanni dei Fiorentini. He was ordained priest and became rector at the Chiesa Nuova. St Philip directed him into ecclesiastical studies and he assisted Baronius in his revision of the *Annales Ecclesiastici*. He also wrote apologetical works, including *De Signis Ecclesiae Dei contra omnes hereses*. He gained especial authority in circles of the Roman Curia and at the invitation of the Pope began to write against Machiavelli. Copies of both *De Signis* and his work against Machiavelli are to be found in the library of St Alban's College Valladolid. In *De Signis* he shows himself familiar with the situation in England and makes reference to Nicholas Sander's *De Visibili Monarchia*, Book 7. Philip Neri when he was living at S. Girolomo is said to have greeted the students of the nearby English College with the words 'Salvete Flores Martyrum' being aware of their fate when they went back as priests to minister in England. It might be that Bozio gained his interest in the Church in England from his association with St Philip.

his *De Signis Ecclesiae Dei contra omnes hereses* he enumerates close on one hundred signs by which we can discern the true Church from false sects and heresies. Among the negative signs which indicate that a body cannot be the true Church he cites what he calls 'impietas hereticorum', 'the wickedness of heretics', and here he singles out Henry VIII and the repudiation of Catherine of Aragon and illicit love of Anne Boleyn as well as Elizabeth's murder of Mary Queen of Scots. Among the positive indications of the true Church he speaks of the sanctity of the contemporary Church militant and this chapter is almost entirely given over to examples from the British Isles. John Fisher and Thomas More were put to death under Henry VIII and then there is a very long list of all those who had suffered for the faith in more recent times. As he is dealing with contemporary history, Bozio cannot rely on any official beatification or canonization lists and so he records those who were known to have suffered in any way for the faith, whether by exile, imprisonment or death. Thus we can get a glimpse of how the situation in England appeared to contemporaries across Europe before it became filtered through the process of scrutiny for beatification or canonization. Bishops Edmund Bonner and Cuthbert Tunstall appear in the list. He makes a particular point about the number of women who suffered for the faith, saying that since the time of Constantine no other age or nation or province had witnessed so many suffer and die for the faith; women of all ranks from Mary Queen of Scots downward. He has a special chapter dealing with the seminary priests, taking them chronologically from Cuthbert Mayne through Campion to those who had died in the year of publication of the work, 1599. The sufferings and death of these English martyrs are a proof of the true Church being the Catholic Church. Bozio's testimony is significant since he relates the persecution in the British Isles to the Church as a whole. The Church has suffered persecution throughout the ages so that persecution is a mark of the Church. In their lives men like Campion defended the truth of the Church against heretics. Bozio is saying that their deaths are an apologetic too, since they point to the place where the true Church can be found.

In 1582 in the brief 'Omnipotens Deus', Gregory XIII had recommended the needs of English Catholics to their fellow religionists. Within a few years, we can see some of the results. Cavalleri's engravings, the apologetic works of Bozio, Yepes' history of the persecution in England drew the attention of continental Catholics to the situation in England. Not only were the persecuted Catholics remembered in the prayers of the faithful, but alms were forthcoming and the most obvious recipients of charity were the seminaries where members of the persecuted church were preparing to go and minister to their suffering people. Ten years after Campion's death, his former companion, Robert Persons, was in Spain setting up the seminaries of Valladolid and Seville.[44] He found a generous

---

[44] For the histories of these colleges, see Michael E. Williams, *St Alban's College Valladolid* (London/New York 1986), and Martin Murphy, *St. Gregory's College, Seville, 1592–1767* (London, 1992) CRS 73.

response from churchmen, nobles and ordinary members of the Church. One can be sure that his own personal connection with Campion had a powerful effect. The generosity of Spanish Catholics towards English Catholics continued into the next century and it was through learning of the sufferings of Campion in particular that a noble lady of Valladolid, Dona Luisa de Carvajal, was moved to a remarkable act.[45] On hearing of the existence of the English College of St Alban and that a former member of staff, Henry Walpole, S.J., who had been converted by Campion's example, had himself suffered death and martyrdom, she resolved to go to England in person to preach the Gospel alongside those former students of the college who were now working there. She was prepared to suffer martyrdom and she took Campion's life as a model to follow. Her presence in London caused a certain amount of embarrassment to the Spanish ambassador and even some English Catholics were nonplussed. She set up a small religious community and was arrested and imprisoned on two occasions. Being a foreigner there was no question of her being executed and it was while awaiting repatriation to Spain that she died in London. Her body was returned and received with some ceremony in her native land. A little later there occurred another example of the effect of knowledge of the martyrdoms in England on the charity and apostolic activity of overseas Catholics. It was through seeing a book of engravings of the sufferings of the English martyrs that a retired Portuguese military man, Dom Pedro Coutinho, decided to endow a college in his native city of Lisbon to prepare Englishmen to go as missionary priests to England.[46] So the opening of an English college in Lisbon was directly related to one of those illustrated books that were published in the years following Campion's death.

But there was a danger. As mentioned above, Acquaviva was aware that concentration on martyrdom might distract students from their calling as missioners, and the aim of the seminary was to provide missioners rather than martyrs.[47] There is even a hint of criticism against Campion of a lack of caution in evading capture. Certainly the ease with which many of the seminary priests were arrested shortly after landing in England did not greatly assist the mission and those Catholics who were eagerly awaiting their ministrations. Allen himself realised that the mission had to be supported by some practical measures to bring about a situation that allowed the priests to exercise their pastoral activity unimpeded. But he did not want his students to be involved in any purely

[45] See Lady Georgiana Fullerton, *The Life of Luisa de Carvajal* (London, 1873) and Camilo María Abad, *Una Misionera Española en la Inglaterra del siglo XVII: Doña Luisa de Carvajal y Mendoza 1566–1614* (Comillas, 1966).

[46] Michael E. Williams, 'The Origins of the English College Lisbon', *Recusant History* 20 (1991), pp. 478–92.

[47] Bossy, 'The Society of Jesus and the Wars of Religion', p. 234. See also his contribution to this volume, 'The Heart of Robert Persons', above.

political scheme. Their task was to preach the Gospel and in order to do this they had to be prepared for death, though not deliberately courting martyrdom.[48]

After the death of Elizabeth there was for a time a slackening off of persecution and there became apparent an aspect of Jesuit training in the seminaries that had not caught the attention of a public that had been mainly concerned with the spectacular manner of their death. Future missionaries had to be introduced to an ascetical way of life. In the seminary they were instructed in a life of contemplation and prayer that was to continue and accompany them in their missionary activity afterwards. Martyrdom was not an inevitable fate, something that would come their way with all its attendant glory because of a natural course of events. In every true martyrdom there was an element of choice and so it called for fortitude and patience and those virtues that are only the fruit of an ascetical life.[49]

This changed aspect is illustrated in another series of paintings. These are to be found in St Alban's College, Valladolid. They are paintings of former alumni associated with the college.[50] The earliest date from 1620 but these have been added to over the years. As distinct from the frescoes at the English College, Rome, these oil paintings do not set out to portray scenes of martyrdom. They are three-quarter length portraits of individuals. While it is true that in the background there is depicted an execution, a gallows or a racking, attention is focused on the main subject who is dressed according to his state as a priest or member of a religious order. It is not a realistic portrait in so far as these people would never have dressed in this way when exercising their mission in England where it was a crime to be a priest. We should also note that on their bodies there are no wounds or marks of suffering. In the oldest pictures there is no symbolic rope around the neck nor dagger piercing the breast as one commonly finds to indicate the death they endured. Each figure is given certain conventional gestures, hands joined in prayer, eyes lifted to heaven, hand on breast in a gesture of humility. Although in some cases there is a heart held in the hands, this is to be taken as a symbol of love rather than a representation of an evisceration or torture. In other words, there is a change of emphasis from the pictures in Rome. The paintings which were displayed on the walls of the seminary in Spain in the first quarter of the seventeenth century were intended to confront the students with persons like themselves, their predecessors, members of the same

---

[48] The way in which a seminary priest's cult of martyrdom could influence the behaviour of the laity is discussed by Claire Cross, 'An Elizabethan Martyrologist and his Martyr: John Mush and Margaret Clitherow,' in Diana Wood, ed., *Martyrs and Martyrologies* (Oxford, 1993), Studies in Church History 30, pp. 271–81.

[49] Michael E. Williams, 'The Ascetic Tradition and the English College Valladolid', in W.J. Sheils, ed., *Monks, Hermits and the Ascetic Tradition* (Oxford, 1985), Studies in Church History 22, pp. 275–83.

[50] Michael E. Williams, 'Images of Martyrdom in Paintings at the English College Valladolid', in M.A. Rees, ed., *Leeds Papers on Symbol and Image in Iberian Arts* (Leeds, 1994), pp. 51–71.

household. Each indicates in their portrait Christian virtues suitable to a missioner. An inscription at the bottom recalls the place of birth and religious order, the fact of being a member of the college and the place, date and manner of death. Over the head of each there is an angel holding a crown of glory and in the background a figure on a gallows, or rack or perhaps just a butcher's knife and a human heart signifying a violent death. One cannot hide the ultimate fate of the person portrayed but that is not the main object of the picture.

Eight of these early 1620 paintings are of College martyrs: Henry Walpole, S.J., Thomas Palaser, Thomas Bensted (Hunt), Mark Barkworth, O.S.B., Thomas Garnet, S.J., William Southerne and Richard Cadwallader. But there are also three others belonging to the set who are not college martyrs. It is these three alone who bear the title 'venerable' before their name. At this time none of those who had suffered during the English reformation had been raised to the altars so one cannot attach any theological signification to the title 'venerable' apart from it indicating persons worthy of great respect. But the choice of the title is interesting. The first of the three is Robert Persons, S.J., the founder of the College. He was not a martyr and so in the background there is no gallows but a group of students indicating his promotion of vocations to the priesthood. Then there is William Weston, S.J. He too was not a martyr but he was imprisoned and a former rector of the college known for his austere life and his efforts to transform the detention centre of Wisbech Castle into a religious community. He is holding a book of exorcisms and there is some scene of exorcism in the background. The third person represented is Edmund Campion, S.J., a martyr and so in the background there are the fires burning the entrails. But Campion, although a martyr, is the only one who is not an alumnus of this seminary of St Alban; in fact he died nine years before it was founded. But he had very close connections with the other two. Not only was he the companion of Persons in the 1580 mission but he was greatly admired by Weston who took as an alias the name Father Edmunds out of respect to Campion.[51] The inclusion of Weston and Persons among the martyrs reminds us that when these pictures were commissioned in the early seventeenth century it was not only to honour martyrdom but also a life of missionary activity and asceticism. There is further evidence that these three names, Campion, Persons and Weston, were held in veneration by Catholics. Fr Francisco de Peralta, the Rector of the English College in Seville, records that there was a common saying among Catholics at the beginning of the seventeenth century: 'If I spoke with the tongue of Fr Campion and wrote with the pen of Fr Persons and led the austere life of Fr Weston and had not charity it would avail me nothing.'[52]

Campion spent only a short time at Douai as a student. He visited the college

---

51 For Henry More's opinion of Weston, see *Elizabethan Jesuits*, pp. 183–87. Weston's own autobiography has been edited and translated by Philip Caraman, S.J., *The Autobiography of an Elizabethan* (London, 1955).

52 Cited in Murphy, *St Gregory's College*, p. 161.

in Rome but the other seminaries in Spain were founded several years after his death. Yet his missionary activities and martyrdom not only inspired future generations of seminary priests, but also his life and death was the occasion of a deepening of understanding of the relationship between mission and martyrdom.

BIBLIOGRAPHY

Printed primary sources

Abbot, Robert. *A Mirrour of Popish Subtilties* (London, 1594), STC 52.

Agricola, Ignaz. *Historiae Provinciae Societatis Jesu Germaniae Superioris*, 4 vols (Augsburg, 1727–46).

Agustí, V., S.J., ed. *Epistolae Mixtae ex variis Europae locis ab anno 1537 ad 1556*, 5 vols (Madrid, 1898–1901), MHSI 12, 14, 17, 18, 20.

[Alfield, Thomas]. *A true reporte of the death & martyrdome of M Campion jesuite* (n.p. n.d. [London, 1582]), ARCR II, no. 4; STC 4537.

Allen, William. *A Briefe Historie of the Glorious Martyrdom of XII Reverend Priests* (n.p. [Rheims], 1582) ARCR II, no. 7; STC 369.5. The most recent edition was edited by John H. Pollen, S.J. (Roehampton, 1908).

———. *An Apologie and True Declaration of the Institution and Endevours of the Two English Colleges* (Mons, 1581), ARCR II, no. 6; STC 369.

Arber, Edward. *A Transcript of the Registers of the Company of Stationers of London, 1554–1640*, 5 vols (London, 1875–94).

Ayre, Rev. John, ed. *The Works of John Jewel*, 4 vols (Cambridge, 1845–50), Parker Society.

Bagshaw, Christopher. *A True relation* (London, 1601), ARCR II, no. 39; STC 1188.

Bain, Joseph, *et al. Calendar of State Papers relating to Scotland and Mary Queen of Scots*, 13 vols in 14 parts (London, 1898–1969).

Baroni, Cesare. *Annales Ecclesiastici*, ed. Oderico Raynaldo and Giov. Laderchi, 37 vols (Paris, 1864–83).

Becccadelli, Ludovico. 'Vita di Reginaldo Polo' in G.B. Morandi, ed., *Monumenti di varia letteratura*, 2 vols (Bologna, 1797–1804).

Bell, Thomas. *A Christian Dialogue* (London, 1609), STC 1816.

———. *The Anatomie* (London, 1603), STC 1814.

Beza, Theodore. *Ad Tractationem de Ministrorum Evangelii Gradibus* (Geneva, 1592).

Bilson, Thomas. *The true difference betweene christian subiection and unchristian rebellion* (Oxford, 1585), STC 3071.

Birch, Thomas, ed. *Memoirs of the Reign of Queen Elizabeth*, 2 vols (London, 1754).

Bluet, Thomas. *Important Considerations* (London, 1601), ARCR II, no. 62; STC 25125.

Bolton, Richard, ed. *The Statutes of Ireland, beginning the third year of King Edward the Second* (Dublin, 1621).

Bombino, Pietro. *Vita et martyrium Edmundi Campiani* (Antwerp, 1618), ARCR I, no. 194.

Bonner, Edmund. *A profitable and necessary doctrine* (London, 1555), STC 3281.5–3283.7.

———. *Certaine homelyes* (London, 1555), STC 3285.1–3285.10.

Bristow, Richard. *A reply to Fulke* (Louvain [vere East Ham], 1580), ARCR II, no. 72; STC 3802.

Brown, Rawdon *et al. Calendar of State Papers and Manuscripts, Relating to English Affairs in the Archives and Collections of Venice*, 38 vols in 40 parts (London, 1864–1947).

Bunny, Edmund. *A booke of Christian exercise, appertaining to resolution, that is shewing how that we should resolve our selves to become Christians in deed: . . . Perused, and accompanied now with a Treatise tending to pacification* (London, 1584), STC 19355.

———. *Brief answer, vnto those idle and friuolous quarrels of R.P. against the late edition of the Resolution* (London, 1589), STC 4088.

Camm, Dom Bede, ed. *Lives of the English Martyrs*, 2 vols (London, 1904–05).

Campion, Edmund. *Rationes decem* (n.p.n.d. [Stonor Park, 1581]), ARCR II, no. 135.1; STC 4536.5.

———. *Opuscula omnia*, ed. Robert Turner (Cologne, 1625), ARCR I, no. 1269.

———. *Ambrosia*, ed. Jos. Simons (Assen, 1969).

Caponetto, Salvatore, ed. *Il Beneficio di Cristo con le versioni del secolo XVI, documenti e testimonianze* (DeKalb-Florence, 1972).

Cervós, F., S.J., ed. *Epistolae PP. Paschasii Broéti, Claudii Jaji, Joannis Codurii, et Simonis Rodericii, S.I.* (Madrid, 1903), MHSI 24.

Cervós, F., S.J., and Nicolau, M., S.J., ed. *Epistolae et Monumenta P. Hieronymi Nadal*, 5 vols (Madrid/Rome, 1898–1964), MHSI 13, 15, 21, 27, 90.

Charke, William. *An answere to a seditious pamphlet lately cast abroade by a jesuite with a discoverie of that blasphemous sect* (London, 1580), STC 5005.

Clark, Andrew, ed. *Register of the University of Oxford* (Oxford, 1887), Oxford Historical Society 10.

Crashaw, William. *The Iesuites Gospell* (London, 1621), STC 6017.

Crowley, Robert. *An Aunswer to sixe Reasons* (London, 1581), STC 6075.

Dasent, John Roche, ed., *Acts of the Privy Council of England*, 46 vols (London, 1890–1964).

Dekker, Thomas. *The Dramatic Works of Thomas Dekker*, ed. Fredson Bowers, 4 vols (Cambridge, 1953–61).

Digby, Kenelm. *A Discourse* (Amsterdam, 1652).

Dolman, R. *A Conference about the Next Succession to the Crowne of Ingland* (n.p. [Antwerp], 1594 [1595]), ARCR II, no. 167; STC 19398.

Donne, John. *Pseudo-Martyr* (London, 1610), STC 7048.

Duncan-Jones, Katherine, and J.A. van Dorsten, eds *Miscellaneous Prose of Sir Philip Sidney* (Oxford, 1973).

Dury, John. *Confutatio responsionis Gulielmi Whitakeri . . . ad Rationes decem . . .* (Paris, 1582), ARCR I, no. 334.

Ecclesiae Anglicanae Trophaea (Rome, 1584), ARCP II, nos. 944–946.

Ely, Humphrey. *Certaine briefe notes upon a briefe apologie* (Paris, 1602), ARCR I, no. 187; STC 7628.

Emden, A.B. *A Biographical Register of the University of Oxford A.D. 1501 to 1540* (Oxford, 1974).

Featley, Daniel. *The Fisher Catched in his owne Net* (London, 1623), STC 10732.

Feuillerat, Albert, ed. *The Complete Works of Sir Philip Sidney*, 4 vols (Cambridge, 1912–26, repr. 1962).

Firpo, Massimo, and Dario, Marcatto, eds *Il processo inquisitoriale del Cardinal Giovanni Morone*, 5 vols (Rome, 1981–89).

FitzSimon, Henry. *The Justification* (Douai, 1611), ARCR II, no. 290; STC 11026.

Forbes-Leith, William, S.J., ed. *Narratives of Scottish Catholics under Mary Stuart and James VI* (Edinburgh, 1885).

French, Nicholas. *The dolefull Fall* (n.p. [Louvain?], 1674).

Frere, W.H., and W.M. Kennedy *Visitation Articles and Injunctions* (London, 1910).

Fulke, William. *A briefe Confutation* (London, 1581), STC 11421.

Garnet, Henry. *A Treatise* (n.p., 1593), ARCR II, no. 322; STC 11617.8.

Gee, John. *The Foot out of the Snare* (fourth edition, London, 1624), STC 11704.

Gerard, John. *The Autobiography of an Elizabethan*, ed. Philip Caraman, S.J. (London, 1951).

Gibbons, John. *Concertatio ecclesiae Catholicae in Anglia* (Trier, 1583), ARCR I, nos. 524–530.

Gibson, Strickland, ed. *Statuta antiqua universitatis oxoniensis* (Oxford, 1931).

de Granada, Luis. *The sinners guide: a worke contayning the whole regiment of a Christian life*, trans. Francis Meres (1598).

———. *Of prayer and meditation* (Rouen, 1584), ARCR II, no. 444.

———. *A memoriall of a Christian life* (Rouen, 1586), ARCR II, no. 439.

Gross, Jorge Calvar, *et al. La Batala del Mar Océano. Corpus Documental de las Hostilidades entre España e Inglaterra (1568–1604)*, 3 vols (Madrid, 1988–1993).

Hanmer, Meredith. *The great bragge and challenge of M. Champion a jesuite* (London, 1581), STC 12745.

Hardy, Thomas Duffus. *Report . . . Upon the Documents in the Archives and Public Libraries of Venice* (London, 1866).

Hicks, Leo, S.J., ed. *Letters and Memorials of Father Robert Persons, S.J.* (London, 1942), CRS 39.

———. *Letters of Thomas Fitzherbert* (London, 1948), CRS 41.

Hide, Thomas. *Consolatorie Epistle* (Louvain [vere East Ham], 1580), ARCR II, nos. 430, 431; STC 13376, 13377.

Historical Manuscripts Commission. *Report on the Manuscripts of Lord De L'Isle and Dudley, preserved at Penshurst Place*, 6 vols (London, 1925–1966).

———. *Calendar of the Manuscripts of the Most Hon. the Marquis of Salisbury preserved at Hatfield House*, 24 vols (London, 1883–1976).

———. *Various Collections*, 8 vols (London, 1901–1914).

Hogan, Edmund, S.J., ed. *Words of Comfort* (Dublin, 1881).

Holinshed, Raphael. *The first and second volumes of chronicles* (London, 1586), STC 13569.

Hughes, Paul L., and James F. Larkin, C.S.V., eds *Tudor Royal Proclamations*, 3 vols (New Haven, 1964–69).

Hughey, Ruth, ed. *The Arundel Harington Manuscript of Tudor Poetry*, 2 vols (Columbus, Ohio, 1960).

Hume, Martin A.S. *Calendar of letters and papers . . . preserved principally in the archives of Simancas*, 4 vols (London, 1892–99).

Humphrey, Laurence. *Iesuitismi pars prima: sive de praxi Romanae curiae contra respublicas et principes, et de nova legatione Iesuitarum in Angliam* (London, 1582), STC 13961.

———. *Iesuitismi pars secunda: Puritanopapismi, seu doctrinae iesuiticae* (London, 1584), STC 13962.

James I. *An Apologie for the Oath of Allegiance . . . Together with a Premonition* (London, 1609), STC 14401.

Jewel, John. *An apologie or aunswer in defence of the Church of England* (London, 1562), STC 14590.

Kenny, Anthony, ed. *The Responsa Scholarum of the English College, Rome*, 2 vols (London, 1962–63), CRS 54, 55.

Ketley, Joseph, ed. *Two Liturgies . . . of the reign of Edward VI* (Cambridge, 1844). Parker Society.

Kidd, B.J, ed. *Documents Illustrative of the Continental Reformation* (Oxford, 1911).

King, E.J., ed. *Six Documents Relating to Queen Mary's Restoration of the Grand Priories of England and Ireland* [London, n. d.], Order of St John of Jerusalem, Historical Pamphlets, no. 7.

Kingdon, Robert W., ed. *'The Execution of Justice in England' By William Cecil and 'A True, sincere, and Modest Defence of English Catholics' By William Allen* (Ithaca, N.Y., 1965).

Knox, Thomas Francis, ed. *The Letters and Memorials of William Cardinal Allen* (London, 1882).

———. *The First and Second Diaries of the English College, Douay* (London, 1878).

Laud, William. *Works*, 7 vols in 9 (Oxford, 1847–60), Library of Anglo-Catholic Theology.

Law, Thomas Graves, ed. *A Historical Sketch of the Conflicts between Jesuits and Seculars in the Reign of Queen Elizabeth* (London, 1889).

Lecina, M., S.J., V. Agustí, S.J., and D. Restrepo, S.J., eds *Sancti Ignatii de Loyola Societatis Iesu Fundatoris Epistolae et Instructiones*, 12 vols (Madrid, 1903–11), MHSI 22, 26, 28, 29, 31, 33, 34, 36, 37, 39, 40, 42.

Lemon, Robert, *et al. Calendar of State Papers, Domestic Series of the Reigns of Edward VI . . .*, 12 vols (London, 1856–1872).

Le Plat, Josse. *Monumentorum ad Historiam Concilii Tridentini*, 7 vols (Louvain, 1781–87).

Lloyd, Charles, ed. *Formularies of the Faith* (Oxford, 1825).

Loarte, Gaspar, S.J. *The exercise of a Christian life* trans. Stephen Brinkley (London, 1579), ARCR II, no. 63; STC 16641.5.

Loomie, Albert J., S.J., ed. *Spain and the Jacobean Catholics*, 2 vols (London, 1973, 1978), CRS 64, 68.

Loyola, Ignatius. *The Autobiography of St Ignatius Loyola* ed. John C. Olin, trans. J.F. O'Callahan (New York, 1974).

———. *Letters of St Ignatius of Loyola*, ed. and trans. William. J. Young, S.J. (Chicago, 1959).

Lutz, Heinrich, ed. *Nuntiaturberichte aus Deutschland. Erste Abteilung 1533–1559*, 15. Band, *Friedenslegation des Reginald Pole zu Kaiser Karl V. und König Heinrich II. (1553–1556)* (Tübingen, 1981).

———. *Nuntiaturberichte aus Deutschland 1533–1559 nebst ergänzenden Aktenstücke*, 14, *Nuntiatur des Girolamo Muzzarelli Sendung des Antonio Agustin Legation des Scipione Rebiba* (Tübingen, 1971).

McCann, Dom Justin, O.S.B., and Dom Hugh Connolly, O.S.B. 'Fr Leander Prichard's Life [of Father Baker]', in *Memorials of Father Augustine Baker* (London, 1933), CRS 33, pp. 53–154.

McCoog, Thomas M., S.J., ed. *Monumenta Angliae*, 2 vols (Rome, 1992), MHSI 142, 143.

———. ed. *English and Welsh Jesuits, 1555–1650*, 2 vols (London, 1994–95), CRS 74, 75.

———. ed. 'The Letters of Robert Southwell, S.J.', *AHSI* 63 (1994), pp. 101–24.

Manzoni, Giacomo, ed. 'Il Processo Carnesecchi', *Miscellanea di storia italiana* 10 (1870), pp. 189–573.

Miller, Liam and Power, Eileen, ed. *Holinshed's Irish Chronicle 1577* (Dublin, 1979).

More, Henry, S.J. *Historia Provinciae Anglicanae Societatis Jesu* (St Omer, 1660).

——. *The Elizabethan Jesuits: Historia Missionis Anglicanae Societatis Jesu (1660)*, translated and edited by Francis Edwards, S.J. (London, 1981).

Munday, Anthony. *A breefe answer made unto two seditious pamphlets* (London, 1582), STC 18262.

Murner, Thomas. *Von dem grossen Lutherischen Narren*, ed. Paul Merker, in *Thomas Murners Deutsche Schriften mit den Holzschnitten der Erstdrucke* ed. Franz Schultz *et al.* (Strasbourg, 1918).

Murphy, Martin. *St Gregory's College, Seville, 1592–1767* (London, 1992), CRS 73.

Nashe, Thomas. *Works of Thomas Nashe*, ed. R.B. McKerrow, 5 vols, 2nd edn (Oxford, 1966).

Neve, Timothy. *Animadversions upon Mr Phillips's History of the Life of Cardinal Pole* (Oxford, 1766).

Nichols, John Gough, ed. *The Diary of Henry Machyn* (London, 1848) Camden Society 42.

Nowell, Alexander and Day, William. *A true report of the Disputation or rather private Conference had in the Tower of London, with Ed. Campion Iesuite, the last of August 1581* and *The three last dayes conferences had in the Tower with Edmund Campion Iesuite, the 18: 23 and 27 of September 1581* (London, 1583), STC 18744.

Official Presentation of Documents on the Martyrdom and Cult of 40 Blessed Martyrs. Sacred Congregation of Rites, Historical Section 148 (Vatican City, 1968).

Pears, Steuart A., ed. *The Correspondence of Sir Philip Sidney and Hubert Languet* (London, 1845).

Peck, Dwight C. ed. *Leicester's Commonwealth: 'The Copy of a Letter Written by a Master of Art of Cambridge' (1584) and Related Documents* (Athens, Ohio, 1985).

Persons, Robert. *The first booke of the Christian exercise, appertayning to resolution* (Rouen, 1582), ARCR II, no. 616; STC 19353.

——. *A Christian directorie guiding men to their salvation* (Rouen, 1585), ARCR II, no. 618; STC 19354.1.

——. *A brief discours contayning certayne reasons why Catholiques refuse to goe to church* (Doway [vere London], 1580), ARCR II, no. 613; STC 19394.

——. *A brief censure vppon two bookes written in answere to M. Edmonde Campions offer of disputation* (Douay [vere London], 1581), ARCR II, no. 612; STC 19393.

——. *A discoverie of J. Nicols minister* (n.p. n.d. [Stonor Park, 1581]), ARCR II, no. 625; STC 19402.

——. *The Christian directory guiding men to eternall saluation* (St Omer, 1607), ARCR II, no. 620; STC 19354.5.

——. *A Christian directory, guiding men to eternall saluation* (St Omer, 1622), ARCR II, no. 622; STC 19354.7.

——. 'Of the Life and Martyrdom of Father Edmond Campian', *Letters and Notices* 11 (1877), pp. 219–42, 308–39; 12 (1878), pp. 1–68.

——. *A Temperate Ward-Word* (Antwerp, 1599), ARCR II, no. 637; STC 19415.

——. *A Review of Ten Publike Disputations* (St Omer, 1604), ARCR II, no. 636; STC 19414.

————. *The Jesuits Memorial, for the Intended Reformation of England*, ed. Edward Gee (London, 1690).

————. *A defence of the Censure, gyven upon two bookes of William Charke and Meredith Hanmer, mynysters* (n.p. [Rouen], 1582), ARCR II, no. 624; STC 19401.

Pocock, Nicholas, ed. *The History of the Reformation of the Church of England by Gilbert Burnet*, 7 vols (Oxford, 1865).

Pole, Reginald. *Reginaldi Poli ad Henricum octavum Britanniae regem, pro ecclesiasticae unitatis defensione* (Rome, 1539).

Pollen, John H., S.J., ed. 'The Notebook of John Southcote, D.D. 1628–36', in *Miscellanea I* (London, 1905), CRS 1, pp. 97–116.

————. 'Memoirs of Father Robert Persons, S.J.', in *Miscellanea II* (London, 1906), CRS 2, pp. 12–218.

————. 'Official Lists of Prisoners for Religion from 1562–80', in *Miscellanea II* (London, 1906), CRS 2, pp. 219–88.

————. 'Notes Concerning the English Mission', in *Miscellanea IV* (London, 1907), CRS 4, pp. 1–161.

————. *Unpublished Documents Relating to the English Martyrs (1584–1603)* (London, 1908), CRS 5.

————. *Campion's Ten Reasons* (London, 1914).

————. 'Recusants and Priests, March 1588', in *Miscellanea XII* (London, 1921), pp. 120–29, CRS 22.

————. *Queen Mary and the Babington Plot* (Edinburgh, 1922), Publications of the Scottish History Society, 3rd series, 3.

————. 'Memoirs of Father William Crichton, S.J. 1584–1589', *The Month* 139 (1922), pp. 317–24.

———— and Richard Challoner D.D., *Memoirs of Missionary Priests* (London, 1924).

———— and MacMahon, William, S.J., eds *The Venerable Philip Howard, Earl of Arundel, 1557–1595* (London, 1919), CRS 21.

Querini, A.M., ed. *Epistolarum Reginaldi Poli*, 5 vols (Brescia, 1744–57).

Ralegh, Sir Walter. *A Religious and Dutifull Advice of a loving Sonne to his Aged Father* (n.p. [London], 1632), STC 20642 and 156.

Renold, Penelope, ed., *The Wisbech Stirs (1595–1598)* (London, 1958), CRS 51.

————. *Letters of William Allen and Richard Barret, 1572–1598* (London, 1967), CRS 58.

Restrepo, D., S.J., ed. *Bobadillae Monumenta* (Madrid, 1913), MHSI 46.

Roberts, George, ed., *Diary of Walter Yonge* (London, 1848), Camden Society, first series, 41.

Robinson, Hastings, ed. *Original Letters Relative to the English Reformation*, 2 vols (Cambridge, 1846–47), Parker Society.

Roper, William. *The Life of Sir Thomas More*, ed. S.W. Singer (London, 1822).

Rupp, E. Gordon, ed. *Luther and Erasmus; Free Will and Salvation* (London, 1969), Library of Christian Classics.

Ryan, Patrick, S.J., ed. 'Some Correspondence of Cardinal Allen 1579–85', in *Miscellanea VII* (London, 1911), CRS 9, pp. 12–105.

Saravia, Hadrian. *Defensio Tractationis de Diversis Ministrorum Evangelii gradibus* (London, 1594), STC 21748.

Schmidl, Joannes. *Historiae Societatis Jesu Provinciae Bohemiae*, 2 vols (Prague, 1747–49).

de Selva, Rasiel (vere Pierre Quesnel, Quesnell of Dieppe, or Charles Gabriel Porée?). *The History of the Wonderful Don Ignatius de Loyola*, 2 vols (London, 1754).

Sheldon, Richard. *The Motives* (London, 1612), STC 22397.

Silos, Giuseppe. *Historiarum clericorum regularium*, 3 vols (Rome, 1650–66).

Skretkowicz, Victor, ed. *The Countess of Pembroke's Arcadia (The New Arcadia)* (Oxford, 1987).

Southwell, Robert, S.J. *Robert Southwell, S.J.: Two Letters and 'Short Rules of a Good Life'*, ed. Nancy Pollard Brown (Charlottesville, Virginia, 1973).

———. *The Poems of Robert Southwell, S.J.*, ed. James H. McDonald and Nancy Pollard Brown (Oxford, 1967).

———. *Spiritual Exercises and Devotions of Blessed Robert Southwell, S.J.*, ed. J.M. de Buck, S.J., trans. P.E. Hallett (London, 1931).

———. *Short Rule of Good Life* (n.p. n.d. [London, 1597?]), ARCR II, no. 721; STC 22968.5.

———. *Saint Peters Complaint, With other Poemes* (n.p. [London], 1595), STC 22955.7.

———. *The Triumphs over Death* (n.p. [London], 1595), STC 22971.

———. *Saincte PETERs Complainte with MARY MAGDALENs blusshe and her Complaint at CHRISTes deathe with other poemes* (n.p. [London], 1595), STC 22956, 22958 and 22959.

———. *An Epistle of Comfort, to the Reverend Priestes, and to the Honorable, Worshipful, and other of the Laye sort restrayned in Durance for the Catholicke Fayth* (Paris, n.d. [vere London, 1587–88]), ARCR II, no. 714; STC 22946.

———. *Marie Magdalens funeral teares* (n.p. [London], 1591), STC 29950.

Spedding, James, R.L. Ellis, and D.D. Heath, eds, *The Works of Francis Bacon*, 14 vols (London, 1858–74).

Starkey, Thomas. *A Dialogue between Pole and Lupset*, ed. T.F. Mayer (London, 1989), Camden Fourth Series, no. 37.

Steen, F.W., ed. *The Life of St Philip Howard* (London, 1857, revised edn 1971).

Stevenson, Joseph, S.J., ed. *Henry Clifford: The Life of Jane Dormer, Duchess of Feria* (London, 1887).

———, et al. *Calendar of State Papers Foreign Series of the Reign of Elizabeth*, 23 vols in 26 (London, 1863–1950).

Strype, John, ed. *Ecclesiastical Memorials*, 3 vols (Oxford, 1721).

———. *Annals of the Reformation and Establishment of Religion*, 4 vols (Oxford, 1820–1840).

Sweet, John. *Monsig' fate voi* (St Omer, 1617), ARCR II, no. 739; STC 23529.

Tanner, Norman, S.J., ed. *Decrees of the Ecumenical Councils*, 2 vols (London and Washington D.C., 1990).

Tellechea Idígoras, J.I. *Fray Bartolomé Carranza. Documentos historicos*, 2 (Madrid, 1963).

———. *Fray Bartolomé Carranza. Documentos historicos* 3 (Madrid, 1966).

Theiner, Augustin, ed. *Annales Ecclesiastici*, 3 vols (Rome, 1856).

Tierney, M.A., ed., *Dodd's Church History of England*, 5 vols (London, 1839–43).

Turner, William H., ed. *Selections from the Records of the City of Oxford Henry VIII to Elizabeth I [1509–1583]* (Oxford, 1880).

Tyler, Royall, et al. *Calendar of State Papers Spanish*, 15 vols in 20 (London, 1862–1954).

Tynley, Robert. *Two Learned Sermons* (London, 1609), STC 24472.

Velez, J.M., S.J., and V. Agusti, S.J., eds *Vita Ignatii Loiolae et rerum Societatis Iesu historia auctore Joanne Alphonso de Polanco*, 6 vols (Madrid, 1894–98), MHSI 1, 3, 5, 7, 9, 11.

Verstegan, Richard. *Theatrum Crudelitatum Haereticorum Nostri Temporis* (Antwerp, 1587), ARCR II, no. 1297.

Vossen, A.F., ed. *Two Bokes of the Histories of Ireland compiled by Edmund Campion* (Assen, 1963).

Walker, George. *The Summe of a Disputation* (London, 1624), STC 24960.

Walsingham, Francis. *A Search* (St Omer, 1609), ARCR II, no. 785; STC 25002.

Ware, James, ed. *The historie of Ireland, collected by three learned authors, viz. Meredith Hanmer, Edmund Campion and Edmund Spenser* (Dublin, 1633). *Ancient Irish Histories: the works of Spencer, Campion, Hanmer and Marleburrough* 2 vols (Dublin, 1809).

Watson, Thomas. *Holesome and catholyke doctryne* (London, 1558), STC 25112–14.

Watson, William. *A Decacordon* (London, 1602), ARCR II, no. 794; STC 25123.

Webbe, George. *Catalogus Protestantium* (London, 1624), STC 25160.7.

Weston, William. *The Autobiography of an Elizabethan*, trans. and ed. Philip Caraman, S.J. (London, 1955).

Whitaker, William. *Ad rationes decem Edmundi Campiani Iesuitae* (London, 1581), STC 25358.

———. *An answere to the ten reasons of Edmund Campion the Iesuit* (London, 1606), STC 25360.

———. *Responsionis ad decem illas rationes . . . Defensio contra Confutationem Ioannis Duraei Scoti, Presbyteri Iesuitae . . .* (London, 1583), STC 23562.

White, John. *The Way to the True Church* (London, 1616), STC 25397.

Willet, Andrew. *An Antilogie* (London, 1603), STC 25672.

Worthington, Thomas. *A Relation* (Douai, 1601), ARCR II, no. 847; STC 26000.9.

Wright, Thomas, ed. *Queen Elizabeth and Her Times*, 2 vols (London, 1838).

Yaxley, Henry. *Morbus et Antidotus* (London, 1630), STC 26090.

Yepes, Diego de. *Historia particular de la Persecucion de Inglaterra* (Madrid, 1599), ARCR I, no. 284.

A Manual or Meditation (Douai, n.d. [vere England], [1580–81]), ARCR II, nos. 664.3, 664.5; STC 17278.4, 17278.5.

Secondary sources

Abad, Camilo María. *Una Misionera Española en la Inglaterra del siglo XVII: Doña Luisa de Carvajal y Mendoza 1566–1614* (Comillas, 1966).

Allison, A.F. 'The Writings of Fr Henry Garnet, S.J. (1555–1606)', *Biographical Studies* (now *Recusant History*) 1 (1951), pp. 7–21.

——— and D.M. Rogers, *The Contemporary Printed Literature of the English Counter-Reformation between 1558 and 1640*, 2 vols (Aldershot, 1989, 1994).

Anstruther, Godfrey. *The Seminary Priests*, 4 vols (Ware/Durham/Great Wakering, 1968–77).

Aries, Philippe. *The Hour of Our Death*, trans. H. Weaver (London, 1981).

Aubenas, Roger and Robert Richard. *L'Église et la Renaissance (1449–1517)* (Paris, 1951), vol. 15 in Augustin Fliche and Victor Martin, eds, *Histoire de l'Église depuis les origines jusqu'à nos jours*, 21 vols and Supplément (Paris, 1938–1964).

Aveling, J.C.H. *Northern Catholics* (London, 1966).

———. *The Handle and the Axe: The Catholic Recusant in England from the Reformation to Emancipation* (London, 1976).

————. *The Jesuits* (London, 1981).

————. 'The English Clergy in the 16th and 17th Centuries', in J.C.H. Aveling, D.M. Loades, H.R. McAdoo and W. Haase, *Rome and the Anglicans* (Berlin, 1982), pp. 55–142.

Aylmer, Gerald. 'The Economics and Finances of the Colleges and University c. 1530–1640', in James McConica, ed., *The Collegiate University. The History of the University of Oxford* vol. 3 (Oxford, 1986), pp. 521–58.

Bainton, Roland. *Here I Stand: Martin Luther* (Tring, 1983 edn).

Bangert, William V., S.J. *A History of the Society of Jesus* (St. Louis, 1972).

————. *Claude Jay and Alfonso Salmerón* (Chicago, 1985).

————. *Jerome Nadal, S. J. 1507–1580. Tracking the First Generation of Jesuits* (Chicago, 1992).

Barton, John. 'The Faculty of Law', in James McConica, ed., *The Collegiate University. The History of the University of Oxford* vol. 3 (Oxford, 1986), pp. 257–83.

————. 'The King's Readers', in James McConica, ed., *The Collegiate University. The History of the University of Oxford* vol. 3 (Oxford, 1986), pp. 285–93.

Basset, Bernard, S.J. *The English Jesuits* (London, 1967).

Beales, A.C.F. *Education Under Penalty* (London, 1963).

Benedict, Philip. *Rouen during the Wars of Religion* (Cambridge, 1981).

Black, J.B. *The Reign of Elizabeth*, 2nd edn (Oxford, 1959).

Blomefield, Francis. *A Topographical History of of the County of Norfolk*, 11 vols (London, 1805–1810).

Bonelli, Giuseppe. 'Un archivio privato del Cinquecento: le Carte Stella', *Archivio storico Lombardo* 34 (1907), pp. 332–86.

Bossy, John. *The English Catholic Community, 1570–1850* (London, 1975).

————. 'English Catholics and the French Marriage 1577–1581', *Recusant History* 5 (1959), pp. 2–16.

————. 'The Character of Elizabethan Catholicism', *Past and Present* 21 (1962), pp. 39–59. Reprinted in Trevor Aston, ed., *Crisis in Europe, 1560–1660* (London, 1965), pp. 235–60.

————. 'The Counter Reformation and the People of Catholic Europe', *Past and Present* 47 (1970), pp. 51–70.

————. 'The English Catholic Community 1603–1625', in Alan G.R. Smith, ed., *The Reign of James VI and I* (London, 1973), pp. 91–105.

————. 'The Society of Jesus in the Wars of Religion', in *Monastic Studies: The Continuity of Tradition*, ed. Judith Loades (Bangor, 1990), pp. 229–44.

————. 'Unrethinking the Sixteenth-Century Wars of Religion', in Thomas Kselman, ed., *Belief in History: Innovative Approaches to European and American Religion* (Notre Dame/London, 1991), pp. 267–85.

Bradshaw, Brendan. *The Irish Constitutional Revolution of the Sixteenth Century* (Cambridge, 1979).

Brady, Ciaran. *The Chief Governors: The Rise and Fall of Reform Government in Ireland* (Cambridge, 1995).

————. 'The Killing of Shane O'Neill: Some New Evidence', *The Irish Sword* 15 (1982), pp. 116–23.

————. ' "Conservative Subversives": The Community of the Pale and the Dublin Administration, 1556–86' in P.J. Corish, ed., *Radicals, Rebels and Establishments: Historical Studies XV* (Belfast, 1985), pp. 11–32.

Brassell, P.V., S.J. *Praeformatio reformationis tridentinae de seminario clericorum* (Roehampton, 1938).

Brigden, Susan. *London and the Reformation* (Oxford, 1989).

Brodrick, James, S.J. *Saint Peter Canisius* (London, 1963 edn).

Brown, Nancy Pollard. 'Paperchase: The Dissemination of Catholic Texts in Elizabethan England', in *English Manuscript Studies, 1100–1700*, ed. Peter Beal and Jeremy Griffiths (Oxford, 1989), I, pp. 120–43.

Buxton, John. *Sir Philip Sidney and the English Renaissance* 2nd edn (London, 1964).

Cameron, Euan. *The European Reformation* (Oxford, 1991).

Campion, Leslie. *The Family of Edmund Campion* (London, 1975).

Canny, Nicholas. *The Elizabethan Conquest of Ireland: A Pattern Established, 1565–76* (Hassocks, 1976).

———. *From Reformation to Restoration: Ireland, 1534–1660* (Dublin, 1987).

Caraman, Philip, S.J. *Henry Garnet (1565–1606) and the Gunpowder Plot* (London, 1964).

———. 'Campion at St John's', *Letters and Notices* 92 (1995), pp. 212–24.

Carrafiello, Michael L. '*Rebus Sic Stantibus* and English Catholicism, 1606–1610', *Recusant History* 22 (1994), pp. 29–40.

———. 'English Catholicism and the Jesuit Mission of 1580–1581', *Historical Journal* 37 (1994), pp. 761–74.

Carro, Venancio D. *El Maestro Fr Pedro de Soto, O. P. y Las controversias politico-teológicas en el siglo XVI* 2 vols (Salamanca, 1931, 1950).

Catto, J.I. 'Wyclif and Wycliffism at Oxford 1356–1430', in J.I. Catto and Ralph Evans, eds, *Late Medieval Oxford, The History of the University of Oxford*, vol. 2 (Oxford, 1992), pp. 175–261.

———. 'Theology after Wycliffism', in J.I. Catto and Ralph Evans, eds, *Late Medieval Oxford, The History of the University of Oxford*, vol. 2 (Oxford, 1992), pp. 263–80.

Chadwick, Hubert, S.J. 'Father William Creichton S.I. and a recently discovered letter (1589)', *AHSI* 6 (1937), pp. 259–86.

de Chastonay, Paul, S.J. *Les Constitutions de l'ordre des Jésuites* (Paris, 1941).

Clancy, Thomas H., S.J. *Papist Pamphleteers* (Chicago, 1964).

———. *English Catholic Books 1641–1700: A Bibliography* (Chicago, 1974).

———. *An Introduction to Jesuit Life* (St Louis, 1976).

———. 'The First Generation of English Jesuits', *AHSI* 57 (1988), pp. 137–62.

———. 'Spiritual Publications of English Jesuits, 1615–1640', *Recusant History* 19 (1989), pp. 426–46.

Cohn, Norman. *The Pursuit of the Millennium* (London, 1957).

Collett, Barry. *Italian Benedictine Scholars and the Reformation: The Congregation of Santa Giustina of Padua* (Oxford, 1985).

Collinson, Patrick. 'If Constantine, then also Theodosius: St Ambrose and the Integrity of the Elizabethan *Ecclesia Anglicana*', in Patrick Collinson, *Godly People: Essays on English Protestantism and Puritanism* (London, 1983), pp. 109–33.

Colthorpe, Marion. 'Edmund Campion's Alleged Interview with Queen Elizabeth in 1581', *Recusant History* 17 (1985), pp. 197–200.

Colvin, Christina. 'Roman Catholicism', in Alan Crossley, ed., *A History of the County of Oxford* (Oxford, 1979), pp. 412–15.

da Costa, Manuel, S.J. 'The Last Years of a Confessor of the Faith: Father David Wolf', *AHSI* 15 (1946), pp. 127–43.

Cox, Virginia. *Renaissance Dialogue* (Cambridge, 1992).

Crehan, Joseph H., S.J. 'Saint Ignatius and Cardinal Pole', *AHSI* 25 (1956), pp. 72–98.

Cross, Claire. 'Oxford and the Tudor State from the Accession of Henry VIII to the death of Mary', in James McConica, ed., *The Collegiate University. The History of the University of Oxford* vol. 3 (Oxford, 1986), pp. 117–49.

———. 'An Elizabethan Martyrologist and his Martyr: John Mush and Margaret Clitherow', in Diana Wood, ed., *Martyrs and Martyrologies* (Oxford, 1993), Studies in Church History 30, pp. 271–81.

Devlin, Christopher, S.J. *The Life of Robert Southwell: Poet and Martyr* (London, 1956).

Dickens, A.G. *The English Reformation*, 2nd edn (London, 1989).

———. 'Robert Parkyn's Narrative of the Reformation', *English Historical Review* 62 (1947), pp. 58–83.

———. 'The First Stages of Romanist Recusancy in Yorkshire', *Yorkshire Archeological Journal* 35 (1943), pp. 157–82.

Dobson, R.B. 'The Religious Orders 1370–1540', in J.I. Catto and Ralph Evans, eds, *Late Medieval Oxford. The History of the University of Oxford* vol. 2 (Oxford, 1992), pp. 539–79.

Driscoll, J.P., S.J. 'The Supposed Source of Persons's "Christian Directory" ', *Recusant History* 5 (1959–60), pp. 236–45.

von Druffel, August. 'Die Sendung des Cardinals Sfondrato an den Hof Karls V, 1547–1548', *Abhandlung der historischer Classe der königlicher Bayerischer Akademie der Wissenschaften* 20, Abt. 2 (1893), pp. 292–362.

Duffy, Eamon. *The Stripping of the Altars* (New Haven, 1992).

———. 'William, Cardinal Allen, 1532–1594', *Recusant History* 22 (1995), pp. 265–90.

Duncan, G.D. 'The Heads of Houses and Religious Change in Tudor Oxford 1547–1558', *Oxoniensia* 45 (1980), pp. 226–34.

———. 'Public Lectures and Professorial Chairs', in James McConica, ed., *The Collegiate University. The History of the University of Oxford* vol. 3 (Oxford, 1986), pp. 335–61.

Duncan-Jones, Katherine. *Sir Philip Sidney: Courtier Poet* (New Haven/London 1991).

Edwards, Francis, S.J. *The Jesuits in England* (London, 1985).

———. *Robert Persons: The Biography of an Elizabethan Jesuit 1546–1610* (St. Louis, 1995).

Edwards, R. Dudley. 'Ireland, Elizabeth I and the Counter-Reformation', in S.T. Bindoff, Joel Hurstfield, and C.H. Williams, eds, *Elizabethan Government and Society: Essays Presented to Sir John Neale* (London, 1961), pp. 315–39.

Ellis, Steven. *Tudor Ireland: Crown and Community and the Conflict of Cultures, 1470–1603* (London, 1985).

———. *Reform and Renewal: English Government in Ireland, 1470–1534* (London, 1985).

Elton, G.R. *The Parliament of England 1559–1581* (Cambridge, 1986).

Emden, A.B. *An Oxford Hall in Medieval Times* (Oxford, 1927).

Evans, G.R. *Problems of Authority in the Reformation Debates* (Cambridge, 1992).

Evans, T.A.R. 'The Number, Origins and Careers of Scholars', in J.I. Catto and Ralph Evans, eds, *Late Medieval Oxford. The History of the University of Oxford*, vol. 2 (Oxford, 1992), pp. 485–538.

Evennett, H. Outram. *The Spirit of the Counter Reformation* (Cambridge, 1968).

Fenlon, Dermot. *Heresy and Obedience in Tridentine Italy: Cardinal Pole and the Counter-Reformation* (Cambridge, 1972).

Flynn, Dennis. 'The English Mission of Jasper Heywood, S.J.', *AHSI* 54 (1985), pp. 45–76.

Firpo, Massimo. *Tra alumbrados e 'spirituali'. Studi su Juan de Valdés e il Valdesianesimo nella crisi religiosa del '500 italiano* (Florence, 1990).

———. 'Gli "spirituali", l'Accademia di Modena e il formulario di fede del 1542: controllo del dissenso religioso e nicodemismo', in *Inquisizione romana e controriforma. Studi sul Giovanni Morone e il suo processo d'eresia* (Bologna, 1992), pp. 9–118.

———. 'Il primo processo inquisitoriale contro il cardinal Giovanni Morone (1552–53)', in *Inquisizione romana e controriforma. Studi sul Giovanni Morone e il suo processo d'eresia* (Bologna, 1992), pp. 177–260.

Fisher, Arthur L. 'A Study in Early Jesuit Government: The Nature and Origins of the Dissent of Nicolás Bobadilla', *Viator* 10 (1979), pp. 397–431.

Foley, Henry, S.J. *Records of the English Province of the Society of Jesus*, 7 vols in 8 (Roehampton/London, 1875–83).

Foster, Michael. 'Thomas Allen, Gloucester Hall and the Survival of Catholicism in Post-Reformation Oxford', *Oxoniensia* 46 (1981), pp. 99–128.

Fouqueray, Henri, S.J. *Histoire de la Compagnie de Jésus en France*, 5 vols (Paris, 1910–25).

Fowler, Thomas. *The History of Corpus Christi College* (Oxford, 1898), Oxford Historical Society 25.

Fragnito, Gigliola. 'Aspetti della censura ecclesiastica nell'Europa della controriforma: L'edizione parigina delle opere di Gasparo Contarini', *Rivista di storia e letteratura religiosa* 21 (1985), pp. 3–48.

Frere, W.H. *The Marian Reaction in its Relation to the English Clergy* (London, 1896).

Fülop-Miller, René. *The Power and Secret of the Jesuits* (London, 1930).

Fullerton, Lady Georgina. *The Life of Luisa de Carvajal* (London, 1873).

Gee, Henry. *The Elizabethan Clergy and the Settlement of Religion* (Oxford, 1898).

Gillow, Joseph. *Biographical Dictionary of the English Catholics*, 5 vols (London, nd [1885]).

Ginzburg, Carlo and Adriano Prosperi. *Giochi di pazienza. Un seminario sul 'Beneficio di Cristo'* (Turin, 1975).

Gleason, Elisabeth G. *Gasparo Contarini: Venice, Rome, and Reform* (Berkeley, 1993).

Gosling, Margaret. 'Berkshire and Oxfordshire Catholics and the Lenten Assize of 1588', *Oxoniensia* 58 (1993), pp. 253–62.

Grafton, Anthony and Lisa Jardine. *From Humanism to the Humanities* (London, 1986).

Graves, Michael A.R. *Thomas Norton: The Parliament Man* (Oxford, 1994).

Greengrass, Mark. 'Mary, Dowager Queen of France', *The Innes Review* 38 (1987), pp. 171–94.

Greenslade, S.L. 'The Faculty of Theology', in James McConica, ed., *The Collegiate University. The History of the University of Oxford* vol. 3 (Oxford, 1986), pp. 295–334.

Gregory, Brad S. 'The "True and Zealouse Seruice of God": Robert Parsons, Edmund Bunny, and *The First Booke of the Christian Exercise*', *Journal of Ecclesiastical History* 45 (1994), pp. 238–68.

de Guibert, Joseph, S.J. *The Jesuits: Their Spiritual Doctrine and Practice*, trans. William J. Young, 2nd edn (St Louis, 1972).

———. *The Jesuits: Their Spiritual Doctrine and Practice*, trans. William J. Young, 3rd edn (St Louis, 1986).

Guilday, Peter. *The English Catholic Refugees on the Continent, 1558–1795* (London, 1914).

Hadfield, Andrew. 'Briton and Scythian: Tudor Representations of Irish Origins', *Irish Historical Studies* 28 (1993), pp. 390–408.

Hagedorn, Maria. *Reformation und Spanische Andachtsliteratur: Luis de Granada in England* (Leipzig, 1934).

Haigh, Christopher. *English Reformations* (Oxford, 1993).

———. 'The Fall of a Church or the Rise of a Sect? Post Reformation Catholicism in England', *Historical Journal* 21 (1978), pp. 182–86.

———. 'The Continuity of Catholicism in the English Reformation', *Past and Present* 93 (1981), pp. 37–69. Reprinted in *The English Reformation Revised* (Cambridge, 1987), pp. 176–208.

———. 'From Monopoly to Minority: Catholicism in Early Modern Europe', *Transactions of the Royal Historical Society*, 5th series, 31 (1981), pp. 129–47.

———. 'The Church of England, the Catholics and the People', in Christopher Haigh, ed., *The Reign of Elizabeth* (London, 1984), pp. 195–219.

Hammer, Carl I., Jr. 'Oxford Town and Oxford University', in James McConica, ed., *The Collegiate University. The History of the University of Oxford* vol. 3 (Oxford, 1986), pp. 69–116.

Hamy, Alfred, S.J. *Province de Lyon, 1582–1762. Noms, Prenoms, Lieu d'Origine, Dates de Naissance, d'Entree, de Degre, Lieu et Date de Mort de Tous les Jesuites Demeures Fideles a Leurs Voeux jusqu'a la Fin* (Paris, 1900).

Hanson, Elizabeth. 'Torture and Truth in Renaissance England', *Representations* 34 (1991), pp. 53–84.

Hibbard, Caroline. 'Early Stuart Catholicism: Revisions and Re-Revisions', *Journal of Modern History* 52 (1980), pp. 1–34.

Hicks, Leo, S.J. *An Elizabethan Problem: Some Aspects of the Careers of Two Exile Adventurers* (London, 1964).

———. 'The Growth of a Myth: Fr Robert Persons, S.J., and *Leicester's Commonwealth*', *Studies* 46 (1957), pp. 91–105.

———. 'Father Robert Persons S.J. and *The Book of Succession*', *Recusant History* 4 (1957–58), pp. 104–37.

Hogan, Edmund, S.J., ed. *Ibernia Ignatiana, seu Ibernorum Societatis Iesu Patrum Monumenta* (Dublin, 1880).

———. 'The Blessed Edmund Campion's "History of Ireland" and its Critics', *Irish Ecclesiastical Record*, 3rd series, 12 (1891), pp. 629–41, 725–35.

Holmes, Peter. *Resistance and Compromise: The Political Thought of the Elizabethan Catholics* (Cambridge, 1982).

———. 'The Authorship and early Reception of *A Conference about the Next Succession to the Crown of England*', *Historical Journal* 23 (1980), pp. 415–29.

Houliston, Victor. 'The Fabrication of the Myth of Father Parsons', *Recusant History* 22 (1994), pp. 141–51.

Howard, Jean E. *The Stage and Social Struggle in Early Modern England* (London, 1994).

Howell, Roger. *Sir Philip Sidney: The Shepherd Knight* (London, 1968).

Hudon, William V. *Marcello Cervini and Ecclesiastical Government in Tridentine Italy* (DeKalb, Illinois, 1992).

Hudson, Elizabeth K. 'The Catholic Challenge to Puritan Piety, 1580–1620', *Catholic Historical Review* 77 (1991), pp. 1–20.

Hughes, Philip. *The Reformation in England*, 3 vols (London, 1952–54).

Hunt, Mary Leland. *Thomas Dekker: A Study* (New York, 1911).

Jedin, Hubert. *A History of the Council of Trent*, trans. E. Graf, 2 vols (London, 1957–61).

———. *Geschichte des Konzils von Trent*, vol. III (Freiburg-im-Breisgau, 1975).

Jones, John. *Balliol College: A History 1263–1939* (Oxford, 1988).

Jones, Norman L. *Faith by Statute; Parliament and the Settlement of Religion, 1559* (London, 1982).

———. *The Birth of the Elizabethan Age* (Oxford, 1993).

Jones, W.R.D. *The Mid-Tudor Crisis 1539–1563* (London, 1973).

Jordan, W.K. *Edward VI: The Young King* (London, 1968).

Kelly, Christine. *Blessed Thomas Belson, His Life and Times 1563–1589* (London, 1987).

Kenny, Anthony. 'From Hospice to College', *The Venerabile* 21 (1962), pp. 218–73.

———. 'Reform and Reaction in Elizabethan Balliol', in John Prest, ed., *Balliol Studies* (Oxford, 1982), pp. 17–51.

Knott, John R., *Discourses on Martyrdom in English Literature, 1563–1694* (Cambridge, 1993).

Knowles, Dom David. *The Religious Orders in England*, 3 vols (Cambridge, 1948–59).

Lake, Peter. 'Anti-popery: the Structure of a Prejudice', in Richard Cust and Ann Hughes, eds., *Conflict in Early Stuart England* (London, 1989), pp. 72–106.

LaRocca, John J., S.J. 'Time, Death, and the Next Generation: The Early Elizabethan Recusancy Policy 1558–1574', *Albion* 14 (1982), pp. 103–17.

Law, Thomas Graves. 'The Spanish blanks and the Catholic Earls', in P. Hume Brown, ed., *Collected Essays and Reviews of Thomas Graves Law* (Edinburgh, 1904), pp. 244–76.

Lechat, Robert. *Les Réfugiés Anglais dans les Pays-Bas Espagnols Durant le Règne d'Élisabeth* (Louvain, 1914).

Lennon, Colm. *Richard Stanihurst the Dubliner* (Dublin, 1981).

———. 'Richard Stanihurst (1547–1618) and Old English Identity', *Irish Historical Studies* 21 (1978), pp. 121–43.

Lewis, Gillian. 'The Faculty of Medicine', in James McConica, ed., *The Collegiate University. The History of the University of Oxford* vol. 3 (Oxford, 1986), pp. 213–56.

Litzenberger, Caroline. 'Richard Cheyney, Bishop of Gloucester: An Infidel in Religion?', *Sixteenth Century Journal* 25 (1994), pp. 567–84.

Loach, Jennifer. *Parliament and the Crown in the Reign of Mary Tudor* (Oxford, 1986).

———. 'Reformation Controversies', in James McConica, ed., *The Collegiate University. The History of the University of Oxford* vol. 3 (Oxford, 1986), pp. 363–96.

Loades, David. *The Reign of Mary Tudor: Politics, Government and Religion in England 1553–1558* (London, 1979); 2nd edition (London and New York, 1991).

———. *Mary Tudor: A Life* (Oxford, 1989).

———. *Essays on the Reign of Edward VI* (Bangor, 1994).

———. 'The Piety of the Catholic Restoration in England, 1553–58', in *Humanism and Reform: the Church in Europe, England and Scotland, 1400–1640*, ed. James Kirk (Oxford, 1992), Studies in Church History Subsidia 8, pp. 289–304.

Loomie, Albert J., S.J. *The Spanish Elizabethans* (New York, 1963).

———. 'The Armadas and the Catholics of England', *The Catholic Historical Review* 59 (1973), pp. 385–403.

Lynch, John. *Spain under the Habsburgs*, 2 vols (Oxford, 1964, 1969).

McCabe, William H., S.J., *An Introduction to the Jesuit Theater* (St Louis, 1983).

McCaffrey, Wallace. *Elizabeth I* (London, 1993).

McConica, James, ed. *English Humanists and Reformation Politics* (Oxford, 1965).

———. *The Collegiate University. The History of the University of Oxford* vol. 3 (Oxford, 1986).

———. 'The Rise of the Undergraduate College', in James McConica, ed., *The Collegiate University. The History of the University of Oxford* vol. 3 (Oxford, 1986), pp. 1–68.

———. 'Studies and Faculties: Introduction', in James McConica, ed., *The Collegiate University. The History of the University of Oxford* vol.3 (Oxford, 1986), pp. 151–56.

McCoog, Thomas M., S.J. 'The Establishment of the English Province of the Society of Jesus', *Recusant History* 17 (1984), pp. 121–39.

———. 'Apostasy and Knavery in Restoration England: The Checkered Career of John Travers', *The Catholic Historical Review* 78 (1992), pp. 395–412.

———. ' "The Flower of Oxford": The Role of Edmund Campion in Early Recusant Polemics', *Sixteenth Century Journal* 24 (1993), pp. 899–913.

———. 'Ignatius Loyola and Reginald Pole: A Reconsideration', *Journal of Ecclesiastical History* (forthcoming).

McDonnell, Michael F.J. 'Edmund Campion, S.J., and St Paul's School', *Notes and Queries* 194 (1949), pp. 46–49, 66–70, 90–92.

McGee, J. Sears. 'Conversion and the Imitation of Christ in Anglican and Puritan Writing', *Journal of British Studies* 15 (1976), pp. 21–39.

McGrath, Patrick. *Puritans and Papists under Elizabeth I* (London, 1967).

———. *Brasenose Priests and Martyrs under Elizabeth I* (Oxford, 1985).

——— and Joy Rowe. 'The Recusancy of Sir Thomas Cornwallis', *Proceedings of the Suffolk Institute of Archaeology* 28 (1961), pp. 226–71.

McNulty, Robert. 'The Protestant Version of Robert Persons' *The First Booke of the Christian Exercise*', *Huntington Library Quarterly* 22 (1959), pp. 271–300.

Manning, Roger B. 'Richard Shelley of Warminghurst and the English Catholic Petition for Toleration of 1585', *Recusant History* 6 (1962), pp. 265–74.

Marc'hadour, Germain. *L'Univers de Thomas More* (Paris, 1963).

Martin, A. Lynn. *Henry III and the Jesuit Politicians* (Geneva, 1973).

———. *The Jesuit Mind* (London, 1988).

Maruyama, Tadataka. *The Ecclesiology of Theodore Beza* (Geneva, 1978).

Mathew, A.H. *A True Historical Relation* (London, 1904).

Mattingly, Garrett. *The Defeat of the Spanish Armada* (London, 1959).

Mas, Bartolomé. 'El p. Bernardino Scotti y la legación de Paulo III a Carlos V en 1548', *Regnum Dei* 3 (1947), pp. 181–95.

Matheson, Peter. *Cardinal Contarini at Regensburg* (Oxford, 1972).

Mayer, Thomas F. *Thomas Starkey and the Commonweal: Humanist Politics and Religion in the Reign of Henry VIII* (Cambridge, 1989).

———. 'A Mission Worse than Death: Reginald Pole and the Parisian Theologians', *English Historical Review* 103 (1988), pp. 870–91.

———. 'Nursery of Resistance: Reginald Pole and his Friends', in Paul A. Fideler and Thomas F. Mayer, eds, *The Commonwealth of Tudor England* (London, 1992), pp. 50–74.

———. 'A Sticking-plaster Saint? Autobiography and Hagiography in the Making of Reginald Pole', in Thomas F. Mayer and D.R. Woolf, eds, *The Rhetorics of*

Life-Writing in Early Modern Europe: Forms of Biography from Cassandra Fedele to Louis XIV (Ann Arbor, 1995), pp. 205–20.

———. 'Il fellimento di una candidatura: la "reform tendency," in Reginald Pole ed il conclave di Giulio III', *Annali dell'istituto storico italo-germanico in Trento*, forthcoming.

Medina, Francisco de Borja, S.J. 'Jesuitas en la Armada contra Inglaterra (1588). Notas para un Centenario', *AHSI* 58 (1989), pp. 3–42.

———. 'La Compañía de Jesús y la Evangelización de América y Filipinas', *Memoria Ecclesiae* V (Oviedo, 1994), pp. 31–61.

Meyer, Arnold Oskar. *England and the Catholic Church under Queen Elizabeth* (London, 1916, repr. London 1967).

Milne, J.G. *The Early History of Corpus Christi College Oxford* (Oxford, 1946).

Milward, Peter, S.J. *Religious Controversies of the Elizabethan Age. A Survey of Printed Sources* (London, 1977).

———. *Religious Controversies of the Jacobean Age* (London, 1978).

Molyneux, Edmund. *Historical Remembrance of the Sidneys, the father and the son (1588)* in Katherine Duncan-Jones, ed., *The Oxford Authors: Sir Philip Sidney* (Oxford, 1989), pp. 311–14.

Morey, Adrian. *The Catholic Subjects of Elizabeth I* (London, 1978).

Morris, John, S.J. *Troubles of our Catholic Forefathers*, 3 vols (London, 1872–77).

———. 'Blessed Edmund Campion at Douay', *The Month* 61 (1887), pp. 30–46.

Neale, J.E. *Elizabeth I and Her Parliaments, 1559–1581* (London, 1953).

———. 'The Elizabethan Act of Supremacy and Uniformity', *The English Historical Review* 64 (1950), pp. 304–32.

Nicholls, David. 'The Theatre of Martyrdom in the French Reformation', *Past and Present* 121 (1988), pp. 49–73.

Nugent, Donald. *Ecumenism in the Age of the Reformation: The Colloquy of Poissy* (Cambridge, Mass., 1974).

O'Day, Rosemary. *The Debate on the English Reformation* (London, 1986).

O'Malley, John W., S.J. *The First Jesuits* (Cambridge, Mass., 1993).

Ong, Walter J., S.J. *Ramus, Method and the Decay of Dialogue* (Cambridge, Mass., 1958).

Osborn, James M. *Young Philip Sidney 1572–77* (New Haven, 1972).

Ozment, Steven E. *The Reformation in the Cities* (New Haven, 1975).

Parente, James A., Jr. 'Tyranny and Revolution on the Baroque Stage: The Dramas of Joseph Simons', *Humanistica Lovaniensia* 32 (1983), pp. 309–24.

Parente, Ulderico. 'Nicolás Bobadilla, 1509–1590', *AHSI* 59 (1990), pp. 323–44.

Pastor, Ludwig Freiherr von. *History of the Popes*, 40 vols (London, 1891–1953).

Pogson, R.H. 'Reginald Pole and the Priorities of Government in Mary Tudor's Church', *Historical Journal* 18 (1975), pp. 3–21.

———. 'The Legacy of the Schism: Confusion, Continuity and Change in the Marian Clergy', in Jennifer Loach and Robert Tittler, eds., *The Mid-Tudor Polity c. 1540–1560* (London, 1980), pp. 116–36.

———. 'Revival and Reform in Mary Tudor's Church: A Question of Money', in Christopher Haigh, ed., *The English Reformation Revised* (Cambridge, 1987), pp. 139–56.

Pollard, A.W. and G.R. Redgrave. *A Short Title Catalogue of Books Printed in England, Scotland, and Ireland and of English Books Printed Abroad, 1475–1640*, 2nd edn revised by W.A. Jackson, F.S. Ferguson and K.F. Pantzer, 3 vols (London, 1976–91).

Pollen, John H., S.J. 'Blessed Edmund Campion's Journey from Rome to England', *The Month* 90 (1897), pp. 243–55.

———. 'Edmund Campion's History of Ireland', *The Month* 106 (1905), 561–76; 107 (1906), 156–69.

———. 'Blessed Edmund Campion's "Challenge" ', *The Month* 115 (1910), pp. 50–65.

———. 'Blessed Edmund Campion's Confessions', *The Month* 134 (1919), pp. 258–61.

Pritchard, Arnold. *Catholic Loyalism in Elizabethan England* (London, 1979).

Procter, F., and W.H. Frere. *A New History of the Book of Common Prayer* (London, 1901).

Puppi, Lionello. *Torment in Art: Pain, Violence and Martyrdom* (New York, 1991).

Quinn, D.B. 'Government Printing and the Publication of the Irish Statutes in the Sixteenth Century', *Proceedings of the Royal Irish Academy* xlix, sect. C (1943), pp. 415–24.

Quinn, Peter A. 'Ignatius Loyola and Gian Pietro Carafa: Catholic Reformers at Odds', *Catholic Historical Review* 67 (1981), pp. 386–400.

Ratzinger, Josef. 'The Papal Primacy and the Unity of the People of God', in *Church, Ecumenism and Politics: New Essays in Ecclesiology* (New York, 1988), pp. 36–44.

Read, Conyers. *Lord Burghley and Queen Elizabeth* (London, 1960).

Redworth, Glyn. *In Defence of the Church Catholic: a Life of Stephen Gardiner* (Oxford, 1990).

Reynolds, E.E. *Campion and Parsons* (London, 1980).

Richgels, Robert W. 'The Pattern of Controversy in a Counter-Reformation Classic: The *Controversies* of Robert Bellarmine', *Sixteenth Century Journal* 11 (1980), pp. 3–15.

Robertson, Jean. *Sir Philip Sidney: The Countess of Pembroke's Arcadia (The Old Arcadia)* (London, 1973).

Rodríguez Salgado, M.J., and Simon Adams eds, *England, Spain and the Gran Armada, 1588–1604* (Edinburgh, 1991).

———. *Felipe II y la crisis Post-Armada: política exterior y rebelión, 1588–1594 / Philip II and the Post-Armada crisis: foreign policy and rebellion, 1588–1594* (Madrid, 1993), Cuadernos monográficos del Instituto de Historia y Cultura Naval, Supplement to No. 20.

———. 'The Anglo-Spanish War: the final episode in the "War of the Roses" ', *England, Spain and the Gran Armada, 1588–1604*, pp. 1–44.

Rose, Elliot E. *Cases of Conscience* (Cambridge, 1975).

Rose-Troup, Frances. *The Western Rebellion of 1549* (London, 1913).

Rowe, K.T. 'Romantic Love and Parental Authority in Sidney's *Arcadia*', *University of Michigan Contributions in Modern Philology* 1–12 (1947–49), pp. 1–58.

Rowlands, Marie B. 'Recusant Women 1560–1640', in Mary Prior, ed., *Women in English Society 1500–1800* (London and New York, 1985), pp. 149–80.

Rowse, A.L. *The England of Elizabeth* (London, 1950).

———. *Eminent Elizabethans* (London, 1983).

Salmon, J.H.M. *Society in Crisis: France in the Sixteenth Century* (London, 1975).

Salter, Rev. H.E. 'Ecclesiastical History', in William Page, ed., *The Victoria History of the County of Oxford* (London, 1907), pp. 1–106.

Scaduto, Mario, S.J. *L'Epoca di Giacomo Lainez. Il Governo. 1556–1565*, Storia della Compagnia di Gesù in Italia, vol. 3 (Rome, 1964).

Scarisbrick, J.J. *Henry VIII* (London, 1968).

————. *The Reformation and the English People* (Oxford, 1984).

Schneider, Burkhart, S.J. 'Der Konflikt zwischen Claudius Aquaviva and Paul Hoffaeus. Ergänzungen und Berichtigungen', *AHSI* 27 (1958), pp. 279–306.

Scribner, R.W. *Popular Culture and Popular Movements in Reformation Germany* (London, 1987).

Signorelli, Giuseppe. 'Il soggiorno di Vittoria Colonna in Viterbo', *Bolletino storico-archaeologico viterbese* 1:4 (1908), pp. 118–51.

Simoncelli, Paolo. *Il caso Reginald Pole: eresia e santità nelle polemiche religiose del Cinquecento* (Rome, 1977).

Simpson, Richard. *Edmund Campion: A Biography* (London, 1867).

————. *Edmund Campion: A Biography*, revised edition (London, 1896).

Southern, A.C. *Elizabethan Recusant Prose, 1559–1582* (London, n.d. [1950]).

Stevenson, W.H., and H.E. Salter. *The Early History of St John's College, Oxford* (Oxford, 1939), Oxford Historical Society.

Stone, J.M. 'Atheism under Elizabeth and James I', *The Month* 81 (1894), pp. 174–87.

Strong, Roy. *The English Icon* (London, 1969).

————. *The Cult of Elizabeth: Elizabethan Portraiture and Pageantry* (London, 1977).

Swan, C.M.J.F. 'The Question of Dissimulation among Elizabethan Catholics', *Report of the Canadian Catholic Historical Association* (Ottawa, 1957), pp. 105–19.

Taunton, Ethelred L. *The History of the Jesuits in England, 1580–1773* (London, 1901).

Taveneaux, Remi. 'The Council of Trent and the Catholic Reformation' in Pierre Chaunu, ed., *The Reformation* (Gloucester, 1989), pp. 266–79.

Tellechea Idígoras, J.I. *Fray Bartolomé Carranza y el Cardenal Pole. Un navarro en la restauración católica (1554–1558)* (Pamplona, 1977).

————. *Sábado espiritual y otros ensayos carrancianos* (Salamanca, 1987).

————. 'Bartolomé Carranza y la restauración católica inglesa', *Anthologia Annua* 12 (1964), pp. 159–282.

————. 'Pole y Paul IV: una celébre Apologia inédita del Cardenal Ingles', *Archivum Historiae Pontificiae* 4 (1966), pp. 105–54.

Thomson, J.A.F. *The Later Lollards, 1414–1520* (Oxford, 1965).

Thurston, Hubert, S.J. 'Catholic Writers and Elizabethan Readers. I. Father Persons' "Christian Directory" ', *The Month* 82 (1894), pp. 457–76.

Treadwell, Victor. 'The Irish Parliament of 1569–71', *Proceedings of the Royal Irish Academy* lxv, sect. C (1966), pp. 55–89.

Trimble, William R. *The Catholic Laity in Elizabethan England 1558–1603* (Cambridge, Mass. 1964).

Tyler, Philip. 'The Significance of the Ecclesiastical Commission of York', *Northern History* 2 (1967), pp. 27–44.

Valentin, Jean-Marie. *Le théâtre des Jésuites dans les pays de langue allemande*, 2 vols (Stuttgart, 1983–84).

Wadkins, Timothy H. 'The Percy-"Fisher" Controversies and the Ecclesiastical Politics of Jacobean Anti-Catholicism, 1622–1625', *Church History* 57 (1988), pp. 153–69.

Walsham, Alexandra. *Church Papists* (London, 1993).

Wallace, M.W. *The Life of Sir Philip Sidney* (Cambridge, 1915).

Wark, K.R. *Elizabethan Recusancy in Cheshire* (Manchester, 1973), Chetham Society, English Remains Historical and Literary, Series 3, No. 19.

Watson, Andrew G. 'Thomas Allen of Oxford and his Manuscripts', in M.B. Parkes and A.G. Watson, eds, *Medieval Scribes, Manuscripts and Libraries: Essays presented to N.R. Ker* (London, 1978), pp. 279–314.

Waugh, Evelyn. *Edmund Campion: Jesuit and Martyr* (London, 1935; reprinted New York, 1956).

Wernham, R.B. *Before the Armada: The Emergence of the English Nation, 1485–1588* (New York, 1966).

———. *After the Armada: Elizabethan England and the Struggle for Western Europe 1588–1595* (Oxford, 1984).

———. *The Return of the Armadas. The Last Years of the Elizabethan War against Spain 1595–1603* (Oxford, 1994).

White, Helen C. *English Devotional Literature [Prose] 1600–1640* (Madison, Wisconsin, 1931).

———. *Tudor Books of Private Devotions* (Madison, Wisconsin, 1951).

Whiting, Robert. *The Blind Devotion of the People* (Cambridge, 1989).

Wickes, George. 'Henry Constable, Poet and Courtier, 1562–1613', *Biographical Studies* [later *Recusant History*] 2 (1953–54), pp. 272–300.

Willen, Diane. 'Women and Religion in Early Modern Europe', in Sherrin Marshall, ed., *Women in Reformation and Counter-Reformation Europe* (Bloomington, 1989), pp. 140–65.

Williams, Cornelius William. 'Conversion IV (Obligation of)', *New Catholic Encyclopaedia*, 16 vols (Washington, 1967–74), IV, pp. 289–90.

Williams, Glanmor. *Renewal and Reformation. Wales c. 1415–1642* (Oxford, 1987).

Williams, Michael E. *St Alban's College Valladolid* (London/New York 1986).

———. 'The Ascetic Tradition and the English College Valladolid', in W.J. Sheils, ed., *Monks, Hermits and the Ascetic Tradition* (Oxford, 1985) Studies in Church History 22, pp. 275–83.

———. 'The Origins of the English College Lisbon', *Recusant History* 20 (1991), pp. 478–92.

———. 'Images of Martyrdom in Paintings at the English College Valladolid', in M.A. Rees, ed., *Leeds Papers on Symbol and Image in Iberian Arts* (Leeds, 1994), pp. 51–71.

———. 'William Allen: The Sixteenth Century Spanish Connection', *Recusant History* 22 (1994), pp. 123–40.

Williams, Penry. *The Tudor Regime* (Oxford, 1979).

———. 'Elizabethan Oxford: State, Church and University', in James McConica, ed., *The Collegiate University. The History of the University of Oxford* vol. 3 (Oxford, 1986), pp. 397–440.

Wing, Donald. *Short-Title Catalogue of Books Printed in England, Scotland, Ireland, Wales, and British America and of English Books Printed in Other Countries 1641–1700*, 2nd edition revised and edited by John J. Morrison, Carolyn W. Nelson and Matthew Seccombe, 3 vols (New York, 1982–94).

Woodman, A. Vere. 'The Buckinghamshire and Oxfordshire Rising of 1549', *Oxoniensia* 22 (1957), pp. 79–82.

Zapico, D. Fernández, S.J. 'La Province d'Aquitaine de la Compagnie de Jésus d'après son plus ancien catalogue (1566)', *AHSI* 5 (1936), pp. 268–292.

Theses

Bartholomew, A.F. 'Lay Piety in the Reign of Mary Tudor' (unpublished M.A. thesis, Manchester University, 1979).

Bossy, John. 'Elizabethan Catholicism: The Link with France' (unpublished D.Phil. thesis, University of Cambridge, 1961).

Davidson, Alan. 'Roman Catholics in Oxfordshire from the Late Elizabethan Period to the Civil War (c. 1580–1640)' (unpublished Ph.D. thesis, University of Bristol, 1970).

LaRocca, John J., S.J. 'English Catholics and the Recusancy Laws 1558–1625: A Study in Religion and Politics' (unpublished Ph.D. thesis, Rutgers University, 1977).

McCoog, Thomas M., S.J. 'The Society of Jesus in England, 1623–1688' (unpublished Ph.D. thesis, University of Warwick, 1984).

McNulty, Robert. 'Robert Persons's *The First Booke of the Christian Exercise* (1582): An Edition and a Study' (unpublished Ph.D. thesis, Columbia University, 1955).

Marmion, J.P. 'The London Synod of Reginald, Cardinal Pole, 1555–56' (unpublished M.A. thesis, University of Keele, 1974).

Milton, Anthony. 'The Laudians and the Church of Rome, c. 1625–1640' (unpublished Ph.D. thesis, University of Cambridge, 1989).

Pogson, R.H. 'Cardinal Pole–Papal Legate to England in Mary Tudor's Reign' (unpublished Ph.D. dissertation, University of Cambridge, 1972).

Questier, Michael. 'The Phenomenon of Conversion: Change of Religion to and from Catholicism in England, 1580–1625' (unpublished D.Phil. thesis, University of Sussex, 1991).

Shell, Allison. 'English Catholicism and Drama, 1578–1688' (unpublished D.Phil. thesis, University of Oxford, 1992).

INDEX

compiled by Susan Hibbert